Creating Sustainable Bioeconomies

T0331319

The growing global demand for food, feed and biobased renewable material is changing the conditions for agricultural production worldwide. At the same time, revolutionary achievements in the field of biosciences are contributing to a transition whereby biobased alternatives for energy and materials are becoming more competitive.

Creating Sustainable Bioeconomies explores the prospects for biosciences and how its innovation has the potential to help countries in the North (Europe) and the South (Africa) to move towards resource-efficient agriculture and sustainable bioeconomies. Throughout the book, the situations of Europe and sub-Saharan Africa will be compared and contrasted, and opportunities for mutual learning and collaboration are explored. The chapters have been written by high-profile authors and deal with a wide range of issues affecting the development of bioeconomies on both continents. This book compares and contrasts the situations of these two regions as they endeavour to develop knowledge-based bioeconomies.

This volume is suitable for those who are interested in ecological economics, development economics and environmental economics. It also provides action plans assisting policymakers in both areas to support the transition to knowledge-based and sustainable bioeconomies.

Ivar Virgin is a researcher at the Stockholm Environment Institute (SEI), Sweden. For the past 20 years at SEI he has done extensive research, managed numerous projects and published extensively in the field of bioscience innovation. A focus of his work has been capacity building and institutional building in third world countries, particularly Africa.

E. Jane Morris is an independent Life Sciences consultant who has spent most of her working life in Africa. She is now based in the UK and has a Visiting Fellowship in the School of Biology at Leeds University. She has expertise that includes bioscience and biotechnology, GMO biosafety and regulatory issues and strategy planning.

Routledge Studies in Ecological Economics

For a full list of titles in this series, please visit www.routledge.com/series/RSEE

Creating Sustainable Bioeconomies

The bioscience revolution in Europe and Africa

Edited by
Ivar Virgin and E. Jane Morris

Routledge
Taylor & Francis Group

LONDON AND NEW YORK

SEI

STOCKHOLM
ENVIRONMENT
INSTITUTE

First published 2017 by Routledge

2 Park Square, Milton Park, Abingdon, Oxfordshire OX14 4RN
52 Vanderbilt Avenue, New York, NY 10017

Routledge is an imprint of the Taylor & Francis Group, an informa business

First issued in paperback 2019

British Library Cataloguing in Publication Data
A catalogue record for this book is available from the British Library

Library of Congress Cataloging in Publication Data
A catalog record for this book has been requested

ISBN: 978-1-138-81853-8 (hbk)
ISBN: 978-0-367-87097-3 (pbk)

Typeset in Times New Roman
by Cenveo Publisher Services

Contents

Figures

Tables

Contributors

Philipp Aerni is Director of the Center for Corporate Responsibility and Sustainability (CCRS) at the University of Zurich, Switzerland. He is an interdisciplinary social scientist and public policy expert with research interests in the fields of public perception, innovation policy and sustainable development. He currently teaches courses related to his research at the University of Zurich, ETH Zurich and the University of Basel.

Yona Baguma is a plant scientist and research manager at the National Agricultural Research Organisation (NARO), Uganda. He has published widely in broad aspects of cassava. He is currently responsible for coordinating and guiding research in NARO.

Joachim von Braun is Director of the Center for Development Research (ZEF), Bonn University, and Professor for economic and technological change. His research is on economic development, science and technology policy, poverty reduction, food and nutrition security, resource economics and trade. He is chair of the Bioeconomy Council of the Federal German Government. He was Director General of the International Food Policy Research Institute (IFPRI) based in Washington, DC, U.S.A., and President of the International Association of Agricultural Economists (IAAE).

Isabelle Schluep Campo is Head of the Sustainable Impact Research Group at the Center for Corporate Responsibility and Sustainability (CCRS) at the University of Zurich, Switzerland. She has expertise in the areas of international trade, public policy, agriculture, and development. She worked for six years in the international trade and economic policy division of the Swiss State Secretariat for Economic Affairs (SECO). She holds M.S. degrees in (agricultural) economics from ETH Zurich, Cornell University and Iowa State University and a PhD from ETH Zurich.

Dirk Carrez is Executive Director of the Biobased Industries Consortium (BIC), representing the private sector in a public-private partnership with the EU known as the Bio-based Industries Joint Undertaking (BBI JU). He is the Founder and Managing Director of Clever Consult, a consulting firm providing a full range of services in the area of the biobased economy such as policy analysis, strategy development, public affairs and business development. He is also a member of several experts groups at international and European level.

Julius Ecuru is a Chemist and Regulatory Science Expert in Uganda at the Uganda National Council for Science and Technology. He has a unique blend of expertise, which includes health, social and environmental safeguards of new technologies. His research work is at the nexus of industry, agriculture and the environment.

Corinda Erasmus is an independent researcher in Food Science and she specialises in the understanding of the factors in the agricultural value chain influencing grain and legume processing and eating quality. She has 25 years experience as an applied scientist, is the holder of a few processing patents and currently works as a project consultant in the South African grains industry.

Torbjörn Fagerström is Professor emeritus of Theoretical Ecology at Lund University, and has also been Deputy Vice Chancellor at the Swedish University of Agricultural Sciences. He is active in the public debate on issues pertaining to science and agriculture, e.g. regarding the problems relating to GM crops in Europe, and the lack of a firm scientific basis for the claims that organic farming should be the route to sustainable agriculture.

Matthew Fielding is a researcher and project manager currently seconded to the Stockholm Environment Institute Asia Office. He has published several articles and reports on agricultural development, extension services, research prioritisation for food security and biofuels. He manages a portfolio of projects all clustered around agriculture, food and resource use.

Jakob Granit is Deputy Director at the Stockholm Environment Institute (SEI) and its Centre Director in Stockholm. He is the International Waters Panel Member of the Global Environment Facility (GEF) and its Scientific and Technical Advisory Panel (STAP). Jakob has a PhD in Geography and over 20 years of expertise gained from working with natural resources, energy management at global, regional and local level.

Holger Hoff is senior scientist at the Stockholm Environment Institute in Sweden and at the Potsdam Institute for Climate Impact Research in Germany. His research includes climate change, integrated natural resources management, and sustainable production and consumption. He works at the interface of science and policy making.

Francis X. Johnson is a Senior Research Fellow at Stockholm Environment Institute (SEI) and is currently based at the SEI Africa Centre in Nairobi. He conducts energy and climate policy analysis and research, with special focus on transitions in biomass and bioenergy use within the context of climate change and economic development goals.

Thomas Kätterer is Professor in ecosystem ecology at the Swedish University of Agricultural Sciences. His research is focused on element cycling in terrestrial ecosystems, in particular the cycling of carbon and nutrients in agroecosystems and how this is affected by climatic and edaphic conditions as well as by management decisions.

John Komen is an independent advisor to research and regulatory organizations and donor agencies on matters of agricultural development policy, capacity development, agricultural research and regulation, and research program management.

Allan Liavoga is a food scientist and currently the program manager of a regional bioscience research and innovation funding initiative (Bio-resources Innovations Network for Eastern Africa Development – Bio-Innovate). He has extensive experience managing research for development programs in Africa focusing on biosciences and bio-policy. He has published in the field of food science and biotechnology.

E. Jane Morris is a Visiting Fellow in the School of Biology at the University of Leeds, and also acts as an independent consultant in the life sciences. Formerly Director of the African Centre for Gene Technologies, her expertise lies in bioscience/biotechnology innovation, building collaborative partnerships, and biosafety of GMOs with an emphasis on developing countries particularly in Africa.

Yacob Mulugetta is Professor of Energy and Development Policy at the Department of Science, Technology, Engineering & Public Policy (STEaPP) at University College London (UCL), UK. He has 20 years of research, teaching and policy advice experience in climate change and development, specializing in the links between energy access, equity and environmental stewardship. He served as a Coordinating Lead Author of the Energy Systems chapter of the IPCC's 5th Assessment Report (Working Group III on Mitigation).

Denis J. Murphy is Professor of Biotechnology at the University of South Wales, UK. He is a Fellow of the Royal Society of Biology and Biotechnology Advisor with the Food and Agriculture Organization. His group works on crop genomics and bioinformatics, including a long standing collaboration on oil palm research with colleagues in Malaysia.

Steffen Noleppa is managing director of HFFA Research GmbH providing scientific consultancy and research on key issues in world agriculture to stakeholders ranging from industry to government, NGOs or academia. He holds a PhD in Agricultural Economics from Humboldt University of Berlin and has special expertise in modeling of agricultural markets and policies, sector analysis and policy simulation. Dr. Noleppa is author and co-author of more than 50 studies, various peer-reviewed scientific articles and two books.

Ephraim Nuwamanya is in charge of the Nutritional and Bio-analytical laboratory at National Crops Resources Research Institute, Uganda. His work is crucial in bridging the gap between crop breeding and food/nutritional security. The emphasis is on compositional analysis, nutritional profiling, product development and standardization. This forms the basis of developing superior crop varieties with applications in food and industry.

Martha M. O'Kennedy is a senior scientist at the Council for Scientific and Industrial Research (CSIR) Biosciences, South Africa. She has published several articles and book chapters on genetic engineering of African cereal crops, as well as presenting several talks nationally and internationally. Her research currently includes veterinary vaccines produced in plants.

Olle Olsson has a PhD in Forest Resource Management and is a Research Fellow at the Stockholm Environment Institute, Stockholm, Sweden. His research is primarily focused on different aspects of bioenergy, specifically issues related to international trade and interactions between bioenergy trade and climate change adaptation.

Ruth K. Oniang'o is a Kenyan food and nutrition scientist. She is Director of Rural Outreach Africa, an NGO working to uplift the lives of resource poor smallholder farmers, especially women. As a policy expert she has served on the board of various international agencies and foundations. She is Editor-in-Chief of the African Journal of Food, Agriculture, Nutrition and Development.

M.E. Chrissie Rey is Professor of Microbiology, University of the Witwatersrand, Johannesburg, South Africa. She has published several articles on cassava and plant viruses, as well as giving lectures and radio/TV interviews on biotechnology and food security around the country. Her research includes genetic engineering of cassava for virus resistance and improved traits, virus diseases of tomato, cassava and sweet potato, plant biotechnology and functional genomics studies of host-virus interactions.

Richard D. Smart is a researcher at the Department for Agricultural Economics at the Technical University of Munich, Freising, Germany. He has published articles on the regulation of transgenic crops, which is the focus of his research.

Sten Stymne is Professor in Plant Breeding and Biochemistry at Swedish University of Agricultural Sciences. His research has been focused on plant lipid biochemistry and genetics and in particular biosynthesis of vegetable oils and he is regarded as one of the leading scientists in this area during the last 20 years. The applied goal of his research is to develop high added value oils for industrial uses in transgenic oil crops and to redirect reduced carbon from starch and sugar in sink tissues such as cereals and tubers.

Melinda Fones Sundell, Senior Research Fellow at the Stockholm Environment Institute, is an Agricultural Economist (MSc) with over 40 years experience of management, analysis and design of rural development programs, primarily in Africa and Latin America. Her fields of specialization include agricultural production economics, bio-energy, environmental impact analysis and gender in agriculture. She is currently Senior Agricultural Advisor to SIANI, the Swedish International Agricultural Network Initiative.

Jens Sundström is an Associate Professor at the Swedish University of Agricultural Sciences and he holds an extension specialist position directed towards plant biotechnology. His research includes gene regulation, plant reproductive development and plant breeding.

Jennifer A. Thomson is Emeritus Professor in the Department of Molecular and Cell Biology at the University of Cape Town, South Africa. Her research involves the development of genetically modified maize resistant to the African endemic maize streak virus and tolerant to drought. She has written three books on GM crops for the interested layperson: *Genes for Africa, Seeds for the Future* and *Food for Africa*.

Ivar Virgin is a Senior Researcher at Stockholm Environment Institute (SEI). He conducts research on matters of agricultural development policy, in particular bioscience innovation and has managed several international programmes on bioscience capacity building.

Justus Wesseler is Professor of Agricultural Economics and Rural Policy, Wageningen University, Netherlands. He has published several articles on bioeconomy economics and policy, as well as appearing as keynote speaker at several international conferences. His research includes regulation of the bio-economy, technical change in agriculture and the contribution of the bioeconomy towards sustainable development.

Harald von Witzke is a Professor emeritus at Humboldt University of Berlin and President of the Humboldt Forum for Food and Agriculture. His work is focused on sustainable world food security and the role of agricultural innovation.

Rosemary Wolson is Senior Intellectual Property Manager at the Council for Scientific and Industrial Research (CSIR) in Pretoria, South Africa. Her experience as an early technology transfer practitioner in a developing country has cultivated an interest in broader policy issues related to the role of innovation and intellectual property rights in promoting development.

Foreword

The scope for bioeconomy cooperation between Africa and Europe

The future of humankind much depends on a secure, sustainable and safe availability of food, energy, water and industrial raw materials. These should be more and more based on renewable resources, with biobased materials playing an important role for sustainability, including mitigation of climate change. Productivity in such a scenario – appropriately measured by inclusion of indirect effects, such as adverse effects of excessive use of agricultural inputs – will increasingly depend on science and innovations around biobased production and processing technologies. This puts the knowledge-based bioeconomy at the centre of a new economic strategy that aims to reconcile humanity with nature.

Bioeconomy is defined as the knowledge-based production and utilization of biological resources, innovative biological processes and principles to sustainably provide goods and services across all economic sectors. So bioeconomy is much more than using biomass for energy. It embraces the sustainable management of ecological systems, understands land, forests and soils as fragile resources that provide wealth through ecosystems services. It learns from nature by employing biomimicry, and utilizes biosciences to transform established economic sectors, such as chemical industries, pharmaceuticals, food and construction, into sustainable ones. The bioeconomy has been rapidly expanding during the past ten years, driven by increased prices of natural resources, such as land and water, by new technological opportunities, and by changed consumer preferences. A first Global Bioeconomy Summit in Berlin in November 2015 was testimony to the accelerated worldwide initiatives in this field. The Paris agreement on climate change lends further impetus to investment in a sustainable bioeconomy.

Bioeconomy means making virtue out of necessity, e.g. using more of what we can sustainably grow on soils, with seed, sun and water, and using it a lot more efficiently and more innovatively, and it entails producing biobased materials even independent of soils. 'Biologisation' of the economy addresses both the efficient use of biological resources in the production of materials and products and the sustainable use of renewable biological raw material instead of fossil carbon sources for industrial processes. A knowledge-based and sustainable bioeconomy contrasts with our current exploitative use of biological and other natural resources, and related effects on water, soils and climate which threatens the future of humankind. While offering prospects of sustainable economic development, bioeconomy is expected to play an increasing and decisive role in addressing some of the big challenges faced by society, such as:

- growing population and higher living standards, leading to increased demand for food, animal feed, fibre for clothing, material for housing, water, energy, health services, etc.;
- declining resources, e.g. degraded ecosystems and loss of ecosystem services, including land degradation and unsustainable ocean fisheries; declining biodiversity due to unsustainable management practices and the effects of climate change on bio-resources;
- adapting to limitation in fossil resources by providing a meaningful substitution of the consumption of such finite resources by the use of biobased and other renewable resources;
- the need to move from production systems that entail waste that may be recycled toward prevention of waste in the first place, i.e. a strategy where 'waste' is designed to act as bioresource for further biological processes.

This book on: *Creating Sustainable Bioeconomies: The Bioscience Revolution in Europe and Africa* addresses all these issues in comprehensive ways. It is a timely and significant contribution to the bioeconomy debate. In particular, it points to the opportunities for strategic partnership between Africa and Europe in the field of bioeconomy: Africa being rich in biomass resources with a growing science capacity, Europe being rich in science capacities but with limited biomass resource base. Biobased economy is a global strategy, where Europe should invest in value addition close to source, e.g. in Africa, and not extract biobased resources from abroad. Science and technology cooperation between Africa and Europe is central for an internationally coherent bioeconomy strategy. Moreover, biomass wealth of Africa is located in close proximity to its rural poor. Thus with improved value chains within Africa, a bioeconomy strategy promises job generation and poverty reduction and thereby supports pro poor development. It must be noted, however, that competition for biomass utilization can increase food prices, as well as indirectly foster competition for land and water. Reconciliation of African food security goals with bioeconomy is a matter of technological and institutional innovations that accelerate sustainable growth in African agriculture. These innovations should be further supported in African – European bioeconomy partnerships.

The fast growth in world biofuel production in recent years is indicative for bioeconomy in the making, but this particular sector has so far not dealt with its negative side effects for food security and landscapes. The biofuels aberration teaches that sound policy impact analyses need to precede hasty policy actions.

Biomass has to be used judiciously for food, energy and industrial products, appropriately adjusting to the local context. The preferred way of increasing agricultural productivity is to intensify farming sustainably on the land that is already used for agriculture where in many cases water is the restricting parameter. Modern bioscience-based breeding technologies able to produce new crop varieties adapted for a resource-efficient and climate-smart food system are important in this regard. It is one of the tasks of a sustainable bioeconomy to create the conditions in which the global provision of foodstuffs can be guaranteed. This also includes measures and technologies to reduce the considerable loss of produce from harvest to market observed today. Socioeconomic behaviour must also be taken into consideration here, to reduce excess consumption and waste of food and biomass. This is also important for promoting good health.

The bioeconomy must ultimately be understood in a context of needed societal, technological and economic change for sustainability. The essence of such change is not just technological (new science) and behavioural (adjusted consumption), but the central issue may very well be institutional, i.e. providing the long-run incentives for sustainable farming, sound bioresource management and industrial development. Facilitating collective actions at international levels and, especially, more sharing of the new knowledge between Europe and Africa about what works in bioeconomy must be one such action. The book concludes with a noteworthy set of action points for Africa and Europe respectively that address the priorities, taking into account the current status on each of the continents. The volume is a 'must read' for scholars and policy advisors in the field of sustainable development.

Joachim von Braun
Chair of the German Government's Bioeconomy Council
and Professor for economic and technical change
and Director of the Centre for Development
Research (ZEF), Bonn University

Preface

Modern bioscience has the potential to meet many of the development challenges confronting the world today, and help to transform societies towards sustainability. The rapid advances of bioscience are contributing to a knowledge-based bioeconomy, where economic growth is founded on the sustainable use of renewable resources. The bioeconomy innovation agenda includes new and effective tools for sustainable agricultural production, waste treatment, energy production and the development of a diverse range of bioresource value chains and novel bioproducts. But, despite its potential to address key development and environmental challenges, there is still a gap between what modern bioscience can do in principle and what has been achieved so far. The promises of modern biosciences will not be fully realised until we broaden the R&D agenda and invest in public R&D platforms to ensure that new bioscience solutions are made available to a wider set of actors than today. There is also a need to address public distrust and skepticism towards modern biosciences, and in particular genetic engineering.

The Stockholm Environment Institute (SEI) has since the early 1990s been heavily engaged in the debate on how bioscience innovation can most effectively contribute to sustainable development. In 1993, SEI established the Biotechnology Advisory Commission (BAC) consisting of an international network of highly reputed experts assisting developing countries with science based information and capacity building for the regulation and use of genetically modified organisms (GMOs). In 1998, the BAC was converted to a broader bioscience capacity building programme with a mission to assist developing countries in adopting modern bioscience to meet local needs. In 1998, building on earlier networking and capacity building efforts, SEI initiated and managed one of the largest African bioscience R&D and innovation platforms ever, the BIO-EARN Programme (*Eastern Africa Regional Programme and Research Network for Biotechnology, Biosafety and Biotechnology Policy Development*). In 2010, BIO-EARN was transformed into the Africa governed Bio-Innovate Programme (*Bio-resources Network for Eastern Africa Development*) where SEI continued to be an active partner. Both the BIO-EARN and Bio-Innovate programme, described in more detail in this book, were made possible through generous support from the Swedish International Development Cooperation Agency

(Sida). Both programmes were in essence bioeconomy programmes with a comprehensive regional network of scientists, private sector actors and policy-makers forming a solid base for bioscience R&D collaboration, innovation and bioeconomy policy development. The collaboration between European and East African scientists was a key feature in both programmes.

This book, developed by SEI and partners in collaboration with Routledge, is building on the SEI legacy of exploring how bioscience innovation can contribute to solve major environmental and development challenges in various parts of the world. The 20 chapters in the book, written by high profile authors, deal with a wide range of issues affecting the development of bioeconomies in particular in Europe and Africa. The book also provides advice and guidance to assist policy-makers, scientists, civil society and the private sector on how to implement the transition towards sustainable bioeconomies. It is my hope that this book will contribute to science based dialogues that foster evidence based governance and innovation, and ultimately move biosciences from the lab to the market where they can make a positive contribution to sustainable development. It is also my hope that the book inspires an increased collaboration between Europe and Africa on how to effectively use modern bioscience as a tool for the development of knowledge based bioeconomies. A particular acknowledgment is extended to Dr. Ivar Virgin who has spearheaded the work on biosciences and the bioeconomy at SEI, and Dr. Jane Morris who together with Ivar has edited this book.

Jakob Granit, PhD
Centre Director, Stockholm Environment Institute,
Stockholm Deputy Director SEI

Part I

Introduction

Why this book?

1   Background and overview of the book

Ivar Virgin and E. Jane Morris

Setting the scene

The world faces an uncertain future with a predicted dramatic increase in demand for renewable resources, otherwise known as bioresources, such as food crops, livestock and biofuels. One of this century's biggest challenges is therefore likely to be how we meet this demand in a way that does not jeopardize current and future generations' quality of life. This is what we mean by sustainable development, defined as 'development that meets the needs of the present without compromising the ability of future generations to meet their own needs' (World Commission on Economic Development, 1987). There have been many elaborations on this basic concept (Kates *et al.*, 2005), but the quest for methods to meet the increasing demand for bioresources in a resource-effective, climate-smart and sustainable manner remains consistently at the top of the agenda for policymakers all around the world.

The task of feeding a global population of over nine billion by 2050 whilst critical resources such as water, energy and land become increasingly scarce generates debate on issues such as the global food supply and 'food vs fuel'. A critical step in meeting rising food demands is to sustainably increase crop yields on the agricultural land already in use. The term 'sustainable agricultural intensification' has been defined by the Montpellier Panel as 'the goal of producing more food with less impact on the environment, intensifying food production while ensuring the natural resource base on which agriculture depends is sustained, and indeed improved, for future generations' (Montpellier Panel, 2013, p.4). While the definition of the Montpellier Panel only addresses food production, the concept is relevant in a broader context if all the demands for bioresources are to be met in a sustainable way. Crop and other bioresource yields must be increased through the use of new technologies, particularly bioscience technologies, while at the same time reducing agricultural inputs (Ringler *et al.*, 2013). Genetic engineering, including genetic modification (GM) and more recently gene editing of crops form key components in the arsenal of technologies available to bioscientists aiming to achieve this goal, yet discussion of their benefits and risks continues to cause considerable debate. At the same time as meeting the increasing demands for food and biofuels, farming systems worldwide also have to meet a rapidly increasing demand for renewable biobased industrial raw materials such as biofuels, green chemicals, biobased oils and plastics, which are changing the conditions for agricultural production. Spectacular achievements in the field of biosciences are contributing to a transition whereby biobased alternatives for energy, chemicals and materials are becoming more economic and more mainstream.

This has led to the development of the term 'knowledge-based bioeconomies', which increasingly are seen as a tool for creating sustainable economic growth based on renewable resources – a growth moving away from the fossil fuel economy and responding to pressing local and global challenges, not least climate change. The development of knowledge-based bioeconomies has also been viewed as a tool to revitalize rural communities, increasing the agricultural and forestry production base and the opportunities for local value addition. It has also been seen as a critical tool for developing a circular economy, recycling energy, material flows and decoupling economic growth from the unsustainable use of scarce resources and emission of greenhouse gases.

To date, more than 40 countries have developed bioeconomy-related strategies or are in different ways promoting the development of bioeconomies to address various challenges such as climate change, promoting sustainability, economic growth and job creation (German Bioeconomy Council, 2015). The European Commission has set a long-term goal to develop a sustainable, competitive, resource-efficient low carbon economy by 2050 (EC, 2011). The development of a low carbon economy would help Europe in shifting its fossil fuel dependent economy to one in which products from the industry and energy to a larger degree than today are derived from renewable biomass. This is also supported and outlined in the European Strategy and Action Plan: *Innovating for Sustainable Growth: A Bio-economy for Europe* (EC, 2012). African countries have been slower than Europe to adopt the concept of a bioeconomy, and it is only South Africa that has a bioeconomy strategy. However a number of countries including Kenya, Uganda and Nigeria have developed bioenergy and/or biotechnology strategies and/or policies, which link to the concept of bioeconomy. It is apparent that for many countries in Africa, sustainable livelihoods and job creation are the overwhelming priorities.

What exactly then do we mean by a 'bioeconomy'? The Organization for Economic Cooperation and Development (OECD) (OECD, 2009) originally defined a bioeconomy quite narrowly as a world where biotechnology contributes to a significant share of economic output. The European Commission widened this to define the bioeconomy as the sustainable 'production of renewable biological resources and the conversion of these resources and waste streams into value added products, such as food, feed, fibre bio-based products and bioenergy' (EC, 2012, p.3). The South African Bio-economy Strategy (Department of Science and Technology, 2013) defines it as activities that make use of bio-innovations, based on biological sources, materials and processes to generate sustainable economic, social and environmental development. During the first Global Bioeconomy Summit held in Berlin (24–25 November 2015) it was agreed that the bioeconomy takes different shapes and is defined in different ways around the world. In the final Summit communiqué another wider bioeconomy definition was offered where it was noted that 'an understanding of *"bioeconomy as the knowledge-based production and utilization of biological resources, innovative biological processes and principles to sustainably provide goods and services across all economic sectors"* is shared by many' (Global Bioeconomy Summit, 2015, p.4). In this book we embrace the term broadly, drawing from all definitions rather than confining ourselves to one.

While sustainability is central in most definitions of knowledge-based bioeconomies, it has been pointed out that the transition to a bioeconomy does not necessarily guarantee sustainability, and that a number of related conditions need to be in place including appropriate policies and governance, necessitating an interdisciplinary approach (Pfau *et al.*, 2014; Global Bioeconomy Summit, 2015).

A key feature of a bioeconomy is that scientific research and knowledge can be applied not only for the production of food, feed and fibre but also for producing a range of agro-industrial and value-added products with potential applications in many sectors, e.g. pharmaceuticals, chemicals and energy sectors. The rising demand for both food and non-food biomass may therefore, at least partly, transform agriculture from a food to a biomass-supplying processing sector. This creates a new production and value chain landscape in which the utilization of the various feedstock crops and intermediate products is more flexible than it was in the past. This is in many cases good news for farmers, increasing the competition for their primary produce and giving them more options to access various value chains and markets. This is by some regarded as a problem, often referred to as a fuel vs food conflict, where use of scarce agricultural land and water for non-food agricultural products may have negative impact on food production, food security and rural livelihoods. Many experts would however argue that there are many ways a bioeconomy can be organized so that production of renewable non-food/ feed products can support food security and livelihoods, and that more diverse uses of biomass would ensure its more efficient use and reduce the problems of waste in the agricultural sector.

In the final communiqué from the Global Bioeconomy Summit in Berlin (2015) a key message was that food security is a fundamental priority in a sustainable bioeconomy. The task for countries, governments, stakeholders and actors is therefore to develop multifunctional bioeconomies where production of renewable non-food/feed products is done in support of an increased production and availability of nutritious food at local and global levels.

The rapid progress in modern biosciences (by which we mean the underlying platform technologies) and biotechnology (by which we mean the application of bioscience to deliver new products or processes), with the potential to revolutionize medicine, agriculture and our use of biological resources, is an important driver of knowledge-based bioeconomies. A key question in this book is therefore to what extent and how the advances in modern bioscience and biotechnology, not least in genetics, genomics and genetic modification, can contribute to sustainable bioeconomies. Our book also focuses on how modern biosciences can assist the development of more productive, resource-efficient crop and agricultural systems that use water, nutrients, energy and agricultural land in a more sustainable manner and enable us to derive more value-added products from biobased materials. While there is much public concern regarding the risks associated with the adoption of new technologies, particularly genetic modification, in this book we do not focus specifically on the issue of biosafety, since we recognize that there are well-established mechanisms in place to assess and ensure safety. Rather, we focus on the opportunities offered by modern bioscience to address the problems faced by the planet in the coming years.

Focus on Europe and Africa

Europe and Africa have different challenges and different opportunities in a global economy and in terms of moving towards a sustainable bioeconomy. The transformation towards a bioeconomy requires a fundamental socioeconomic transition and must comprise changes not only in technology but also in markets, user practices, policy, culture and institutions (Urmetzer and Pyka, 2014).

There are many aspects that make a comparison between Africa and Europe interesting. For better or worse, due to the colonial history, the relations between the two continents have always been intertwined in terms of cultural, linguistic, legal, and political and economic influences. Trade between Africa and Europe has a long history, but during the last decade trade between the two continents has increased rapidly, and there are prospects for further integration of African and European economies. The increasing migration flow from Africa to Europe, while it creates its own challenges, is also creating new opportunities for linkages and collaboration.

In Europe, while the European Commission has expressed exciting prospects for a bioeconomy, the reality is gloomier. Resistance against GM crops and novel crop breeding techniques limits the options. Precise and efficient crop breeding technologies are needed in the development of resource efficient and climate-smart agricultural production systems for food, feed and also renewable industrial products. Modern breeding is increasingly based on GM and other molecular technologies. The scepticism about GM crops and other modern breeding technologies, combined with demanding regulatory frameworks and insufficient R&D funding, has led European plant breeding and life science companies to move their advanced bioscience research efforts to countries such as the United States or Brazil. The loss of skills and private sector actors able to invest in and develop bioscience applications for European farming systems may therefore be a limitation in the transition of European countries towards modern bioeconomies where a wide variety of agricultural products and tailor-made agriculture systems provide food and feed but also renewable raw material for the industry. A more positive outcome though can be envisaged where European bioeconomies are based on opportunities in other areas, such as health, advanced value chains and environmental remediation.

Africa lags behind much of the rest of the world, both scientifically and economically, and faces many challenges. However, many countries in sub-Saharan Africa (SSA) are well endowed with a diverse range of renewable bio-resources that through the application of modern biosciences and bioscience innovation systems could be used as a basis for economic growth, food security and improving livelihoods. Despite the lack of technological and infrastructural capacity in Africa, many African countries may be more willing to embrace rapid change than European countries. While SSA is not yet in a position to meet its own food needs, Europe at the same time faces energy constraints and food production limitations, and is already looking to Africa for sources of renewable energy (Showers, 2014).

There is now a growing recognition in both Europe and Africa that bioscience innovations could contribute to new resource-efficient and environmentally friendly agro-processing opportunities, value chains and diversified production systems creating an increased demand for local crops, thereby potentially improving rural livelihoods. The importance of moving towards a knowledge-based bioeconomy is emphasized by the fact that the current trajectory of economic development on the African continent is ecologically unsustainable, particularly in SSA which is one of the regions where the environment and ecosystem services are most threatened by human impacts.

European scientists and European aid/donor organizations have for the last 20 years been deeply involved in building scientific capacity in Africa to adapt and adopt the modern bioscience to the needs of various African sectors. At the same time, regulatory systems for modern biotechnology, specifically concerning the introduction of GM crops in Africa, have to a great extent adopted a European precautionary approach. Both Europe and Africa have largely lagged behind other regions such as North and South America and Asia.

In this book we explore the trajectories being followed by both African and European countries using modern biosciences in their attempt to develop their bioeconomies, comparing and contrasting their situations but also highlighting synergies and productive instances of cooperation, and we draw on these experiences to distil key messages for stakeholders in both Africa and Europe.

The chapters

In the introductory section of the book, Chapter 2 (Virgin *et al.*) elaborates on the global threats and challenges and the urgent need to adjust our development path to a direction that respects our planetary boundaries. Agricultural production needs to increase by 70% by the year 2050, and most of this increase will have to be achieved without increasing the area of land devoted to agriculture. Together with developments in bioscience, appropriate strategies and policy interventions will be required.

Chapter 3 (Morris) highlights the role of bioscience in delivering a new 'green revolution' in agriculture, by means of a 'gene revolution'. The chapter provides an overview of the exciting developments in bioscience, highlighting the current state of the art, but also some of the challenges that lie ahead.

Part II of the book addresses some of the challenges faced by Europe and Africa in achieving sustainable food security. In Chapter 4 (von Witzke and Noleppa) it is pointed out that agricultural yield growth is levelling off in Europe, to a large extent due to neglect of agricultural research. Europe is a net importer of food and agricultural products, and if it is to realize its ambitions of moving towards a bioeconomy then attention must be paid to achieving productivity growth through investment in modern bioscience. Similarly in Chapter 5 (Thomson) the need for African farmers to increase productivity by embracing modern technology, including the use of GM crops, is highlighted and some encouraging examples given of development of GM crops that have the potential to benefit African agriculture if regulatory hurdles can be overcome. Chapter 6 (Schluep Campo *et al.*) brings the issues facing the two continents together, since both are in a situation of food trade deficit. The need for policy alignment and investment in capacity for public sector agricultural innovation is stressed, as is the negative impact of Europe's anti-GM policies on the adoption of modern crop breeding technologies, including GM crops in Africa.

Whereas Part II of the book dealt with many of the challenges facing Europe and Africa, Part III outlines the future potential for bioscience innovations, if they were to be applied, to contribute towards resource-efficient economies. Chapter 7 (Olsson *et al.*) uses the example of wheat to demonstrate how, by improving nitrogen-use efficiency and introducing perenniality, modern bioscience has the potential to contribute significantly to climate change mitigation. In Chapter 8, Stymne describes significant opportunities for increased use of biobased feed-stocks to meet the needs of the European chemicals and materials industries (in preference to biofuel production), but expresses concern that tailoring crops to meet the needs of the chemical industry will require significant investment in genetic engineering and is unlikely to be realized in the current European political climate. In Chapter 9 (Morris *et al.*), a number of bioscience innovations under development in Africa are described, ranging from improved crops to novel agro-processing technologies and reduction of post-harvest losses, and finally showing the potential for production of plant-based pharmaceuticals in Africa. Chapter 10 (Nuwamanya *et al.*) homes in on one particular crop of importance to Africa, namely cassava. Cassava has value as both a food security crop and as a source of added value processed products. The chapter provides case studies on a number of initiatives that are under way across the continent to improve the production of, and value addition to, cassava. Chapter 11 (Johnson and Mulugetta) charts the history of biofuels development in both Europe and Africa and looks to the future where cooperation between the continents in both science and policy domains could improve the chances for biofuels to become a vibrant part of the bioeconomy.

Part IV of the book explores a range of ideas that will affect the future develop-ment of bioeconomies in both Europe and Africa. The section starts with a longer term view of the future of modern bioscience in Chapter 12 (Murphy), outlining opportunities that could revolutionize our current perspectives on what could be delivered by the bioeconomy. In Chapter 13 Komen and Ecuru demonstrate how modern bioscience is already diffusing into small farming systems in Africa and catalysing growth of bioenterprises in the region. In Africa, there is a dominant role for public-sector organizations, often working in international public-public and public-private bioscience programmes. Expanded European and African collaboration could result in significant benefits for the development of an African bioeconomy. Chapter 14 (Smart and Wesseler) addresses some extremely important questions regarding the socioeconomic challenges that face both Europe and Africa as they move towards bioeconomies, including issues such as what drives the development of a bioeconomy, how the benefits (and risks) are distributed, how innovations are diffused in different socioeconomic contexts, and how issues such as globalization and governance impact on the development of bioeconomies. The section concludes with Chapter 15 (Virgin and Liavoga) demonstrating the positive role that a sustained investment in African bioscience can have on bioeconomic development in Africa, in this case through two Swedish-funded programmes in East Africa, BIO-EARN and Bio-Innovate.

Part V moves us into an analysis of policies and strategies that influence the development of bioeconomies on the two continents. Chapter 16 (Carrez) outlines the elements of the European bioeconomy strategy and the strategies of some individual member states. The striking issue highlighted is the mismatch between bioeconomy strategies and policy regimes in Europe, where policies are often uncoordinated (e.g. a focus on biofuels providing market distortion against other uses of biomass) and in some areas even stifling (e.g. policies on GMOs). Chapter 17 (Ecuru) details a number of pan-African policies that could support the development of African bioeconomies, but that are too broad in scope and deficient in implementation. The need to build a functioning African bioscience innovation system with a critical mass of appropriately trained scientists is stressed. As discussed in Chapter 18 (Wolson), one important component of training is in the area of intellectual property (IP), where a strong cohort of IP-literate and IP-articulate African stakeholders is needed. Chapter 19 (Komen) returns to the issue of policy incoherence in Europe by highlighting the negative impact on African development.

Finally, in Part VI the book concludes with Chapter 20, which gives some recommendations on how countries in Europe and Africa can collaborate and share experiences. The chapter, and the book, ends with a ten-point action plan for each continent for how bioscience innovation could be further fostered and become a more effective tool in progressing towards successful and sustainable European and African bioeconomies.

References

Department of Science and Technology. 2013. *The Bio-Economy Strategy*. [Online]. Pretoria: Department of Science and Technology. [Accessed 4 May 2016]. Available from: http://www.dst.gov.za/images/ska/Bioeconomy%20Strategy.pdf

EC (European Commission). 2011. *A Roadmap for Moving Towards a Competitive Low Carbon Economy in 2050*. [Online]. [Accessed 8 December 2015]. Available from: http://eur-lex.europa.eu/legal-content/EN/TXT/?uri=CELEX:52011DC0112

EC (European Commission). 2012. *Innovating for Sustainable Growth: A Bioeconomy for Europe*. [Online]. [Accessed 4 December 2015]. Available from: http://ec.europa.eu/research/bioeconomy/pdf/201202_innovating_sustainable_growth_en.pdf

German Bioeconomy Council. 2015. *Bioeconomy Policy (Part II). Synopsis of National Strategies Around the World*. [Online]. [Accessed 8 December 2015]. Available from: http://gbs2015.com/fileadmin/gbs2015/Downloads/Bioeconomy-Policy_Part-II.pdf

Global Bioeconomy Summit. 2015. Communiqué: Making bioeconomy work for sustainable development. [Online]. [Accessed 4 December 2015]. Available from: http://gbs2015.com/fileadmin/gbs2015/Downloads/Communique_final_neu.pdf

Kates, R.W. *et al.* 2005. What is sustainable development? Goals, indicators, values and practice. *Environment: Science and Policy for Sustainable Development* 47(3), pp.8–21.

Montpellier Panel. 2013. *Sustainable Intensification: A New Paradigm for African Agriculture*. London: Agriculture for Impact.

OECD (Organisation for Economic Co-operation and Development). 2009. *The Bioeconomy to 2030: Designing a Policy Agenda*. [Online]. [Accessed 4 December 2015]. Available from: http://www.oecd.org/futures/long-termtechnologicalsocietalchallenges/thebioeconomyto2030designingapolicyagenda.htm

Pfau, S.F. *et al.* 2014. Visions of sustainability in bioeconomy research. *Sustainability* 6(3), pp.1222–49.

Ringler, C. *et al.* 2013. Sustainable agricultural innovation: the promise of innovative farming practices. In: *2013 Global Food Policy Report*. Washington, DC: International Food Policy Research Institute.

Showers, K.B. 2014. Europe's long history of extracting African renewable energy: contexts for African scientists, technologists, innovators and policy-makers. *African Journal of Science, Technology, Innovation and Development* 6(4), pp.301–13.

Urmetzer, S. and Pyka, A. 2014. *Varieties of Knowledge-based Bioeconomies*. FZID Discussion Paper 91-2014. Stuttgart: Forschungszentrum FZID, Universität Hohenheim.

World Commission on Environment and Development. 1987. *Our Common Future*. New York: Oxford University Press.

2 Benefits and challenges of a new knowledge-based bioeconomy

Ivar Virgin, Matthew Fielding,
Melinda Fones Sundell, Holger Hoff and
Jakob Granit

Introduction

Feeding a world population of well over 9 billion without significantly expanding the land area devoted to agriculture is one of the greatest challenges in this century. Apart from the dramatic increase in global food and feed demand, there is also a rapidly growing demand for non-food, non-feed agro-industrial products for applications spanning many sectors — industry, chemicals and energy. Meeting this demand will be a great test for human ingenuity to drastically increase the productivity on the fertile soils already in production, without causing land degradation. Climate change, water resource scarcity, increased climate variability and geopolitical uncertainties are however already today limiting agricultural production at a global scale. The era of plentiful and under-priced resources is hence slowly coming to an end and agricultural land, biodiversity, terrestrial, aquatic and marine ecosystems and corresponding ecosystem services are under increasing pressure (UNEP, 2014). A key question is therefore how humanity will meet a future massive bioresource demand in a resource-efficient, climate-smart and sustainable manner.

What today is considered as conventional high-input agriculture has been very successful in meeting an increased food and feed demand in most parts of the world, except in regions such as sub-Saharan Africa. This is largely due to a continuous improvement of crop productivity derived from crop genetic improvements but also through greater use of external inputs such as energy, fertilizers, pesticides and irrigation. This increased use of external inputs is also placing a burden on the environment and contributes to a significant part of global greenhouse gas (GHG) emissions. Agriculture is also the largest consumer of water and the main source of nutrient pollution of groundwater and surface water. Pesticide use is in many places a serious threat to human and environmental health. The increasing costs of inputs such as fertilizer, agrochemicals and energy also account for a large part of total production cost for farmers all over the world. Modern precision agriculture demonstrates promising opportunities to reduce inputs and improve resource and cost efficiency but such technologies are expensive and so far mostly used by farmers in the North.

As a response to high-input conventional agriculture, alternative low-input agriculture systems, such as organic and agro-ecological farming, have gained increased attention not least by farmers and consumers in Europe and United States. There is today increasing demand for organically produced food products in advanced economies demonstrating a promising commercial future for these production systems and their products. With particular crops and growing conditions, good management practices, input of nutrients from conventional systems and high labour input, organic farming can nearly match the yields of conventional systems (Seufert *et al.*, 2012). However, for many crops, particularly cereals, organic agriculture results in low yields and would therefore need more land to produce the same amount of food as conventional farms. Such an expansion of land could in many cases result in deforestation and biodiversity loss, which would undermine the environmental benefits of organic practices. When impacts on indirect land use change are taken into account, low-intensity agricultural systems often have higher GHG emissions per unit product and are therefore often less climate smart than high-input agriculture systems (Leifeld *et al.*, 2013; Tuomisto *et al.*, 2012). Low-intensity agricultural systems are therefore deemed by many scientists to be insufficient to sustainably produce the bulk of the globe's cereal-based food and feed demand (Seufert *et al.*, 2012). They will thus not be able to provide sufficient agro-based goods and services to fully support the livelihoods of an expanding global population and the accompanying changes in lifestyles of an increasingly affluent world population.

An alternative and additional route to meet the rising demand for agricultural produce in a resource-efficient and climate-smart manner is to make more use of modern biosciences, including genetic engineering of crops. The benefits of this are exemplified in many chapters in this book, but in essence, through the rapid advances in bioscience it is possible to tailor make:

- highly productive crops and crop production systems tolerant to biotic and abiotic stress, including disease and drought, and with an enhanced ability to absorb nutrients, limiting the use of pesticides and increasing the efficiency of fertilizers;
- food and feed with improved nutritional characteristics, improving human health and animal feeding efficiencies, reducing waste and livestock-related GHG emission and making agriculture more climate smart;
- productive and resource-efficient crop production systems able to efficiently provide ecosystem services, sequester carbon and mitigate climate change.

Advances in biosciences can also result in crops or other biological systems (algae, microorganisms, etc.) engineered to produce raw material direct for industry. This is propelling a transition whereby biobased alternatives for energy, chemical and materials are slowly becoming more economic and mainstream and available in larger quantities. This has led to the development of the term 'knowledge-based bio-economies' or 'KBBE' (EC, 2012). The development of bioeconomies is increasingly seen as a tool for creating sustainable economic growth

Table 2.1 A selection of national bioeconomy strategies

Countries	Bioeconomy-related actions and strategies
Austria	Bioeconomy Background Paper (2013)
Canada	Blueprint Beyond Moose and Mountains (2011)
China	Bioindustry Development Plan (2012)
Denmark	Agreement on Green Growth (2009)
EU Commission	A Bioeconomy for Europe (2012)
Finland	The Finnish Bioeconomy Strategy (2014)
Germany	National Policy Strategy on Bioeconomy (2013) National Research Strategy BioEconomy 2030
Ireland	Delivering our Green Potential (2012)
Korea	Bio-Vision 2018 plan
Malaysia	Bioeconomy Transformation Programme (2012)
Netherlands	Framework Memorandum on the Biobased Economy (2012)
South Africa	South Africa – the Bioeconomy Strategy (2013)
Sweden	Research and Innovation Strategy for Bio-based Economy (2012)
USA	National Bioeconomy Blueprint (2012)

Source: German Bioeconomy Council (2015)

based on renewable resources and can support a transition away from the fossil fuel economy. The development of KBBEs has also been seen as a tool to revitalize rural communities, supporting job creation and increasing the production base and the opportunities for local value addition and agro-processing.

Governments around the world are now developing their bioeconomy strategies. A compilation of some recent national strategies related to the development of knowledge-based bioeconomies is shown in Table 2.1. Further information on European bioeconomy strategies is provided in Chapter 16.

This chapter aims to describe the various challenges and issues a KBBE in Europe and Africa has to respond to. The chapter will also try to explain why modern biosciences, resource-efficient agricultural production systems, innovative agro-processing and value chains are important for both Europe and Africa.

What a knowledge-based bioeconomy needs to respond to

Optimizing the use of biomass

Ultimately, a KBBE is largely about optimizing the production and use of bioresources and biomass. The total annual global primary production of biomass is around 200 billion tonnes (Rosillo-Calle, 2012) and of this roughly some 12 billion tonnes are extracted for human use. Around 58 per cent of this is used for animal feed, 15 per cent for direct food consumption, 10 per cent as biobased industrial feedstock and 17 per cent as energy carriers (Piotrowski *et al.*, 2015). The most important biobased industrial products are today paper, cellulose, building materials and fuel and to a lesser degree, green chemicals, bioplastics, composites, lubricants and pharmaceuticals. The demand for the latter type of products may change as industries, not least in the chemical sector, are increasingly looking at phasing out fossil-fuel-based raw material in favour of biobased renewables in their future production schemes. Markets for various types of biobased raw material for biofuels will also probably increase in the future. In this context it is however important to add that the world's energy demands cannot be met by biomass alone, but need to rely largely on other renewable energy sources such as hydropower, solar and wind.

In discussing the structure and features of a modern bioeconomy there is an opportunity to address sustainable increase in biomass production at full landscape scale, rather than the common focus on agricultural areas only. This would include discussions on improved, resource-efficient and climate-smart production under different regimes in different landscapes, including forests, grasslands, aquatic productions systems and multifunctional landscapes.

Putting the bioeconomy into a broader context

A general goal of a KBBE is to enable economic growth to be combined with ecological and social sustainability. It therefore needs to be a core element of sustainability concepts such as the 'green economy', decoupling economic development from resource use and environmental pressures. It also needs to be a central part of a circular economy, reusing and recycling existing resources with the aim of reducing waste and closing material loops.

The development of the bioeconomy is indeed receiving increasing attention, and the transition towards a bioeconomy is often associated with increased sustainability (EC, 2012). However, there is also a controversy in scientific and public fora on whether or not such a transition necessarily will lead to a better, more sustainable future. Frequently mentioned problems are the competition between food and fuel production and the potential negative environmental and social effects of land use change and intensification (Pfau *et al.*, 2014). It is clear that a KBBE is not a silver bullet solution to food security and increased agricultural productivity and cannot be considered as something self-evidently sustainable. Instead it needs to be designed, planned, regulated and supported in such a way that it effectively functions as a driver of sustainability in the development, use and reuse of bioresources.

There are also a number of other drivers affecting the production and use of biomass besides the continuously growing demand, which interact with the bioeconomy agenda both locally and globally. This includes drivers such as global trade, urbanization, increasingly complex global food and bioproducts value chains, public debate and political responses on sustainability issues related to agricultural and forestry production regimes.

Lastly, while increasing food production and crop productivity is important, it is also crucial to address the logistical challenges (e.g. inadequate road infrastructure, lack of storage and agro-processing facilities leading to post-harvest losses) and socioeconomic challenges (e.g. weak markets and poor market access) which currently severely limit access to food for many food insecure.

Biophysical and environmental challenges

Some of the most critical biophysical and environmental challenges and the potential response not least through using modern biosciences are described below. In a KBBE these challenges will have to be addressed in an integrated manner assessing the potential synergies and trade-offs between the different climate-, land-, water- and ecosystem-related challenges.

Climate change

Climate change is and will increasingly be a key factor decisive for agricultural production on a global and local scale. Although some agricultural regions will benefit from climate change, negative effects such as droughts, new pests and diseases are expected to dominate on a global level (Foley *et al.*, 2011; Smith *et al.*, 2014). Thus, adapting crop production to a changing climate is imperative for any KBBE to keep providing a growing human population with food, fibre and fuel in the coming decades. The other challenge besides adaptation is mitigation which requires a drastic decrease in GHG emissions. According to the International Panel on Climate Change (IPCC), the AFOLU (agriculture, forestry and other land use) sectors were responsible for approximately 24 per cent of total anthropogenic GHG emissions in 2010 (Foley *et al.*, 2011; Smith *et al.*, 2014).

An important task goal in a KBBE should therefore be to decrease our dependence on fossil energy and decrease GHG emissions. Here, bioscience innovation could help in the development of agro-industrial crop production systems replacing fossil fuel products (described in Chapters 8–12 in this book). Modern biosciences could promote land use and agricultural systems reducing agricultural GHG emissions but also more adapted to climate change. In the long run, modern biosciences could promote agricultural systems that even may act as net sinks of CO_2. This would include an increased application of agro-ecological principles, smarter feeding systems for livestock improving livestock productivity or converting annual crops to perennial crops (described in Chapters 7, 9 and 12 in this book). However, there remain environmental and socioeconomic risks. If biomass is produced and harvested unsustainably, ecosystems will be damaged and potential reductions of GHGs will be reversed.

Increasing the efficiency of nutrient use

Modern agriculture is dependent on fertilizers. Production of nitrogen fertilizers is energy-intensive and results in additional GHG emission. The European fertilizer industry has made significant advances in reducing GHG emissions through minimizing N_2O emissions in its fertilizer production processes. Further improvements are possible – although still not commercially viable – by using renewable energy sources in the production process. Phosphorus, a key component in fertilizers, is extracted at few places in the world and is likely to become more scarce and expensive in the coming decades. Fertilizer run-off causing eutrophication and anoxic zones in lakes and the seas is also a problem in many areas of the world. Therefore, it is crucial to develop agricultural systems that minimize nitrogen and phosphorus leaching and recycle nutrients. In large parts of Africa, the problem is the reverse, with nutrient mining and nutrient depleted soils and very limited use of fertilizers. So there is significant potential to improve overall biomass production while respecting the integrity of ecosystems through redistribution of fertilizer use from surplus to deficit regions. In this regard, systems and technologies that recycle nutrients and close nutrient loops between urban and rural farming areas will be important.

An important task in a KBBE is to create crop production systems that assimilate nitrogen and other nutrients more efficiently and hence are able to produce more biomass with less fertilizer input. Such crops are described in more detail in Chapter 7 of this book.

Water scarcity

Water is increasingly scarce in many agricultural production areas. Improved irrigation techniques have a high potential for reducing water demand while increasing food production (Jägermeyr *et al.*, 2016). Climate change will however aggravate that trend in many areas of the world, which may be increasingly affected by severe droughts and extreme weather conditions.

A central task in a KBBE is to create crop production systems with reduced irrigation demand which are more tolerant to climate change stresses, including drought, pathogens and new emerging diseases. Modern biosciences can support agro-processing and agricultural value chains to improve their water and other resource efficiencies and convert agro-waste and urban waste that today pollutes freshwater sources to useful products such as bioenergy and fertilizers. Bioscience-based crops tolerant to drought and waste conversion technologies are described in Chapters 3, 5, 9, 12 and 15 in this book.

Land scarcity, land degradation and ecosystem services

At the global scale, agricultural land is becoming scarce and ecosystems and their services are under pressure in both Europe and Africa. Land use changes are cumulatively a major driver of global environmental change. The most important form of land conversion is an expansion of crop and pastoral land often at the expense of forests and other ecosystems providing environmental services, resilience and biotic diversity (Lambin and Meyfroidt, 2011). Overexploitation of agricultural and forestry land involves a risk of soil erosion, land degradation and at worst desertification. Converting woodlands, savanna and shrubland to agricultural land often leads to environmental problems such as loss of biodiversity and additional GHG emissions. All this limits the manoeuvring space for expanding and intensifying the use of arable land.

In Europe agricultural productivity and input intensity is very high. Agricultural expansion has mostly come to a halt in Europe, while most natural ecosystems have been modified or converted long ago. The situation is different in Africa, which has been claimed to have more room for agricultural land expansion (Deininger *et al.*, 2011), but where expansion may have associated environmental and socioeconomic impacts. Conversion of natural land and land degradation is ongoing in Africa and is in many places accelerating, while input intensity and productivity are still very low. Accordingly, bioresource production solutions have to be adapted to the respective context where inclusive innovation systems, benefit sharing mechanisms, knowledge and technology transfer will be important.

An important task in a KBBE is thus to develop highly productive crops and bioresource production systems which can meet the increasing demands with minimal expansion of agricultural areas, in order to keep ecosystems and their broad range of services intact. It is also equally important to develop bioresource production systems that contribute to preserving existing ecosystem services. A KBBE could also help to rehabilitate degraded land and improve soils. For a more extensive discussion on these tasks see Chapters 4 and 6 in this book.

Development challenges and opportunities

Broadening the innovation agenda

Today a large part of the funding for bioscience R&D is targeted to the health sector. The promise of a modern bioeconomy is, however, to a large degree connected to agricultural biosciences supporting sustainable and productive agricultural systems. To realize the potential of a modern bioeconomy, increased public and private sector investments are needed on such things as i) modern breeding platforms for crops more tolerant to drought, pests or poor soils, ii) climate-smart, environmentally friendly, resource-efficient agricultural production systems, value chains and agro-processing systems.

An important part of the bioeconomy innovation agenda is the potentially increasing role for new types of highly productive and resource-efficient production systems for biobased synthetic food and feed (e.g. vegetal, algae, insect or microbial substitutes for meat or other livestock products).

An increasing proportion of bioscience R&D and innovation for a modern bioeconomy is developed in the private sector, and often by large multinational companies. Their primary interest is in developing and marketing bioscience technologies for high-profit markets and 'global crops' such as maize, soybean and cotton in which they can control parts of the value chain. These multinational companies are, however, often less interested in low-profit, bioscience innovations of crucial importance to smallholder farmers. Governments and public sector actors therefore have a crucial role in promoting bioscience innovation in support of a broader innovation agenda.

In knowledge intensive areas such as biosciences, the existence of a strong public sector research base is therefore important to ensure that promising bioscience technologies are made available to a broad set of actors and for the public good. The public sector has a key role in promoting a broad use and uptake of innovations supporting inclusive economic growth and markets for more equal benefit sharing. In Africa in particular, public research organizations and universities are central in adapting modern biosciences to broader societal needs, including the needs of smallholder farming systems and local agro-processing actors. Unfortunately, although public R&D is important for inclusive knowledge development, public research organizations and universities have not been effective in moving ideas and technologies beyond research into the market space. Linking public research organizations, universities and market actors is therefore key in improving the chances that the benefits of bioscience innovation also reach smallholder farmers, resource-poor communities and a broader set of market actors.

The path from innovation to market is treacherous, and is likely to be even more so with innovations in biosciences. In the case of promoting new bioscience-based agro-industrial pathways, current business models, often based on fossil fuel input, need to be altered. The barriers of doing so could be so high that many promising technologies fall by the wayside and fail to deliver their potential. Policies and government support are therefore needed to support the transition to knowledge-based bioeconomies. This could be through providing incentives, such as supportive regulations, government procurement regimes, new infrastructures, financing support, tax reductions and business incubation supporting biobased SMEs and start-ups.

New value chains and converting waste to useful products

Modern agro-processing and value chains are key components of a modern bioeconomy and have the potential to add economic value to primary agricultural production and convert biowaste to useful products, creating new opportunities for farmers and agro-processing actors.

Bioprocessing and agro-processing industries are entering a dynamic phase offering new opportunities for a multitude of new value chains, recycling energy and material flows both in Europe and Africa. In both these regions, there are large untapped bioresource production opportunities that offer building blocks for expanded utilization of bioresources and the growth of agro-processing industries. This includes the development of new biorefinery industries where modern biotechnology can add value to the primary production and convert agro-waste into valuable products such as feed, enzymes, fuel and at the same time minimize environmental impact.

While traditionally modern biosciences have been developed and implemented by industries, there are opportunities for much more rural participation in the innovation processes leading towards a KBBE. This is particularly true for countries in Africa, with large farming communities in search of new livelihood opportunities. For instance there may well be new products that could be derived through value addition to various horticultural products, traditional grains or natural products.

The European farming sector would greatly benefit from a larger variety of crop alternatives and value chains, which would support crop rotation and new value chain possibilities for farmers and agro-processing actors. In many parts of Africa there is great need to add value and reduce post-harvest losses by processing and preserving crops of great importance for the smallholder farming sector. This includes crops such as traditional grains, vegetables, fruits, legumes and tubers, staple crops and crops more tolerant to climate variability and change such as cassava, millet and sorghum.

Broadening the value addition opportunities for crops and other bioresources would help revitalize farming communities in both Europe and Africa. Increasing local value addition opportunities to primary production would also be a method to support rural participation in knowledge-based bioeconomies. Since it is often inefficient to transport biomass long distances, it should ideally be processed close to the site where it is harvested or acquired. This may in many cases overturn the traditional economy of scale model in favour of economy of numbers where local production plants are integrated with other complementary industries. It is important, particularly in Africa, that a KBBE supports broad-based bioresource production and local value addition to primary produce that can be marketed in local, regional and rapidly emerging urban markets.

Resource allocation disputes

The central feature of a KBBE is that agricultural systems are not only producing food and feed but to an increasingly large extent also agro-industrial products in applications spanning many sectors. In the development of new non-food/feed biomass production areas conflicts of interest around resource allocation may arise, such as the food vs fuel disputes. In Europe there is the political debate on a ceiling for crop-based biofuels. This debate reflects a fear of increased GHG emissions and negative socioeconomic impacts resulting from indirect land use change that may occur when increased demand for biofuel crops displaces other crops to new areas. Disputes such as these need to be addressed, assessed and governed in an interdisciplinary manner.

In an African context, it is crucial that the development of agricultural systems producing a wider range of products, including bioenergy, does not negatively affect the ability of Africa to feed itself. Ideally, the development of an African KBBE and a linking of African farmers to a diversity of agri-business opportunities should instead lead to resilient production systems, increased food crop productivity and food production. In the long run this would assist African farmers to be more profitable and able to invest in higher production, increasing supplies of locally affordable food on African markets.

Social, policy and governance issues

Successful development of a sustainable bioeconomy will be determined not only by technical and scientific developments, but also by government policies, public opinion, cultural norms, and perceived social, economic, environmental, health risks and benefits. Ideally, a KBBE should bring prosperity to the parts of the globe where biomass is concentrated.

The KBBE is often connected to new large-scale production regimes and foreign direct investment (FDI) in agricultural land. The increase of FDI in agricultural land has caused concerns relating to the perceived negative effects on local food security and livelihoods. International investments may however, if done right, catalyse the development of KBBEs and bring much needed infra-structural investments, technology transfer and new agribusiness opportunities from which all can benefit (Hoff *et al.*, 2012). The question is therefore how investments in large-scale land use in a KBBE, including FDI, can be optimized to minimize the inherent risks for all involved and also bring benefits to local communities. Ideally the development of KBBEs and investments in new land use regimes and agro-value chains should be guided by governance mecha-nisms taking account of local interests and safeguarding local livelihoods and food security. Institutions responsible for governing land use should be appro-priately resourced for the task of attracting valuable investments whilst simul-taneously monitoring and ensuring the interest and rights of those with customary tenure of the land (Fielding *et al.*, 2015). This is not a small task and may necessitate cumbersome and technical processes such as amending existing and/or developing new regulations to frame monitoring and implementation of activities.

A KBBE requires effective governance of innovation, transparent decision-making and coherent well-anchored visions and strategies balancing risk and benefits. This includes the regulation of investments and production and trade of biomass and biomass products for inclusive social development and mini-mized environmental footprints. In the context of biosciences and particularly genetic modification, it will be important to find a balance between public pres-sure for stringent and demanding regulations and effective regulatory oversight not stifling bioscience innovation. To support such governance, there needs to be more interdisciplinary assessments and a consideration of insights from a broad set of scientific disciplines, including environmental, social and economic disciplines, to build up a joint knowledge base and tackle sustainability issues. When measuring success in a bioeconomy it is important that this is not only limited to monetary or production measures. The hope for a bioeconomy is that success can be achieved through a promotion of equitable profit sharing, improvements in access to healthcare and education, and the introduction of social safety nets.

Getting towards a KBBE in Europe

Europe, with its advanced agricultural, forestry, agro-processing and chemical sectors, has a great potential to become a globally competitive bioeconomy that shares knowledge and technologies with other regions globally, such as Africa.

As discussed in other parts of this book, crop productivity growth and food and feed self-sufficiency in Europe are lagging behind many other parts of the world, due to a range of factors, including limited public investments in agricultural innovation and incoherent agricultural policies.

There is at the same time an increasing understanding and also demand within the EU that the high-input agricultural system in Europe needs to be made more resource efficient, climate smart and sustainable. Within the European farming community, there is also a demand for a greater diversity of crop alternatives and connected value chains improving crop rotation opportunities and profitability for farmers and agro-processing actors. The tools of modern biosciences and a modern bioeconomy are well suited to respond to these demands, addressing breeding targets of importance to European farmers, the forestry sector and biobased industries. These include:

- crops tailored to lower levels of pesticide use and to agricultural practices requiring less energy, water, crop nutrients and labour input (e.g. low tillage and perennial grains);
- agro-industrial crops tailor-made to enhance the production of certain desirable compounds or renewable components for an expanding biobased industrial sector;
- a more productive, sustainable and knowledge-intensive forestry sector converting biomass to a range of renewable products.

The development of such bioresource production systems would assist Europe in shifting its fossil fuel dependent economy to one in which health, fibre, industrial products and energy are to a larger degree than today derived from renewable biomass resources. This is also to a large extent outlined in the European Strategy and Action Plan *Innovating for Sustainable Growth: A Bio-economy for Europe* (EC, 2012).

Bioscience-based breeding including genetic engineering is an important part of a KBBE. There is however great political and consumer-based resistance in Europe against bioscience-based breeding and genetic modification. This together with challenging and costly regulations stifling bioscience innovation have led many European plant-breeding, life science and biotechnology companies to move their advanced bioscience innovation to other parts of the world. This has resulted in the interesting dichotomy that while many Europeans want to see a shift towards a biobased economy, Europe is losing some of the key tools in getting towards such a bioeconomy. Converting the promises of modern biology to accepted and widely distributed tools driving the development of a European bioeconomy will therefore be a challenging and long process. The process will require well-anchored visions and strategies, political leadership, participatory governance, knowledge-driven decision-making and transparent systems of weighing risk and benefits with the various technologies and biobased production regimes.

Getting towards a KBBE in Africa

Africa overall is endowed with abundant natural resources, including arable land. These resources are however unevenly distributed, and the variety in agro-ecological niches and biomass production conditions (such as availability of water, land, infrastructure, markets, etc.) varies widely across the continent. Encouragingly enough, agricultural productivity in large parts of Africa is showing signs of steady improvement (AGRA, 2015), albeit from very low levels. Continued improvements in sustainable agricultural productivity, combined with viable agribusiness that adds value to farmers' production and improved access to markets, can drive broader biobased economic growth across the continent and improve food security across Africa.

In Africa, there is growing recognition that transition into middle-income nations, a key goal for many African countries, can be assisted through investment in and transformation into knowledge-based bioeconomies. This is broadly captured by Professor Calestous Juma (Juma, 2011) who argues that modern biosciences can do for Africa what information technology has done for India.

Smallholders are the major producer of food in Africa for the foreseeable future. These smallholders, to a large extent both poor and vulnerable, are under increasing pressure to produce more and better quality food, but are facing severe difficulties to do so. African farmers are facing a host of challenges, including a serious lack of improved high quality planting material. African breeding institutions able to adapt modern biosciences to local needs, opportunities and cultivars would thus greatly contribute to food security and improved livelihoods on the continent.

The agro-processing sector is in many African countries a vital part of the economy and also crucial for creating demand and value chain opportunities for African farmers. This sector however runs at a suboptimal level and produces large amounts of waste and severe environmental problems. Transforming the African agro-processing sector so that it effectively adds value to the primary production and converts waste to valuable products in an environmentally friendly manner will be central in improving agricultural productivity in Africa. A more dynamic, resource-efficient agro-processing sector is also important for creating new jobs and raising profitability for farmers and agribusinesses in the region.

The transition to African knowledge-driven bioeconomies will require an increased focus on agricultural innovation in areas such as sustainable agricultural intensification, effective food and agro value chains, resource-efficient agro-processing and market diversification. It would also include agricultural innovation transforming traditional staple crops, livestock, agro-processing waste and other bioresources to commercially attractive bioproducts. For this to materialize, African countries need to tap into modern biosciences.

Capacities to adapt and use modern biosciences in various sectors are emerging in Africa, such as the Biosciences Eastern and Central Africa Hub (BecA) in Nairobi, Kenya. For countries in Africa to transform into knowledge-based bioeconomies, well-developed strategies linked to effective priority setting and targeted efforts are needed. Such efforts include increased funding for research and innovation, business incubation, techno-economic-environment assessment, market creation, policy development, institutional reforms, access to capital and increased international collaboration, not least with Europe. Well-targeted funding from European donors and the EU could play a catalytic role here. Donor support can also play a role in supporting broad assessments and interdisciplinary analysis supporting African development efforts, stimulating engagement, coherence and collaboration between different sectors (e.g. energy, agriculture and industry).

Collaboration and joint efforts

For Europe and Africa there is great potential to foster sustainable intensification of biomass production through increased cooperation. Trade between the two continents could be defined and regulated from a sustainability perspective. This would include the opportunities for sourcing and trading biomass from where it is most efficiently produced, which in some cases may be in Europe and in other cases in Africa.

There are promising examples of collaboration between Europe and Africa, which could be nurtured and further developed. Horizon 2020 is a European Commission programme through which research initiatives are being commissioned during the period 2014–20. While Horizon 2020 focuses on European issues and competitiveness of Europe, there are also opportunities for European-African collaboration. Issues central to modern bioeconomies such as clean energy, low carbon economies, linking farmers to value chains, resource-efficient agricultural intensification and agro-processing are part of the Horizon 2020 agenda. Another example of successful collaboration is the Sida-supported programmes, BIO-EARN and Bio-Innovate, which are African-European programmes establishing collaborative bioscience innovation platforms in support of modern African bioeconomies (these programmes are described in Chapter 15 in this book).

While the European support to build bioscience and technical capacity in the African public R&D sector has been significant, there has been limited support for bioeconomy business development in Africa. The African private sector is still too weak to grasp the opportunities of emerging African markets. The European agro-processing and biobased private sectors have so far, with some exceptions, made limited attempts to establish themselves in African markets. European–African private sector partnerships are also rare. There are however significant opportunities for increased collaboration. Many countries in Africa are *de facto* bioeconomies but with a highly inefficient production and use of their bioresources and with lots of potential for improvements. Europe has a broad base of advanced life science and biobased companies with a high capacity to develop resource-efficient food production and processing, modern value chains and technologies converting agro-waste to useful products suitable for African and European markets. Africa is also endowed with a rich diversity of genetic resources, agro-ecological niches and rapidly growing markets. Thus, the conditions for more investments in Africa by the European private sector, and increased European–African private sector collaboration are becoming increasingly attractive. Efforts towards incubating and supporting European–African private sector partnerships and also broader collaboration engaging public R&D actors in Europe and Africa would therefore facilitate a transition to KBBEs, both in Europe and in Africa.

Concluding remarks

In this chapter we have discussed the potential of KBBEs to meet a rapid increase in bioresource demand in a resource-efficient, climate-smart and sustainable manner. We have also discussed the potential for countries in Africa and Europe to transform to KBBEs.

Bioscience innovation systems will be a crucial part of such a transition. In both Europe and Africa there is a multitude of potentially useful bioscience innovations in the public R&D pipeline but also in the private sector. To date the large majority of these R&D efforts have not moved beyond research due to a number of reasons including, weak market demand, negative public opinions, stifling policies and regulations, lack of business incubation, lack of capital and poor market communication.

To unleash the potential of the new biology and the promises of modern bioeconomies in Africa and in Europe, more emphasis needs to be placed on moving innovation from the R&D stage into practical use addressing societal needs.

Throughout this book there are many examples of current or new technology applications and policy measures that could help countries in Europe and Africa to move towards KBBEs.

References

AGRA (Alliance for a Green Revolution in Agriculture). 2015. *Africa Agriculture Status Report: Youth in Agriculture in sub-Saharan Africa*, Issue No. 3. [Online]. [Accessed 26 February 2016]. Available from: http://www.agra.org/our-results/agra-status-reports

Deininger, K. *et al.* 2011. *Rising Global Interest in Farmland: Can it Yield Sustainable and Equitable Benefits?* [Online]. Washington, DC: World Bank Publications. [Accessed 26 February 2016]. Available from: http://siteresources.worldbank.org/DEC/Resources/Rising-Global-Interest-in-Farmland.pdf

EC (European Commission). 2012. *Innovating for Sustainable Growth: A Bioeconomy for Europe.* [Online]. [Accessed 26 February 2016]. Available from: http://ec.europa.eu/research/bioeconomy/pdf/201202_innovating_sustainable_growth_en.pdf

Fielding, M. *et al.* 2015. *Agricultural Investment and Rural Transformation: A Case Study of the Makeni Bioenergy Project in Sierra Leone. SEI Report 2015-09.* [Online]. [Accessed 26 February 2016]. Available from: http://www.sei-international.org/mediamanager/documents/Publications/Climate/SEI-PR-2015-09-Makeni-Project-LR.pdf

Foley, J.A. *et al.* 2011. Solutions for a cultivated planet. *Nature* 478(7369), pp.337–42.

German Bioeconomy Council. 2015. *Bioeconomy Policy (Part II). Synopsis of National Strategies Around the World.* [Online]. [Accessed 8 December 2015]. Available from: http://gbs2015.com/fileadmin/gbs2015/Downloads/Bioeconomy-Policy_Part-II.pdf

Hoff, H. *et al.* 2012. Green and blue water in Africa: how foreign direct investment can support sustainable intensification. In: Allan J.A. *et al.* (eds). *Handbook on Land and Water Grabs in Africa.* London: Routledge, pp.359–75.

Jägermeyr, J. *et al.* 2016. Integrated crop water management might sustainably halve the global food gap. *Environmental Research Letters* 11(2). doi: http://dx.doi.org/10.1088/1748-9326/11/2/025002

Juma, C. 2011. *The New Harvest: Agricultural Innovation in Africa.* New York: Oxford University Press.

Lambin, E.F. and Meyfroidt, P. 2011. Global land use change, economic globalization, and the looming land scarcity. *Proceedings of the National Academy of Sciences* 108(9), pp.3465–72.

Leifeld, J. *et al.* 2013. Organic farming gives no climate change benefit through soil carbon sequestration. *Proceedings of the National Academy of Sciences* 110(11), E984.

Pfau, S.F. *et al.* 2014. Visions of sustainability in bioeconomy research. *Sustainability* 6(3), pp.1222–49.

Piotrowski, S. *et al.* 2015. Global bioeconomy in the conflict between biomass supply and demand. *Industrial Biotechnology* 11(6), pp.308–15.

Rosillo-Calle, F. 2015. Overview of biomass energy. In: Rosillo-Calle, F. *et al.* (eds). *The Biomass Assessment Handbook: Bioenergy for a Sustainable Environment,* Second Edition. London: Earthscan, pp.1–25.

Seufert, V. *et al.* 2012. Comparing the yields of organic and conventional agriculture. *Nature* 485(7397), pp.229–32.

Smith, P. *et al.* 2014. Agriculture, forestry and other land use (AFOLU). In: Edenhofer, O. *et al.* (eds). *Climate Change 2014: Mitigation of Climate Change Contribution of Working Group III to the Fifth Assessment Report of the Intergovernmental Panel on Climate Change.* Cambridge: Cambridge University Press, pp.812–922.

Tuomisto, H.L. *et al.* 2012. Does organic farming reduce environmental impacts? – A meta-analysis of European research. *Journal of Environmental Management* 112, pp.309–20.

UNEP (United Nations Environment Programme). 2014. *Annual Report 2014.* [Online]. [Accessed 26 February 2016]. Available from: http://www.unep.org/annualreport/2014/en/index.html

3 The gene revolution

What can and can't be done with modern biosciences?

E. Jane Morris

Introduction

The so-called 'green revolution' that resulted in significant increases in agricultural production, was led by the development of high-yielding varieties of maize, wheat and rice, produced largely through conventional breeding. In combination with modern agricultural practices, including use of synthetic agricultural chemicals and fertilizers, world agricultural production doubled. In Western Europe, cereal yields more than doubled in the period from 1960 to 1990. However the green revolution largely bypassed African countries. African production increased over the same period, but this was largely through an increase in area harvested while yield remained static (FAOSTAT, 2015). This was in part because breeding strategies were not focused on Africa's needs, but also because the strategy of agricultural intensification was not appropriate where population densities were low and/or market infrastructure was poor (Pingali, 2012).

In the years since the green revolution it has become obvious that there have been downsides as well as upsides. Not only have the benefits not been seen in all countries, but where modern varieties have been introduced, along with associated farming practices, there have been environmental costs due to increased use of agrochemicals, irrigation water and accompanying soil degradation. This has resulted in calls for a second green revolution or a 'doubly green revolution' (Conway, 1997), that would protect the environment at the same time as boosting output and would lead countries to develop sustainable bioeconomies. This can only be achieved through the intervention of modern biosciences, otherwise known as the 'gene revolution'.

For environmental sustainability, we need to develop plants that are better adapted to environmental stresses, and plants that can alter and 'improve' environments (Brummer *et al.*, 2011). Durable disease resistance, abiotic stress tolerance and nutrient- and water-use efficiency are important. In addition, crops are needed that can be grown in marginal land areas, and there needs to be greater emphasis on improving minor or 'orphan' crops that are not traded around the world and have so far received little research attention (Collard and Mackill, 2008). Most plant breeding programmes focus on the development of high-yielding varieties under high-input production systems, whereas for sustainability, particularly in the developing world, crop breeding programmes are needed that focus more on nutrient economy and local environmental fitness (Fess *et al.*, 2011). Livestock production is also an important component of agriculture, and livestock breeding needs to harness the latest technologies to address issues such as greenhouse gas emissions and water use by animals (Hume *et al.*, 2011; Scholtz *et al.*, 2013).

For the development of sustainable bioeconomies we need to harness the potential of agriculture to produce not only food and feed but also biofuels, pharmaceuticals and many industrial products.

This chapter highlights the role of modern bioscience in shaping agricultural bioresource production systems in both the developed and the developing world, both now and in the coming years.

Where do we stand with the technology?

Tissue culture techniques

Although plant tissue culture was first developed early in the last century, it has steadily increased in importance as techniques have improved and new opportunities have opened up, making it one of the most important tools in agricultural biotechnology. Not only has it enabled the production of disease-free planting material, particularly important for vegetatively propagated crops such as banana, but techniques such as embryo rescue have enabled the production of interspecific and intergeneric hybrids. The induction of haploidy and production of doubled haploids have facilitated their use in hybrid breeding programmes (Thorpe, 2007), and a new technique termed genome elimination could potentially expand the possibilities for hybrid induction particularly for the breeding of staple food crops such as bananas and cassava that are currently mainly vegetatively propagated (Comai, 2014). Tissue culture forms the basis for the majority of modern techniques for crop improvement described below.

Marker assisted selection (MAS)

Typical crop breeding programmes involve thousands or millions of individual plants, may take five to ten years for elite lines (i.e. inbred lines with many genes for desirable agronomic traits) to be identified, and involve considerable expense (Collard and Mackill, 2008). This has led to efforts to speed up and refine the process through the use of DNA markers, which can be used to detect the presence of allelic variation (i.e. alternative forms of a gene) in genes associated with desired traits. The identification of molecular markers such as Restriction Fragment Length Polymorphisms (RFLPs), Simple Sequence Repeats (SSRs) and single nucleotide polymorphisms (SNPs) has become standard practice. The association of a marker with a particular trait (marker validation) enables rapid selection of individual plants with the desired trait.

TILLING (Targeting Induced Local Lesions IN Genomes) is a reverse genetics technique (i.e. a technique to identify the function of a gene by analysing the phenotypic effects of changes in the gene) that employs mutagenesis followed by identification of resulting SNPs in specific genes that are expected or known to correspond to a trait of interest. EcoTILLING applies a similar approach but identifies naturally occurring mutations (Till *et al.*, 2007). TILLING populations have been developed for several crop plants, such as rice, wheat, sorghum, oat, Brassica, chickpea and pearl millet (Varshney *et al.*, 2014), but so far TILLING has not been extensively applied to orphan crops (Esfeld *et al.*, 2013).

Collard and Mackill (2008) point out that despite its potential, MAS has so far had a limited impact on plant breeding programmes. They put forward a number of reasons for this, including problems in the transfer of technology between molecular biologists and plant breeders. However, for less studied crops sufficient molecular markers are generally not yet available for trait mapping and MAS (Gao *et al.*, 2012), though in recent years progress is being made with a number of crops such as pulses (Bohra *et al.*, 2014) and a range of other orphan crops such as groundnuts, cassava and banana (Gedil *et al.*, 2014) utilizing genomic information as described below. Although costs are coming down, MAS remains relatively expensive and technology intensive, and this is likely to constitute a significant hurdle for its use in developing countries.

In livestock breeding, genomic selection, which enables prediction of the genetic merit of animals from genome-wide SNP markers, has already been adopted by the dairy industry and could in future be applied to a broader selection of traits, including reduced methane production in cattle. However, a significant problem for livestock breeders, particularly in developing countries, is the need to assemble large enough reference populations to make accurate predictions because thousands to tens of thousands of phenotyped individuals are required (Hayes *et al.*, 2013; van Marle-Köster *et al.*, 2015).

High throughput genotyping and genome-wide selection

The development of rapid next generation sequencing (NGS) over the past few years has enabled the expanded availability of genome sequences of many crop plants. Candidate genes of agronomic importance can more rapidly be identified than before, and resequencing (where a reference genome sequence is already known) to determine crop variation is leading to the development of new molecular markers and the construction of saturated molecular genetic maps, enabling the simultaneous selection of multiple desirable traits (Van *et al.*, 2013; Gao *et al.*, 2012). To date, genome sequences of most crops that are of importance to the developing world, particularly Africa, have not become available, but with the continuing decrease in cost of whole genome sequencing, this is likely to change. Genome sequencing of pigeon pea (*Cajanus cajan*), tef (*Eragrostis tef*), banana (*Musa acuminata*), African rice (*Oryza glaberrima*) and cassava (*Manihot esculenta*) has been completed or is under way (CoGePedia, 2015) and is also described in Chapter 12. The African Orphan Crops Consortium has as its goal the sequencing, assembly and annotation of 100 traditional African food crops (World Agroforestry Centre, 2015). Since there has been a lack of focus on conventional plant breeding for the so-called 'orphan' crops, a bottleneck in further development may well be the lack of carefully chosen and designed breeding populations that sample genetic variation particularly for complex characters (Powell and Barsby, 2013).

In livestock, genome sequences are available for nearly all the major food animals, including cows, pigs, chickens, sheep and goats. NGS techniques are allowing researchers to compare different breeds and/or populations from different geographical regions (sometimes called landscape genomics), which might enable selection for local environments. A particular challenge for the developing world is the need for selection of animals that are able to perform well under suboptimal conditions including limited feed, drought, disease and heat stress (Rothschild and Plastow, 2014).

Transcriptome analysis

NGS is increasingly being used in RNA sequencing (RNA-seq) experiments to collect transcriptomic data on multiple samples from different tissues, over time or undergoing different treatments, allowing for identification of key genes involved in specific cellular responses (Strickler *et al.*, 2012; Wilson and Roberts, 2014). RNA-seq is increasingly replacing older techniques of transcriptomic analysis such as microarrays and serial analysis of gene expression (SAGE) in many applications. It can be used in non-model species where sequence data is not available, although this requires *de novo* sequence assembly. One of the greatest challenges lies in data analysis of the large quantity of data (Strickler *et al.*, 2012) and the development of new bioinformatics tools is a priority.

Transgenesis

Much has been written already concerning the introduction of genetically modified (GM) crops, produced through the introduction of DNA from a different species, which have now been commercially grown for almost 20 years. While the first generation GM crops focused on the genetically simple traits of herbicide tolerance and resistance to insect pests that were of benefit to the farmer, the next generation of GM crops is likely to include traits that provide more benefits to the consumer. Examples include golden rice to address vitamin A deficiency, high oleic oil soybean, canola/rapeseed or other oilseeds with enhanced omega-3 fatty acid content, and rice with increased iron content (Chen and Lin, 2013; Usher *et al.*, 2015). As discussed later in this chapter, GM plants are now increasingly being developed as plant factories to produce a range of pharmaceuticals and other valuable products.

The development of GM crops with complex traits has proved much more difficult than the modification of simple, often single-gene, traits. Attempts to improve nutrient-use efficiency, enhanced photosynthesis, or stress tolerance have encountered many challenges and will necessitate large collaborative research programmes over an extended timescale (Rothstein *et al.*, 2014). Nevertheless, some success is being achieved in the development of a first generation of drought-tolerant crops, both by the private sector and by public–private partnerships such as the Water Efficient Maize for Africa (WEMA) project as described in Chapter 5.

A variety of transgenic animals have also been produced, but the process is costly and there is considerable public resistance to the concept. The closest to the market is the AquAdvantage salmon, engineered to have an enhanced growth rate. Forabosco *et al.* (2013) provide a comprehensive summary of the GM animals that are in development with relevance to agriculture. A limited number of pharmaceuticals produced in transgenic animals (most often in the milk) have been approved for commercial use, but the products have not made a major impact in the marketplace, and the companies developing them have struggled to keep afloat (Thayer, 2012).

More recently, techniques have been introduced whereby transgenesis is used as an initial step in the breeding process to induce traits that are useful to breeders such as early flowering in plants, but the transgene is segregated out during further breeding and is therefore not present in the final product (null segregants). A transgene encoding an RNA interference (RNAi) construct or a dominant negative protein is inserted which may lead to gene silencing. Where the RNAi construct induces an epigenetic effect through methylation of the DNA, the change of methylation pattern will be inherited even in the absence of the inserted gene in subsequent generations, but the epigenetic effect will eventually die out (see section on epigenetics below). The regulatory status of null segregants is still unclear (Lusser and Davies, 2013).

Cisgenesis and intragenesis

Transfer of a gene (cisgenesis) or DNA fragment (intragenesis) between organisms of the same species or from a cross-compatible species differs from transgenesis in that it can be conceived as a process that could occur naturally. Whereas cisgenesis may lead to a new organism that is indistinguishable from a conventional cross, intragenesis leads to an organism that is not obtainable by conventional crosses. Crops modified by cisgenesis or intragenesis should be free of markers and any vector backbone, so that it is only DNA from the compatible species that is introduced. At present crops modified using these methods are regulated as GMOs worldwide, but there is a considerable body of opinion that they should be deregulated (Holme *et al.*, 2013). One argument supporting deregulation of such crops is the fact that they can only be detected if information about the modification has been provided by the developer (Lusser *et al.*, 2012).

Targeted genome editing

Programmable nucleases enable targeted genetic modifications by inducing site-specific DNA cleavage in the genome, leading to targeted genetic modifications including gene disruption, insertion or deletion of new genes or small sequences (known as indels), changes in specific bases and chromosomal rearrangements. The first programmable nucleases were zinc-finger nucleases but, as described further in Chapter 12, the technology is evolving rapidly and the new clustered, regularly interspaced, short palindromic repeats (CRISPR)-associated system is opening up a range of possibilities.

These techniques enable directed mutagenesis of specific genes for gene silencing, increasing expression levels or stacking of multiple genes at a single locus, with enough specificity to be able to target either single or multiple copies of a particular gene. They offer the potential for metabolic engineering to increase the production of valuable plant products, for example by upregulating or silencing specific pathway genes, cooperative or competing pathway genes, or transcription factors (Wilson and Roberts, 2014).

Programmable nucleases enable the development of modified crops and livestock without necessarily introducing new genetic material, hence potentially avoiding much of the controversy surrounding GM crops and animals. Already they have shown potential to eliminate allergens and enhance disease resistance. As described in Chapter 12, the majority of crops produced using these techniques cannot be distinguished from crops derived through mutagenesis induced by chemicals or irradiation, and are unlikely to be regulated as GMOs in many countries (Lusser and Davies, 2013).

Epigenetics and epigenomics

Epigenetics involves the study of heritable information that is not fully explained by DNA sequence variation. The memory of gene expression states may apparently be transmitted across generations (meiosis) or during morphological development (mitosis), providing a mechanism for the transmission of acquired characteristics that would allow for flexible adaptations to the environment. There are a variety of molecular mechanisms that may contribute to epigenetic inheritance, including stable changes in protein structure (prions), small RNAs, chromatin modifications including DNA methylation, and histone modifications. The term epigenomics is used to describe the genome-wide distribution of such modifications.

A recognition of the role of epigenetic information is leading to complexities but also opportunities for plant breeders. It is often difficult to disentangle the various contributions of genetic and epigenetic information; the stability of epigenetic traits is highly variable; and such traits may or may not exhibit Mendelian inheritance. While much remains to be discovered, epigenetic mutagenesis shows potential to lead to gain-of-function variants through loss of epigenetic silencing, which would be particularly attractive in species that are clonally propagated, have severe germplasm bottlenecks or to generate variation in genomic regions where recombination is very rare (Springer, 2013).

Focus areas for new technology applications

Environmentally sustainable crops

For environmental sustainability, it will be necessary to improve the nutrient-use efficiency of plants and reduce the input of chemical fertilizers. This implies the need to enhance carbon utilization through photosynthesis; to improve utilization of nitrogen, phosphorus and minerals such as zinc, iron and selenium; and to improve water productivity (i.e. the amount of water required per unit of biomass produced).

One approach to reducing the use of nitrogenous fertilizers is to understand the signalling events underpinning the formation of nitrogen fixing nodules in legumes, so that this trait may be engineered into non-legume crops. An alternative approach is to directly engineer nitrogen fixation into cereals through the introduction of a nitrogenase, although the complexity of the enzyme and its mode of action present significant hurdles. While progress has been made with respect to both possibilities, they are unlikely to provide results in the short term (Oldroyd and Dixon, 2014).

In future years, phosphorus shortages are likely to be an increasing concern limiting the use of chemical fertilizers, since rock phosphate is a limited global resource. Phosphorus scarcity has been identified as a global threat to food security (Cordell and Neset, 2014). A number of efforts are underway to develop plants with improved phosphorus acquisition efficiency and phosphorus-use efficiency. Plants acquire phosphate from the soil either directly via the roots, or via symbiosis with mycorrhizal fungi. Modern genomic, transcriptomic and proteomic tools are being used to study phosphorus uptake and utilization in crops and in plant species adapted to soils with low available phosphorus. While the hope is to eventually use this knowledge to modify crop plants, this goal remains some years away (Baker *et al.*, 2015).

Crops also need to be developed that can be grown on marginal land; traits such as salt and aluminium tolerance are important in this context. At this stage, limited progress has been made in developing salt-tolerant cultivars using modern molecular techniques. The situation is complicated by the fact that tolerance at one stage of plant development may be poorly correlated with tolerance at other developmental stages (Ashraf and Foolad, 2013). Aluminium toxicity is a particular problem in acid soils prevalent in developing countries in the tropics and sub-tropics, and significant progress is being made in identifying aluminium resistance genes as well as gaining an understanding of the induction of gene expression and modification of protein function by aluminium that occurs during the onset of aluminium resistance responses (Liu *et al.*, 2014). However, much remains to be done before this information can be fully utilized in crop breeding programmes.

Crops can also be developed to remove toxic chemicals such as mercury, or to improve industrially degraded soils such as mine spoils (Brummer *et al.*, 2011). A number of plants are known to hyper-accumulate particular metals and progress has been made in identifying candidate genes involved. However, only a few species have the required agronomic traits, and genetic modification may be required to address this issue. Phytoextraction shows considerable promise but is very much in its infancy (Hunt *et al.*, 2014).

Crops to withstand climate change

Climate change is likely to result in extreme fluctuations in agricultural conditions, with plants being exposed to unpredictable (both in extent and duration) heat and cold stresses, as well as drought or flooding. Overall, global warming is predicted to reduce yields in many crops, to the extent of about six per cent and five per cent average yield loss per 1°C increase in C_3 and C_4 crops, respectively (Yamori *et al.*, 2013). The complex polygenic basis of the response to most abiotic stresses leads to considerable difficulty in breeding for stress tolerance; this is further complicated by crosstalk between the response pathways of different stresses (Hu and Xiong, 2014). It is likely that most success will be achieved through transgenic or cisgenic pyramiding of a number of genes. At the same time, to avoid negative effects on plant growth it will be necessary to restrict expression of the introduced genes to a specific tissue or stress, via the use of tissue-specific and stress-inducible promoters (Bita and Gerats, 2013).

Biofuel crops

The 'food versus fuel' debate has resulted in many polarized viewpoints in an environment of rising food prices that have a particular impact on people in the developing world. This debate has led to growing consideration of the possibility of breeding multi-use crops, where part can be used for biofuel (bioethanol, biodiesel or biogas) while the remainder is used for food or feed. Jatropha (*Jatropha curcus*) has been widely hailed as a biofuel crop, yet there is a pressing need to bring modern bioscience and molecular breeding to bear on the crop to increase seed yield, oil content, biotic and abiotic stress tolerance, and to remove toxic substances like curcin and phorbol esters from the seeds (Edrisi *et al.*, 2015). Molecular breeding techniques incorporating NGS are now being used to identify varieties that lack phorbol esters so that the seed cake after extraction of oil can be used for animal feed (King *et al.*, 2013). The genus *Miscanthus*, a perennial grass, also shows potential as a biofuel crop and here breeding targets include reduction in lignin concentration, regulation of flowering time to increase the vegetative phase, and abiotic stress tolerance (Yamada *et al.*, 2015).

Other promising biofuel crops with multipurpose uses are sweet sorghum (*Sorghum bicolor*) and cassava (see Chapter 10). Sorghum can potentially be used for food (grains), feed (stems) as well as fuel (sugars and potentially cellulosic biomass). Amongst more obvious traits for biofuel production such as a high content of fermentable sugars, there is a need for a wide range of maturity classes to allow for extended harvesting periods that better fit the requirements of a processing industry. Again, genomics and molecular breeding tools are being brought to bear to address the multiple characteristics that are needed (Rao *et al.*, 2014; Mullet *et al.*, 2014). There are now opportunities for wide hybridization that could lead to the development of perennial sorghum x C_4 grass crosses. The perennial trait would provide additional opportunities for use as a biofuel crop (Mullet *et al.*, 2014).

Pharmaceuticals from plants

The production of recombinant pharmaceuticals in plants is commonly referred to as molecular pharming and is described further in Chapter 9. The first product was approved for use in humans in 2012, a form of human glucocerebrosidase for the treatment of the lysosomal disorder Gaucher's disease (Stoger *et al.*, 2014). A number of other products are in clinical trials, such as collagen produced in plants for wound healing (Shilo *et al.*, 2013).

In some cases where pharmaceuticals are naturally produced in plants, metabolic engineering is being used to increase production levels. An example is the anti-cancer drug paclitaxel, originally extracted from the bark of *Taxus brevifolia*, but currently produced in plant cell culture. Although upregulation of key pathway genes has led to an increase in paclitaxel production, the results are not always predictable, emphasizing the need for a detailed understanding of the biosynthetic pathway and regulatory mechanisms in the plant (Wilson and Roberts, 2014).

Plant-based production systems offer a number of advantages, including opportunities for the production of proteins required in very small amounts for a limited market, or in very large amounts (such as human serum albumin); in both of these cases costs of production by fermentation are likely to be prohibitive. Although the cost of downstream purification and processing can be high, there are advantages over production in mammalian cells in that there is no risk of contamination by mammalian viruses or prions (Stoger *et al.*, 2014).

Other products from plants

Few non-clinical products from transgenic plants have yet reached the market other than some limited products approved for diagnostic use. However modern bioscience is increasingly being brought to bear to increase the production of many valuable metabolites that are naturally produced in plants, such as nutraceuticals (Saxena and Cramer, 2013), cosmeceuticals (including a variety of skin treatments) (Draelos, 2011), dyes and pigments (Islam *et al.*, 2013), novel sweeteners, etc. For instance there is interest in enhancing the production of anthocyanin pigments in plants by up-regulating biosynthesis using transcription factors, or modifying the pathway to produce new colours for the colourants and food industries (Zhang *et al.*, 2014). Low-calorie or zero-calorie natural sweeteners from plants are increasingly in demand, including thaumatin, glycyrrhizic acid, monatin, brazzein, mogroside V, stevioside and rebaudioside A. The biosynthetic pathways for some of these are better known than for others, but RNA-seq offers opportunities to speed up the process of pathway elucidation, providing opportunities for more efficient production in either plant or recombinant microbial systems (Philippe *et al.*, 2014).

Flavours and fragrances from plants offer another avenue for biotechnological intervention. The most well-known plant flavour extract is vanillin, but the production of vanilla beans and the isolation of vanillin from vanilla pods is a costly and laborious process. Production of 1 kg of vanillin requires around 500 kg of vanilla pods corresponding to the hand pollination of approximately 40,000 vanilla orchid flowers (Gallage and Møller, 2015). Accordingly, the majority of vanillin sold is now produced by chemical synthesis, which is not environmentally benign. The demand for 'natural' vanillin has led to the recent identification of the vanillin synthase enzyme from the vanilla orchid using transcriptomic and proteomic techniques (Gallage *et al.*, 2014) and may offer new opportunities to introduce this enzyme into other plants either by genetic engineering or mutation breeding.

As described in Chapter 8, there is a strong need to develop biobased alternatives to petrochemical feedstocks used by the chemical industry to produce a wide range of modern chemicals and polymers. Plant fatty acids, oils and waxes show potential as replacements, but it will be necessary not only to dramatically increase productivity in current oil crops, but also to develop some of the major oil plants to produce industrial oil compositions that go beyond their natural within-species variation. Metabolic engineering approaches using the full spectrum of the latest technologies are being brought to bear to accelerate progress in this important area (Vanhercke *et al.*, 2013).

The challenges ahead

Many of the opportunities described above may not be realized because of resistance to the technology. Much of the negative propaganda is directed not so much at the technology itself, but at the multinational companies who are seen as imposing proprietary control on the agro-food system. Yet for the 'doubly green revolution' to occur, the regulatory regimes in the target countries need to be targeted towards facilitating the introduction of publicly funded crop improvements, rather than towards blocking the multinationals.

While many developing countries, including most African countries, have not yet got to grips with the regulatory requirements for GMOs, at the same time the technology is developing at a faster rate than the regulators can deal with. An enhanced dialogue between scientists and regulators is essential if progress is to be maintained.

Finally, much more emphasis needs to be placed on public sector research and facilitating research into use. The 'doubly green revolution' will certainly not be achieved if it is left in the hands of the private sector alone. There is significant scope here for collaboration between European and African countries and the fact that many of the genomic technologies are becoming increasingly affordable offers new opportunities for African scientists to engage in cutting edge research and development.

References

Ashraf, M. and Foolad, M.R. 2013. Crop breeding for salt tolerance in the era of molecular markers and marker-assisted selection. *Plant Breeding* 132, pp.10–20.

Baker, A. *et al.* 2015. Replace, reuse, recycle: improving the sustainable use of phosphorus by plants. *Journal of Experimental Botany* 66(12), pp.3523–40.

Bita, C.E. and Gerats, T. 2013. Plant tolerance to high temperature in a changing environment: scientific fundamentals and production of heat stress-tolerant crops. *Frontiers in Plant Science* 4, 273.

Bohra, A. *et al.* 2014. Genomics-assisted breeding in four major pulse crops of developing countries: present status and prospects. *Theoretical and Applied Genetics* 127, pp.1263–91.

Brummer, E.C. *et al.* 2011. Plant breeding for harmony between agriculture and the environment. *Frontiers in Ecology and the Environment* 9(10), pp.561–8.

Chen, H. and Lin, Y. 2013. Promise and issues of genetically modified crops. *Current Opinion in Plant Biology* 16(2), pp.255–60.

CoGePedia. 2015. *Sequenced Plant Genomes*. [Online]. [Accessed 13 February 2016]. Available from: https://genomevolution.org/wiki/index.php/Sequenced_plant_genomes

Collard, B.C.Y. and Mackill, D.J. 2008. Marker-assisted selection: an approach for precision plant breeding in the twenty-first century. *Philosophical Transactions of the Royal Society B* 363, pp.557–72.

Comai, L. 2014. Genome elimination: translating basic research into a future tool for plant breeding. *PLoS Biology* 12(6), e1001876.

Conway, G. 1997. *The Doubly Green Revolution: Food for All in the Twenty-first Century.* London: Penguin Books.

Cordell, D. and Neset, T.-S.S. 2014. Phosphorus vulnerability: a qualitative framework for assessing the vulnerability of national and regional food systems to the multi-dimensional stressors of phosphorus scarcity. *Global Environmental Change* 24, pp.108–22.

Draelos, Z.D. 2011. The art and science of new advances in cosmeceuticals. *Clinics in Plastic Surgery* 38, pp.397–407.

Edrisi, S.A. *et al.* 2015. Jatropha curcas L.: a crucified plant waiting for resurgence. *Renewable and Sustainable Energy Reviews* 41, pp.855–62.

Esfeld, K. *et al.* 2013. Application of TILLING for orphan crop improvement. In: Jain, S.M. and Dutta Gupta, S. (eds). *Biotechnology of Neglected and Underutilized Crops.* Dordrecht: Springer, pp.83–113.

FAOSTAT. 2015. Food and Agriculture Organization of the United Nations Statistics Division Website. [Online]. [Accessed 30 December 2015]. Available from: http://faostat3.fao.org/compare/E

Fess, T.L. *et al.* 2011. Crop breeding for low input agriculture: a sustainable response to feed a growing world population. *Sustainability* 3, pp.1742–72.

Forabosco, F. *et al.* 2013. Genetically modified farm animals and fish in agriculture: a review. *Livestock Science* 153, pp.1–9.

Gallage, N.J. and Møller, B.L. 2015. Vanillin – bioconversion and bioengineering of the most popular plant flavour and its *de novo* biosynthesis in the vanilla orchid. *Molecular Plant* 8(1), pp.40–57.

Gallage, N.J. *et al.* 2014. Vanillin formation from ferulic acid in *Vanilla planifolia* is catalysed by a single enzyme. *Nature Communications* 5, article number 4037. doi:10.1038/ncomms5037.

Gao, Q. *et al.* 2012. Recent progress using high-throughput sequencing technologies in plant molecular breeding. *Journal of Integrative Plant Biology* 54(4), pp.215–27.

Gedil, M. *et al.* 2014. Biotechnology success stories by the Consultative Group on International Agriculture Research (CGIAR) system. In: Wambugu, F. and Kamanga, D. (eds). *Biotechnology in Africa. Emergence, Initiatives and Future.* Switzerland: Springer Science Policy Report, pp.95–114.

Hayes, B.J. *et al.* 2013. The future of livestock breeding: genomic selection for efficiency, reduced emissions intensity, and adaptation. *Trends in Genetics* 29(4), pp.206–14.

Holme, I.B. *et al.* 2013. Intragenesis and cisgenesis as alternatives to transgenic crop development. *Plant Biotechnology Journal* 11, pp.395–407.

Hu, H. and Xiong, L. 2014. Genetic engineering and breeding of drought-resistant crops. *Annual Reviews of Plant Biology* 65, pp.715–41.

Hume, D.A. *et al.* 2011. The future of animal production: improving productivity and sustainability. *Journal of Agricultural Science* 149, pp.9–16.

Hunt, A.J. *et al.* 2014. Phytoextraction as a tool for green chemistry. *Green Processing and Synthesis* 3, pp.3–22.

Islam, S. *et al.* 2013. Perspectives for natural product based agents derived from industrial plants in textile applications – a review. *Journal of Cleaner Production* 57, pp.2–18.

King, A.J. *et al.* 2013. Linkage mapping in the oilseed crop *Jatropha curcas* L. reveals a locus controlling the biosynthesis of phorbol esters which cause seed toxicity. *Plant Biotechnology Journal* 11(8), pp.986–96.

Liu, J. *et al.* 2014. The role of aluminum sensing and signalling in plant aluminum resistance. *Journal of Integrative Plant Biology* 56(3), pp.221–30.

Lusser, M. and Davies, H.V. 2013. Comparative regulatory approaches for groups of new plant breeding techniques. *New Biotechnology* 30(5), pp.437–46.

Lusser, M. *et al.* 2012. Deployment of new biotechnologies in plant breeding. *Nature Biotechnology* 30(3), pp.231–9.

Mullet, J. *et al.* 2014. Energy *Sorghum* – a genetic model for the design of C_4 grass bioenergy crops. *Journal of Experimental Botany* 65(13), pp.3479–89.

Oldroyd, G.E.D. and Dixon, R. 2014. Biotechnological solutions to the nitrogen problem. *Current Opinion in Biotechnology* 26, pp.19–24.

Philippe, R.N. *et al.* 2014. Biotechnological production of natural zero-calorie sweeteners. *Current Opinion in Biotechnology* 26, pp.155–61.

Pingali, P.L. 2012. Green Revolution; impacts, limits and the path ahead. *Proceedings of the National Academy of Science* 109(31), pp.12302–8.

Powell, W. and Barsby, T. 2013. Germplasm diversity and genetics to drive plant breeding for Africa. In: Bennett, D.J. and Jennings, R.C. (eds). *Successful Agricultural Innovation in Emerging Economies.* Cambridge: Cambridge University Press, pp.83–94.

Rao, S.P. *et al.* 2014. Prospect of sorghum as a biofuel feedstock. In: Wang, Y-H. *et al.* (eds). *Genetics, Genomics and Breeding of Sorghum.* London and New York: CRC Press, pp.303–30.

Rothschild, M.F. and Plastow, G.S. 2014. Applications of genomics to improve livestock in the developing world. *Livestock Science* 166, pp.76–83.

Rothstein, S.J. *et al.* 2014. The challenges of commercializing second-generation transgenic crop traits necessitate the development of international public sector research infrastructure. *Journal of Experimental Botany* 65(19), pp.5673–82.

Saxena, A. and Cramer, C.S. 2013. Metabolomics: a potential tool for breeding nutraceutical vegetables. *Advances in Crop Science and Technology* 1(2), p.106.

Scholtz, M.M. *et al.* 2013. Livestock breeding for sustainability to mitigate global warming, with the emphasis on developing countries. *South African Journal of Animal Science* 43(3), pp.269–81.

Shilo, S. *et al.* 2013. Cutaneous wound healing after treatment with plant-derived human recombinant human recombinant collagen flowable gel. *Tissue Engineering: Part A* 19(13–14), pp.1519–26.

Springer, N.M. 2013. Epigenetics and crop improvement. *Trends in Genetics* 29(4), pp.241–7.

Stoger, E. *et al.* 2014. Plant molecular pharming for the treatment of chronic and infectious diseases. *Annual Review of Plant Biology* 65, pp.743–68.

Strickler, S.R. *et al.* 2012. Designing a transcriptome next-generation sequencing project for a nonmodel plant species. *American Journal of Botany* 99(2), pp.257–66.

Thayer, A.M. 2012. Transgenic firms struggle to keep going. *Chemical and Engineering News* 90(36), pp.34–8.

Thorpe, T.A. 2007. History of plant tissue culture. *Molecular Biotechnology* 37, pp.169–80.

Till, B.J. *et al.* 2007. TILLING and EcoTILLING for crop improvement. In: Varshney, R.K. and Tuberosa, R. (eds). *Genomics-Assisted Crop Improvement: Vol.1: Genomics Approaches and Platforms*. Springer, pp.333–49.

Usher, S. *et al.* 2015. Field trial evaluation of the accumulation of omega-3 long chain polyunsaturated fatty acids in transgenic *Camelina sativa*: making fish oil substitutes in plants. *Metabolic Engineering Communications* 2, pp.93–8.

Van, K. *et al.* 2013. Next-generation sequencing technology for crop improvement. *SABRAO Journal of Breeding and Genetics* 45(1), pp.84–99.

Vanhercke, T. *et al.* 2013. Metabolic engineering of plant oils and waxes for use as industrial feedstocks. *Plant Biotechnology Journal* 11, pp.197–210.

Van Marle-Köster, E. *et al.* 2015. Genomic technologies for food security: a review of challenges and opportunities in Southern Africa. *Food Research International* 76(4), pp.971–9.

Varshney, R.K. *et al.* 2014. Harvesting the promising fruits of genomics: applying genome sequencing technologies to crop breeding. *PLoS Biology* 12(6), e1001883.

Wilson, S.A. and Roberts, S.C. 2014. Metabolic engineering approaches for production of biochemicals in food and medicinal plants. *Current Opinion in Biotechnology* 26, pp.174–82.

World Agroforestry Centre. 2015. *African Orphan Crops Consortium*. [Online]. [Accessed 2 August 2015]. Available from: http://africanorphancrops.org/

Yamada, T. *et al.* 2015. Candidate gene approach in Miscanthus spp. for biorefinery. In: Budak, H. and Spangenberg, G. (eds). *Molecular Breeding of Forage and Turf*. Springer International Publishing, pp.85–92.

Yamori, W. *et al.* 2013. Temperature response of photosynthesis in C3, C4 and CAM plants. *Photosynthesis Research* 119(1–2), pp.101–17.

Zhang, Y. *et al.* 2014. Engineering anthocyanin biosynthesis in plants. *Current Opinion in Plant Biology* 19, pp.81–90.

Part II

Towards sustainable food security

4 A European perspective

The case for a highly productive and innovative agriculture in Europe

Harald von Witzke and Steffen Noleppa

Rising prices of agricultural commodities and food

The times of plenty in food and agriculture are over. The European Union and the world have entered a new era of scarcity. This chapter will lay out the causes and consequences of these and related changes. It will lead us to conclude that the response to the challenges ahead in Europe and elsewhere must be different today from what many Europeans continue to think to be appropriate.

From about 1870 to the turn of the millennium, agricultural commodity prices and the price of food tended to decline. During that period world agriculture produced ever more food for ever more humans at ever declining prices. This mega-trend in world agriculture has come to an end. The turn of the millennium marks a mega-trend reversal in international agricultural commodity prices. Since 2000, prices have tended to rise – albeit with large fluctuations as in the past. Contrary to public perception price volatility has not changed in more than 50 years (Wright, 2011). What has changed, however, is the direction of the long-term price trend, which will continue to point upward (von Witzke *et al.*, 2009; USDA, 2015).

The reason for this is simply that since the turn of the millennium, global demand growth for agricultural commodities has been outpacing the growth in supply. Demand growth for food may be expected to occur almost exclusively in developing and newly industrializing countries. However, demand for goods of the green economy will grow in both developing and developed countries. The growth in demand is driven by two variables, population growth and per capita consumption growth.

Our estimates suggest that global demand will increase by about 120 per cent in the first half of the twenty-first century. It is based on more recent population projections which suggest a scenario of the world population being closer to 10 rather than 9 billion by 2050 (UN, 2011). This is roughly in line with the FAO (2009) which expects a 70 per cent population growth between 2005/7 and 2050 and assumes a world population of 9.1 billion in 2050.

The other key variable on the demand side is the result of economic reforms in many developing and newly industrializing countries, which act to increase per capita incomes. According to Engel's Law, income growth leads to a significant per capita food consumption growth in these countries. In addition there is an expected rapid growth in the demand for biobased goods of the emerging bioeconomy. The growing middle class in developing and newly industrializing countries will be a key driver of demand growth while people at the lower end of the income scale will suffer from rising prices.

The rapid demand growth could, in principle, be met by increasing the acreage used for agricultural production or by producing more on the land being farmed already. The first option, expanding the acreage, is not really available, as the land that could be used for farming is limited. The most productive land is being farmed already. In many parts of the world, including Europe, there are no major land reserves left that could be used for farming. In some regions of the world, including parts of Europe, there still is some unused land with the potential for farming. In other parts of the world there are fairly sizeable land reserves. However, a lot of them should not be converted into farm land for environmental reasons such as the need to preserve tropical rain forests and other valuable ecosystems. In the last half decade about 80 per cent of global supply growth has been the result of yield growth. FAO (2009) estimates that 90 per cent of future production growth must come from yield growth and only 10 per cent could be realized through the expansion of the agricultural acreage.

Agricultural productivity is levelling off in Europe

Yield growth in world agriculture is declining and is expected to continue to do so in the decades ahead (FAO, 2012). Therefore, achieving a sufficiently large yield growth to meet the rapidly growing needs of the world may be difficult. The European Union apparently was particularly successful in neglecting productivity growth because average yield growth is significantly lower than in the world at large (von Witzke and Noleppa, 2010). This is depicted for wheat in Table 1.

A key reason for the decline in productivity growth is the result of a general neglect of agriculture and in particular of agricultural research aimed at generating productivity gains. This began in the late 1970s when both the European Union and the United States had begun to produce surpluses (Pardey, 2009). The public perception during that time was that there were ample land and other resources to produce enough food for the growing needs of the world. The political solution to the problem of surplus production on both sides of the Atlantic was seen in a combination of production controls and land set-aside programmes.

Table 4.1 Wheat yields: world and EU-28

	Av. 1982/84 (MT/ha)	Av. 1992/94 (MT/ha)	Av. 2012/14 (MT/ha)	% p.a. 82/84–92/94	% p.a. 92/94–12/14
World	2.10	2.50	3.18	1.8	1.2
EU-28	4.10	5.22	5.50	2.4	0.3

Source: Own calculations based on ADM (2014)

Yield growth was seen as leading to just more surplus production and to a further intensification of land use with the potential of damages to the environment.

The problem with reversing the trend of declining productivity growth is the long time lag between initial research investment and yield growth on the farms. Research shows that this time lag may be 25 years or even longer (Pardey, 2009).

Besides the land constraint and declining yield growth, there are additional impediments to growing production. They include increasing water scarcity, an increasing energy price, and increasing competition for the scarce natural resources in world agriculture between the production of food crops on the one hand and non-food crops on the other hand such as cotton, flowers and ornamental plants, rubber, biofuel crops and crops for the bioeconomy. The growth in the production of bioeconomy goods is in part fuelled by government programmes.

Biofuels are seen by many as the main culprit in this regard. However, the impact of biofuel production, globally and in the European Union, continues to be fairly limited. Von Witzke and Noleppa (2014) estimate that between 2.9 and 3.5 per cent of the global cropland is presently being used for the production of bioenergy crops. Let this number be at 3.2 per cent. In most models the price elasticity of demand for agricultural commodities in aggregate is assumed to be at or around -.03. A price elasticity of demand of -0.3 implies that a 1 per cent increase in price acts to reduce demand by 0.3 per cent. Assume further that the land used for bioenergy crops is as productive as any other cropland. This would reduce production by 3.2 per cent and raise commodity price in aggregate by 10.7 per cent.

The assumptions of this calculation, however, are fairly conservative and act to overstate the actual price effect of bioenergy crop production, as it neglects three important aspects. The first is that about 20 million hectares of bioenergy acreage has come at the expense of land that was idled under government land set-aside programmes. The second is that land used for bioenergy crops tends to be less productive than average cropland. The third is that bioenergy production results in by-products, such as animal feed, which tend to reduce the price increasing effect of growing bioenergy production. Accounting for all three effects would reduce the overall commodity price effect of global bioenergy production to less than 4 per cent (von Witzke and Noleppa, 2014). A EU share of 20 per cent in global bioenergy acreage implies that EU bioenergy production accounts for less than a 1 per cent increase in aggregate agricultural commodity prices. Given that prices have risen by more than 100 per cent on many commodity markets since the turn of the millennium, this is in the range of white noise.

The above back of the envelope calculation, incidentally, is in line with findings by Grethe *et al.* (2013) and Hamelinck (2013). In essence, the public debate about the food price effects of biofuels and other goods of the bioeconomy distracts from the root causes of high, and rising, prices of agricultural commodities and food and their contribution to global hunger.

Climate change also matters in this regard. While some regions gain, others will lose. On balance agricultural production may be expected to decline, all other things being equal (Sundström *et al.*, 2014).

Table 4.2 Real world market prices of selected agricultural commodities, 2003/5–2015/17

Market	2003/5 (US$/MT)	2015/17 (US$/MT)	2015/17 in % of 2003/5 (projected)
Wheat	158	272	172
Corn	106	219	207
Other grains	91	137	151
Oilseeds	288	492	197
Sugar	250	493	197

Source: Von Witzke *et al.* (2009)

Continuing price increase

Economic analysis has been able to predict the rise in commodity prices fairly well (e.g. OECD/FAO, 2012, 2013). Our price projections (Table 4.2) for the time period 2003/05– 2015/17 have also been reasonably close to actual price increases (von Witzke *et al.*, 2009). On the demand side the main driving forces of the rapidly rising prices during the time period analysed turned out to be population and consumption growth. On the supply side the most important variables were the price of energy and declining agricultural productivity growth. Recent price projections suggest that the longer-term trend in prices will continue to point upward. USDA (2014, 2015) correctly emphasizes that the short-term outlook is for lower prices, as high prices in the past have mobilized resources to expand production. As a consequence, stocks have been replenished. However, USDA (2014, 2015) price projections also show that prices will be rising again in the longer term. The magnitude of price increases, however, will also depend on the price of energy which is difficult to predict, as it is at times fairly volatile and also affected heavily by political events and decisions.

The European Union: a net importer of virtual agricultural land

The poor countries of the world used to be net exporters of food and agricultural products when it came to trade with the rich countries. Today they are net importers. The net food imports of the poor countries are estimated by FAO (2003) to quintuple between 2000 and 2030. It would, of course, be desirable if the poor countries were in a position to contribute more towards their own food security. However, these countries are, for the time being, caught in the Malthusian Trap. Demand growth is outpacing the growth in supply.

This rapidly growing import gap of the poor countries, therefore, can only be closed if the newly industrializing and the rich countries, including the European Union, increase both production and exports. Much would be gained if the EU would cease to be one of the largest net importers of food and agricultural products when the trade flows are converted back to the commodity level; i.e. when the value added of the food industry is subtracted. Von Witzke and Noleppa (2010) have developed a method which permits the conversion of the net imports of the EU into the agricultural acreage used abroad to produce these net imports. They refer to this phenomenon as the net import of virtual agricultural land.

The results of such calculations for 2000–13 are summarized in Figure 4.1. As is evident, the EU has consistently been a net importer of virtual agricultural land during that time. Net imports have tended to increase in the 2000–7 time period, but after this period they began to decline. There are three main reasons for the decline in EU imports of virtual agricultural land after 2007.

The least important of these reasons is that – although EU productivity growth is lagging – there have been increasing yields which obviously have acted to reduce the net import of virtual agricultural land. The lesson in this regard is that EU agricultural productivity matters and that it has the potential to significantly reduce the land footprint of EU food and agriculture.

A second and more important reason has been the gain in efficiency in food processing. This effect is intuitively plausible. Rising agricultural commodity prices increase the input cost in the food industry. Hence, it is not surprising that the industry has looked for ways to get more final good out of the commodities by increasing technical efficiency and by reducing waste.

The most important reason, however, has been the growth in yields outside the EU. Hence, the EU has reduced its imports of virtual agricultural land not so much by EU agriculture becoming more productive but because the EU food industry and farmers outside the EU have managed to realize productivity gains. This last mentioned effect is also caused by the fact that EU production is small

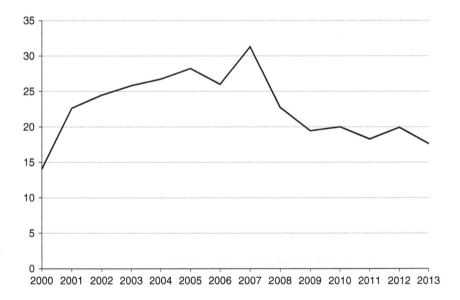

Figure 4.1 EU net import of virtual agricultural land (in million ha), 2000–13

relative to the rest of the world and small productivity gains in the rest of the world may have a significant effect on EU net imports of virtual land.

The EU net import of virtual agricultural land must not be interpreted such that the EU should return to a Common Agricultural Policy of trade protection. On the contrary, a liberal international agricultural trade regime is a necessary condition for sustainable world food security, as it makes the most out of the scarce resources in world agriculture. Rather, the results reported here demonstrate three things. First, there is a need for highly productive agriculture in the EU, as this acts to reduce the EU's land footprint in the rest of the world, thus slowing down the global expansion of the agricultural acreage. Second, it illustrates that both international trade patterns and international resources also depend on agricultural research investment. And third, it shows that productivity gains in the entire value chain in food and agriculture matter.

Diminishing agricultural productivity growth contributes to global warming and harms the world's natural resources

Rising prices of agricultural commodities and food also act to increase the incentives to expand the agricultural acreage. Already today the expansion of the global agricultural acreage through deforestation or the conversion of pasture into cropland contributes 18 per cent to the global greenhouse effect. This is more than global manufacturing or transportation each of which account for 14 per cent of the human-made part of global warming (e.g. Stern, 2007).

It is obvious that rising productivity in agriculture in a resource-efficient and sustainable way is the key in the fight against hunger around the globe. The majority of undernourished people live in the countryside of poor countries. They are landless farm workers as well as smallholders who do not produce enough food to feed their families, let alone produce a surplus for the market. Productivity growth in small-scale farming systems in particular when they are connected to a functioning value chain has the potential to significantly increase welfare in rural regions of developing countries. It also reduces the price of food for the urban poor. Hunger, incidentally, is most prevalent in regions in which farmers have the least access to productive technologies which have successfully been employed in rich countries for a long time. These technologies are fairly basic such as mineral fertilizer, modern crop protection and high-yielding crop varieties (von Witzke, 2014).

In addition, productivity growth is key in the fight against global warming and crucial also for the preservation of natural habitats and biodiversity around the globe. If EU and world agriculture succeed in producing more food on the land being farmed already, the global agricultural acreage would have to be expanded by less to meet the world's rapidly growing needs in food and agriculture. Eastern Europe has the potential to do a lot of catching up.

The lesson of the analysis in this chapter is that productivity growth in EU agriculture has many benefits to society in both the EU and the world at large. With productivity growth the EU and the world could afford more of everything:

more food, more feed, more bioenergy and other goods of the growing bioeconomy, more natural habitats, more biodiversity and –along with it – reduced CO_2 emissions which result from the expansion of the agricultural acreage.

Noleppa *et al.* (2013) have quantified these benefits. The results of their analysis suggest that every percentage point increase in EU crop yields raises the traditional measure of social welfare by about €500 million. This is the market effect of productivity growth. It is the result of two distinct effects. When production increases, the price declines. This is beneficial for consumers, as they can enjoy more food at a lower price. In addition, there is a benefit to producers, as they can produce more food at lower cost. Both effects are traditionally being quantified with standard economic methods of welfare economics.

However, when it comes to quantifying the social welfare effects of agricultural yield growth, additional aspects have to be included as well. Several but certainly not all of them are intangibles and cannot yet be quantified in terms of social welfare.

Noleppa *et al.* (2013) have quantified several of the additional effects of every percentage point increase in crop yields in the EU. One of them is that this would provide food for about 10 million people globally. Another effect is that this would reduce the EU import of virtual land by 1.2 million hectares and at the same time would preserve natural and semi-natural habitats by the same acreage. The reduced expansion of the global agricultural acreage resulting from a 1 per cent yield growth would act to reduce CO_2 emissions by 220 million tonnes. Estimates of the social cost of CO_2 emission vary widely. Ackerman and Stanton (2012) have reviewed the literature on this issue. They report estimates which range from US$28 per tonne to almost US$900 per tonne. In a recent study by Moore and Diaz (2015) the social cost of CO_2 emissions is reported to be at US$220 per tonne. At a conservative number for the cost to society of €50 per tonne of CO_2 emissions saved, this would be a value to society at large of €11 billion. This far exceeds the traditional market effect of productivity growth on social welfare and demonstrates why it is important to also include greenhouse gas emissions in the analysis of productivity growth in agriculture.

Yet another aspect in this regard is that when natural habitats are preserved biodiversity is preserved as well. Noleppa *et al.* (2013) also have quantified the effect of yield growth on biodiversity. Their results suggest that every percentage increase in EU yields would preserve global biodiversity equivalent to about 600,000 hectares of tropical rainforest.

Critiques of modern agriculture may argue that all this might be so, but that increasing yields necessitate intensifying use of agricultural land; i.e., that it would be necessary to use more inputs per hectare (such as fertilizer, crop protection, etc.), and that this would be undesirable. However, this frequently used claim does not hold much water. Anything done in agriculture now and in the future will have to be sustainable at any rate. In the long run, yield growth only makes sense when it is possible to sustain it.

The authors of this paper have analysed the causes of yield growth in German agriculture (Noleppa and von Witzke, 2013). The results are listed in Table 4.3.

Table 4.3 Annual yield growth: intensification vs innovations. The case of Germany, 1991–2010

Crop	Yield growth, per cent change (MT/ha) p.a.	Tfp growth (innovation), per cent change p.a.
Wheat	1.1	1.1
Corn	2.0	1.9
Oilseed rape	1.7	1.7
Sugar beet	1.6	1.6
Potato	2.4	2.3

Source: Based on data in Noleppa and von Witzke (2013)

Tfp: Total factor productivity per hectare. Tfp is the part of yield growth which is the result of innovation rather than increasing input. Innovation typically is the result of investment in research.

The gain in yields per hectare in column 2 of Table 4.3 could have been the result of intensification of land use or of innovation. Innovation is measured by the change in total factor productivity per hectare. This is the portion of yield growth that is not attributable to increasing intensity of land use; i.e., not the consequence of more inputs per hectare. As seen from the table, the annual percentage change in yields per hectare is essentially identical to the change in total factor productivity per hectare. Therefore, the entire yield growth during the 20-year period of analysis was the result of innovation and not of increasing intensity of land use.

For the US, total factor productivity is reported to have grown more than yields in roughly the same period of time (Fuglie, 2012). Farmers in the US, thus, have been able to increase yields with declining intensity of land use. There are two probable causes for this difference between Germany and the US. One is that the use of precision farming practices has grown significantly in the US during the time period analysed. Adoption in Germany is lagging because precision farming has fairly high fixed cost and in many parts of the country farms are small. Therefore this technology is being adopted more slowly than in the US. In addition, genetically modified (GM) crops have become increasingly popular with US farmers which resulted in declining intensity of land use because it reduces tilling and simplifies crop protection (e.g. less energy, less crop protection per hectare) while German farmers are not permitted to grow them.

The results reported by Fuglie (2012) and in Table 4.3 also suggest that the concept of *sustainable intensification*, which is so popular in the public debate about EU agriculture, is grossly misleading. The reason is simply that it suggests that yield growth can only be achieved by intensification and not by innovation. The above results suggest that, in fact, it has been innovation rather than intensification of land use which has been driving yield growth in agriculture in Europe and the US.

Innovation does not fall from heaven like manna. Rather it is the result of investment in agricultural research. Time and again research finds that investment in agricultural research is highly profitable (e.g. Fuglie, 2012). Noleppa and von Witzke (2013) find that the social rate of return to plant breeding in Germany is in the range of about 40–80 per cent annually and, thus, in line with findings for other countries and agricultural R&D activities. However, the actual social rate of return may be much higher, as the authors assumed the social cost of CO_2 emissions to be at only €12.50 per tonne.

Conclusion

The very high value of modern, highly productive and innovative agriculture to society is certainly good news for the agricultural science profession around the globe. However, this is at the same time bad news because such high benefits to society of modern agriculture imply that there is severe underinvestment in agricultural research (e.g. Ruttan, 1980; Alston *et al.*, 1998). Therefore, there is a need for increasing investment in agricultural research. Unfortunately, the opposite has happened in many countries where public agricultural research has faced cutbacks. In addition, agricultural research in the private sector is being discouraged by agricultural regulation and research policy. As a consequence, Europe is losing scientists and research facilities. This is particularly true for crop genetic engineering.

In conclusion, extensification and land set-aside programmes may have been reasonable political strategies during times in which the EU and other countries were producing mounting surpluses. In the new era of scarcity such policies are anachronistic. What is needed is a modern, highly productive and innovative agriculture around the globe, and a global agricultural research system that generates innovation to support a sustained and sustainable productivity growth. Only with modern and science-based farming practices will the world feed 9 or even 10 billion people by 2050 and, at the same time, preserve the world's natural resources.

References

Ackerman, F. and Stanton, E.A. 2012. Climate risks and carbon prices: revising the social cost of carbon. *Economics* 6, 2012-10.

ADM. 2014. *Statistical Information About the Grain and Feedstuff Market.* [Online]. [Accessed 27 February 2016]. Available from: http://www.adm.com/en-US/worldwide/germany/Documents/Statistikbroschuere%202014.pdf

Alston, J.M. *et al.* 1998. Financing agricultural research: international investment patterns and policy perspectives. *World Development* 6, pp.1050–71.

FAO (Food and Agriculture Organization). 2003. *World Agriculture Towards 2015/30.* London: Earthscan.

FAO (Food and Agriculture Organization). 2009. *How to Feed the World in 2050.* Rome: FAO.

FAO (Food and Agriculture Organization). 2012. *World Agriculture Towards 2030/2050: The 2012 Revision.* ESA Working Paper 12-03. Rome: FAO.

Fuglie, K.O. 2012. Productivity growth and technology capital in the global agricultural economy. In: Fuglie, K.O. *et al.* (eds). *Productivity Growth in Agriculture: An International Perspective.* Oxfordshire: CABI International.

Grethe, H. *et al.* 2013. *Biofuels: Effects on Global Agricultural Prices and Climate Change.* Hohenheim: University of Hohenheim.

Hamelinck, C. 2013. *Biofuels and Food Security: Risks and Opportunities.* Utrecht: Ecofys.

Moore, F.C. and Diaz, D.B. 2015. Temperature impacts on economic growth warrant stringent mitigation policy. *Nature Climate Change* 5, pp.127–31.

Noleppa, S. and von Witzke, H. 2013. *Die gesellschaftliche Bedeutung der Pflanzenzüchtung in Deutschland.* HFFA Working Paper 02/2013.

Noleppa, S. *et al.* 2013. *The Social, Economic and Environmental Value of Agricultural Productivity in the European Union.* HFFA Working Paper 3/2013.

OECD (Organisation for Economic Co-operation and Development)/FAO (Food and Agriculture Organization). 2012. *Agricultural Outlook 2012–2021.* Paris: OECD.

OECD/FAO (Organisation for Economic Co-operation and Development)/FAO (Food and Agriculture Organization). 2013. *Agricultural Outlook 2013–2022.* Paris: OECD.

Pardey, P. 2009. *Determinants of Agricultural Productivity Growth.* Paper presented at the HFFA meeting in Davos, Switzerland, February 1–3.

Ruttan, V.W. 1980. Bureaucratic productivity: the case of agricultural research. *Public Choice* 35, pp.529–46.

Stern, N. 2007. *The Economics of Climate Change: The Stern Review.* Cambridge: Cambridge University Press.

Sundström, J.F. *et al.* 2014. Future threats to agricultural food production posed by environmental degradation, climate change, and animal and plant diseases. *Food Security* 6, pp.2012–15.

UN (United Nations). 2011. *World Population Prospects: The 2010 Revision.* New York: United Nations.

USDA (United States Department of Agriculture). 2014. *USDA Agricultural Projections for 2014–2023.* Washington, DC: USDA.

USDA (United States Department of Agriculture). 2015. *USDA Agricultural Projections for 2015–2024.* Washington, DC: USDA.

von Witzke, H. 2014. Sicherung der Welternährung, Innovation und Produktivitätswachstum vs. Extensivierung und Flächenstilllegung in der Europäischen Union. In: Härtel, I. (ed.). *Nachhaltigkeit, Energiewende, Klimawandel, Welternährung.* Baden-Baden: Nomos.

von Witzke, H. *et al.* 2009. *Global Agricultural Market Trends Revisited.* Working Paper 89/2009, Department für Agrarökonomie, Humboldt Universität zu Berlin.

von Witzke H. and Noleppa, S. 2010. *EU Agricultural Production and Trade: Can More Production Efficiency Prevent Increasing 'Land-grabbing' Outside of Europe?* OPERA Research Centre, University of Piacenca.

von Witzke, H. and Noleppa, S. 2014. *Biofuels: Agricultural Commodity Prices, Food Security, and Resource Use.* Agripol Research Paper 2014-02.

Wright, B.D. 2011. The economics of grain price volatility. *Applied Economic Perspectives and Policies* 33, pp.32–58.

5   An African perspective

New biosciences making African
agriculture more productive and
resilient

Jennifer A. Thomson

Introduction

The global crisis in food production and climate change is raising the status of
Africa as a source of growth and investment in the eyes of many countries looking to feed their people. In the eyes of many agriculture in Africa is viewed as big
business. African farmers will, in the future, move away from subsistence to
large-scale and commercial farming. But in order to do this they will have to
embrace modern technology, including biotechnology, to boost the currently low
productivity, and amongst the tools of biotechnology lies the adoption of genetically modified (GM) crops. However, no single technology can be viewed as a
'silver bullet' and together with increasing crop productivity must come improvements in infrastructure, including road and rail transportation, energy and education. African farmers must become educated in new technologies as well as in the
economics of food production, and one of the best ways to ensure food security
for future generations is to invest in the education of women.

Hand-in-hand with new technologies, such as GM crops, must come social
acceptance. Much of the current antagonism to this particular technology lies in
the belief by many Africans and, indeed, by many African leaders, that this is
something that has been foisted upon them by greedy Western companies wishing to make a quick profit at the expense of human and environmental safety. This
chapter looks at the successful uptake of various GM crops in some African
countries, considers what new crops are in the pipeline and how these could be
introduced to improve the competitiveness of farmers, as well as providing food
safety for those living on this continent.

Insect resistance

Cotton

Insect-resistant cotton is the largest GM crop by area in Africa. Cotton is a shrub
native to tropical and subtropical regions around the world, including Africa,
India, Australia and the Americas. It was independently domesticated in the Old
and New Worlds and is an important trading commodity in many African

countries. Unfortunately the larvae of certain lepidopterans, such as the cotton bollworm, *Helicoverpa armigera*, bore into the cotton bolls causing extensive damage which can often reach staggering proportions with farmers losing most of their crops. Most insecticides are rather ineffective against these pests that burrow into plant tissues where they are protected against the spray. However, there is a biotechnological approach which has been extremely effective in many cotton-growing countries and is now being used in parts of Africa.

Bacillus thuringiensis is a naturally occurring soil bacterium that produces proteins, called Bt proteins, that are toxic to certain insects (Schnepf *et al.*, 1998). They cause little or no harm to most non-target organisms, including humans and wildlife due to the specificity of their mode of action. The toxin binds to specific cells in the lining of the insect's gut, where it causes lysis and rapid death. It has been used in sprays in conventional and organic agriculture for decades with little or no ill effects on human health or the environment.

However, it is not very effective as the toxin protein is sensitive to UV light and hence decays on exposure to sunlight. Scientists have therefore taken the gene(s) encoding one or more of the more than 30 Bt toxins and introduced them into crops such as cotton to produce plants that can protect themselves from larval attack.

Bt cotton in South Africa

Bt cotton has been grown commercially in South Africa since 1999. An analysis of the benefits of adoption by both small- and large-scale farmers was published by Gouse *et al.* (2004). They found the yield increase of large-scale farmers who irrigated was 18.5 per cent, those who did not: 13.8 per cent, and small-scale farmers: 45.8 per cent. Besides the yield benefits, the adoption of Bt cotton also caused a decrease in the volume of insecticides sprayed, with associated cost benefits. Because small-scale farmers do most of their spraying by hand, this reduction usually meant more time for weeding and other farm management activities.

According to Gouse *et al.* (2004, p.192) 'a high percentage of large-scale farmers have indicated that peace of mind about bollworms is a very important benefit of Bt cotton'. This peace of mind gave farmers managerial freedom to devote time to other crops or general farming activities. These farmers also noticed increased populations of beneficial insects, such as ladybirds and lacewings, in Bt cotton fields, indicating a possible environmental benefit due to reduced insecticide applications.

In recent years plantings of cotton, whether Bt or not, have decreased partly due to the worldwide drop in cotton prices.

Bt cotton in Burkina Faso

In 2009 Burkina Faso became the third country in Africa to commercialize a GM crop, but they did it in grand style. By planting just over 125,000 hectares of insect-resistant cotton they introduced the largest biotechnology crop onto the continent (Vitale *et al.*, 2011). But this did not happen overnight; the commercial release was made possible through a joint collaboration between their national cotton companies and Monsanto that began in May 2000. The genetic construct they introduced is Bollgard II® (BGII), which encodes Cry1Ac and Cry2Ab from *B. thuringiensis*, and Monsanto helped to transfer it to the two regional cotton varieties, STAM 59 and STAM 103. But even before then the various cotton stakeholders in the country had been coordinating their efforts to satisfy the technical, legal and business requirements before any commercial release could be effected.

Burkina Faso's national agricultural research centre, Environmental Institute for Agricultural Research (INERA), played an important role as since 2003 they have been testing the efficacy of Bt cotton by conducting environmental assessments as part of the inputs required to satisfy biosafety protocols and to monitor the socioeconomic impacts of BGII (Vitale *et al.*, 2011). To determine the impact they conducted a survey of 160 rural households in ten villages where Bt cotton had been planted since 2009 (Vitale *et al.*, 2011). The area planted averaged 3.2 hectares and the average households contained 14.1 persons, with 8.6 actively engaged in the family's farming operations. It was found that average yield increases in different zones of the country varied from 36.6 per cent to 16.5 per cent and 14.3 per cent. The yield differences could have been due to a combination of factors including environmental characteristics, pest pressure, and secondary pest spray differences (Vitale *et al.*, 2011).

However, yield increase is not the only factor that could improve cotton farmers' lives in Burkina Faso. The overall economic benefits are what really count and in the period under review BGII increased incomes by an average of approximately US$62 per hectare (Vitale *et al.*, 2011). More significantly, Bt cotton enabled producers surveyed to move from a negative return of approximately -US$23 per hectare generated by conventional cotton to a positive return of approximately US$39 per hectare. Vitale *et al.* (2011, p.329) concluded that 'in relative terms, BGII's economic impact in 2009 corresponded to more than a doubling of the income that would have been earned by conventional cotton, a 270 per cent increase in cotton income'. This was partly due to the fact that production costs had no significant effect on cotton income as costs were nearly the same between BGII and non-Bt cotton.

In 2014 73.8 per cent of the 648,469 hectares planted to cotton was Bt. This represents a 5 per cent increase of adoption since 2013. Farmer benefits included a 20 per cent yield increase compared to conventional cotton, and pesticide use reduction of about 67 per cent. Cotton profits rose by approximately US$64 per hectare (James, 2014).

As pointed out by Vitale *et al.* (2011) continued monitoring will be required to determine whether Bt cotton will be technically and economically viable in the long term. They concluded that 'experience from other parts of the world suggests that benefits can change significantly from one year to another due to differences in weather, pest density, and economic conditions' (p.334). An extremely important aspect of such monitoring will be the assessment of farmer compliance with the use of refugia to prevent the build-up of pest resistance. If the BGII experience in Burkina Faso is positive it will be interesting to see whether neighbouring cotton-producing countries such as Mali and Benin will follow suit.

Bt cotton in Sudan

Bt cotton was approved for commercial release in Sudan in June 2012. In 2014 of the 109,200 total cotton hectarage, 80 per cent was Bt, planted by nearly 30,000 farmers having an average of 1 to 2.5 hectares of land (James, 2014). Most of Sudan's cotton is exported as lint, however the industry has been in a slump in recent years. The average export earnings during the 1970s were approximately US$270 million, while those in 2001 were a mere US$42 million (James, 2014). Earnest efforts are now being made by the Sudanese government to revive both cotton production and the domestic textile industry. The Bt cotton programme is one such effort that responds to the real need and is poised to position Sudan back on the global map as a major player in the world cotton trade (James, 2014).

Maize and post-harvest fungus resistance

Maize, although technically a grain, is used in cooking as a vegetable or starch. In many African countries it is the staple food where people can eat it three times a day. White maize is consumed by humans, yellow maize is fed to livestock and poultry. South Africa is the only African country growing commercial GM maize, most being consumed locally, with commercial farmers producing about 96 per cent of the crop.

GM maize was introduced in South Africa in 1997 but only became commercially adopted on a major scale in 2000. Since then GM plantings have increased dramatically. Maize can be severely damaged by the larvae of the maize stalk borer, *Busseola fusca*, and, as with cotton, there are genes coding for varieties of the Bt toxin that can be introduced to this crop to protect it. In 2014 it was estimated that some 86 per cent of commercial maize plantings were GM. Of this 28 per cent carried the single Bt gene, while the rest comprised either herbicide resistance or both traits stacked (see below). The adoption was very similar for white and yellow maize and it was noted that adoption is reaching saturation. This is because not all plantings require Bt insect resistance as not all are subject to severe stalk borer pressure. Over 92 per cent of commercial maize samples tested were positive for GM traits, either pure GM or co-mingled. Some traders import or contract farmers for non-GM grain for certain customers (James, 2014, p.107).

An unexpected side effect has been noticed especially by smallholder farmers in South Africa planting Bt maize. They often store their annual crop of maize in storage cribs that are open to the air. If the cobs have been 'nibbled' by insect borers their kernels will have holes in them. These are perfect breeding grounds for fungi under rainy and sunny conditions alike. Many of these are *Aspergillus* species which produce aflatoxins, a known human carcinogen that has been linked to liver cancer (Environmental Health Trust, 2015). Many women instead of using such infected maize directly for food will ferment it to form beer. As aflatoxins have also been implicated in oesophageal cancer it is little wonder that this disease is widespread in parts of Africa where homebrewed maize beer is widely consumed.

Cowpea

Cowpeas are one of the most important food legume crops in the semi-arid tropics. They are rich in protein and are consumed by approximately 200 million people in Africa. In addition, they are drought tolerant and hence well adapted to the drier regions of the tropics. Being a legume the plant fixes atmospheric nitrogen through its root nodules, but unlike many other legumes, its green leaves and pods can also be eaten before crop maturity, which helps to bridge the hunger gap between harvests. It grows well in poor soils with more than 85 per cent sand and with less than 0.2 per cent organic matter and low levels of phosphorus (Singh, 2003). In addition, it is shade tolerant and can therefore be used in intercropping, a farming method popular in many parts of Africa. Cowpeas can be intercropped with maize, millet, sorghum, sugarcane and cotton.

Unfortunately, however, cowpeas are often infested by the borer *Maruca vitrata*, which decreases the yield from a potential 2–2.5 to 0.05–0.5 tonnes per hectare. Control through spraying with insecticide has not been widely adopted by farmers due to the prohibitive costs and health hazards associated with spraying. Fortunately, *Maruca*, being an insect, is sensitive to the Bt toxin. Scientists at the Commonwealth Scientific and Industrial Research Organization (CSIRO) in Australia have transformed cowpea with the Bt *cry1Ab* gene for *Maruca* resistance. They have formed a partnership with the African Agricultural Technology Foundation (AATF), based in Nairobi, to conduct field trials in West Africa, where cowpeas are a major crop. The AATF was founded in 2003 as a not-for-profit organization that facilitates and promotes public/private partnerships for the access and delivery of appropriate agricultural technologies for sustainable use by smallholder farmers in sub-Saharan Africa through innovative partnerships and effective stewardship along the entire value chain. It acts as a one-stop-shop that provides expertise and know-how that facilitates the identification, access, development, delivery and utilization of agricultural technologies (AATF, 2015a).

Field trials conducted in Nigeria and Burkina Faso have shown encouraging results. There is a clear and striking difference between the non-transgenic and transgenic plants. The level of floral, pod and leaf damage is pronounced in the former and no damage has been observed in the latter. Only dead first instar larvae were observed inside the flowers of transgenic events, showing that these plants are resistant to *Maruca* infestation (Thomson 2013, pp.137–9).

Herbicide tolerance in maize

Weeds compete with crops for moisture, nutrients and light. Uncontrolled weed growth can thus result in significant losses in yield. Farmers have therefore been spraying herbicides on their crops for decades. As with insecticidal sprays, this is often done using aeroplanes, with the result that a great deal of the spray drifts away from the target sites.

The best-known example of transgenic herbicide tolerance is Monsanto's Roundup Ready®. The active ingredient in the herbicide Roundup is glyphosate which acts on an enzyme found in many plants, including maize and its weeds. Using Roundup on conventional maize fields is a tricky operation as the herbicide must not make contact with the crop. Roundup Ready® maize produces a naturally occurring form of the target enzyme, 5-*enol*pyruvylshikimate-3-phosphate synthase (EPSPS) that is resistant to glyphosate and hence to the herbicide. The gene encoding the glyphosate-resistant form of EPSPS was derived from *Agrobacterium tumefaciens*, coincidentally the bacterium that is used to genetically manipulate plants.

In South Africa in 2014 86 per cent of the maize crop was GM. The total GM maize crop of 2.14 million hectares consisted of 19 per cent herbicide tolerant (HT) while 53 per cent was planted to stacked Bt and HT traits (James, 2014). One of the positive environmental impacts of herbicide-tolerant maize is the use of no-till cultivation or conservation tillage. With conventional maize, farmers would till the soil to allow weeds to grow, spray with herbicide and then wait a sufficient time for it to degrade before planting. Now they can allow weeds and maize to grow together before spraying. This means less soil erosion and better retention of moisture in the soil. In addition, Roundup is more readily degradable by bacteria than many other herbicides (Balthazor and Hallas, 1986). In a recent report the World Health Organization's International Agency for Research on Cancer (IARC) reported that glyphosate is 'probably carcinogenic to humans'. However, according to an article published by the Genetic Literacy Project (Porterfield, 2015), all that the IARC looks at is potential hazard, but the risk depends on exposure. For instance, electricity can be extremely hazardous, but our risk is low because of the steps we take to prevent exposure to enough of it to harm us. In fact, the lethal dose measure of glyphosate is about the same as common table salt. Porterfield notes that the classification that IARC assigned to glyphosate, 2A, is the same classification it gave to grapefruit juice, apples and working the night shift.

Bacterial resistance in bananas

To most Westerners bananas are soft and sweet, the so-called 'dessert banana'. However, in Africa the banana cultivars grown are of a firmer, starchier consistency and are called plantains or 'cooking bananas'. Banana is a major staple crop in East Africa produced mostly by smallholder subsistence farmers. More bananas are produced and consumed in East Africa than in any other region of the world. Uganda is the world's second foremost grower with a total annual production of about 10.5 million tonnes. The average daily per capita consumption in Uganda ranges from 0.61 to over 1.6 kg, one of the highest in the world (Tripathi *et al.*, 2014). Cultivated bananas are parthenocarpic, which literally means virgin fruit; the fruit are produced without fertilization and are thus seedless and sterile. Propagation involves farmers removing and planting a sucker, a vertical shoot that develops from the base of the plant. If the sucker is removed before it has elongated the process is even easier as these suckers can be left out of the ground for up to two weeks.

Banana *Xanthamonas* wilt (BXW), caused by *Xanthamonas campestris*, threatens the livelihoods of millions of farmers in Ethiopia, Uganda, the Democratic Republic of Congo (DRC), Rwanda, Tanzania, Kenya and Burundi. The crop devastation can be both extreme and rapid. Banana bacterial wilt is caused by the bacterium *Xanthomonas campestris*. It threatens the livelihood of millions of farmers in the Great Lakes region who rely on this crop as a staple food and for income generation. The disease was first identified in Uganda in 2001 and subsequently reported in the DRC, Rwanda, Tanzania and Kenya. It is very destructive, infecting all banana varieties. Prospects of developing varieties with resistance to bacterial wilt through conventional breeding are limited, as no source of germplasm exhibiting resistance against the disease has been identified. Therefore scientists at the International Institute for Tropical Agriculture (IITA) in Uganda and Kenya have turned to a transgenic approach.

The genes were obtained from Academia Sinica, Taiwan, and royalty-free licenses were obtained from the patent holder by the AATF. They originated from the sweet pepper, *Capsicum annuum*, and encode a plant ferrodoxin-like protein (PFLP) and a hypersensitive response-assisting protein (HRAP). The former mediates electron transfer and the latter prevents the spread of pathogens by causing the rapid death of cells in the local area surrounding the infection (Tripathi *et al.*, 2010; Namukwaya *et al.*, 2012).

Resistant banana lines (65) expressing either the Hrap or Pflp gene were subjected to confined field trials in Uganda for two successive crop cycles, artificially infected with *X. campestris* (Tripathi *et al.*, 2014). All non-transgenic controls died while the majority of the transgenic lines had a significantly higher ($P \leq 0.05$) resistance. Transfer of this resistance from mother to progeny occurred in all except two lines and all lines produced fruits that appeared normal. Eleven showed 100 per cent resistance which was retained in the ratoon crop, suggesting that this approach could provide a solution to farmers for controlling BXW. This trial will be expanded to multiple locations and subjected to food and environmental safety evaluations (Tripathi *et al.*, 2014).

Virus resistance

Maize streak virus (MSV) is one of the most significant viral pathogen of maize in Africa, resulting in crop yield losses of up to 100 per cent in epidemic years. It is a geminivirus which, unlike most plant viruses so far discovered, contains

DNA not RNA as its genetic material. There is evidence that resistance due to coat protein-mediated transgene silencing, effectively used for the latter group, including such excellent examples as the Hawaiian papayas resistant to papaya ringspot virus (Gonsalves, 2014), would not be a successful approach to use for resistance to MSV (Shepherd *et al.*, 2009).

Scientists at the University of Cape Town have therefore tested three different approaches. MSV has a small (2.7 kb), single-stranded circular DNA genome encoding the coat protein, movement protein, and two replication-associated proteins, Rep and RepA. The multifunctional Rep protein is essential for viral replication, is required early in the viral lifecycle and functions as a multimer, making it an ideal target for pathogen-derived resistance. The rationale behind the approach was that by making transgenic maize plants constitutively express mutant Rep proteins, these over-expressed non-functional Reps would bind to any newly-synthesized viral Reps and prevent the complex from binding to the viral origin of replication. Thus, the replication of the incoming viral DNA would be inhibited and consequently the maize plant would be resistant to MSV.

A number of different mutants were made including deletions in motif III required for virus replication and in the retinoblastoma-related protein-binding domain (RBR), a motif that is important in the viral lifecycle. Transgenic maize plants were tested for virus resistance and the phenotypes included no symptom development, delayed and mild symptoms (Shepherd *et al.*, 2007).

The second approach was used to circumvent possible negative effects on plant growth of constitutive expression of MSV-derived resistance genes, and to avoid placing an unnecessary metabolic load on uninfected transgenic plants. The mechanism tested, called the 'split gene cassette', was used for inducible expression. In this case the mutant *rep* gene was split into two exons flanked by two viral intergenic regions containing the origin of replication and the Rep binding and nicking sites. Upon viral infection the cassette serves as a template for rolling circle replication during which removal of the intergenic regions results in the reconstitution of the mutant *rep*$^{1-219}$ gene (Shepherd *et al.*, 2014).

The third approach uses the process of gene silencing, whereby small pieces of RNA can cause genes to be inactivated. Post-transcriptional gene silencing (PTGS) occurs when translation of a targeted mRNA is prevented by translational inhibition or cleavage, with subsequent degradation of the mRNA. Given that it is a natural defence mechanism used by plants to reduce the accumulation of viral RNA, gene silencing is an attractive option for the development of MSV resistance. (Even though MSV is a DNA virus, there is substantial evidence that PTGS is triggered in host plants by geminivirus infection.) The target chosen for this approach was a portion of the *rep* gene, chosen because of the indispensable role of the Rep protein in viral replication (Owor *et al.*, 2011).

When we published the work on the first strategy (Shepherd *et al.*, 2007) it was followed up by an article in *Science* (Sinha, 2007) entitled 'GM technology develops in the developing world'. It had the sub-heading: 'The first genetically modified crop developed entirely in Africa is gearing up for field trials. Its success would be a milestone'. Sadly those field trials have not yet materialized.

Why? In 2011 CropLife International published an analysis of what it took in time and money to bring an idea for a GM crop to market (Phillips McDougall, 2011). They estimated that it took at least 13 years and cost about US$136 million. But the stark fact that underlies these estimates is the burden of regulation. This component, according to their calculations, accounts for 37 per cent of the time and 42 per cent of the costs. Although regulations are necessary, they are becoming such a burden that it is almost impossible for any organization other than a multinational company to afford them.

Drought tolerance

In recent years severe droughts have been affecting many parts of Africa, particularly countries such as Somalia, Ethiopia and Kenya in East Africa. This is threatening the livelihood of many millions of people resulting in a huge refugee problem. With the onset of climate change this situation can only get worse and therefore many groups worldwide are working to develop drought-tolerant crops. One of these is a partnership called WEMA, Water Efficient Maize for Africa, funded by the Bill and Melinda Gates and Howard Buffet Foundations and managed by the AATF. The gene being used is *csp*B which has been donated royalty free by Monsanto and encodes a cold shock protein from the bacterium *Bacillus subtilis* (Castiglioni *et al.*, 2008). This has been shown by the company to confer tolerance to dehydration in transgenic maize in the USA.

The gene has been introduced into African maize varieties by the International Maize and Wheat Improvement Center, CIMMYT, which, although based in Mexico, also has centres in Africa. These plants are being put through confined field trials (CFTs) by the National Agricultural Research Services of some of the partner countries, Kenya, Mozambique, South Africa, Tanzania and Uganda (Thomson, 2013, p.142).

NEWEST rice

Rice (Oryza spp.) is an important staple food crop in parts of Africa. However, production, largely by small-scale farmers, is not sufficient for the demand with the result that about 40 per cent of sub-Saharan rice is imported. The average yield in Africa is about 50 per cent less than the world average. This affects the well-being of over 20 million smallholder farmers who depend on rice as their main food (AATF, 2015b).

Soil nitrogen deficiency and drought have been cited as major constraints to rice production. In addition high salinity is also becoming a major problem in coastal lowlands and mangrove swamps. To counter these problems, the AATF is embarking on CFTs of their NEWEST rice: Nitrogen-Use-Efficient (NUE), Water-Use-Efficient (WUE) and Salt Tolerant (ST) in Ghana, Uganda and Nigeria. The genes have been donated by Arcadia Biosciences in Davis, California, and the International Centre for Tropical Agriculture (CIAT) is carrying out seed increase and agronomic trait assessment.

Vitamin enrichment

Vitamin A deficiency is common in developing countries. One of its earliest manifestations is night blindness which is often found in malnourished pregnant women and children. Many of these children die within a year of becoming blind. Vitamin-enriched rice was produced by Ingo Potrykus and Peter Beyer (Ye *et al.*, 2000) using genes from the daffodil and a soil bacterium to produce β- carotene, a precursor to vitamin A. The resultant product is yellow in colour, hence the name Golden Rice, and was developed mainly for Asian communities. Vitamin A deficiency is also a problem in Africa leading to blindness in children and night blindness and maternal mortality in pregnant women.

In 2005 the Bill and Melinda Gates Foundation funded the African Biofortified Sorghum (ABS) project, run by an international consortium under the leadership of Africa Harvest, an African-based international non-profit organization. Sorghum is Africa's second largest crop, producing about 20 million tonnes per annum, approximately one-third of the world crop. It is the only viable food grain for many of the world's most food insecure people, as it is uniquely adapted to Africa's climate, being both drought resistant and able to withstand periods of water-logging. The African biofortified sorghum contains the gene for a high-lysine storage protein from barley and has increased levels of Vitamin A, iron and zinc. In 2013 the ABS initiative received a 'Patents for Humanity Award' from the USA Patent and Trademark office for its efforts to improve nutrition, production and availability of sorghum in Africa (The Biofortified Blog, 2014).

Conclusion

As stated in the introduction, GM crops are not a 'magic bullet' to improve food security for Africans or to provide a source of income for commercial farmers. However, it is one technology that has proven to work in some African countries and could be profitably employed by many others. It would be an indictment on society if opinions held by anti-GMO, well-fed European countries were to prevent African farmers from testing this technology on their own soil.

References

AATF (African Agricultural Technology Foundation). 2015a. *Pod Borer Resistant Cowpea* [Online]. [Accessed 1 May 2015]. Available from: http://cowpea.aatf-africa.org
AATF (African Agricultural Technology Foundation). 2015b. *Nitrogen-Use Efficient, Water-Use Efficient and Salt-Tolerant Rice Project* [Online]. [Accessed 1 May 2015]. Available from: http://newest.aatf-africa.org
Balthazor, T.M. and Hallas, L. 1986. Glyphosate-degrading microorganisms in industrial waste treatment biosystems. *Applied and Environmental Microbiology* 51, pp.432–4.
Castiglioni, P. *et al.* 2008. Bacterial RNA chaperones confer abiotic stress tolerance in plants and improved grain yield in maize under water-limited conditions. *Plant Physiology* 147, pp.446–55.

Environmental Health Trust. 2015. *Aflatoxin facts.* [Online]. [Accessed 14 April 2015]. Available from: http://ehtrust.org/fact-sheetsfaqs/aflatoxin-facts/

Gonsalves, D. 2014. Hawaii's transgenic papaya story 1978–2012: a personal account. In: Ming, R. and Moore, P.H. (eds). *Genetics and Genomics of Papaya.* New York: Springer, pp.115–42.

Gouse, M. *et al.* 2004. The distribution of benefits from Bt cotton adoption in South Africa. *AgBioForum* 7(4), pp.187–94. [Online]. [Accessed 14 April 2015]. Available from: http://www.agbioforum.org

James, C. 2014. *Global Status of Commercialized Biotech/GM Crops: 2014.* ISAAA Brief No. 46. Ithaca, NY: ISAAA.

Namukwaya, B. *et al.* 2012. Transgenic banana expressing *Pflp* gene confers enhanced resistance to Xanthomonas wilt disease. *Transgenic Research* 21, pp.855–65.

Owor, B.E. *et al.* 2011. A *rep*-based hairpin inhibits replication of diverse maize streak virus isolates in a transient assay. *Journal of General Virology* 92, pp.2458–65.

Phillips McDougall, 2011. *The Cost and Time Involved in the Discovery, Development and Authorization of a New Plant Biotechnology Derived Trait.* [Online]. Brussels: CropLife International. [Accessed 14 April 2015]. Available from: https://croplife.org/wp-content/uploads/2014/04/Getting-a-Biotech-Crop-to-Market-Phillips-McDougall-Study.pdf

Porterfield, A. 2015. Why regulators conclude glyphosate safe while IARC, alone, claims it could cause cancer? [Online]. Genetic Literacy Project. [Accessed 14 December 2015]. Available from: http://www.geneticliteracyproject.org/2015/07/24/

Schnepf, E. *et al.* 1998. *Bacillus thuringiensis* and its pesticidal crystal proteins. *Microbiology and Molecular Biology Reviews* 62, pp.775–806.

Shepherd, D.N. *et al.* 2007. Maize streak virus-resistant transgenic maize: a first for Africa. *Plant Biotechnology Journal* 5, pp.759–67.

Shepherd, D.N. *et al.* 2009. Transgenic strategies for developing crops resistant to geminiviruses. *Plant Science* 176, pp.1–11.

Shepherd, D.N. *et al.* 2014. Inducible resistance to maize streak virus. *PLoS ONE* 9(8): e105932. doi:10.1371/journal.pone.0105932.

Singh, B. 2003. Improving the production and utilization of cowpea as food and fodder. *Field Crops Research* 84, pp.150–69.

Sinha, G. 2007. GM technology develops in the developing world. *Science* 315, pp.182–3.

Thomson, J. 2013. *Food for Africa: The Life and Work of a Scientist in GM Crops.* Cape Town: UCT Press.

The Biofortified Blog. 2014. Q&A about biofortified sorghum. [Online]. [Accessed 1 May 2015]. Available from: http://biofortified.org/2014/03/qa-about-biofortified-sorghum

Tripathi, L. *et al.* 2010. Expression of sweet pepper *Hrap* gene in banana enhances resistance to *Xanthomonas campestris* pv. *Musacearum. Molecular Plant Pathology* 11, pp.721–31.

Tripathi, L. *et al.* 2014. Field trial of *Xanthomonas* wilt disease-resistant bananas in East Africa. *Nature Biotechnology* 32, pp.868–970.

Vitale, J.D. *et al.* 2011. The commercial application of GMO crops in Africa: Burkina Faso's decade of experience with Bt cotton. *AgBioForum.* [Online]. 13(4), pp.320–32. [Accessed 14 April 2015]. Available from: http://www.agbioforum.org

Ye, X. *et al.* 2000. Engineering the provitamin A (beta-carotene) biosynthetic pathway into (carotenoid-free) rice endosperm. *Science* 287, pp.303–5.

6 Europe and Africa

Addressing the food security challenges

Isabelle Schluep Campo, Philipp Aerni and Ruth K. Oniang'o

Introduction

Global food supply over the past 50 years has increased faster than world population growth even though today more than half of the world's population live in urban areas and less than 40 per cent earn their livelihoods from agriculture (Alston and Pardey, 2014b). To a large extent this has been made possible by improvements in agricultural productivity through technological change and the resulting expansion of agricultural trade, allowing food to become more abundant and cheaper. Further, this enabled countries to cope with rising populations, to reduce poverty, improve food security and stimulate broad-based economic growth. Poor farmers as well as the non-farming poor benefited alike from agricultural innovation. It enabled increases in productivity and a reduction in harvest losses and food waste due to improved management of biotic and abiotic stress factors in agriculture. Alston *et al.* (2014) showed that a sustained period of higher agricultural productivity growth always leads to a reduced vulnerability of rural households to poverty and destitution. The non-farming poor, in return, benefit indirectly from agricultural productivity increases due to increases in food supply and thus improved access to food through lower prices (Alston and Pardey, 2014b).

In Europe, where the population is well fed and the share of income spent on food is declining (constituting between 7 and 15 per cent of household expenditures), benefits from agricultural productivity increases through innovation seem irrelevant. As a consequence, the public narrative on agriculture is not about producing food anymore but about cultural and environmental benefits (Aerni, 2011). Productive agriculture nevertheless matters in the European Union (EU) because it generates various benefits for the rural economy and society as a whole (Noleppa *et al.*, 2013). The EU agricultural production and food consumption levels also have an impact on global food security and climate change. The current EU agricultural policy focuses on promoting low-input 'sustainable' farming and the ban on genetically modified crops is not conducive to further productivity gains in European agriculture. The EU has already started to increase its dependence on food and feed imports. Moreover, a shift to low-input agriculture also has consequences for farm incomes. It is estimated that in Germany a full conversion to low-input agriculture would reduce farm incomes by a third (Noleppa *et al.*, 2013).

Agricultural productivity developments in world regions 1961–2011

Past trends in agricultural productivity in sub-Saharan Africa (SSA) are unsettling: Alston and Pardey (2014a) showed that the real value of agricultural output per capita declined by 0.17 per cent per year from 1961 to 2011. Even though SSA had a reasonably rapid growth rate in real agricultural output of 2.6 per cent per year during that period, it was outpaced by a more rapid population growth rate of 2.8 per cent per year (Alston and Pardey, 2014a). Figure 6.1 shows that productivity in SSA continues to lag far behind other regions and this productivity gap is widening compared with emerging country regions such as Latin America, Asia and Pacific, and the Middle East and North Africa. In the Western Europe country group the per capita agricultural production between 1961 and 2011 has been flat since 1980, while productivity rates increased in Northern America. Over the same period of time, countries comprising the former Soviet Union and Eastern Europe saw production collapsing following the dissolution of the Soviet Union in 1989 and are still on a recovery path (Alston and Pardey, 2014a).

Most agricultural output growth in SSA has been the result of an increase in the use of land and labour, but there has been very little improvement in yields and barely any change in production techniques (NEPAD, 2013). Although growth in cereal production in SSA can be almost entirely attributed to growth through area expansion, with very slow yield growth, these general dynamics

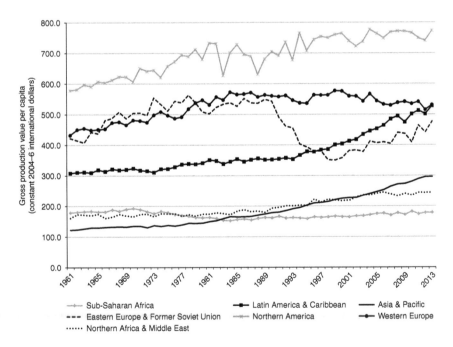

Figure 6.1 Per capita agriculture production by region, 1961–2013 (Calculations based on FAOSTAT, 2015)

vary considerably from one region to another, both across the continent and within the different regions. In general, growth rates of crop yields and land and labour productivity in much of the world have slowed. Taking China out of the equation, land and labour productivity growth rates were slower in the period 1990–2011 compared to 1961–1990 (Alston and Pardey, 2014a).

SSA probably faces the biggest challenge in achieving sustained, long-term productivity growth in agriculture considering its high population and urbanization growth rates, its unsustainable low-input agricultural practices that lead to nutrient depletion, soil erosion and deforestation, the lack of means and capacity to invest in agricultural innovation and the absence of a dependable infrastructure necessary to commercialize agricultural surpluses. Furthermore, adverse macro-economic environments, corruption and poor infrastructure also contribute to high transaction costs in regional agricultural trade and market development. Armed conflicts and public health challenges (e.g. HIV/AIDS, malaria) are also affecting agricultural productivity due to a loss in skilled labour.

Yet, despite all these challenges, Africa has a great potential to increase its agricultural productivity without further depleting its natural resources if it promotes sustainable intensification through technological change.

The need for sustainable intensification

Sustainable intensification is a practical approach that can allow smallholder African farmers to tackle food insecurity while preserving their natural resource base. The Montpellier Panel Report (2013, p.1) defines sustainable intensification as 'the goal of producing more food with less impact on the environment, intensifying food production while ensuring the natural resource base on which agriculture depends is sustained, and indeed improved, for future generations'.

Sustainable intensification encompasses a range of goals that must be achieved simultaneously. To realize sustainable intensification at scale, the report outlines a variety of practical examples under three headings: *Ecological intensification* is the utilization and intensification of ecological processes to create sustainable forms of crop and livestock production. One such form of ecological intensification is intercropping, which grows two plants together in a way that reduces competition and increases mutual benefits between them. *Genetic intensification* is the concentration of beneficial genes within crop varieties and livestock breeds; for this, game-changing technologies have to be developed and utilized. One ongoing project, Water Efficient Maize for Africa (WEMA), released 16 new drought-tolerant maize hybrids in 2013. They are marketed royalty-free to smallholder farmers in Kenya, Mozambique, South Africa, Uganda and Tanzania. *Socioeconomic intensification* is the process of developing innovative and sustainable institutions that provide more incentives to invest in sustainable and productive farming and commercialization at the level of farm communities as well as across regions and nations as a whole. African smallholder farmers require improved access to input and output markets as well as assistance to become better integrated into remunerative commercial food value chains.

Markets can offer poor farmers better access to inputs, knowledge and credit while also helping to increase their income from selling surplus crops. To link smallholder farmers to markets, one solution is to work with farmer associations to create and run village-level 'grain banks', where farmers can safely deposit their grain (Montpellier Panel, 2013). The storage facilities are usually fumigated against pests in order to preserve the quality of the grain. Such institutions help farmers to cope with market price fluctuations and help to improve local food availability throughout the year. In Kenya, such storage facilities are linked to a countrywide network of small and large markets. This network is supported by the Kenya Agricultural Commodity Exchange (KACE), a private sector firm that provides farmers with prices and other market intelligence accessible to smallholders using simple mobile phone texts (Montpellier Panel, 2013).

Research and development (R&D) and agricultural innovation

The accumulation of past and present research spending plays an important role in stimulating present and future productivity growth in agriculture (Alston and Pardey, 2014a). In 2009 a total of about US$35 billion (in 2005 dollars converted at Purchasing Power Parity exchange rates) was spent on public sector agricultural and food research worldwide (Pardey *et al.*, 2012a). Even though the social rates of return from agricultural R&D investments are high and productivity is slowing down, public support in high-income countries (including Europe) has slowed down and a diversion of funds away from farm productivity enhancement – towards off-farm issues such as health and nutrition, food safety, biofuels technology and the environment – can be observed (Alston and Pardey, 2014a). By 2009 high-income countries (USA plus Other High Income) accounted for 48 per cent compared with 58 per cent in 1960 (Figure 6.2). As a result, public agricultural research capacity in many high-income countries has decreased in the past two decades, infrastructure has depreciated and the majority of scientists in the field are close to retirement age (Alston and Pardey, 2014a). Around 90 per cent of private R&D – estimated to be in the range of US$20–22 billion per year – took place in the high-income countries and, for the high-income countries (including Western Europe) at least, almost half of that research was concerned with producing off-farm innovations, primarily those related to food processing (Alston and Pardey, 2014a).

The Agricultural Science and Technology Indicators (ASTI) show that after a decade of stagnation in the 1990s, public agriculture R&D spending in SSA increased by more than one-third in real terms, from US$1.2 billion in 2000 to US$1.7 billion in 2011, measured in constant 2005 PPP (Purchasing Power Parity) dollars (Beintema and Stads, 2014). However, about half of these investments were made in just three countries – Nigeria ($394 million), South Africa ($237 million) and Kenya ($188 million). In 2011, Africa invested 0.51 per cent of agricultural output in agricultural research (public research intensity ratio), far below the African Union's target of 1 per cent or more (Beintema and Stads, 2014). The target was met in South Africa and Kenya but not in Nigeria.

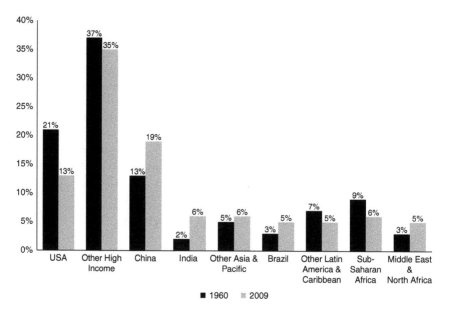

Figure 6.2 Global trends in public agricultural R&D spending, 1960 and 2009 (Data from Pardey *et al.*, 2012a, in Pardey *et al.*, 2012b)

Note: Eastern European and Former Soviet Union countries are excluded. High-income countries are excluded from each geographical region. For example, Other Asia & Pacific excludes Japan and Singapore.

Yet, it is not the increase in spending for agricultural R&D as such, but the potential of this research to lead to agricultural innovation that enables farmers to produce more with less that matters. Most tropical regions have developed national or even regional agricultural innovation systems but in most cases their capacity to translate their R&D expenses into commercially viable agricultural innovation has been missing, because of a lack of involvement of private sector collaboration (Aerni *et al.*, 2015). The main problem is that many of the institutions involved in agricultural research and extension in SSA are highly dependent on donor and development bank funding which is highly volatile and vulnerable to funding shocks (Beintema and Stads, 2014).

Dissatisfied with the slow progress of agricultural and food market liberalization policies, several SSA countries have made public commitments to increasing input use via the Abuja Declaration and, more broadly, under the Comprehensive Africa Agriculture Development Programme (CAADP) of the African Union (AU) in the New Partnership for Africa's Development (NEPAD). CAADP has been a catalyst for African-owned initiatives in setting national priorities in agriculture, as well as for Africans regaining control of the dialogue with technical and financial partners, and to reclaim ownership of agricultural policy.

Nevertheless, public commitment to boosting agriculture has been limited and has often failed to match the set targets and benchmarks. In terms of the CAADP targets, only four countries (Ethiopia, Malawi, Burkina Faso and Niger) have since allocated at least 10 per cent of their annual budgets to agriculture. In terms of sectorial growth, only Ethiopia, Angola, Tanzania, Burkina Faso and The Gambia have attained the 6 per cent annual target (Aerni, 2013).

Trade policy and food security

Africa's food trade deficit had started in the mid-1970s and since then the dependence on food imports has increased. In its report *Africa Can Help Feed Africa: Removing Barriers to Regional Trade in Food Staples* the World Bank (2012) shows that it is not inter-continental trade but intra-continental trade that represents the major bottleneck to improved agricultural production and commercialization in Africa. The nearest source of demand is often across the border, yet fragmented regional markets, high transaction costs and lack of predictable trade policies deter much needed private investments. As most cross-border food trade in Africa takes place in informal value chains outside the legal system, and formal sector trade involves cumbersome procedures, the development of efficient and predictable procedures that allow large- and small-scale traders to compete more effectively with each other and with global commodities should be a priority.

As the variability in production is expected to increase with climate change, facilitating cross-border trade for food staples and crop inputs is more important than ever to meet the rapidly growing food demand (Keyser, 2015). Equally important would be the harmonization of genetically modified organism (GMO) regulations across African countries. In the case of fertilizer, African regional trade is severely constrained by countries insisting on their own unique product formulations, by lengthy product-testing requirements and by special input subsidy programmes in different countries. To improve the regional trade situation for seed, Common Market for Eastern and Southern Africa (COMESA), Economic Community of West African States (ECOWAS) and Southern African Development Community (SADC) have taken steps to develop harmonized systems for seed registration and seed certification. The ECOWAS system was formally adopted by member countries in 2008 but has not yet been put into practice. This is also the case for SADC and COMESA (Keyser, 2015).

African countries have taken several measures to promote regional integration, a major part of which is intra-regional trade. These include the establishment of the AU and the creation of various Regional Economic Communities (RECs) designed to promote trade integration, create customs unions and, eventually, a common market. Generally, intra-regional trade enhances competition in the local market leading to increases in productivity, efficiency and price convergence across countries and regions. It also promotes more foreign direct investment, the transmission of technological innovation and the creation of enhanced capacity to compete with more advanced economies on the international market (UNCTAD, 2013). Although in 2012 the average intra-African trade was just 12 per cent compared with 61 per cent for the EU (Anyanwu, 2014), it has grown at a rate of 10.9 per cent in the period since 1995 (see Table 6.1).

Reducing the time and cost required to transport agricultural goods without impairing their quality requires more reliable electricity supply systems, better run port facilities, road construction and maintenance and air transport infrastructure. The positive effects of such investments would not just improve intra-continental but also inter-continental trade and thus enhance the ability to export at competitive terms to OECD countries (Anyanwu, 2014). The International Trade Centre (ITC) estimates that the improvement of transport infrastructure within Africa could boost exports by up to 51 per cent beyond the export growth that would otherwise occur based on current trends. Intra-African trade would mostly benefit (ITC, 2012).

The evolution of African trade patterns

History and proximity lead African countries to prioritize relations with the EU. But, given its future market prospects, Africa is already engaged with other partners. Overall, Africa's trade with the rest of the world has grown over fourfold since 2000 (EY Africa, 2014). China has been at the forefront of this growth, and is now the continent's single largest trading partner, although the EU with its 27 member states remains the largest trading partner on the aggregated level (see Figure 6.3, Table 6.1).

In 2012 nearly half of Africa's agricultural exports (US$26 billion) went to Europe. This amounts to just 3.9 per cent of Europe's agricultural imports, although it is an improvement from 2.7 per cent in 2005. Europe in turn exported US$20 billion in agricultural products to Africa, 35.4 per cent of Africa's agricultural imports in 2012 – down from 50.4 per cent in 2005 (AfDB *et al.*, 2014).

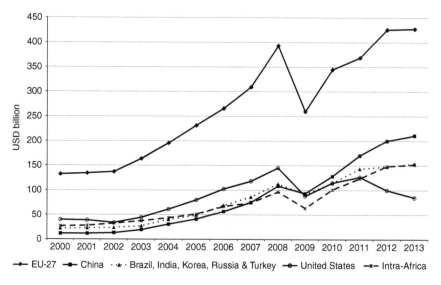

Figure 6.3 Africa's total trade flows with selected partners, 2000–2013 (UN COMTRADE, in AfDB *et al.*, 2015)

Table 6.1 SSA exports

Partner country	Exports US\$ billion (2013)	Exports US\$ billion (2014)	Compounded average growth rate in per cent (1995–2014)
South Asia	18.7	7.4	14.7
SSA	71.6	44.6	10.9
Middle East & North Africa	9.7	7.8	9.8
East Asia & Pacific	46.9	29.5	8.9
Europe & Central Asia	91.1	44.9	5.5
North America	21.0	10.0	5.5
Latin America & the Caribbean	11.4	1.7	4.1

Source: Calculations based on UN COMTRADE

The need for sustainable technological change in Africa versus European perception

One way to improve sustainable intensification and consequently food security in Africa is to ensure that plant and animal breeding techniques derived from modern biotechnology are being used to their full potential. Agricultural biotechnology, which comprises a wide range of biological disciplines, offers great potential to speed up the development of plant varieties with traits such as drought tolerance, pest and virus resistance, improved nutrient efficiency, increased shelf life and nutritional value, among others. Yet, Europe's anti-GMO policies also impact Africa, as it is the greatest donor to African governments. Close to 50 per cent of all bilateral Official Development Aid to Africa originates from Western Europe (OECD, 2015). As a consequence, many genetically improved orphan crops that have been successfully tested in the field in Africa have failed to pass approval for commercial release due to burdensome and often dysfunctional biosafety regulations. These regulations are mostly the product of European-funded 'capacity building' programmes (Paarlberg, 2008).

Similarly, in animal production there is substantial opportunity for development of vaccines and diagnostics targeting diseases that constrain livestock production in developing regions of the world (UNCTAD, 2004). While biotechnology does not provide the 'silver bullet' for poverty alleviation, it does enhance the effectiveness of other disciplines such as plant breeding, integrated pest and nutrient management, post-harvest management, and livestock breeding, feeding and disease management. Importantly, because the use of these technologies, as any other, is associated with risks, African scientists need to have access to scientific insights gained from publicly funded risk assessment projects, and acquire capacities for the safe use of the technology. But they also need to make use of a scientific infrastructure that allows them to develop and propagate improved and locally adapted varieties.

Even when it comes to the most controversial tool of agricultural biotechnology, genetic engineering, a meta-analysis on genetically modified (GM) crops found that gains for public health, the environment and small-scale farmers far outweigh the potential risks that are well known from conventional agriculture (Klümper and Qaim, 2014).

The main barriers to maximize the benefits and minimize the risks of modern agricultural biotechnology for society and the environment are not technical but regulatory in nature (Juma, 2011). Preventive regulation of agricultural biotechnology must be understood as a policy response to public rather than scientific concerns about the development and use of genetically modified organisms (GMOs) in agriculture. On the basis of negative public attitudes towards agricultural biotechnology, the majority of governments in Europe decided to ban the use of GM crops in domestic agriculture. This is so despite the fact that numerous publicly funded risk assessment studies on the national level, such as the Swiss National Research Programme (NRP) on the risks and benefits of GM crops (NRP 59, 2013) and the EU-level research on GMOs (EC, 2010), did not confirm these concerns. Nonetheless, new legislation officially approved by the European Parliament in January 2015 is making it legal for member states to prohibit the cultivation of GMOs without the need to respect their own scientific risk assessments and those made by the European Food Safety Authority (EFSA). The justification to ban GM crops is thus no longer based on scientific concerns about biosafety but merely on the argument that public attitudes in Europe remain hostile to the use of GMOs in food and agriculture. Science does not matter anymore in the risk debate on GMOs in Europe. This was confirmed by the decision of the President of the European Commission (EC) Jean-Claude Juncker in November 2014 to abolish the post of the science advisor to the EC, held by Professor Anne Glover who dared to rebut the claims of Greenpeace and other organizations that GMOs are unsafe (Wildson, 2014). Although by the end of 2015 a new High Level Group of Scientific Advisors to the EC was appointed, it needs to be seen what its stance on GMOs is.

There is radical refusal to see any potential in a platform technology such as biotechnology to address the global agricultural sustainability challenges of the twenty-first century. Platform technologies enable the development of new products and services in various industries that have prior competences and capacities to make use of the new technology. This stands in strong contrast to the reality that about 70 per cent of the soybean meal that is needed as feed for the EU's livestock industry is imported and about 80 per cent thereof is genetically modified (transparenzGentechnik, 2015). It also contradicts the EC's own strategy and action plan of 2012 called *Innovating for Sustainable Growth: A Bioeconomy for Europe* (EC, 2012), the reform efforts of the Common Agricultural Policy (CAP) to promote rural development through innovation and entrepreneurship and its Global Food Security 2030 strategy (JRC, 2015), which recognizes the value of sustainable intensification of agriculture for rural development as well as the environment.

The EU's restrictive policy toward GM foods imposes negative externalities. For example, firms underinvest in R&D in agricultural biotechnology because they fear a loss in public reputation, regulatory uncertainty and a shrinking market. Moreover, not only private but also public R&D in agricultural biotechnology is being curtailed due to low prospects of use in the field. This clearly reduces the contribution biotechnology could make to increase global food supplies (Kerr, 2014). In addition, many African nations have reservations about the commercial production of GM crops because they fear that their financially lucrative and economically vital crop export markets in the EU as well as generous European aid will be at risk if GM crops are approved for commercial release (Paarlberg, 2008).

The attempts by European governments to tacitly tie funding and market access to the condition to refrain from the use of modern agricultural biotechnology is, however, contrary to the Paris Declaration on Aid Effectiveness, which they have signed as OECD countries. This Declaration is supposed to commit donors to align their funding with the priorities of the recipient countries, rather than shaping recipient priorities in a way that is in line with European priorities (Aerni *et al.*, 2015).

Learning from New Zealand: treating farmers as entrepreneurs

European policy makers may eventually have to apply innovation policy rather than social policy instruments to agriculture if they want to move toward more sustainable and less patronizing agricultural policies. In this context, they could learn from New Zealand (NZ). The NZ government decided to liberalize its export-oriented agricultural system in the 1980s and fared surprisingly well with this paradigm shift in agricultural policy. Rather than continuing to be the 'nanny' of farmers, the government assumed the role of a coach that supports farmers in their efforts to innovate and commercialize new agricultural products and services. The objective was to reconcile sustainability goals with national competitiveness. As a very attractive tourist destination, its government is anxious to preserve the country's image of being 'clean and green' while ensuring prosperity of its agricultural economy in rural areas. It did so by making innovation and entrepreneurship the drivers of sustainable change in agriculture. Rather than following the conventional social planning approach of multifunctional agriculture, NZ's government decided to promote an adaptive approach based on a continuing process of trial and error. In other words, NZ embraced sustainability as a dynamic concept.

Europe might learn from the adaptive approach by New Zealand. It does not mean that the European governments should stop supporting their farmers at all, but should rather do so in a different way. Rather than just assuming the role of a rational social planner that aims at allocating public resources in accordance with social preferences, European governments could become facilitators of sustainable change in agriculture by supporting farmers and agricultural researchers in their efforts to become innovation-driven entrepreneurs that generate their own revenues through the creation of new markets and simultaneously address social and environmental problems through their innovations and increased trade (Aerni, 2009).

This adaptive approach may also be the best way for African countries to lift rural people out of poverty and simultaneously enable a more sustainable use of natural resources in agriculture (Juma, 2011). In short, empirical evidence suggests that Europe should revisit its views about sustainable agriculture and embrace entrepreneurship and innovation as positive forces of sustainable change. It would bring its agricultural and environmental policies more in line with its own vision to create a bioeconomy, and it would bring its development policies more in line with its genuine commitment to the Paris Declaration on Aid Effectiveness. In the process, it would assist all those African countries who tend to be bound by Europe's stand on sustainable agriculture.

Concluding remarks

Even if SSA continues to manage to increase its agricultural productivity at the rate of population growth, consumption increases due to elevated income and changing food habits, will still have to be met through imports. This is why high-income EU countries can no longer ignore the importance of agricultural productivity and trade for sustainable development. The EU has a responsibility to limit the negative externalities of its anti-GM policy which does not comply with its legal obligations under the WTO, and which increasingly deprives Africa of an important option in its fight against food insecurity, its efforts to generate more off-farm employment, and the promotion of growth-enhancing structural change.

Innovation does not only encompass the uptake of new technologies (product innovation) but also organizational changes (process innovation). The economist Paul Collier (Collier, 2015) argues that if Africa wants to escape the Malthusian disaster – meaning that population growth will accelerate faster than food production – agriculture has to scale up. In that respect Africa could learn from Brazil where by 2006/7 76.4 per cent of the value generated in agriculture was due to commercial farming against 23.6 per cent contributed by family agriculture.

South–South trade, such as with China and Brazil, has the potential to empower SSA countries through science, innovation and trade and to become more independent from the patronizing European approach in its trade, aid and R&D priorities. Yet, for SSA to further integrate into regional or even global value chains, it will also require more political and macroeconomic stability, improved governance and heavy domestic investments in infrastructure to connect farmers to markets as well as trade facilitation.

References

Aerni, P. 2009. What is sustainable agriculture? Empirical evidence of diverging views in Switzerland and New Zealand. *Ecological Economics* 68(6), pp.1872–82.

Aerni, P. 2011. Food sovereignty and its discontents. *African Technology Development Forum Journal (ATDF)* 8(1/2), pp.23–40.

Aerni, P. 2013. *Tropical Agriculture Platform (TAP). Assessment of Current Capacities and Needs for Capacity Development in Agricultural Innovation Systems in Low Income Tropical Countries*. Synthesis Report. Rome: FAO.

Aerni, P. *et al*. 2015. Making agricultural innovation systems (AIS) work for development in tropical countries. *Sustainability* 7(1), pp.831–50.

AfDB (African Development Bank), OECD (Organisation for Economic Co-operation and Development) and UNDP (United Nations Development Programme). 2015. *African Economic Outlook 2015. Regional Development and Spatial Inclusion.* [Online]. [Accessed 29 May 2016]. Available from: http://www.oecd-ilibrary.org/development/african-economic-outlook-2015_aeo-2015-en;jsessionid=1ih4aqjftgyq2.x-oecd-live-02

Alston, J.M. *et al* 2014. Influences of agricultural technology on the size and importance of food price variability. In: Chavas, J.-P., Hummels, D. and Wright, B.D. (eds). *The Economics of Food Price Volatility.* Chicago and London: The University of Chicago Press, pp.13–58.

Alston, J.M. and Pardey, P.G. 2014a. Agriculture in the global economy. *Journal of Economic Perspectives* 28(1), pp.121–46.

Alston, J.M. and Pardey, P.G. 2014b. *Agricultural R&D, Food Prices, Poverty and Malnutrition Redux.* Staff Paper P14–01, Department of Applied Economics, University of Minnesota.

Anyanwu, J.C. 2014. *Does Intra-African Trade Reduce Youth Unemployment in Africa?* Working Paper No. 201, African Development Bank Group.

Beintema, N. and Stads, G.-J. 2014. *Taking Stock of National Agricultural R&D Capacity in Africa South of the Sahara.* ASTI Synthesis Report. Washington, DC: IFPRI.

Collier, P. 2015. *Achieving Sustainability: Should People Be Fitted to Policies, or Policies to People?* Lecture at the Center for Corporate Responsibility and Sustainability CCRS, University of Zurich, 19 March. [Accessed 15 February 2016]. Available on videostream from: https://cast.switch.ch/vod/clips/2osar1ci3b/streaming.html

EC (European Commission). 2010. *A Decade of EU Funded GMO Research (2001–2010).* Directorate-General for Research and Innovation, [Online]. [Accessed 15 February 2016]. Available from: http://ec.europa.eu/research/biosociety/pdf/a_decade_of_eu-funded_gmo_research.pdf

EC (European Commission). 2012. *Innovating for Sustainable Growth: A Bioeconomy for Europe.* Directorate-General for Research and Innovation. [Online]. [Accessed 15 February 2016]. Available from: http://ec.europa.eu/research/bioeconomy/pdf/bioeconomycommunicationstrategy_b5_brochure_web.pdf

EY Africa. 2014. *Africa 2030: Realizing the Possibilities.* [Online]. [Accessed 15 February 2016]. Available from: http://www.ey.com/Publication/vwLUAssets/EY-Africa-2030-realizing-the-possibilities/$FILE/EY-Africa-2030-realizing-the-possibilities.pdf

FAO (Food and Agricultural Organization). 2014. *The State of Food and Agriculture 2014 (SOFA): Innovation in Family Farming.* [Online]. [Accessed 15 February 2016]. Available from: http://www.fao.org/3/a-i4040e.pdf

FAOSTAT. 2015. FAO Statistics Division [Online]. [Accessed 16 February 2016]. Available from: http://faostat3.fao.org/

ITC (International Trade Centre). 2012. *Africa's Trade Potential: Export Opportunities in Growth Markets.* Technical Paper Document No. MAR-12-226.E, Geneva.

JRC (Joint Research Centre). 2015. *Global Food Security 2030. Assessing Trends with a View to Guiding Future EU Policies.* JRC94867, Foresight Series, European Commission, Brussels. [Online]. [Accessed 15 February 2016]. Available from: http://publications.jrc.ec.europa.eu/repository/bitstream/JRC94867/lbna27252enn.pdf

Juma, C. 2011. *The New Harvest: Agricultural Innovation in Africa.* New York: Oxford University Press.

Kerr, W.A. 2014. Food security and trade: some supply conundrums for 2050. *The Estey Centre Journal of International Law and Trade Policy* 15(2), pp.115–32.

Keyser, J.C. 2015. Regional trade of food staples and crop inputs in Africa. In: Gillson, I. and Fouad, A. (eds). *Trade Policy and Food Security. Improving Access to Food in Developing Countries in the Wake of High World Prices.* Washington, DC: The World Bank, pp.153–88.

Klümper, W. and Qaim, M. 2014. A meta-analysis of the impacts of genetically modified crops. *PLOS ONE* 9(11): e111629. doi:10.1371/journal.pone.0111629.

Montpellier Panel. 2013. *Sustainable Intensification: A New Paradigm for African Agriculture.* [Online]. [Accessed 15 February 2016]. Available from: http://ag4impact. org/publications/montpellier-panel-report2013/

NEPAD (New Partnership for Africa's Development). 2013. *Agriculture in Africa. Transformation and Outlook.* [Online]. [Accessed 15 February 2016]. Available from: http://www.un.org/en/africa/osaa/pdf/pubs/2013africanagricultures.pdf

Noleppa, S. *et al.* 2013. *The Social, Economic, and Environmental Value of Agricultural Productivity in the European Union.* HFFA Working Paper 03/2013, Berlin.

NRP (National Research Programme) 59. 2013. *Benefits and Risks of the Deliberate Release of Genetically Modified Plants.* [Online]. [Accessed 16 February 2016]. Available from: http://www.nfp59.ch/e_index.cfm

OECD (Organisation for Economic Co-operation and Development). 2015. *Development Aid at a Glance, Statistics by Region, 2. Africa.* 2015 Edition. [Online]. [Accessed 15 February 2016]. Available from: http://www.oecd.org/dac/stats/documentupload/2%20 Africa%20-%20Development%20Aid%20at%20a%20Glance%202015.pdf

Paarlberg, R. 2008. *Starved for Science: How Biotechnology Is Being Kept Out of Africa.* Cambridge, MA: Harvard University Press.

Pardey, P.G. *et al.* 2012a. *Global Food and Agricultural R&D Spending, 1960–2009.* InStePP Report. St. Paul, MN: University of Minnesota.

Pardey, P.G. *et al.* 2012b. *Agricultural Production, Productivity and R&D over the Past Half Century: An Emerging New World Order.* [Online]. Paper presented at the International Association of Agricultural Economists (IAAE) Triennial Conference, Foz do Iguaçu, Brazil, 18–24 August. [Accessed 15 February 2016]. Available from: http:// ageconsearch.umn.edu/bitstream/131824/2/PardeyEtAlFinal.pdf

transparenzGentechnik. 2015. *Eiweisslücke und Futtermittelimporte: Europa ist auf gentechnisch veränderte Sojabohnen angewiesen.* [Online]. [Accessed 15 February 2016]. Available from: http://www.transgen.de/lebensmittel/einkauf/1095.doku.html

UNCTAD (United Nations Conference on Trade and Development). 2004. *The Biotechnology Promise.* UNCTAD/ITE/IPC/2004/2, Geneva.

UNCTAD (United Nations Conference on Trade and Development). 2013. *Economic Development in Africa Report 2013: Intra-African Trade: Unlocking Private Sector Dynamism.* UNCTAD/ALDC/AFRICA/2013, Geneva.

Wildson, J. 2014. Juncker axes Europe's chief scientific adviser. *Guardian*, 13 November. [Online]. [Accessed 15 February 2016]. Available from: https://www.theguardian.com/ science/political-science/2014/nov/13/juncker-axes-europes-chief-scientific-adviser

World Bank. 2012. *Africa Can Help Feed Africa: Removing Barriers to Regional Trade in Food Staples.* [Online]. [Accessed 15 February 2016]. Available from: http://siteresources. worldbank.org/INTAFRICA/Resources/Africa-Can-Feed-Africa-Report.pdf

Part III

Towards resource-efficient economies

Broadening the base of agriculture

7 A European perspective

Potential of crop biosciences to support resource-use efficiency, climate change mitigation and adaptation in European agriculture

Olle Olsson, Torbjörn Fagerström, Jens Sundström, Thomas Kätterer and Ivar Virgin

Introduction

The impact of modern agriculture on the environment in general and our climate in particular has become a major global concern. Population growth and expanding demand for agricultural products constantly increase the pressure on production systems and ecosystem resources and cause environmental problems. A major issue of concern for many intensively managed agricultural systems with high external inputs is how to increase the resource-use efficiency, especially for agricultural inputs such as nitrogen. A high input combined with limited efficiency in growth and uptake ultimately results in environmental problems such as eutrophication and high emissions of greenhouse gases (GHGs). Consequently, there is a need for a transition of current agricultural systems into highly resource-use efficient systems that are productive, but at the same time ecologically sound, socially acceptable and climate smart. As a certain extent of future climate change is inevitable – as a result of historical emissions – 'climate smart' entails not only reduced GHG emissions from agriculture but also adaptation of agricultural systems to a changed climate.

In the past and present, increased productivity of the major plant production systems has been derived from genetic improvement but also through greater use of external inputs such as energy, fertilizers, pesticides and irrigation water. From a climate change perspective, improving resource-use efficiencies and maintaining a high crop yield with less external input is of key importance. At the same time, crop breeding strategies must become responsive to a changing climate.

In this chapter, we illustrate the potential of modern bioscience to contribute to climate change mitigation and adaptation in wheat production. For that purpose, we look at the two concrete crop innovations under development: nutrient use efficient (NUE) wheat and perennial wheat. If eventually commercialized in the European Union (EU), where roughly half of the total grain production is based on wheat cultivation, these products could make a significant contribution to reducing European GHG emissions. However, the current regulatory environment discourages many breeding companies to invest in these innovations, no matter how great the potential benefits would be for farmers and the environment.

The role of bioscience in reducing climate change risks

Given the intrinsic dependence of agriculture on geophysical conditions – not least weather patterns – a changing climate will also change conditions for agriculture. Although some agricultural regions will benefit from climate change, negative effects are expected to dominate on a global level (Porter *et al.*, 2014). For Europe, the effects will vary between regions. Whereas we expect longer periods of droughts and elevated temperatures in Southern Europe, Northern Europe will benefit from longer vegetation periods but risk irregular precipitation and emerging new crop diseases (Sundström *et al.*, 2014). Thus, *adaptation* to a changing climate is imperative for agriculture to keep providing a growing human population with food, fibre and fuel in the coming decades.

Agriculture is also a key sector when it comes to climate change *mitigation*, i.e. minimization of the extent of climate change through reduction of GHG emissions and enhancement of carbon sinks. The agricultural sector is responsible for 10–12 per cent of total global GHG emissions, mainly as methane from livestock and rice cultivation and nitrous oxide from manure and soils. Including CO_2 emissions caused by land use change (conversion of forest and grassland into cropland), drainage and cultivation of organic soils and consumption of fossil energy, the agriculture, forestry and other land use (AFOLU) sector was responsible for approximately 24 per cent of total anthropogenic GHG emissions in 2010. Remaining GHG emissions are coming from electricity and heat production (25 per cent), industry (21 per cent), transport (14 per cent), fossil fuel extraction and processing (10 per cent) and on-site energy generation in buildings (6 per cent) (Foley *et al.*, 2011; Smith *et al.*, 2014).

In essence, the final goal of mitigation and adaptation is the same: to minimize the negative effects of anthropogenic climate change. To ensure that this goal can be reached effectively, adaptation and mitigation strategies should not work in conflict with each other. In other words, a strategy for climate change adaptation must not lead to increased GHG emissions and a strategy for climate change mitigation must not increase societal and ecosystem-related vulnerabilities to climate change.

Below we discuss the potential of modern bioscience to contribute to climate change mitigation and adaptation in the agricultural sector, with special focus on the situation in Europe. We address two cases where successful implementation of modern plant breeding has the potential to make significant contributions to reducing GHG emissions, and in both cases we use wheat, as the crop of study.

The first case is primarily focused on the mitigation aspect, reviewing the potential to increase nitrogen use efficiency (NUE) in wheat. Improved NUE would reduce the need for nitrogen fertilization, connected to a large portion of life cycle GHG emissions from wheat cultivation. The second case is focused on the prospects for perennial wheat to support mitigation of, as well as adaptation to, climate change. Annual crops are in general quite vulnerable to drought and also increase the vulnerability of agricultural lands to soil erosion whereas perennial crops tend to be more resilient to outside disturbances, reduce the risk of erosion, improve soil water retention and support build-up of soil organic matter. Perennial wheat could thus provide positive effects for both adaptation and mitigation.

It should also be mentioned that apart from these two cases there are other interesting bioscience research efforts to mitigate GHG emissions resulting from crop production. This includes a better understanding and utilization of plant–microbe interactions in the design of a new generation of crop cultivars with optimization of these interactions leading to lower GHG emissions (Su *et al.*, 2015).

European wheat cultivation and climate change: impacts, emissions and adaptation

Impact of climate change on wheat cultivation in Europe

Climate change is expected to entail serious challenges to European agriculture, including wheat cultivation where drought, heat stress, extreme weather events and increased risks of damage from pests and pathogens can threaten productivity (Moore and Lobell, 2014; Trnka *et al.*, 2014). It has been estimated that an increase in average temperatures by 2°C could result in 30 per cent yield reductions for wheat (Moore and Lobell, 2014).

Therefore, it is essential that measures are taken to ensure that crop cultivation systems are adapted to climate change. Here, technologies enabling fast, efficient and precise breeding of crops tolerant to emerging diseases, drought, floods and elevated temperatures and with suitable agro-processing characteristics will be an important part of European climate change adaptation strategy.

Carbon sequestration in European wheat cultivation systems

All photosynthesizing organisms, including wheat, sequester carbon as they grow. Since soil carbon balances are mainly driven by net primary production (NPP), management practices which result in increased NPP will also result in increased soil Carbon (C) sequestration (Kätterer *et al.*, 2012). The increase of NPP through application of N fertilizer has been shown to increase soil C by 1–2 kg C for each kilogram of N fertilizer applied (Kätterer *et al.*, 2012). Minimizing the time with bare soil conditions through intercropping or cover crops and fertilization are also means of increasing total NPP and soil C sequestration during the growing season in cropland (Poeplau *et al.*, 2015).

Soil tillage may stimulate the turnover of organic matter, thus leading to increased CO_2 emissions. Reduced tillage is often mentioned as an effective measure to reduce CO_2 emissions, but evidence is accumulating that this is only the case under certain climatic conditions. Reduced tillage may increase emission of N_2O (Basche *et al.*, 2014) and its effect on soil carbon sequestration depends on climatic conditions, being often positive in dry regions where NPP is stimulated compared to moist climate regions where effects often are negligible (Virto *et al.*, 2012).

Whereas natural ecosystems such as forests and grasslands have perennial life cycles extending over decades and centuries, wheat is an annual crop, which means that each year the wheat crop is harvested and the land is re-cultivated. This difference between annual and perennial life cycles is crucial when it comes to carbon sequestration. If land use is changed from permanent grassland to crop-land, the soil carbon content usually drops and vice versa (Kätterer *et al.*, 2012). Crop rotations including perennial forage crops accumulate more carbon in soil than rotations dominated by cereals (Bolinder *et al.*, 2010). The main reason for this is that perennials allocate more of their carbon resources than annual plants to roots and rhizomes for surviving during cold or dry periods. According to a review by Bolinder *et al.* (2007) the proportions of NPP allocated below ground are about 50 per cent for perennial forage crops and about 20 per cent for wheat. Moreover, roots contribute relatively more to soil organic matter than corre-sponding carbon input from above-ground residues (Kätterer *et al.*, 2011). Thus, it is not surprising that soil carbon stocks increase significantly with the frequency of perennial crops in rotation (Kätterer *et al.*, 2012).

A highly interesting future pathway for increasing carbon sequestration of crop cultivation systems is based on converting annual crops, for example wheat, into perennials. This would result in wheat farming in the future being conducted much like today's cultivation of perennial forage crops, with a permanent plant cover which admittedly is harvested annually, but not tilled – a 'virtual prairie'. The potential climate effect for such perennial wheat productions is discussed below.

Greenhouse gas emissions from European wheat cultivation systems

When it comes to GHG emissions from wheat cultivation in the EU, fertilizer production and use are together by far the most important GHG emission sources, as has been shown in the recent decade in a number of studies (Meisterling *et al.*, 2009; Röös *et al.*, 2011; Tidåker *et al.*, 2007). The vast majority of life cycle fertilizer-related GHG emissions are in the form of nitrous oxide, N_2O, which is emitted both in the fertilizer production process and from agricultural soils. An important issue to be aware of is that the extent of emissions can vary greatly from case to case.

*   In the production stage, the European fertilizer industry has made significant advances in recent years, reducing GHG emissions to less than 4 kg CO_2eq/kg N, compared to a global average of 9.5 kg CO_2eq/kg N. Further improve-ments are possible – although still not commercially viable – by using renewable energy in the production process (Tunå *et al.*, 2014).
*   The amount of nitrogen added to soils in the form of fertilizer is commonly used (e.g. by the International Panel on Climate Change (IPCC)) as an esti-mator of ensuing N_2O emissions from cropland. The data provided herein are therefore also based on this assumption. However, it is important to note that this is only a rough estimator as actual emissions depend on a rather wide

and complex set of factors, including soil moisture, soil organic carbon, soil pH and soil temperature (Linquist *et al.*, 2012). This means that the actual extent of these emissions is very difficult to quantify with satisfactory precision (Röös *et al.*, 2011). We therefore urge the reader to be aware of these uncertainties in our estimation below of the total GHG emissions related to fertilization of EU wheat.

In order to estimate total fertilizer-related emissions from European wheat cultivation, we use data from Brentrup and Pallière (2014), who estimate fertilizer-related (i.e. including both production and use) emissions in European crop cultivation to be 8.88–11.19 kg CO_2eq/kg N, depending on the actual fertilizer product, see Figure 7.1 (Brentrup and Pallière, 2014). According to the International Fertilizer Industry Association (IFA), 3.022 million tonnes of N were consumed in wheat cultivation in the EU-27 in 2010–11(Heffer, 2013). Multiplying these yields, an estimate of total GHG emissions from fertilization of EU wheat will be between ($8.88 \times 3.022 \approx$) 26.8 and ($11.19 \times 3.022 \approx$) 33.8 million tonnes CO_2eq. As a point of comparison, this is slightly more than half of the total GHG emissions of the entire country of Denmark.

Thus, GHG emissions from N fertilization of EU wheat are a non-negligible contributor to the total emissions of the European Union. For this reason, increasing the nitrogen use efficiency of crop production systems should be seen as an

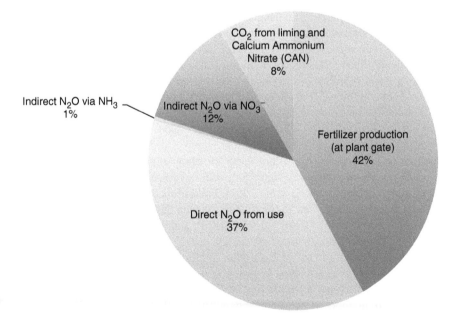

Figure 7.1 Emissions from production and use of Ammonium Nitrate in kg CO_2eq/kg N (Data from Brentrup and Pallière 2014) (CAN = Calcium Ammonium Nitrate)

important tool in EU climate change mitigation efforts. Improved NUE can be achieved by pursuing different strategies. Improved management systems and reduced emissions in the actual fertilizer production stage are important components. But Ussiri and Lal (2013) highlight that the use of modern breeding techniques and bioscience to improve NUE of the crops also has significant potential.

Wheat with increased ability to assimilate nitrogen

Background on NUE wheat

NUE is a complex trait with several co-occurring definitions (Good *et al.*, 2004). It may be affected by plant growth (Garnett *et al.*, 2009) as well as microbial interactions, e.g. mycorrhizal symbioses and nitrogen fixating rhizobia (Beatty and Good, 2011). From a plant perspective, N usage can be divided into two distinct steps: uptake and utilization, where utilization can be further subdivided into assimilation and translocation/remobilization (Masclaux-Daubresse *et al.*, 2010). The main source of N for agricultural plants is in the form of water-soluble nitrate (NO_3^-, most abundant) and ammonium (NH_4^+), although N uptake in organic forms may be more important in natural systems (Gardenas *et al.*, 2011). Ultimately, both N uptake and utilization are dependent on carbon uptake related to photosynthesis rates. Nitrogen is stored in large quantities in photosynthetic proteins, such as Rubisco.

Several of the enzymes involved in N usage have been characterized and attempts in model organisms have been made to increase NUE by either over-expressing or down-regulating key enzymes (McAllister *et al.*, 2012). Although promising, the success of this approach has been limited to laboratory-scale experiments. Further testing of multiple traits and traits under the control of tissue-specific promoters is imperative to determine if this strategy will work under field conditions. One alternative approach could be to change the activity of regulatory transcription factors that determine the activity of the enzymatic genes (Kurai *et al.*, 2011; Yanagisawa *et al.*, 2004) or proteins that help to increase nitrogen uptake. One interesting example of the latter is tissue specific expression of a barley gene encoding an alanine aminotransferase enzyme (AlaAT) in *Brassica napus*, which resulted in increased yield and biomass under N-limiting conditions (Good *et al.*, 2007). Field trials employing this technology in both wheat and barley are currently being run by the Commonwealth Scientific and Industrial Research Organisation (CSIRO), and the patent holding US-based company Arcadia (McAllister *et al.*, 2012).

The AlaAT example above highlights that enzymes and proteins other than those primarily being involved in nitrogen uptake may be targeted to increase plant NUE. In addition, selection of traits linked to NUE, such as improved root proliferation in modern short-strawed cultivars, photosynthetic efficiency, N remobilization and drought-tolerant phenotypes may also be used to address NUE (Hawkesford, 2014).

Benefits of NUE wheat

Above, we estimated the total GHG emissions related to nitrogen fertilization of wheat in Europe to be approximately 34 million tonnes CO_2eq. The question is to what extent one could use NUE wheat technology to reduce GHG emissions. As a rough thought experiment we can elaborate on two cases.

The first case is based on farmers using less fertilizer and producing the same yields as today; the second case is based on using the same amount of fertilizer resulting in a higher yield. In the first case, early field trials on NUE wheat indicate that nitrogen fertilization can be reduced by up to 50 per cent with maintained yields. Assuming this could be scaled up and implemented in all EU wheat cultivation, the ensuing GHG emission reductions would – all else being equal – be around 17 million tonnes CO_2eq, equal to total emissions from all road traffic in Sweden in 2012.

The second case is based on field trials with NUE wheat, which indicates that using the same amount of fertilizer results in a higher yield of NUE wheat in comparison to its conventional counterpart. Assuming that grain yield could be increased by 20 per cent, e.g., from 6.5 (Swedish average) to 7.8 tonnes/ha given the same amount of fertilizer, annual carbon (C) input to soil through roots would probably increase by about 0.3 tonnes C/hectare (ha) according to Bolinder *et al.* (2007). If one-third of this extra C is retained in soil in a longer time perspective (Kätterer *et al.*, 2011) then about 0.1 tonnes C/ha and year would be sequestered. This would, if this was an effect on the total yield in all EU countries, amount to roughly some 2–3 million tonnes C equivalent to 9 million tonnes CO_2eq sequestered every year over several decades. Future cultivars of perennial cereals may probably lead to much higher C sequestration rates due to high root/shoot ratios of perennial plants in general (Bolinder *et al.*, 2007). It should be pointed out that increasing wheat yields and productivity in itself has value, given the need for the EU to maintain and also increase crop productivity, which is discussed more elaborately in Chapters 4 and 6 in this book.

There is great potential for improved NUE in wheat and other crops to reduce not only agricultural GHG emissions but also eutrophication of waterways. However, it is important to note that going from potential and prospects to implementation is a long and cumbersome process. In practice, there are large uncertainties pertaining partly to the science component but probably even more so when it comes to the broad-scale introduction of new crop varieties. It is yet uncertain to what degree field trials can be replicated on a large scale and in varying conditions when it comes to climate, soil and management systems. Regarding the latter, we discussed above that NUE wheat can be implemented by means of two different strategies: either to reduce nitrogen fertilization at maintained yields or to increase yields at maintained level of fertilization. Both these strategies will entail environmental benefits, but have somewhat different characteristics. In the end, the choice is made by the individual farmer, and this choice can obviously vary depending on site conditions, but also economic considerations. The relative prices of wheat, fertilizer and possibly also carbon credits (gained by reducing GHG emissions) will likely be a key determinant here.

It is evident that the technical conditions for a successful implementation of NUE wheat look very promising. However, in order to succeed within a reasonable timeframe, best available techniques, including genetic engineering, must be employed and sufficient resources in basic research and development need to be invested. The current emphasis by European legislators and funding agencies to unilaterally support farming systems that prohibit the use of new molecular breeding technologies blocks this development. Hence, a future introduction of a NUE wheat bred for European conditions is not so much a technical issue as a policy issue, since the regulatory burden put on the technology rather than the marketed products (Fagerström *et al.*, 2012) effectively hinders the European breeding sector to invest in NUE wheat varieties that are bred using modern molecular breeding technologies.

The virtual prairie and possibilities with perennial wheat

Description of perennial crops

In several places in the United States, including at the Land Institute in Kansas, researchers work on transforming a selection of major agricultural crops into perennial varieties. Maize, wheat, sorghum, sunflower and rice are examples of annual crops that most certainly can be turned into perennial agricultural plants. In the United States, preliminary field trials on perennial wheat have yielded 70 per cent of the harvest of conventional wheat, which is probably already a commercially profitable harvest level, given that the farmer will save a large part of the costs for tractor fuel, herbicides and other inputs (Glover *et al.*, 2007; Glover, pers. comm.).

No-till cropping systems based on perennial plants have the advantage over those based on annuals that long-term interactions between plants and microorganisms in the soil can be established. Measurements made at the Land Institute reveal that the native perennial grass species of the prairie capture more nitrogen and carbon from the air and soil and convert it into more protein and carbohydrates in harvested hay than today's farmers are able to capture in the harvested grain on the corresponding land (Glover, 2010).

The interesting question is of course where the grasses get their nutrients from. Weathering of soil and downfall from the air is not enough, even if one also accounts for all the nitrogen that may be captured from the air by nitrogen-fixing legumes. The answer to the puzzle is the nitrogen-fixing bacteria in the soil. They can handle their own needs by capturing atmospheric nitrogen. They may share a little nitrogen with the plants while they are alive, but this changes when they die: once they are disintegrated, the nitrogen is released into the soil and is absorbed by plant roots. In soils that are interwoven with deep roots the released nitrogen is rapidly absorbed, but in fields where annuals are grown – whether spring or autumn sown – the soil microorganisms break down organic matter and release nitrogen in the soil solution long before and long after there are any plant roots that can take care of the nitrogen (Culman *et al.*, 2010).

Benefits with perennial wheat

We have no experience yet of a transition from annual to perennial grain crops at large scale. But there is good reason to believe that the perennial ley, in most respects, can be used as a model for perennial grain crops. In both cases we are dealing with grasses, and in both cases the crop is harvested before autumn and overwinters as stubble.

We will therefore use data from field trials on perennial leys to estimate the environmental effects of a transition from annual to perennial grain crops. Perennial crops bind significantly more carbon than the annuals do. According to results from Canadian long-term field experiments perennial grass cover resulted in about 0.6 tonnes higher soil carbon content/ha and year compared to annual cropping systems (Van den Bygaart *et al.*, 2010). Similar effects were also reported for the US (Glover *et al.*, 2007). Forage-based crop rotations, which under Nordic conditions often include perennial leys that are kept for more than three years, have also been shown to result in increased soil carbon stocks compared with annual crops of 0.5 tonnes carbon/ha and year (Kätterer *et al.*, 2013).

As a thought experiment to demonstrate the theoretical potential of perennial crops we extrapolate these figures to perennial wheat production in the EU. The total acreage of wheat in the EU covers around 25 million ha. Using the figure of 0.5 tonnes carbon/ha, which corresponds to about 1.8 tonnes of carbon dioxide, and assuming that future perennial wheat will behave similarly to perennial forage crops, means that an additional 45 million tonnes of carbon dioxide per year would be bound by perennial wheat.

Using data from field trials on nitrogen leaching in Sweden (Rune Andersson and Lars Bergström, pers. comm.) enables us to estimate a rough figure on the potential for decreased nitrogen leaching as a result of conversion from annual to perennial wheat. The total annual leaching of N from cereal production is estimated to be 50,000 tonnes, of which some 25 per cent could be avoided by a conversion to perennial crops. Extrapolating this to the wheat acreage in the EU shows that a transition from annual to perennial wheat could theoretically reduce nitrogen leaching by some 300,000 tonnes. Even though the fields with perennial wheat would have to be ploughed regularly for soil loosening, and for getting rid of or reducing weeds and pests, it remains a valid notion that there is no other single measure to reduce nitrogen leaching from arable land that comes even close to such a large effect.

Finally, a transition to perennial grain crops would reduce energy consumption for tractors, estimated to consume 40 litres of diesel/ha. Applying this to the thought experiment of an EU-wide transition to perennial wheat would result in some 1 billion litres of diesel saved annually. In addition, a number of further positive effects are expected. These may include reductions in the release of phosphorus, ammonia and nitrous oxide, increased humus content of the soils and positive impacts on the fauna and flora of the agricultural landscape. Perennial crop systems are also often more drought resistant than annual crops, and thus perenniality is potentially an asset to help adapt crop production systems to anticipated enhanced climate variations. The cumulative environmental effects of these and other factors are expected to be highly positive, but we still lack data to quantify these effects in a reasonably reliable way.

Breeding of perennial crops – the role of modern biosciences

Research on perennial cereals, grain legumes and oilseeds, along with the cropping systems into which they will be assembled, can greatly benefit from modern bioscience-based breeding technologies, including genetic engineering that have been well developed for staple grains grown currently. But to succeed, those methods must be supplemented by knowledge and experience, new and old, that applies uniquely to perennial crops.

Genomic studies of the cereal model species *Brachypodium* may eventually lead to the molecular characterization of the traits regulating perenniality in cereals. This would enable perenniality to be engineered into wheat either through transgenics or through genome editing. Currently, efforts are being made to introduce perenniality into wheat by making hybrids between the annual bread-wheat used today and perennial wild wheat relatives. Traits that need to be selected for in such wide crosses are e.g. semi-dwarf plant height, seed shattering, seed size, self-fertility, grain yield and disease resistance (Larkin and Newell, 2013).

Issues and challenges with perennial crops

While there is little doubt that perennial crops present characteristics that are worthwhile exploring, there are also potential drawbacks that have to be investigated and accounted for. These drawbacks include an array of issues pertaining to plant protection, e.g. the difficulty of mastering perennial grass weeds that are likely to become a major problem in a perennial cereal crop. Another potential drawback is the possible difficulty of producing perennial varieties where the axes ripe simultaneously, and where the quality of the seeds are acceptable – not least important in wheat. A third question mark relates to the profitability for the breeding industry. Who wants to develop and market a product (i.e. perennial seeds) which has a much lower demand on the market than the competing product (i.e. annual seeds)? On the other hand, if it would be possible to simultaneously improve the productivity and the quality (taste, baking properties, health profiles, etc.) of perennial grains they may become attractive for the agro-processing sector and then also for the breeding industry. A fourth question mark is yield stability which often is a challenge in perennials as the subsequent years often result in reduced yields.

These and other factors suggest that perennial wheat might be primarily relevant for those regions in the world where climatic and other factors limit the yields to low or moderate levels, say in the order of a couple of tonnes/ha. There are vast wheat-growing regions that fall into that category, including in Australia and central Asia, but also in Africa. In addition perennial crop varieties seem to be a case where publicly financed research and development should be mobilized within the EU, both to speed up the availability of such crops for developing countries and for overcoming the drawbacks of these varieties with regard to assembling them in the high yield systems that typically prevail in the EU countries.

Concluding remarks

In this chapter we have discussed the imminent need to transform current agriculture into a resource-use efficient system with reduced environmental impact and increased production. Future agriculture needs to adapt to increased global temperatures to sustain production, but also holds the potential to mitigate climate change through reduction of greenhouse gas emissions. We have provided two examples where modern bioscience may provide tangible solutions to these challenges.

Given the current understanding of both NUE and perenniality, a combination of current and new breeding technologies has the potential to produce wheat varieties holding either of these traits. Ironically, the largest obstacle to meet this end seems to be legislative and connected to the current emphasis of European research and development within the agricultural sector on low-input/low-yield farming systems, which *in fact* to a large extent excludes the use of modern breeding technologies.

In many parts of Africa, a major cause for the low crop productivity is the limited use of fertilizers. For most African small-scale farming systems, the high cost of fertilizer in connection with poor access to markets is a major barrier for increased crop productivity.

With recurring droughts in many parts of Africa, soil erosion and soil instability is another huge problem. Perennial crop systems with strong interlocking root systems would make a large difference here and even if they did not grow at all while waiting for the rains, they would at least stabilize the soil and reduce soil erosion.

Hence, crop and cropping systems using inputs such as fertilizers and water in a highly efficient manner are therefore of high value to African farmers. In this context, breeding platforms incorporating NUE traits and perenniality in African crops would be a useful tool in increasing crop productivity in the region. For African countries it is therefore of strategic value to develop capacity, regulations and policies encouraging bioscience innovation and adaption of these types of traits into crops of key importance for farmers in the region (Fagerström *et al.*, 2016).

References

Basche, A.D. *et al.* 2014. Do cover crops increase or decrease nitrous oxide emissions? A meta-analysis. *Journal of Soil and Water Conservation* 69(6), pp.471–82.

Beatty, P.H. and Good, A.G. 2011. Plant science. Future prospects for cereals that fix nitrogen. *Science* 333(6041), pp.416–17.

Bolinder, M.A. *et al.* 2007. An approach for estimating net primary productivity and annual carbon inputs to soil for common agricultural crops in Canada. *Agriculture Ecosystems & Environment* 118(1–4), pp.29–42.

Bolinder, M.A. *et al.* 2010. Long-term soil organic carbon and nitrogen dynamics in forage-based crop rotations in Northern Sweden (63–64 degrees N). *Agriculture Ecosystems & Environment* 138(3–4), pp.335–42.

Brentrup, F. and Pallière, C. 2014. *Energy Efficiency and Greenhouse Gas Emissions in European Nitrogen Fertilizer and Use* [Online]. [Accessed 23 February 2016]. Available from: http://www.fertilizerseurope.com/fileadmin/user_upload/publications/agriculture_publications/Energy_Efficiency__V9.pdf

Culman, S.W. *et al.* 2010. Long-term impacts of high-input annual cropping and unfertilized perennial grass production on soil properties and belowground food webs in Kansas, USA. *Agriculture Ecosystems & Environment* 137(1–2), pp.13–24.

Fagerström, T. *et al.* 2012. Stop worrying; start growing. Risk research on GM crops is a dead parrot: it is time to start reaping the benefits of GM. *EMBO Reports* 13(6), pp.493–7.

Fagerström, T. *et al.* 2016. Biotechnology – the tool Africa cannot afford to ignore. *The African Technopolitan* 5, pp.56–65.

Foley, J.A. *et al.* 2011. Solutions for a cultivated planet. *Nature* 478(7369), pp.337–42.

Gardenas, A.I. *et al.* 2011. Knowledge gaps in soil carbon and nitrogen interactions – from molecular to global scale. *Soil Biology & Biochemistry* 43(4), pp.702–17.

Garnett, T. *et al.* 2009. Root based approaches to improving nitrogen use efficiency in plants. *Plant, Cell & Environment* 32(9), pp.1272–83.

Glover, J.D. 2010. Harvested perennial grasslands: ecological models for farming's perennial future. *Agriculture Ecosystems & Environment* 137(1–2), pp.1–2.

Glover, J.D. *et al.* 2007. Future farming: a return to roots? *Scientific American* 297(2), pp.82–9.

Good, A.G. *et al.* 2004. Can less yield more? Is reducing nutrient input into the environment compatible with maintaining crop production? *Trends in Plant Science* 9(12), pp.597–605.

Good, A.G. *et al.* 2007. Engineering nitrogen use efficiency with alanine aminotransferase. *Canadian Journal of Botany-Revue Canadienne De Botanique* 85(3), pp.252–62.

Hawkesford, M.J. 2014. Reducing the reliance on nitrogen fertilizer for wheat production. *Journal of Cereal Science* 59(3), pp.276–83.

Heffer, P. 2013. *Assessment of Fertilizer Use by Crop at the Global Level 2010–2010/11.* Paris: International Fertilizer Industry Association (IFA), pp.1–9.

Kätterer, T. *et al.* 2011. Roots contribute more to refractory soil organic matter than aboveground crop residues, as revealed by a long-term field experiment. *Agriculture, Ecosystems & Environment* 141, pp.184–92.

Kätterer, T. *et al.* 2012. Strategies for carbon sequestration in agricultural soils in northern Europe. *Acta Agriculturae Scandinavica* 62(Section A), pp.181–98.

Kätterer, T. *et al.* 2013. Influence of ley-arable systems on soil carbon stocks in Northern Europe and Eastern Canada. In: Helgadóttir, A. *et al.* (eds) *The Role of Grasslands in a Green Future – Threats and Perspectives in Less Favoured Areas. Proceedings of the 17th Symposium of the European Grassland Federation.* Akureyri: Grassland Science in Europe, pp.47–56.

Kurai, T. *et al.* 2011. Introduction of the ZmDof1 gene into rice enhances carbon and nitrogen assimilation under low-nitrogen conditions. *Plant Biotechnology Journal* 9(8), pp.826–37.

Larkin, J.P. and Newell, M.T. 2013. Perennial wheat breeding: current germplasm and a way forward for breeding and global cooperation. In: C. Batello (ed.). *Perennial Crops For Food Security*. Rome: FAO, pp.39–53.

Linquist, B. *et al.* 2012. An agronomic assessment of greenhouse gas emissions from major cereal crops. *Global Change Biology* 18(1), pp.194–209.

Masclaux-Daubresse, C. *et al.* 2010. Nitrogen uptake, assimilation and remobilization in plants: challenges for sustainable and productive agriculture. *Annals of Botany* 105(7), pp.1141–57.

McAllister, C.H. *et al.* 2012. Engineering nitrogen use efficient crop plants: the current status. *Plant Biotechnology Journal* 10(9), pp.1011–25.

Meisterling, K. *et al.* 2009. Decisions to reduce greenhouse gases from agriculture and product transport: LCA case study of organic and conventional wheat. *Journal of Cleaner Production* 17(2), pp.222–30.

Moore, F.C. and Lobell, D.B. 2014. Adaptation potential of European agriculture in response to climate change. *Nature Climate Change* 4(7), pp.610–14.

Poeplau, C. *et al.* 2015. Effect of perennial ryegrass cover crop on soil organic carbon stocks in southern Sweden. *Geoderma Regional* 4, pp.126–33.

Porter, J.R. *et al.* 2014. Food security and food production systems. In: Field, C.B. *et al.* (eds). *Climate Change 2014: Impacts, Adaptation, and Vulnerability. Part A: Global and Sectoral Aspects. Contribution of Working Group II to the Fifth Assessment Report of the Intergovernmental Panel on Climate Change*. Cambridge: Cambridge University Press, pp.485–533.

Röös, E. *et al.* 2011. Uncertainties in the carbon footprint of refined wheat products: a case study on Swedish pasta. *The International Journal of Life Cycle Assessment* 16, pp.338–50.

Smith, P. *et al.* 2014. Agriculture, Forestry and Other Land Use (AFOLU). In: Edenhofer, O. *et al.* (eds). *Climate Change 2014: Mitigation of Climate Change. Contribution of Working Group III to the Fifth Assessment Report of the Intergovernmental Panel on Climate* Change. Cambridge: Cambridge University Press, pp.812–922.

Su, J. *et al.* 2015. Expression of barley SUSIBA2 transcription factor yields high-starch low-methane rice. *Nature* 523(7562), pp.602–6.

Sundström, J. *et al.* 2014. Future threats to agricultural food production posed by environmental degradation, climate change, and animal and plant diseases – a risk analysis in three economic and climate settings. *Food Security* 6(2), pp.201–15.

Tidåker, P. *et al.* 2007. Environmental impact of wheat production using human urine and mineral fertilisers – a scenario study. *Journal of Cleaner Production* 15, pp.52–62.

Trnka, M. *et al.* 2014. Adverse weather conditions for European wheat production will become more frequent with climate change. *Nature Climate Change* 4(7), pp.637–43.

Tunå, P. *et al.* 2014. Techno-economic assessment of nonfossil ammonia production. *Environmental Progress & Sustainable Energy* 33(4), pp.1290–7.

Ussiri, D. and Lal, R. 2013. Conclusions: towards managing agricultural soils for mitigating nitrous oxide emissions. In: *Soil Emission of Nitrous Oxide and its Mitigation*. Dordrecht: Springer Netherlands, pp.347–67.

Van den Bygaart, A.J. *et al.* 2010. Soil organic carbon stocks on long-term agroecosystem experiments in Canada. *Canadian Journal of Soil Science* 90, pp.543–50.

Virto, I. *et al.* 2012. Carbon input differences as the main factor explaining the variability in soil organic C storage in no-tilled compared to inversion tilled agrosystems. *Biogeochemistry* 108(1–3), pp.17–26.

Yanagisawa, S. *et al.* 2004. Metabolic engineering with Dof1 transcription factor in plants: improved nitrogen assimilation and growth under low-nitrogen conditions. *Proceedings of the National Academy of Sciences USA* 101(20), pp.7833–8.

8 A European perspective

A renewable resource base for the European chemical industry – getting to a European bioeconomy

Sten Stymne

Introduction

On its website's homepage, the European Commission describes the bioeconomy as 'a more resource efficient society that relies strongly on renewable biological resources to satisfy consumers' needs, industry demand and tackle climate change' (EC, 2016). I will not in this chapter echo all the thousands of pages from the European Commission that describe all the initiatives that will be taken to achieve the Grand Goal of the EU Bioeconomy. I will instead rather critically review the EU's strategies to reach its goals. In particular, I will stress the opportunities that modern plant science and breeding could offer to increase the use of renewable biological feed stocks in the chemical industry, which for complex political reasons have been left out of these strategy plans.

We need new, innovative methods to increase overall agricultural production

The productivity increase in global agriculture has been impressive over the last 50 years with a more than 100 per cent yield increase per ha for the major crops, maize, wheat, rice and soybean (Long *et al.*, 2015), thereby more than keeping up with the pace of the global population growth. This productivity increase is largely due to a combination of the development of new crop varieties that respond with a greatly increased harvest index on application of fertilizer and the intense use of synthetic fertilizers and crop protection chemicals, methods that led to what we call the Green Revolution.

It has been projected that we need to further increase global agricultural production by 80 per cent by 2050 if we should meet the demand of a still growing global population as well as the shift to much more animal products in the diet of the rapidly developing former 'third world' countries (Long *et al.*, 2015). If a major expansion in using agricultural products for biofuel to replace fossil carbon sources will take place, there is no upper limit in the increase in productivity needed to satisfy this demand.

The rapid productivity increase as a consequence of the Green Revolution during the last 50 years is now ceasing with, for example, the rice and wheat yields plateauing (Grassini *et al.*, 2013). The potential of increasing yield with the methods developed during the Green Revolution have thus more or less reached their limits in the major crops. In addition to this, we are losing arable land due to water shortage, salinity and soil erosion. In addition to the productivity issue, agriculture is today a major greenhouse gas (GHG) emitter and a main global polluter of the aquatic systems (EPA, 2015; Moss, 2008). Thus, we desperately need a second Green Revolution where both productivity and environmental issues are dealt with, the latter much neglected during the first Green Revolution. Such sustainable increase in productivity can only be achieved by applying new innovative technologies.

Should primary biomass production for energy really be a part of the bioeconomy?

An increased use of renewable biobased products for energy can be achieved by increased production and/or better utilizing the biomaterial produced today. The latter is rather non-controversial and includes the use of waste products for combustion or biogas production instead of letting them ferment on landfill. It also includes using usually non-harvest biomass such as straw from the agricultural fields and roots, stumps, bark and twigs from the forests. However, it should be noted that some part of the organic carbon in these materials would, if not collected and utilized, contribute to organic matter in the soil, thereby capturing CO_2 and improving soil quality. Actually, there can be a severe conflict in mitigating climate change and utilizing biological material for energy, at least when calculated over several decades. The most drastic of such examples are the boreal forests. They have in Europe a re-generation time from 30 to over 100 years (compared to 5–10 years for tropical forests) and thus if the trees are utilized for energy purposes, net CO_2 savings will usually not be achieved until beyond 2050. It can be questioned if biological material with such a long period of re-capturing the released CO_2 should be used for energy purposes in view of the immediate urgency to mitigate net CO_2 emissions.

Today food products are used for fuel production, such as starch from cereals and oils from oil crops, creating a direct conflict between food and non-food uses and often with small net savings in CO_2 emissions compared to using fossil oil. An exception to this appears to be ethanol from sugar cane, which has greater net GHG saving than other crops. Great expectations have therefore been coupled to the development of the so-called 'next generation' biofuels where the sugar from the cellulose in lignocellulose from energy crops such as switch grass, miscanthus and poplar is released and fermented to ethanol. In order to improve the economy of such a facility the concept of 'biorefinery' has been developed where residual products are converted to high-value products after the cellulosic sugars has been utilized. However, since there is no high-value product in any quantity in lignocellulose biomass, the residual products have to be extensively processed, either by chemical means or microbial processing, both costly methods. There is a saying among natural product chemists: 'You can make everything out of lignin, except money'. There are many facts that cause severe concerns regarding the viability of lignocellulosic ethanol production (Ohlrogge *et al.*, 2009): 1) a loss of about 50 per cent energy in the distillation of the ethanol from the water after fermentation; 2) the very limited progress in energy-efficient conversion of ligno-cellulose to sugars that can be used *for* fermentation to ethanol despite huge investments in this research; 3) gasoline/ethanol-fuelled cars are in Europe and elsewhere in sharp decline in favour of lean diesel cars. Unfortunately, the development of more energy-efficient motors has not resulted in corresponding reduction in carbon dioxide emissions since many customers have shifted to cars with more powerful engines. However electricity-fuelled cars are on the brink of large-scale global market penetration and the first hydrogen-fuelled cars are now on the market. It should however be noted that so far no-one has suggested any realistic alternative to the energy-dense liquid fuels in aeroplanes and ships other than biobased fuels such as hydro-treated vegetable oils (HVO) and dimethyl-esters.

The fossil oil prices more than halved during the year 2014 due to the rapidly expanding fracking technology for producing natural gas and oil. Since the threshold for a profitable fracking is around 60 US$/barrel and many of the present big oil-exporting countries with easily accessed oil reserves can make profit at a much lower price, it can be anticipated that the oil price will be more or less balanced at that price for a long time. Thus, the prediction of sky-rocketing fossil oil prices that have motivated many of the efforts in producing biofuels has been totally shattered. It should be noted that plants are not very good at capturing sunlight energy into chemically bound energy. Only a maximum 2 per cent is captured in crops (Grassini *et al.*, 2013) and thus can be utilized by us as energy and heat, where most will be lost to heat, regardless if the biomass is directly burned for electricity or converted to liquid biofuel. In short, for energy, there are other carbon dioxide-neutral alternatives with much better economy and efficiency such as solar, hydro, wind power and geothermal heat. In addition to these alternatives to fossil energy sources, developing more energy-efficient processes is of paramount importance. The development of LED lights is an example of how scientific progress and innovation can lead to leapfrogging in energy efficiency in a relatively short time. However, these alternatives do not preclude that bioenergy will play a significant role in the palette of future carbon dioxide-neutral and cost-effective energy sources in certain regions and cases.

How biobased feedstocks for the chemical and material industry can be more cost effective than fossil oil

Before the First World War biological feedstocks dominated in the chemical industry, but increasing prices and shortages of agricultural products, cheap fossil oil and advancement of organic chemistry led to a shift to be nearly totally dependent on fossil oil. Today about 8 per cent of the fossil oil consumed serves as feedstock for the chemical industry, corresponding to about 320 million tonnes yearly. Much of the fossil-based chemical industry is built on converting the crude oil to a limited number of small reactive building blocks (reactive olefins) that are then converted by advanced organic chemistry into the myriad of fossil oil products we are surrounded with today. This consumes a lot of energy and requires huge investment costs in the processing.

Although the biobased products have lost most of their importance as feedstocks in the chemical industry, they still maintain major roles in delivering materials and household products that in price and functionality outcompete fossil oil-based products. Such examples are wood for furniture, buildings and paper, cotton, wool and leather for clothing and vegetable oils for soap, detergents and personal care products. The common feature of these products is that they utilize the complex molecules already formed in the organisms with very little downstream processing and thus, despite their higher price compared to crude fossil oil, the much lower downstream processing makes them economically competitive. The value of the products made from the 8 per cent of fossil oil used by the chemical industry is the same as the value of all fuel made from the remaining 92 per cent. Thus, if the biomolecules already in a crop are optimized for the chemical and material industry, much of this ten-fold added value can already be captured in the field.

By genetic engineering, novel pathways can be introduced into plants to create novel and societally desired molecules, and carbon metabolism can be manipulated to achieve very high levels of such molecules in the cells. Thus, in this concept we do not build a chemical factory to produce wanted molecules but the plant cells themselves are the factories, a self-replicating factory fuelled by the sun and using carbon dioxide and water as input molecules; once constructed it will never wear out. Huge industrial and public investments have been made in advanced engineering of microorganisms that produce high-value molecules, mainly for the pharmaceutical sector, that would be very expensive to do with organic chemistry from fossil oil. There are also a few examples of bacteria that produce some lower value products such as lactic acid (Li and Cui, 2010) and 1,2-propane-diol (Clomburg and Gonzalez, 2011) for plastic manufacturing and that are used in commercial production and thus are directly competing with fossil oil-based plastics. However, it should be noted that production by microorganisms will always have a relative high cost since they have to be maintained in a controlled environment and supplemented with nutrients such as sugars, which in their turn are agricultural products.

If the desired molecules instead could be produced in high amounts directly in agricultural crops, the cost for their production would be at least a magnitude lower than those produced by microbes. If totally novel molecules are going to be produced in our crops it requires the use of genetic engineering. However, little investment has so far been made in such research and development, globally mainly due to high costs for de-regulation for commercial production of such genetically modified (GM) crops, but in the EU also due to the political resistance to use any GM plants in its own agriculture. This has created a total stalemate for using GM technology for any plant trait in the EU. It should also be pointed out that the investments made by the chemical companies in the infrastructure to process fossil oil are huge and long term and therefore the use of *in-planta* 'pre-made' products that do not need this infrastructure will not necessarily be endorsed by this industry, even if the regulatory hurdles did not exist.

Tailor-made plant oils for the chemical industry

Despite the very modest resources, almost only from public sources, that have been allocated to genetically engineer crops to produce added value products for the chemical and material industry, there have been very promising advances in this research. I will give below some examples of what has been done from my own field of research, i.e. plant oils, and what can be expected in the future if the investments in this area could be substantially increased.

Vegetable oil is the agricultural product that chemically most resembles fossil oil. Plant oils are composed of long hydrocarbon chains similar to the bulk molecules of fossil oil. Everything you do with fossil oil, you can also do with vegetable oil and it is only a price issue. About 10 per cent of the vegetable oils (15 million tonnes) are today used in the chemical industry for making several hundred different products such as soap, detergents, paints, ink, etc. Because of the low downstream processing to the final product, they are economically more favourable to use than crude fossil oil in these applications, despite their higher price. Plant oils have, in contrast to fossil oil, hydrocarbons chains (fatty acids) of defined carbon number and unsaturation (or other modifications) at specific carbons in the chain. Taking advantage of the already totally homogeneous chemical structure of a particular fatty acid, limited chemical steps can convert these fatty acids to a variety of useful products with defined chemical structures. Metathesis chemistry is in this respect particularly suited for the conversion of fatty acids into a range of high-value chemicals (Dupé *et al.*, 2012). Seed oils from our annual oil crops contain only five dominant types of fatty acids, which restricts the number of products that can be economically produced. However, there are hundreds of different fatty acids with great interest for the chemical industry produced in high amounts in the seed oil in many wild plants (Badami and Patil, 1980). These plants have too poor an agronomic performance to be economically cultivated. Genetic engineering can transfer the biosynthetic machinery for the production of these valuable fatty acids into high-yielding oil crops (Table 8.1).

Oils from our annual oil crops are composed of fatty acids of 16 carbons and longer. Shorter chain fatty acids have great use in the chemical industry. By transferring only one gene from a wild plant to rape seed, rape seed oil with over 60 per cent of a 12 carbon fatty acid (lauric acid) was produced (Wiberg *et al.*, 2000). However, present commercial sources of lauric acid, i.e. coconut and palm kernel fat, are relatively cheap and abundant, and the lauric acid producing rape could not compete due to higher cultivation costs. Of more interest is producing 8 and 10 carbon fatty acids in oil crops, which have wide use in industry and are today made from fossil oil. About 7 per cent and 29 per cent of 8 carbon and 10 carbon fatty acids, respectively, have been reported to be achieved in oils from GM rape seeds (Wiberg *et al.*, 2000). In order to achieve much higher amounts, a whole suite of genes has to be transferred from the wild plants, which can accumulate over 90 per cent of these fatty acids in their seed oil (Table 8.1). The rapid advancement in molecular biology knowledge and methods that have taken place during the last decade makes it realistic to soon achieve these levels also in productive oil crops.

Table 8.1 Industrial valuable unusual fatty acids occurring in high amounts in seed oils of wild plant species. All these fatty acids have been produced in various amounts in transgenic plants (Dyer *et al.*, 2008)

Plant species	Dominant fatty acid	% of seed oil fatty acids	Main industrial uses
Cuphea painteri	Caprylic acid (8:0)	73%	Aromatic esters, polymers, bactererdicides
Cuphea koehneana	Capric acid (10:0)	95%	Aromatic esters, lubricants, rubber, dyes, polymers, pharmaceuticals
Castor bean (*Ricinus communis*)	Ricinoleic acid (12-OH-18:1Δ12Z)	90%	Lubricants, coatings, polymers, rubber, inks, cosmetics
Tung tree (*Aleurites fordii*)	α-Eleosteric acid (18:3Δ,9Z,11E,13E)	88%	Paints, varnishes
Vernonia galamensis	Vernolic acid (12-epoxy-18:1Δ,9Z)	80%	Paints, coatings, polymers

Plant oils are composed of triacylglycerol molecules, i.e. three fatty acids attached to a glycerol molecule. These oils have excellent lubrication properties but have a major drawback in that the molecules decompose under high temperature and pressure, conditions that prevail in most lubrication applications. The spermaceti whale was hunted for its spermaceti oil, which was widely used in lubrication formulas. The spermaceti oil is composed mainly of wax ester molecules, which have as good lubrication properties as triacylglycerols but can also withstand very high temperatures and pressures and can be used, for example, in lubricants for combustion engines. There is only one plant known to produce wax ester oil in its seed, the desert plant jojoba (*Simmondia chinensis*). It is a low-yielding plant that is commercially cultivated on a limited scale to produce jojoba oil, a very expensive oil only used in high-value cosmetic products. By transferring genes from jojoba to the model plant mouse ear cress (*Arabidopsis thaliana*), this plant produced wax ester in its oil (Lardizabal *et al.*, 2000). The EC-sponsored project ICON followed up this research by transferring jojoba genes into the industrial oil crops *Crambe abyssinica*, *Brassica carniata* and *Camelina sativa* (EC FP7 project ICON, 2008). Crambe plants with 22 per cent of wax esters in their seed oil have now been grown in the field in Sweden during two seasons and have an oil yield similar to non-GM Crambe (Zhu *et al.*, 2016). Work to further enhance the levels of wax esters in the oil is continuing with support from the Swedish Foundation for Strategic Research.

One of the most successful reports of developing industrial oil by genetic engineering is the production of 86 per cent acetyl-triacylglycerol in *Camelina sativa* seed oil (Liu *et al.*, 2015). These GM plants were grown in the field without significant penalty in oil yield compared to non-GM Camelina. This oil, which is composed of molecules with two long chain fatty acids and one two-carbon acid (acetic acid) attached to a glycerol, has drastic reduced melting points and viscosity compared with other plant oils. Although the specific application of this oil awaits further application tests, it demonstrates how total novel oil qualities in high amounts can be introduced by modern plant-breeding technologies.

In addition to the above oil qualities, work is progressing on producing other types of industrially interesting fatty acids in GM seed oils, such as epoxy- and hydroxy-fatty acids, conjugated fatty acids and cyclopropane fatty acids, with incremental increase of success reported each year (Napier *et al.*, 2014).

How biotechnology can increase global plant oil production

It is a great challenge to substantially increase plant oil production for industrial uses in addition to the increase in global plant oil production needed for food uses. Plant oil is the agricultural product that has shown the highest increase in global production during the last decades. The production has nearly tripled during only the two last decades (Figure 8.1). If we can keep up the same pace of increase over the next two decades, we will be able to both satisfy the demand for the food and feed sector as well as replace 40 per cent of the feed stock in the chemical industry with plant oils (Figure 8.1). However, the major oil crops that we have today have little prospect for any substantial increase in production except for oil palm, the expansion of which has to be at the expense of the tropical rainforests. Also, here plant biotechnology can offer radical solutions.

Science has made great progress just during the last few years in understanding the regulation of global plant cell metabolism. Of particular interest are the networks of activation genes, so-called transcription factors, that orchestrate the activity of the genes encoding the enzymes involved in carbon allocation. By manipulating these by genetic engineering, the sugars from photosynthesis used in sink tissues can be diverted into oil instead of starch in, for example, our

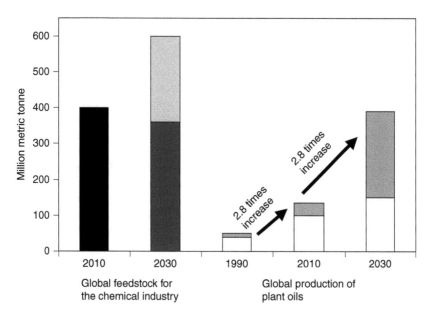

Figure 8.1 Actual and forecasted global feedstock needs for the chemical industry and plant oil production required for replacement of 40 per cent of feedstock for the chemical industry by 2030 (Adopted from Carlsson *et al.*, 2011)

Note: Values at 2030 have been forecasted assuming yearly increases in the amount of feedstock needed by the chemical industry and the amount of oil needed for food of about 2 and 1.5 per cent, respectively. Black bar areas indicate fossil oil, grey areas indicate plant oils for chemical industry and white bar areas indicate plant oils for food and feed. It is assumed that no plant oils will be used for biofuels.

cereals. If maize were to be engineered to produce 30 per cent of oil in its kernels, this alone would triple the global plant oil production. An even more spectacular scenario is to accumulate oil directly in the leaves and thereby circumvent any need for the crop to build a sink tissue. Tobacco leaves have been engineered to produce up to 15 per cent oil as a per cent of dry weight (Vanhercke *et al.*, 2014), and even up to 30 per cent has now been reported in a conference by the same research group (Vanhercke, 2014). If translated into field production of tobacco, this would correspond to 6 tonnes of oil per ha, three times higher than the top yield of winter rape and similar to the oil palm, the most productive oil crop we have today. However, the latter research is an example of *what is possible to achieve in greenhouse*, but it is not known how such a radical re-programming of a plant metabolism would affect the agronomic performance and if such types of plants will ever be used in agriculture. Thus, although the potential for changing quality and quantity of plant oils using biotechnology is immense as shown under controlled cultivation conditions, the technology has in most cases to prove its viability under field conditions.

A lost opportunity for the European chemical industry

Regardless of political decisions governing the fate of European agriculture, science and technology in agriculture will progress globally and will eventually have major impact on competitiveness, sustainability and power structures of the world's agriculture. The political decisions that seem reasonable in Europe today might be regarded as bizarre just a decade later. If agriculture in the EU is going to contribute to satisfying the global increased demand for food, feed and non-food products, it also has to adopt the powerful modern plant-breeding technologies, including genetic engineering and the recently developed genome editing technology (Jacobs *et al.*, 2015). Although these technologies will be pivotal for all agriculture production and thus food security, I have in this chapter focused on their potential role in re-shaping the chemical industry from a fossil-dependent to a more biobased industry.

The chemical industry is one of Europe's strongest industrial sectors, a pillar of the European economy (more than 29,000 companies in Europe) and a world-wide leader; 41.6 per cent of global trade is generated by the EU chemical industry. Although the use of fossil oil in the global chemical industry is approximately 320 million tonnes per year, it is estimated that less than 10 per cent of these chemical feedstocks are derived from biological sources (CEFIC, 2014). Therefore, innovation and expansion in the usage of raw material from renewable resources by the chemical industry will provide Europe with a sustainable alternative to the fossil economy. Compared to the economically rather unrealistic projects to produce low-value biofuels, like lignocellulosic ethanol, algal oil and hydrogen-producing microorganisms, where many millions of euros and dollars have already been spent in research, the investment in developing crops with added value bioproducts has been marginal.

Therefore the time is now right for the industry to reap great economic benefits by heavily investing in this commercially virgin but scientifically already advanced area. Unfortunately, due to the political forces now governing the development of EU agriculture, this is not likely to happen here. Much of the pioneering plant biotechnology research was done in Europe. After 30 years of development of biotech crops, which today cover 12 per cent of the global arable land, Europe has totally denied itself a technology that it once developed. It is probably the most tragic example of how the exploitation of a new technology has been successfully undermined by lies about the consequences of the technology and further hindered by pure political and populistic reasons.

References

Badami, R.C. and Patil, K.B. 1980. Structure and occurrence of unusual fatty acids in minor seed oils. *Progress in Lipid Research* 19, pp.119–53.

Carlsson, A.S. *et al.* 2011. Replacing fossil oil with fresh oil – with what and for what? *European Journal of Lipid Science and Technology* 13, pp.812–31.

CEFIC (European Chemical Industry Council). 2014. The European chemical industry facts and figures. [Online]. [Accessed 16 February 2016]. Available from: http://www.cefic.org/Facts-and-Figures/

Clomburg, J.M. and Gonzalez, R. 2011. Metabolic engineering of *Escherichia coli* for the production of 1,2-propanediol from glycerol. *Biotechnology and Bioengineering* 108, pp.867–79.

Dupé, A. *et al.* 2012. Methyl ricinoleate as platform chemical for simultaneous production of fine chemicals and polymer precursors. *ChemSusChem* 5, pp.2249–54.

Dyer, J.M. *et al.* 2008. High-value oils from plants. *Plant Journal* 54, pp.640–55.

EC (European Commission). 2016. What is the bioeconomy? [Online]. [Accessed 21 February 2016]. Available from: http://ec.europa.eu/research/bioeconomy/

EC FP7 project ICON. 2008. [Online]. [Accessed 21 February 2016]. Available from: http://icon.slu.se/ICON/

EPA (US Environment Protection Agency). 2015. Global greenhouse gas emissions data. [Online]. [Accessed 21 February 2016]. Available from: http://www.epa.gov/climatechange/ghgemissions/global.html

Grassini, P. *et al.* 2013. Distinguishing between yield advances and yield plateaus in historical crop production trends. *Nature Communication* 4, 2918. [Online]. [Accessed 21 February 2016]. Available from: http://www.nature.com/ncomms/2013/131217/ncomms3918/full/ncomms3918.html

Jacobs, T.B. *et al.* 2015. Targeted genome modifications in soybean with CRISPR/Cas9. *BMC Biotechnology.* [Online]. 15(1), p.16. [Accessed 21 February 2016]. Available from: http://www.biomedcentral.com/content/pdf/s12896-015-0131-2.pdf

Lardizabal, K.D. *et al.* 2000. Purification of a jojoba embryo wax synthase, cloning of its cDNA, and production of high levels of wax in seeds of transgenic Arabidopsis. *Plant Physiology* 122, pp.645–55.

Li, Y.B. and Cui, F. 2010. *Microbial lactic acid production from renewable resources.* In: Singh, O. and Harvey, S. (eds). *Sustainable Biotechnology: Sources of Renewable Energy.* Dordrecht: Springer, pp.211–28

Liu, J. *et al.* 2015. Metabolic engineering of oilseed crops to produce high levels of novel acetyl glyceride oils with reduced viscosity, freezing point and calorific value. *Plant Biotechnology Journal* 13(6), pp.858–65.

Long, S.P. *et al.* 2015. Meeting the global food demand of the future by engineering crop photosynthesis and yield potential. *Cell* 161(1), pp.56–66.

Moss, B. 2008. Water pollution by agriculture. *Philosophic Transactions of the Royal Society Biological Sciences* 363, pp.659–66.

Napier, J.A. *et al.* 2014. Understanding and manipulating plant lipid composition: metabolic engineering leads the way. *Current Opinion in Plant Biology* 19, pp.68–75.

Ohlrogge, J. *et al.* 2009. Driving on biomass. *Science* 324(5930), pp.1019–20.

Vanhercke, T. 2014. Maximizing TAG accumulation in plant leaves by combinatorial metabolic engineering (W068). ISPL Conference, 6–11 July, Guelph, Canada.

Vanhercke, T. *et al.* 2014. Metabolic engineering of biomass for high energy density: oilseed-like triacylglycerol yields from plant leaves. *Plant Biotechnology Journal* 12, pp.231–9.

Wiberg, E. *et al.* 2000. The distribution of caprylate, caprate and laurate in lipids from developing and mature seeds of transgenic *Brassica napus L. Planta* 212, pp.33–40.

Zhu, L.-H. *et al.* 2016. Dedicated industrial oilseed crops as metabolic engineering platforms for sustainable industrial feedstock production. *Scientific Reports* 26(6) 22181. doi: 10.1038/srep22181.

9 An African perspective

Using the new biosciences to support the African development agenda

E. Jane Morris, Corinda Erasmus and
Martha M. O'Kennedy

Introduction

In June 2014 at the African Union Summit, the Science, Technology and Innovation Strategy for Africa 2024 (STISA-2024) was adopted as an ambitious continental framework. The mission of STISA-2024 is to 'accelerate Africa's transition to an innovation-led, knowledge based economy', with bioscience, agriculture and food security highlighted as priority areas (African Union, 2014).

The Comprehensive Africa Agriculture Development Programme (CAADP) of the African Union was established in 2003, and consists of four pillars, of which Pillar 4 is agricultural research. Despite the CAADP and other initiatives, there has been insufficient innovation in the agricultural sector as evidenced by the poor performance of the sector over many years. In spite of efforts to increase the budget allocation to research and development (R&D), spending on agricultural R&D in most African countries remains low in global terms, and moreover in many cases does not translate into implemented innovation. Bioscience innovation can apply to many fields of high relevance to Africa, ranging from food to biofuels and health. In this chapter a number of exciting bioscience applications that support the African development agenda are presented, highlighting opportunities and progress towards implementing bioscience innovations in Africa, but also illustrating some of the hurdles that need to be overcome.

Bioscience innovation for production of bioresources

Improving African crops through genetics and genomics-assisted breeding

Marker assisted selection (MAS), involving the identification of DNA markers and their association with a particular trait, has been described in Chapter 3. MAS offers the opportunity to provide increased precision to plant breeders and to accelerate the selection of desirable genotypes. To date MAS has had limited impact on plant breeding programmes, particularly in Africa. However, some programmes, such as the Generation Challenge Program of the CGIAR, have had a degree of success in changing this situation for crops including pigeonpea, groundnuts, cowpeas, cassava, maize and chickpeas. Breeding populations and markers have been developed, and a web-based Integrated Breeding Platform (The Integrated Breeding Platform, 2014) provides information on genetic resources, genomics and genetic databases. Deployment and sustainable adoption of this integrated breeding platform remain as major challenges.

MAS is being used in efforts to develop provitamin-enriched maize under the CGIAR's HarvestPlus Program (Prasanna *et al.*, 2014). Broadening the scope to non-food crops, Eucalyptus trees are grown in several countries in East and Southern Africa and have potential as a future biofuel crop. The recent sequencing of the genome of *Eucalyptus grandis* by a team led by a South African scientist (Myburg *et al.*, 2014) will aid in future efforts to accelerate Eucalyptus breeding through genome-wide evaluation.

Some new varieties developed through MAS are starting to reach the farmer. Recently Mohamed *et al.* (2014) described the development and mapping of markers for sorghum resistance to the parasitic weed Striga (*Striga hermonthica* (Del.) Benth.) and the subsequent release of new high-performing sorghum varieties in sub-Saharan Africa (SSA). MAS also assisted in the development of bacterial blight resistance in common beans, with the release of one cultivar with improved resistance (Fourie *et al.*, 2011).

African crops for biofuels: the case for bird-proof (high tannin) sorghum

Biofuel production is discussed in detail in Chapter 11; this short section highlights a few recent developments in the production of an African indigenous cereal crop suitable for cost-effective local production of biofuel.

One of the best candidates for the production of biofuel starch feedstock is high tannin sorghum, valued for its so-called 'bird-proof' qualities. In the semi-arid regions of Southern Africa, the high tannin varieties have been cultivated by the local population for many years mainly as a source of malt for indigenous sorghum beer brewing. Structured cultivar breeding has more recently been undertaken by public sector researchers using conventional breeding and marker assisted selection to improve a range of qualities including yield, stress tolerance and fermentability of the sorghum.

High tannin sorghums are quite hardy and can survive many environmental stress factors, giving a crop yield where other crops will fail. The resistance to bird damage is of particular concern with wild seed-eating red-billed Queleas (*Quelea Quelea*) being one of the worst culprits. The birds descend in large flocks and can decimate an entire crop within minutes. Up to 20 per cent of the total crop of small grains (wheat, rice, millet and sorghum) is destroyed by these birds every year. To date, no significant biological control programmes have been developed and implemented. It is currently one of the most devastating factors threatening food security throughout the African continent (Oduntan *et al.*, 2015).

Therefore, bird-proof varieties of sorghum are of interest as bioethanol crops with projects being undertaken especially in South Africa, sponsored by government as well as private industry (The Industrial Development Corporation, 2016; The Protein Research Foundation, 2016; The Southern African Grain Laboratory, 2016).

Research focusing on a biological intervention to develop a sustainable way to address the Quelea bird problem will have an enormous positive impact on food security, and can revolutionize the current smallholder farmer economies in the majority of African countries affected, but sadly this problem has never been addressed on a large enough scale with the required resources and sufficient international collaborative focus and global funding. It is an area where Africa and Europe can collaborate to find permanent solutions and where biotechnology can play a significant role.

High tannin sorghums are more challenging to process and ferment into ethanol than their low tannin cousins. The high tannins inhibit the production of Free Amino Nitrogen (FAN) during the malting and mashing stages. The fermentation by yeast cells needs a high FAN content in order to develop vigorously and if the FAN levels are too low, ethanol production is significantly reduced. The use of various exogenous proteases from industrial enzyme suppliers has demonstrated the ability to reduce or even eliminate the problem of low FAN levels (Dlamini *et al.*, 2015). Biotechnology interventions including gene mapping of sorghum cultivars and selected yeast strains for the improvement of fermentation efficiency and cost reduction can enable the use of the crop to move from beer fermentation, where ethanol levels are comparatively low to fermentation for bioethanol, where maximum ethanol production is the goal. An ideal cultivar would be one that is bird-proof, very hardy (drought and heat resistant), high yielding in the field, and easy to ferment with the optimum yeast strain and protease enzyme combination. Research in this area is still limited and needs to expand.

Seaweed aquaculture

More than 95 per cent of the world's seaweed production is from aquaculture, however Africa contributes less than 1 per cent of the production. There is a rapidly growing market, increasing from 3.8 million tonnes in 1990 to 19 million tonnes in 2010. This is driven by a number of factors, including its use in integrated fish farming systems as well as the production of seaweed products such as carrageenan and agar, but also increasing potential for the production of agrochemicals, animal feed supplements, nutraceuticals, biofuels, plastics and surfactants.

Amosu *et al.* (2013) provided a comprehensive review of the potential for seaweed aquaculture in South Africa and in other coastal African nations. The main countries with an aquaculture industry are Tanzania (Zanzibar), Madagascar, South Africa, Mozambique and Namibia. Integration of aquaculture with seaweed production not only provides the marine animals (molluscs such as abalone in particular) with feed, but also reduces nutrient release to the environment by using the seaweed as a biofilter, significantly reducing greenhouse gas emissions. Although South Africa has a very successful abalone farming sector, feed is still often imported.

In Tanzania the main seaweed farming industry is focused on production of red seaweed for extraction of carrageenan, which is used in a variety of food and cosmetic products. Dried seaweed is largely exported to Europe and the USA rather than being further processed within Tanzania. The seaweed aquaculture industry has been negatively affected by a complex bacterial disease known as 'ice-ice' that affects the most valuable of the two main cultivated species, *Kappaphycus alvarezii*, which leads the seaweed to disintegrate and die causing seaweed farmers to leave the sector (Msuya, 2013). Research in the Philippines has focused on tissue culture and selection of disease-resistant cultivars, and application of biostimulants to enhance disease resistance, however more research is needed (Hurtado *et al.*, 2015).

Bioscience innovation is needed not only to optimize production and solve disease problems but also to develop new uses for seaweed derivatives. Biogas and/or biodiesel production from seaweed have formed the subject of considerable research over many years, and though it has not yet reached the stage of commercial production, there is a potential opportunity for production of renewable energy (Hughes *et al.*, 2012). This could be an area of opportunity for collaboration between Europe and Africa. The involvement of the private sector and investment in the industry will be crucial if Africa is to fully develop this opportunity.

Bioscience innovation in agro-processing and agro-waste conversion

Bananas and banana waste

Banana is an important staple food and a cash crop in many African countries; approximately a third of the annual world production of 104 million tonnes is produced in Africa and bananas and plantains supply more than 25 per cent of the carbohydrate requirements for over 70 million people. Uganda is the largest producer with a total production of around 9.8 million tonnes of bananas and plantains, followed by Tanzania at around 3.3 million tonnes (FAOSTAT, 2015).

In Uganda in the past few years, a number of private sector and development projects tried to explore ways of processing bananas into dried slices for export, but the initiative has been hampered by the fact that the quantity and quality of the exported produce is insufficient for the European market (van Asten *et al.*, 2010). A study in Tanzania showed that only a small amount of banana processing is undertaken in that country, the main products being sweet banana chips (the only export product), banana juice ('mulamba'), banana beer ('rubisi'), banana wine, roasted bananas, banana crafts, pastries ('balagara'), and baked banana products (Mgenzi *et al.*, 2010). These authors identified a number of gaps in the innovation chain, with little coordination provided by research institutes, universities and NGOs, and a lack of linkage between farmers, processors and the market place.

Since every bunch of bananas peeled generates around a third as much in waste, efforts to increase banana processing present a significant waste disposal challenge (Tumutegyereize *et al.*, 2011). Experimental work has been done to evaluate the potential of banana waste for biogas production in anaerobic bioreactors as well as for the production of animal feed and fibre for paper making. A project under the auspices of the East African Bio-Innovate Programme has demonstrated considerable success in generating biogas from banana winery effluent (Olomi, 2013; see also Chapter 15).

Considerable efforts are being made to address problems of declining yields of bananas in east Africa, including improving the quality of banana planting material through tissue culture and development of disease-resistant cultivars including the use of genetic modification (GM) technology. It is important that attention should be paid to the whole banana value chain, from production through to processing of both the bananas themselves and banana waste. A concerted effort to integrate the efforts of all the role players (producers, processors, market actors, scientists and government) could offer a major opportunity for economic growth and sustainable development.

Enzyme technology for agro-processing

The process of barley malt replacement in brewing has accelerated since the beginning of the twentieth century (Taylor *et al.*, 2013). Today, there are several totally non-barley lager beers being brewed across the world of which important ones are in Africa, for example Nile Breweries in Uganda (Eagle beer brand from sorghum) and lager beer from cassava in Ghana (also under the Eagle beer brand). Drivers of barley malt replacement such as grain cultivation, government policies promoting import replacement and support for local farmers have led to a new interest in using sorghum malt to replace barley malt. In Nigeria, a temporary ban on barley and barley malt imports from the mid 1980s to 1999 resulted in the general use of sorghum and maize in lager beer brewing. Lower taxation to favour locally grown cereals has helped the development of sorghum lager brewing in East African countries such as Uganda. Another driver is the enormous growth of grain bioethanol production based predominantly on maize, which is resulting in major developments in commercial enzyme technology. Although brewing beer with cereals other than barley malt is straightforward, economic process efficiency and producing a consumer-acceptable product presents an ongoing research challenge. These challenges including different gelatinization temperatures, changes in mashing enzyme combinations, challenges with crosslinked prolamine proteins in sorghum and persisting sorghum endosperm cell wall components such as arabinoxylans after malting are discussed in depth by Taylor *et al.* (2013). The availability of new unique enzymes has revolutionized the use of local crops for use in beer brewing and, as a spin-off, also created sustainable livelihoods for small-scale farmers who supply these crops as part of collective groups on contract to companies such as SABMiller (SABMiller plc, 2014). This model, where resource-poor farmers around a large processing facility are capacitated to supply raw materials on fixed contracts is becoming an increasingly popular system for sustainable development in Africa, because of its high success rate. However, the technological challenges specifically relating to dealing with raw materials of widely varying quality remain high, although a company such as Novozymes producing tailor-made enzymes has revolutionized agro-processing in this field (van Aswegen, 2014).

Other novel technologies using new enzymes to improve existing systems in Africa include enzyme cleaning of coffee flesh to replace the traditional wasteful fermentation process to remove the coffee fruit flesh from the nuts before roasting (projects in Ethiopia and Kenya, Duza and Mastan, 2013) and novel waste benefi- ciation such as producing glucose syrups from waste bread collected from baker- ies and restaurants in South Africa (van Aswegen, 2014).

Fermentation technology improving storage and nutrition of food products

The vast complexity and opportunities in the field of fermentation are too many to discuss in depth but one area worthy of mentioning is the use of probiotic organisms in foods. Due to a lack of refrigeration facilities in less developed environments in a hot climate, many African traditional foods rely heavily on lactic acid fermentation as a means of food preservation and shelf-life extension. Therefore, products such as drinking yoghurt-type foods (for example a product called mageu made from maize) made from cereal ingredients are commonplace. In South Africa, such products have been commercialized on a large scale. The low pH and high acidity of mageu contribute to its bacteriostatic and bactericidal properties. The typical starter cultures for mageu are strains of *Lactobacillus delbrueckii*, a non-probiotic lactic acid bacterium. The need to develop a probi- otic mageu is part of a drive to promote the concept of food as a health-promoting substance, beyond basic nutrition, to add more value for consumers (Nyanzi *et al.*, 2010).

An African workshop on capacity building for microbiome and probiotic research was held in Nairobi, Kenya and the full report is available online (Reid *et al.*, 2014). In this report the rapid expansion and opportunities for microbiome research between Africa, Europe, Canada and the USA are discussed in depth. Following from the so-called 'Human Microbiome' project (Turnbaugh *et al.*, 2007), that has transformed our perception of human health and disease, an African microbiome project is being proposed and developed by the participants from the Nairobi workshop. The commercialization of unique microbiota enhanc- ing human health has great potential for collaboration between Africa and indus- trialized countries providing that intellectual property issues can be addressed satisfactorily.

The case for African biorefineries

Biorefineries for the chemical industry are described in Chapter 10. In this section the link between biofuel production and the feed/food chain is highlighted.

Biofuel crops produce a significant amount of by-products, often with a high protein content. This is particularly true for crops such as soybeans, where the oil content is only 18–20 per cent (Priolli *et al.*, 2015). Studies done under contract for the South African Government have shown that it is not possible to survive financially by relying on the production of biofuels alone from a specific crop. The by-product stream utilization in the form of animal feed of excellent quality using high protein by-products (for example press-cake or Distillers Dried Grains with Solubles (DDGS)) is essential for a business to survive (The Protein Research Foundation, 2016).

In the Southern Africa region particularly, there is a chronic and often severe shortage of high-protein animal feed to the extent that a country such as South Africa imports up to 1 million tons of oil cake (mostly soya cake) per annum (The South African Grain Information Service, 2016). The situation is quite different compared with for example Europe, where waste streams are available in large quantities to warrant the development of efficient biorefinery plants. In South Africa, all wastes from cereals and oilseed crops are utilized mainly by the animal feed industry and what is left are only the truly unuseable wastes such as spoilt products with high levels of mycotoxins or some other safety prohibition.

The replacement of costly imports of oil cake and other by-products can be alleviated by the biorefinery plant, producing a range of high-value animal feeds alongside its biofuel streams. Unfortunately, the sophistication of the animal feed market is often poorly understood by investors and especially newcomers into the business. Low-quality feeds produced by start-up companies are then not taken up by the commercial livestock producers and lead to bankruptcy.

In the case of high tannin sorghum as an illustration, the DDGS fraction may be problematic for animal feed, reducing the value of the commodity. Monogastric animals are quite sensitive to high dietary levels of tannins, therefore limiting the by-product stream to certain ruminant feed applications with reduced selling prices. There is ongoing research focusing on processing refinement to address the problem, for example incorporating decortication steps before starch cooking (Nkomba *et al.*, 2016). The decortication step reduces the tannin levels of the sorghum itself but in turn produces a dust fraction with extremely high levels of tannin. One novel use of the high tannin fraction is for the production of nutraceuticals, as some of the polyphenols therein have been shown to alleviate diabetes (Links *et al.*, 2016). The challenge to combine a processing plant that incorporates bioethanol, high-quality animal feed and nutraceutical production from the same source of sorghum will require a novel design for the biorefinery and appropriate total quality management throughout the value chain.

Biorefinery development in sub-Saharan Africa will have to be built on and support increased local food production and agro-processing, but may provide an attractive opportunity for investment in an industry sector based on renewable biomass, delivering a range of products serving growing local and regional markets.

Biocontrol to reduce post-harvest losses

Worldwide estimates for post-harvest losses typically range at around 30 per cent of harvested produce. This is an average figure and losses are usually higher in developing countries. A recent survey done in the Limpopo province of South Africa showed that post-harvest losses are much higher in the informal sector, in this case 50 per cent. Losses are mainly due to over-ripening as a consequence of lack of proper storage facilities and appropriate technologies for extending shelf life outside of the cold chain (Mashau *et al.*, 2012). This is the case in spite of the fact that Limpopo Province produces a significant percentage of South Africa's fruit and includes a number of large commercial producers supplying fruit to the export markets, particularly Europe.

Elaborate computerized modelling in west Africa evaluating post-harvest losses of tomatoes in Ghana and Burkina Faso in the informal market and transporting systems also revealed losses of 30–50 per cent (Venus *et al.*, 2013), confirming the general trend on the continent. Biological control using microbial antagonists such as bacteria and yeasts has emerged as one of the promising technologies to inhibit fungal growth on fruit and vegetables, one of the main reasons for post-harvest decay and short shelf life (Mari *et al.*, 2014). After three decades of study and promising results, only a few biological control agents (BCAs) are available on the market for industrial application to control post-harvest decay.

There are several reasons for this situation. Some are due to intrinsic problems of BCAs such as their inconsistency, and the variability of their effectiveness under commercial conditions. There are also regulatory barriers to BCA registration in different countries that hamper their dissemination.

Research is very active in Africa and examples include *Bacillus amyloliquefaciens* to control anthracnose and phomopsis rot of papayas during storage, a collaborative project between Sudan and South Africa (Osman *et al.*, 2011), and yeast antagonists to control *Penicillium digitatum* in oranges (Mekbib *et al.*, 2011). The use of chemical fungicides has problems such as residue retention on the fruit and also the development of fungicide-resistant microorganism populations. Therefore the use of yeast antagonists is gaining much interest as an alternative, but the actual mechanism by which yeasts inhibit the target pathogen microorganisms is still not clear. There are currently only three commercial yeast biocontrol products available on the market. A comprehensive review by Mari *et al.* (2014) summarizes the issues and innovative approaches in this field.

Towards plant-based production of biopharmaceuticals

Biopharmaceutical proteins and vaccines are traditionally produced in bacteria, eggs, yeast and animal cell cultures and are well-established industries. More recently, these molecules are being produced in plants, a method known as biopharming. Plant-based production systems have the advantages of eukaryotic protein processing, inherent safety due to a lack of adventitious agents, substantial cost reduction and facile scalability. The latter was demonstrated in two therapeutic and industrial enzyme techno-economic case studies (Tusé *et al.*, 2014). These advantages however are molecule/product-specific and depend on the relative cost-efficiency of alternative sources of the same product (biosimilars) or improved products (biobetters). Nevertheless, plant-based manufacturing is estimated to reduce the running costs (20–25 per cent) and capital expenses (40 per cent) compared with animal cell-based processes. Plants are grown in enclosed greenhouse or growth room facilities, with highly regulated downstream processes to ensure product quality. A facility with the capacity of 1 tonne of antibody per year would cost less than US$50 million and operation costs for the first three years would amount to US$45–60 million (Gleba and Giritch, 2012). Such a relatively low financial entry barrier represents a very attractive opportunity for manufacturers in developing countries. In addition, the Defence Advanced Research Projects Agency (DARPA) recognizes that plant-based transient systems overall represent the best manufacturing technologies when dealing with bioterrorism and pandemics.

Biopharming is advancing fast and numerous reviews cover the latest developments concerning vaccines (Rybicki, 2014), antibodies (Whaley *et al.*, 2014), purification strategies (Buyel and Fischer, 2014) and manufacturing platforms (Gleba and Giritch, 2012; Klimyuk *et al.*, 2014).

Plant-based antibodies, vaccines and biologics globally

Since the first biopharming (Barta *et al.*, 1986; Hiatt *et al.*, 1989) two to three decades ago, the commercial production of antibodies, vaccines and other pharmaceutical proteins in plants was only a dream. The first initiatives in *Nicotiana benthamiana*, closely related to tobacco, spiralled out to production in strawberries, spinach, lettuce and duckweed. Since then the US Food and Drug Administration (FDA) has approved vegetable cell-based treatment enzymes (Protalix produced in carrot cells for the treatment of Gaucher's disease in humans) and edible interferon for dogs produced in strawberries. Kushnir *et al.* (2012) describe many more plant-based vaccines in pre-clinical and clinical trials.

The magnitude of the Ebola outbreak in West Africa focused the attention on ZMapp, a plant-based cocktail of three humanized monoclonal antibodies which proved successful in non-human primates (Qui *et al.*, 2014). Registration of ZMapp will pave the way for numerous other plant-based mAbs.

Vaccination remains the most effective way to control, prevent and eradicate infectious diseases (Kushnir *et al.*, 2012). Virus-like particle (VLP) vaccines consisting of assembled viral capsid proteins and void of the viral genome offer safe and effective new generation vaccines. VLPs as prophylactic vaccines against target viruses are developed in bacteria, insect, yeast, mammalian and recently in plant cell systems (Kushnir *et al.*, 2012). Insect cell-produced VLP-based vaccines currently on the market are human papillomavirus (HPV) (Cervarix and Gardisil) and Hepatitis B (Engerix and Recombivax).

The leaders globally in the development of plant-based VLPs to serve as vaccines in human health are Fraunhofer and Medicago. Both Medicago and Fraunhofer have proprietary VLP products for pandemic and seasonal influenza in advanced clinical trials. Other plant-produced products of Medicago include prophylactic rabies, rotavirus and HIV vaccines. Fraunhofer's portfolio includes vaccines and antibodies for malaria, Sleeping sickness, Yellow fever, bioterror agents, hookworm and HPV.

A European Union (EU) FP7-funded research project (2014–16) has opened up a radical new era in the world of vaccine discovery and production. The PLAPROVA (Plant Production of Vaccines) consortium focused on plant-based vaccines against diseases such as avian influenza, bluetongue, foot and mouth disease, and porcine reproductive and respiratory syndrome. Similarly, CoMoFarm, also funded by the EU FP7 programme, supported the development of high-yielding plant-based expression systems, with a specific focus on consistent homogeneous material and establishing current good manufacturing practice (cGMP) facilities.

Plant-based vaccines, antibodies and biologics – a role for Africa

The burden of tropical disease in Africa necessitates a government contingency plan to be in place. Cost-effective treatments and preventative measures for diseases unique to Africa are imperative. Apart from first generation live attenuated vaccines produced in South Africa, the majority of vaccines are imported for human and animal health.

The South African Department of Science and Technology (DST) Bio-Economy strategy priorities include the manufacturing of high-value protein products such as biopharmaceuticals and vaccines. DST invested in developing plant-made antibodies, vaccines and biologics during the last decade. The Greenpharm concept was developed at the CSIR as a commercial vehicle for plant-produced products in South Africa. One of the exciting products is RabiVir™, consisting of a cocktail of two antibodies against rabies. The product is equal to the gold standard in industry. The product was validated by World Health Organization Collaborating Centre on Rabies Research (WHO CCRR) and the potential to protect against various strains of rabies confirmed. Clinical-grade material was manufactured under cGMP conditions by the CSIR's global partner Kentucky Bioprocessing (KBP). Therapeutic antibodies for use as anti-HIV agents in microbicides are close to registration (Rybicki, 2014) and perhaps rabies antibodies will follow.

Pandemic response to human influenza

Globally, plant-based vaccines are being developed for a response to a human influenza pandemic. Both Medicago and Fraunhofer have *N.benthamiana*-produced avian (H1N1) and swine (H5N1) influenza vaccines, respectively, in Phase I clinical trials. Thirty million doses of the VLP vaccine could be produced within three months (D'Aoust *et al.*, 2008 and 2010) once the hemagglutinin (HA) sequence of the latest strain is available.

The CSIR in South Africa, as part of a global consortium including KBP and Touro University, developed a highly effective antigen carrier, TMV, presenting target influenza HA antigens (Mallajosyula et al., 2014). Recombinant HA subunit protein vaccines are often of low potency and require high dose or boosting to generate a sustained immune response. The TMV-HA conjugate compared to a commercial H1N1 vaccine showed an increase in mice survival rates from 10 per cent to 50 per cent and even to 100 per cent if combined with an adjuvant. The consortium facilities are positioned to respond to a pandemic outbreak of influenza with a rapid and scalable plant production in place. Similarly, successful work is being undertaken for a highly pathogenic avian influenza A subtype (H5N1) (Mortimer et al., 2012).

Veterinary vaccines for Africa

In South Africa the Tshwane Animal Health Innovation Cluster of the Technology Innovation Agency (TIA) invested more than US$8–10 million in developing animal vaccines and related products for the period 2012–17. A number of these products are plant based. The incremental learning of bringing veterinary vaccines to the market will pave the way for human health vaccines in Africa. The length and rigour of vaccine development and clinical testing for human health compared to animal vaccines is a huge obstacle to commercial production of novel biopharmed vaccines (Rybicki, 2014). Nevertheless, plant-produced monoclonal antibodies and animal vaccines may provide affordable vaccines for Africa. Furthermore, biosafety concerns in secondary crops and enclosed production facilities for edible crops are negligible.

The need for a cGMP production facility

Proof of principle of various vaccines for the African continent has been shown, but a cGMP facility for the production, downstream processing and specialized purification techniques for large-scale and end-stage production is lacking in Africa. Currently, South Africa is relying on international research partners to produce cGMP-grade target products. A portfolio of validated plant-based products with sustainable income potential may convince stakeholders and investors to fund such a facility in the near future.

Conclusion

The bioscience innovations described in this chapter cover a wide range of valuable applications. All are technologically difficult and are based on advanced R&D and functional innovation structures. Yet with adequate support they could all be implemented on the continent to the benefit of the African development agenda as a whole. Innovation, particularly bioscience innovation, is needed throughout the agricultural value chain, involving all the steps from production to the delivery of value-added products to the consumer. The success stories demonstrate the importance of collaboration and of long-term commitment, as well as the involvement of the private sector and resource-poor farmers. Successful bioscience innovation needs to be linked to capacity development, improved income and food security, and health status of the general population. Countries in Africa are facing a range of challenges in their efforts to address these issues as they move towards sustainable bioeconomies.

References

African Union. 2014. *On the Wings of Innovation. Science, Technology and Innovation for Africa. 2024 Strategy, STISA-2024*. Addis Ababa: African Union.

Amosu, A.O. *et al.* 2013. South African seaweed aquaculture: a sustainable development example for other African coastal countries. *African Journal of Agricultural Research* 8(43), pp.5268–79.

Barta, A. *et al.* 1986. The expression of a nopaline synthase – human growth hormone chimaeric gene in transformed tobacco and sunflower callus tissue. *Plant Molecular Biology* 6, pp.347–57.

Buyel, J.F. and Fischer, R. 2014. Generic chromatography-based purification strategies accelerate the development of downstream processes for biopharmaceutical proteins produced in plants. *Biotechnology Journal* 9(4), pp.566–77.

D'Aoust, A-M. *et al.* 2008. Influenza virus-like particles produced by transient expression in *Nicotiana benthamiana* induce a protective immune response against a lethal viral challenge in mice. *Plant Biotechnology Journal* 6, pp.930–40.

D'Aoust, A-M. *et al.* 2010. The production of hemagglutinin-based virus-like particles in plants: a rapid, efficient and safe response to pandemic influenza. *Plant Biotechnology Journal* 8, pp.607–19.

Dlamini, B.C. *et al.* 2015. Effect of sorghum type and malting on production of free amino nitrogen in conjunction with exogenous protease enzymes. *Journal of the Science of Food and Agriculture* 95(2), pp.417–22.

Duza, M.B. and Mastan, S.A. 2013. Microbial enzymes and their applications – a review. *Indo-American Journal of Pharmaceutical Research* 3(8), pp.6208–19.

FAOSTAT. 2015. *Food and Agriculture Organization of the United Nations Statistics Division website*. [Online]. [Accessed 25 January 2016]. Available from: http://faostat3.fao.org/faostat-gateway/go/to/download/Q/QC/E

Fourie, D. *et al.* 2011. Improvement of common bacterial blight resistance in South African dry bean cultivar Teebus. *African Crop Science Journal* 19(4), pp.377–86.

Gleba, Y.Y. and Giritch, A. 2012. *Vaccines, antibodies, and pharmaceutical proteins*. Oxford: Academic Press, Elsevier.

Hiatt, A. *et al.* 1989. Production of antibodies in transgenic plants. *Nature* 342, pp.76–8.

Hughes, A.D. *et al.* 2012. Biogas from macroalgae: is it time to revisit the idea? *Biotechnology for Biofuels* 5, p.86.

Hurtado, A.Q. *et al.* 2015. Developments in production technology of *Kappaphycus* in the Philippines: more than four decades of farming. *Journal of Applied Phycology* 27, pp.1945–61.

Klimyuk, V. *et al.* 2014. Production of recombinant antigens and antibodies in *Nicotiana benthamiana* using 'Magnifection' Technology: GMP-compliant facilities for small- and large-scale manufacturing. *Current Topics in Microbiology and Immunology* 375, pp.127–54.

Kushnir, N. *et al.* 2012. Virus-like particles as a highly efficient vaccine platform: diversity of targets and production systems and advances in clinical development. *Vaccine* 31(1), pp.58–83.

Links, M.R. *et al.* 2016. Kafirin microparticle encapsulated sorghum condensed tannins exhibit potential as an anti-hyperglycaemic agent in a small animal model. *Journal of Functional Foods* 20, pp.394–9

Mallajosyula, J.K. *et al.* 2014. Single-dose monomeric HA subunit vaccine generates full protection from influenza challenge. *Human Vaccines & Immunotherapeutics* 10(3), pp.586–95.

Mari, M. *et al.* 2014. Control of fruit postharvest diseases: old issues and innovative approaches. *Stewart Postharvest Review* 10(1), pp.1–4.

Mashau, M.E. *et al.* 2012. Assessment of post harvest losses of fruits at Tshakhuma fruit market in Limpopo Province, South Africa. *African Journal of Agricultural Research* 7(29), pp.4145–50.

Olomi, A.R. 2013. Technology diffusion from university to the private sector – integrating waste management and bio-energy production – the case of Bio-Innovate. [Online]. Presentation at First Bio-Innovate Regional Scientific Conference, Addis Ababa, Ethiopia, 25–27 February. [Accessed 1 February 2016]. Available from: http://www.slideshare.net/ILRI/bio-innovate2013-mdbanana.

Mekbib, S.B. *et al.* 2011. Efficacy and mode of action of yeast antagonists for control of *Penicillium digitatum* in oranges. *Tropical Plant Pathology* 36(4), pp.233–40.

Mgenzi, S.R.B. *et al.* 2010. Banana (*Musa* spp.) processing businesses: support environment and role in poverty reduction in rural Tanzania. In: T. Dubois *et al.* (eds). *International Conference on Banana and Plantain in Africa on Harnessing International Partnerships to Increase Research Impact, Mombasa, Kenya, 2008/10/05-09. Acta Horticulturae 879.* Leuven: ISHS, pp.249–55.

Mohamed, A. *et al.* 2014. First products of DNA marker-assisted selection in sorghum released for cultivation by farmers in sub-Saharan Africa. *Journal of Plant Science and Molecular Breeding* 3, p.3.

Mortimer, E. *et al.* 2012. Setting up a platform for plant-based influenza virus vaccine production in South Africa. *BMC* Biotechnology 12, p.14.

Msuya, F.E. 2013. Social and economic dimensions of carrageenan seaweed farming in the United Republic of Tanzania. In: Valderrama, D. *et al.* (eds). *Social and Economic Dimensions of Carrageenan Seaweed Farming.* Fisheries and Aquaculture Technical Paper No. 580. Rome: FAO, pp.115–46.

Myburg, A.A. *et al.* 2014. The genome of *Eucalyptus grandis. Nature* 510, pp.356–62.

Nkomba, E.Y. *et al.* 2016. The influence of sorghum grain decortication on bioethanol production and quality of the distillers' dried grains with solubles using cold and conventional warm starch processing. *Bioresource Technology* 203, pp.181–9.

Nyanzi, R. *et al.* 2010. Consumer acceptability of a synbiotic version of the maize beverage mageu. *Development Southern Africa* 27(3), pp.447–63.

Oduntan O.O. *et al.* 2015. Human-wildlife conflict: a view on red-billed Quelea (*Quelea quelea*). *International Journal of Molecular Evolution and Biodiversity* 5(2), pp.1–4.

Osman, M.S. *et al.* 2011. Effect of biocontrol agent *Bacillus amyloliquefaciens* and 1-methyl cyclopropene on the control of postharvest diseases and maintenance of fruit quality. *Crop Protection* 30(2), pp.173–8.

Prasanna, B.M. *et al.* 2014. Molecular marker-assisted breeding for tropical maize improvement. In: Wusiruika, R. *et al.* (eds). *Genetics, Genomics and Breeding of Maize.* London: CRC Press, pp.89–119.

Priolli, R.H.G. *et al.* 2015. Association mapping of oil content and fatty acid components in soybean. *Euphytica* 203(1), pp.83–96.

Qui, X. *et al.* 2014. Reversion of advanced Ebola virus disease. *Nature* 514, pp.47–53.

Reid, G. *et al.* 2014. Harnessing microbiome and probiotic research in sub-Saharan Africa: recommendations from an African workshop. *Microbiome* 2, p.12.

Rybicki, E.P. 2014. Plant-based vaccines against viruses. *Virology Journal* 11(1), p.205.

SABMiller plc. 2014. *Sustainable Development Summary Report.* [Online]. [Accessed 3 April 2015]. Available from: http://www.sabmiller.com/docs/default-source/investor-documents/reports/2014/sustainability-reports/sustainable-development-report-2014.pdf?sfvrsn=14

Taylor, J.R.N. *et al.* 2013. The science of the tropical cereals sorghum, maize and rice in relation to lager beer brewing. *Journal of the Institute of Brewing* 119(1–2), pp.1–14.

The Industrial Development Corporation. 2016. [Online]. [Accessed 15 January 2016]. Available from: https://www.idc.co.za/

The Integrated Breeding Platform. 2014. [Online]. [Accessed 1 February 2016]. Available from: https://www.integratedbreeding.net/

The Protein Research Foundation. 2016. [Online]. [Accessed 15 January 2016]. Available from: https://www.proteinresearch.net/

The South African Grain Information Service. 2016. [Online]. [Accessed 15 January 2016]. Available from: http://www.sagis.org.za/

The Southern African Grain Laboratory. 2016. [Online]. [Accessed 15 January 2016]. Available from: https://www.sagl.co.za/

Tumutegyereize, P. *et al.* 2011. Optimization of biogas production from banana peels: effect of particle size on methane yield. *African Journal of Biotechnology* 10(79), pp.18243–51.

Turnbaugh, P.J. *et al.* 2007. The human microbiome project. *Nature* 449, pp.804–10.

Tusé, D. *et al.* 2014. Manufacturing economics of plant-made biologics: case studies in therapeutic and industrial enzymes. *BioMed Research International* Article ID 256135, p.16. doi:10.1155/2014/256135.

Van Asten, P.J.A. *et al.* 2010. Opportunities and constraints for dried dessert banana (*Musa* spp.) export in Uganda. In: T. Dubois *et al.* (eds). *International Conference on Banana and Plantain in Africa on Harnessing International Partnerships to Increase Research Impact, Mombasa, Kenya, 2008/10/05–09. Acta Horticulturae 879.* Leuven: ISHS, pp.105–12.

Van Aswegen, J. 2014. *Personal communication to Corinda Erasmus*, Novozymes SA.

Venus, V. *et al.* 2013. Development and validation of a model to estimate postharvest losses during transport of tomatoes in West Africa. *Computers and Electronics in Agriculture* 92, pp.32–47.

Whaley, K.J. *et al.* 2014. Emerging antibody-based products. In: *Plant Viral Vectors.* Heidelberg: Springer, pp.107–26.

10　An African perspective

Developing an African bioresource-based industry – the case for cassava

Ephraim Nuwamanya, Yona Baguma and M.E. Chrissie Rey

Introduction

There is an urgent need for transformation of sub-Saharan Africa's (SSA)'s economic structures to cope with future challenges such as increased food demand, shortages of food and rising unemployment. Increased agricultural production is thus required, not only to feed the growing populations, but also to expand employment into industrial sectors and provide markets for a wider array of processed agricultural products (Snodgrass, 2014). Cassava (*Manihot esculenta* Crantz) has a high potential to meet the above demands in addition to contributing to economic transformation in SSA. More than 90 per cent of cassava produced in SSA is being used as food (Philips *et al.*, 2006). Food security in SSA depends on different farming systems, and cassava is the main crop for both calories and income. Approximately 150 million people depend on cassava as a staple crop, with about 27.8 million tonnes produced annually in eastern Africa (FAOSTAT, 2015). Many West African countries rely on cassava as a food crop, and Nigeria is the world's largest producer with 54 million tonnes in 2014 (FAOSTAT, 2015). Thailand with a production of 30 million tonnes, and Brazil producing 23 million tonnes, are the two highest cassava-producing countries in Asia and South America, respectively (FAOSTAT, 2015). Despite being the largest producer of cassava, Nigeria, unlike other large producers such as Thailand, does not currently export cassava, but plans to supply China with about 3.2 million tonnes of dry cassava chips in the future (Centre for Management Technology, 2014). Thailand's market share of cassava exports in 2009 was 83 per cent, followed by Vietnam, Indonesia, China and Brazil (Poramacom *et al.*, 2013). In Southern Africa, cassava is grown to a lesser extent in Zambia and Zimbabwe, but widely cultivated in Mozambique, accounting for about 30 per cent of total national calorie intake (FAOSTAT, 2015). In South Africa, a small number of subsistence farmers grow cassava (Daphne, 1980), and recently national germplasm trials have commenced to select suitable varieties for small-scale farmers. Despite wide cultivation of cassava in many SSA countries, overall yields are low (Nigeria produces 7.72 tonnes/ha compared with Thailand which produces 22.2 tonnes/ha) (FAOSTAT, 2015), due to small-scale and subsistence farming systems that are not efficiently managed (Lopez and El-Sharkawy, 1995). Reversing this trend would provide huge potential for increased productivity and production in Africa.

Cassava produces edible tuberous roots as storage units (with high starch content, ~85 per cent) and its leaves, having a considerable amount of calcium and protein, are utilized as a vegetable in some African cultures. Globally, in terms of production volumes it is ranked as the seventh most important crop behind sugar cane, maize, rice, wheat, potato and soybeans (FAOSTAT, 2015). Over the period 1980–2014, cassava has had the highest increase in global harvest area amounting to a 78 per cent expansion. In this same period, global cassava production has increased from 124 million tonnes to 270 million tonnes (FAOSTAT, 2015). In the wake of climate change, cassava has become a vital crop for food security in sub-Saharan Africa. The crop does well in poor soils with low rainfall, and, because it is perennial, it can be harvested as required over time. However, rapid post-harvest deterioration of the tubers once out of the ground remains a challenge. The importance of cassava to many Africans is epitomized in the Ewe (a language spoken in Ghana, Togo and Benin) name for the plant, *agbeli*, meaning 'there is life'.

The cassava crop combines a number of attributes that give it superiority over other crops such as resilience to both biotic and abiotic stresses, high biomass and calorie content and its ability to fit in various cropping systems. In SSA, these attributes have been harnessed and the number of hectares under cassava has increased by over 90 per cent in the last ten years (FAOSTAT, 2015). The market price of cassava has increased too, and with a steady increase in demand, the number of cassava-processed products has increased tremendously by over 50 per cent (Kleih *et al.*, 2012). Importantly too, the number of research interventions into cassava by National Agricultural Research Centres and other regional research organizations and academia has increased, with emphasis on development of high-yielding, biotic and abiotic stress-resilient cassava varieties.

However, despite the recognition of the value of cassava, African countries have to a limited degree responded to opportunities presented, and from 1992 to early 2000s, there was only a minor export of cassava starch from Africa (Prakash, 2005). While commercial enterprises in cassava have been successful in countries such as Brazil and Thailand, many past attempts to exploit cassava as an industrial crop in Africa have failed, although commercial application of cassava starch is increasing. In Malawi, for example, policy and institutional support to expand the food security basket has included the promotion of diversified applications of cassava in the non-food sector which has also propelled cassava production in non-traditional growing areas (Kambewa, 2010). In this chapter we focus on lessons learnt from the past and opportunities, which need to be factored into strategic planning for future development of cassava as a broad bioresource for the African continent. We present some case studies showcasing critical factors that have been instrumental in recent successful commercial endeavours.

Opportunities for cassava commercialization: increased utilization and new value chains for diverse cassava products in Africa

The exploitation of cassava offers attractive opportunities for SSA countries given its food-processing qualities and potential value chains such as cassava chips, flour and alcoholic beverage production. It also has a large potential for other industrial applications in pharmaceuticals, paper and textile manufacturing, animal feed or pellets and for the bioethanol sectors (Tonukari, 2004). Furthermore, problematic cassava waste, a product of industrial processes, can be converted to useful products such as bioenergy and biofertilizer used for cassava cultivation and irrigation, a sustainable way of using cassava.

Several strategic factors/issues crucial for development of cassava value chains include:

Market and trade opportunities

One of the constraints in identifying and adopting opportunities for cassava product markets is information gaps on market needs for raw and processed products, efficient processing for specific markets and established market linkages (FAOSTAT, 2015), lack of trade facilitation and information about marketing and distribution channels (SADC Trade, 2012). In addition, cassava trading and agro-processing industrial sectors in SSA should consider building capacity to supply international markets in the face of competition from established cassava-producing countries that have benefited from earlier high-level investment in cassava production through direct government support. Increased production of cassava and connected value chains in SSA countries should also focus on national and regional markets taking advantage of rapidly rising populations and *per capita* income increases, stimulating the local demand.

Financial resources

Commercialization of cassava requires increased cultivation areas and investments in production technologies. Most countries in SSA do not have financial resources to facilitate increased cassava production and commercialization and investments will need farmer, government and industrial partnerships.

Suitable germplasm and cultivation practices

The international starch market is extremely competitive and is dominated by maize and potato starch products, which have an established technological advantage related to starch production compared with cassava (Wang, 2007). However, cassava starch has some unique properties such as high density and amenability to modification, which are highly desirable for industry. Cassava's future prospects are also rooted in enhancing its supply side in terms of increased productivity by improving farming management practices, and adopting more high-yielding varieties tailored to industrial needs and resistant to pests. The challenge therefore is development of an industrial cassava variety combining enhanced starch, viral disease resistance and abiotic stress tolerance.

Farming practices for sustainable cassava production, marketing and utilization

Fundamental to any prospects of cassava industrialization in SSA is scale-up of cassava cultivation from subsistence to small-scale (~5 ha) or commercial (>1,000 ha) enterprises. A continuous rotating high volume supply of cassava root is needed all year round in order for factories to be economically viable. In addition, yields of cassava roots need to be minimally above 20 tonnes per hectare, but ideally 2–3 times higher with strategic irrigation and fertilization. This requires sound financial, technical and agronomic management of cassava enterprises.

Cassava agro-processing strategies and their role in the bioeconomy

Current agro-processing strategies

Cassava processing in most African countries is carried out to control deterioration after harvest and to decrease the toxicity due to cyanogens in fresh cassava products. Processing, through fermentation, accounts for 20–30 per cent of the products in typical cassava-consuming communities, while dried chips account for 10–15 per cent. Industrial-purpose products, like starch and high quality cassava flour (HQCF), and traditional products account for 5 per cent (Kleih *et al.*, 2012). Flour from primary processing is used for food and other minor uses in paper industries, ethanol and even mosquito coils carrying insect repellants. Thus agro-processing in SSA is basic and occupies a small proportion of industrial processing. However, recent approaches are encouraging large-scale manufacturing, although the type and amount of products mainly serving the local market, fetching a low premium price at regional or export markets (Quaye *et al.*, 2009).

Shifting the fresh cassava value chain towards industrial development (food, feed, fibre)

In Africa, the local cassava value chain has shifted from fresh value chains in the 1980s to highly evolved flour and fermentation products aimed at adding value (Chiwona-Karltun, 1998). This has been due to improved technologies and equipment fabrication for flour processing from chipped/chopped cassava (Kleih *et al.*, 2012).

In many countries in SSA two main markets for cassava occur, i.e. the fresh cassava and the dried cassava products markets. In the fresh cassava market, cassava (from small-scale farmers) is purchased by retailers at 10–15 US$/100 kg, transported and sold at 30–40 US$/100 kg to urban centres for direct consumption. The dried cassava products (chips, chops and flour) market involves commercial farmers and middlemen, who are linked to millers and wholesalers of cassava flour. These in turn sell to the local market or export to neighbouring countries. It is this market that supplies cassava for processed food, animal feeds and industries and, in some countries, as the mainstay food in schools. Such a value chain can potentially result in a number of new cassava products, such as fuel (Nuwamanya *et al.*, 2011) or livestock feed, but which to date have been less exploited.

Environmentally friendly products such as biodegradable plastics and specialty green chemicals that can be produced from cassava would be a driver for cassava production and can increase profitability for cassava farmers. These would have considerable beneficial impacts on the economy in cassava-producing countries. High value chains and cassava products produced and marketed for local, regional and international use would link African farmers to expanding markets allowing them to be part of a global economy. Modification of cassava starch to suit various local and regional markets has not been fully undertaken in SSA although cassava starch has unique industrial processing qualities and can be easily modified using cheaper semi-traditional procedures. Fermentation technologies for producing flour from cyanogenic varieties are needed to exploit cassava for production of high grade unmodified starches for various industrial applications. These, if undertaken, will propel diversified uses of cassava for various food, feed and agro-industrial applications.

Case study: The C:AVA (Cassava: Adding Value for Africa) project – Uganda and NARO (National Agricultural Research Organisation)

With increasing cassava production, lack of efficient processing or post-harvest handling methods has been identified to be a major limiting factor. The increments in production have also encouraged the shift from traditional roles to commercial roles such as sale as food, planting material and primary products such as flour and fermented products (Kleih *et al.*, 2012). Both research and policy institutions in Uganda allude to cassava as a key strategic crop and as such have implemented various strategies to allow for its exploitation. An analysis of the cassava value chain in the C:AVA project (Kleih *et al.*, 2012) in Uganda found that cassava commercialization was dependent on consistent fresh root availability and production of high quality products. The potential for up to 20 per cent substitution of wheat flour with cassava flour is envisaged in the food industry. For starch-based adhesives, 100 per cent substitution is possible as long as continuous starch production is guaranteed. With the government-led national cassava utilization initiative aimed at reducing imports of locally available materials such as corn starch, support is assured. This process is partly driven by a pressure group known as the 'cassava platform' that promotes technical guidelines to support inclusion of cassava in various products. In addition, through various projects and other lobby groups, government has changed its position and is implementing policies and strategies allowing for increased cassava utilization (Museveni, 2012). Such strategies have been adopted by research institutions undertaking research in cassava variety development, seed production, agricultural mechanisation, post-harvest management and seed production.

Case study: Nigeria's cassava transformation

Nearly 90 per cent of cassava production in Nigeria goes to the domestic food market and marginally to the beverage or industrial food markets. Cassava for the Nigerian agro-processing industry is not competitive with imported alternatives. Nigeria has recently adopted a coalition strategy of subsidiarity and partnership to rehabilitate cassava production while linking farmers to markets to unlock cassava's potential. Partnerships with technology developers, non-government organizations, developmental agencies, as well as private sector and civil society, have already been initiated (Adekanye *et al.*, 2013). Trials with improved varieties, including high starch, have commenced to raise productivity to 20 tonnes/ha. Public and private sector investments in value-added products like HQCF, starch, fuel ethanol, and high quality traditional processed cassava foods such as gari, lafun and abacha are ongoing.

A Cassava Market and Trade Development Corporation (CMTDC) has been established to facilitate cooperation between farmers and the private sector. Commercialization by two large industrial bakers of 20 per cent and 40 per cent cassava flour-substituted bread and pastries, respectively, has led to savings of about 1 million tonnes of imported wheat a year. Objectives of the CMTDC will be to plan, mobilize, activate and regulate holistic growth and development of the Nigerian cassava economy, such that all the operators in the cassava value chain are motivated to contribute their best and benefit from this industry. The successful execution of this organization is intended to facilitate Nigeria in its aim to double its cassava production and utilization by 2020.

Positioning of a sustainable cassava biofuel industry

Production of biofuel for clean energy interventions is crucial despite the potential negative effects on food production that are anticipated. Henceforth, specific and well-tailored studies for sustainable biofuel production processes (simulation, sustainability analysis, economic evaluations and life-cycle assessments) are needed. Establishment of a successful cassava biofuel industry requires implementation of local biorefineries to increase cassava value and industrial relevance. These should be well-organized bioprocesses promoted for their suitability and assessed for a number of functionalities. They should be based on the biorefinery concept for production of various biobased products from biomass, including food, feed and chemicals and energy in form of heat and fuel (Star-COLIBRI, 2011).

Case study: The EU-BIOPOL biorefinery project: how can SSA benefit from such interventions in their bid to set up bioresource-based refineries?

Given the energy/chemical supply situation in SSA, which is dependent on an inadequate access to fossil fuels, there is a need to improve energy and chemical supply using biorefineries. Borrowing from the European bioeconomy strategy, harnessing of versatile biomass supply chains from agricultural residues, lignocellulosic crops and algal and aquatic biomass is necessary for a revitalized competitive and knowledge-intensive rural economy. Sustainable production of industrial feedstocks at a local level, and the locating of industries where biomass can easily be produced, is crucial for setting up a bioindustry. However, sustainability of such small-scale industries, dependent on season-based biomass sources and a small capital base, is not guaranteed as they can fail to compete internationally and are vulnerable to price fluctuations.

In the EU-BIOPOL biorefinery project, it was realized that demonstration/model biorefineries need to be put in place with an inherent food and feed security component to augment the already existing systems (O'Connell *et al.*, 2007). Therefore, SSA countries will require a research and development agenda to develop an agricultural-based energy/chemical strategy to utilize crops such as cassava as feedstocks amidst food and feed insecurity. Currently, most interventions are aimed at making biofuels (Wang *et al.*, 2013), but alternative plans to develop other affordable biobased products must be explored. Already existing ethanol production processes can be harnessed for production of key chemical constituents such as fertilizers and biodiesel/bioethanol by-products. Research and development will have specific roles in adopting, integrating and supporting deployment of technologies at commercial scale via upscaling processes in laboratories and training centres.

Particular aspects such as sustainable resource mobilization and cost-efficient preparation of harvested biomass (O'Connell *et al.*, 2007) will be high on the agenda for sustainable use of cassava. Issues including development of amenable feedstocks, improved logistics and storage for continuous supply, integration of already existing feedstocks into optimized systems, and cost-effective production technologies need to be addressed. Other key issues revolve around management and addressing of societal challenges related to cassava biorefineries such as use of clustering and networking models for cottage-based biorefineries. The standards and regulatory teams working with country-specific and industry regulations will have to be put in place before relevant biorefineries are set up.

Case study: cassava production and agro-processing in South Africa

As a food crop, cassava in Southern Africa has not been as well exploited compared with East and West African countries. Subsistence cultivation in Southern Africa has been erratic due to higher reliance on, and preference for, maize. In South Africa, interest in commercial cassava exploitation was stimulated in 1948 by Dr Lloyd who established links with a company extracting starch for adhesive paste, and several trials in the eastern Transvaal (now Mpumalanga) province were undertaken (Daphne, 1980). The economic climate at the time was not auspicious for pioneering new crops. Since then there have been periodic surges of interest in cassava, pioneered by African Products Manufacturing Company (now part of Tongaat Hulett Starch) in the 1980s. The agricultural operations closed down in 1990 due to difficulties identified as i) lack of suitable germplasm, ii) labour-intensive planting of material, iii) time gaps between bulking up of material and iv) losses through either soil erosion or water logging, drought, or pests and diseases. Process technology was also deemed to be problematic due to i) low starch yields for cost-effective processing, ii) high levels of fibre by-products that were expensive to dry, iii) high water usage and iv) disposal of liquid effluent. Since then, the political climate, and competition with the maize and sugar industries, has not supported sustainable attempts to realize cassava's potential as an industrial crop. While low winter temperatures are limiting for cassava growth in South Africa, intermittent germplasm trials in warmer subtropical Limpopo, KwaZulu-Natal and Mpumalanga provinces show promise. Several workshops engaging government, industry and academia have taken place over the past few years, culminating in the registration of the Cassava Industry Association in Southern African Development Community (SADC).

Trait requirements and improvement of cassava germplasm for industrialization

Plant breeding and introgression of traits from wild cassava or landraces is an important approach, but this will not be sufficient in future to ensure an economically viable cassava industry within critical timeframes. Therefore, bioscience innovation for improved crop traits is critical if large commercial-scale cultivation for cassava value addition is to be realized. Several integrated molecular platforms (see Chapter 3), such as marker assisted breeding, directed genome targeting, genomic and post-genomic tools are important in cassava improvement programmes (Ayling *et al.*, 2012). Efficient high-throughput genetic transformation capabilities are required for development of varieties with desired traits.

Cassava genetic engineering capacity is largely restricted to advanced laboratories, but recently, significant strides have been made in assisting research programmes in South Africa (Chetty *et al.*, 2013) and East Africa (Taylor *et al.*, 2012a; Nyaboga *et al.*, 2013) to establish genetic transformation platforms for local farmer-preferred cultivars on several important traits critical for sustainable commercialization of a cassava starch industry.

Virus resistance

Cassava mosaic disease (CMD) is endemic in all cassava-growing regions in SSA, and cassava brown streak disease (CBSD) has spread rapidly in East Africa over the past two decades (Legg *et al.*, 2011). Both diseases cause major yield losses and are significant threats to productivity. The VIRCA (Virus Resistant Cassava for Africa) collaborative project, and efforts at Plant Biotechnology, ETH Zurich, are helping in production of cassava with dual resistance to both CMD and CBSD using pathogen-derived RNAi (RNA interference) technology (Vanderschuren *et al.*, 2007; Ogwok *et al.*, 2012). In addition to delivery of royalty-free improved planting materials for farmers, VIRCA capacity-building activities are enhancing indigenous capability for crop biotechnology in East Africa (Taylor *et al.*, 2012b).

Starch yields and properties

Starch yields are important for viable cassava commercialization, starch modification and value addition. The concept of plant-based biorefineries for starch is important in future cassava improvement programmes. Having plants with ability to produce specialized starches such as waxy starchy, high amylose starches and other forms of starch is possible through breeding techniques such as mutation breeding and exploitation of enzymes involved in synthesis of starch in cassava (Baguma *et al.*, 2008; Beyene *et al.*, 2010). Other specific studies (Bahaji *et al.*, 2014) have highlighted inhibition or optimization of enzymes such as lipases, glucoamylases and proteases in order to improve the quality and quantity of cassava starch. Various methods for modification of starch are available (Tran *et al.*, 2007) including starch composites production, nanotechnology and specialized fermentation technologies. These methods in addition to blended starch and starch films are critical for production of industrial grade starches. These technologies need to be employed to produce specific industrial starches for targeted markets.

Post-harvest physiological deterioration (PPD)

This problem could be overcome by developing improved varieties with reduced PPD, though genetic modification (Morante *et al.*, 2010) or local on-site basic processing before transport to larger down-scale value-adding/modifying processing plants.

Drought tolerance

Studies on drought tolerance in cassava have so far identified specific selection criteria for identifying varieties with ability to withstand moisture stress. Such traits include the stay green trait as identified by Turyagyenda *et al.* (2013) and the resurrection-like early recovering traits (Nuwamanya *et al.*, 2014a). The studies have resulted in a set of criteria for early selection of drought-tolerant and temperature or stress-related tolerant cassava (Nuwamanya *et al.*, 2014b). Identified varieties are usually with farmers although they can be harnessed on a large scale by industrial-based farms. In West African countries, specific breeding schemes with broad targeted goals have been in place for a while, with quantitative trait loci (QTLs) and specific markers for drought tolerance being sought (Okogbenin *et al.*, 2013). Other desired traits for cassava improvement include resistance to bacterial blight and insect pests such as cassava mite, mealybug and whitefly (Bellotti *et al.*, 2012).

Case study: The Mozambique experience: success story for cassava farmers

Cassava cultivation in Mozambique is subsistent for food security, and commercialization remains in its formative stages. Strategic investment in a set of key public goods (breeding, food sciences and food safety) can help to shape this transition in ways that benefit both commercial interests and food security. Recently, SABMiller invested in setting up a viable brewery in Mozambique and has set up a farming system model (hub-and-spoke) comprising financial, technical and agronomic support where contracted farmers supply the central hub for processing. Cassava-derived ethanol can be used in cooking stoves, and a project involving the Mozambique government, universities, farmers and the private sector focusing on this process has been running for a few years.

An issue that could potentially inhibit or reduce the ability of farmers to become integrated into the value chain is limited access to infrastructure and technology to allow them to process cassava into storable products. One of the key players in unlocking the industrial potential of cassava is processing the raw starch into cassava cakes which can be further exploited in downstream processing plants. A mobile cassava-processing unit has been developed by the Dutch Agricultural Development and Trading Company and has been adopted in Nigeria and Mozambique. This game-changing technology opens up the opportunities for use by small-scale farmers in remote areas to process cassava into easily transportable products which can be stored for six months.

Concluding remarks

The increasing awareness in SSA of the potential of cassava in agro-processing and biorefinery processes is evidenced by its uptake in several SSA countries to create a platform for development of value-added products. Key issues, such as infrastructure, government–academia–industry partnerships, and technology development need to be addressed in order to produce specific industrial packages for niche markets. Sharing and learning from the European bioeconomy strategy could enhance harnessing of versatile products from cassava-derived biomass. Integrated financial, technical and agronomic management, and training of farmers, in addition to research and development, will play multiple roles in bringing cassava agro-processing technologies closer to commercial scale, contributing to a growing bioeconomy in SSA.

References

Adekanye, T.A. *et al.* 2013. An assessment of cassava processing plants in Irepodun local government areas, Kwara State, Nigeria. *World Journal of Agricultural Research* 1(1), pp.14–17.

Ayling, S. *et al.* 2012. Information resources for cassava research and breeding. *Tropical Plant Biol*ogy 5, pp.140–51.

Baguma, Y. *et al.* 2008. Sugar-mediated semidian oscillation of gene expression in the cassava storage root regulates starch synthesis. *Plant Signaling & Behavior* 3(7), pp.439–45.

Bahaji, A. *et al.* 2014. Starch biosynthesis, its regulation and biotechnological approaches to improve crop yields. *Biotechnology Advances* 32(1), pp.87–106.

Bellotti, A. *et al.* 2012. Cassava production and pest management: present and potential threats in a changing environment. *Tropical Plant Biology* 5, pp.39–72.

Beyene, D. *et al.* 2010. Characterization and role of *Isoamylase1* (*Meisa1*) gene in cassava. *African Crop Science Journal* 18, pp.1–8.

Centre for Management Technology. 2014. *Cassava World Africa*. [Online]. [Accessed 2 August 2015]. Available from: http://www.cmtevents.com/eventposts.aspx?feedid=1750&ev=140312&

Chetty, C.C. *et al.* 2013. Empowering biotechnology in southern Africa: establishment of a robust transformation platform for the production of industry-preferred cassava. *New Biotechnology* 30, pp.136–43.

Chiwona-Karltun, L. *et al.* (1998). The importance of being bitter – a qualitative study on cassava cultivar preference in Malawi. *Ecology of Food and Nutrition* 37, pp.219–45.

Daphne, P. 1980. Cassava: a South African venture. *Optima* 1, pp.61–8.

FAOSTAT. 2015. *Food and Agricultural Organisation of the United Nations Statistics Division website*. [Online]. [Accessed 11 February 2016]. Available from: http://faostat3.fao.org/

Kambewa, E. 2010. Cassava commercialization in Malawi. Michigan State University, International Development Working Paper No. 109. [Online]. [Accessed 11 February 2016]. Available from: http://fsg.afre.msu.edu/papers/idwp109.pdf

Kleih, U. *et al.* 2012. *Cassava market and value chain analysis: Ugandan case study, Final report*. [Online]. [Accessed 2 August 2015]. Natural Resources Institute, University of

126   *Ephraim Nuwamanya* et al.

Greenwich, UK and Africa Innovations Institute, Uganda. Available from: http://cava.
    nri.org/images/documents/publications/UgandaCassavaMarketStudy-FinalJuly2012_
    anonymised-version2.pdf

Legg, J.P. *et al.* 2011. Comparing the regional epidemiology of the cassava mosaic and
    cassava brown streak pandemics in Africa. *Virus Research* 159, pp.161–70.

Lopez, J. and El-Sharkawy, M.A. 1995. Increasing crop productivity in cassava by fertiliz-
    ing production of planting material. *Field Crops Research* 44, pp.151–7.

Morante, N. *et al.* 2010. Tolerance to postharvest physiological deterioration in cassava
    roots. *Crop Science* 50, pp.1333–8.

Museveni, Y. 2012. Speech by H.E. Yoweri Kaguta Museveni, President of the Republic of
    Uganda, at the official opening of the second scientific conference on the Global Cassava
    Partnership of the 21st century, Speke Resort Hotel, Munyonyo, Kampala, 18 June.

Nuwamanya, E. *et al.* 2011. Bio-ethanol production from non-food parts of cassava
    (*Manihot esculenta* Crantz). *Ambio* 41(3), pp.262–70.

Nuwamanya, E. *et al.* 2014a. Influence of spectral properties on cassava leaf development
    and metabolism. *African Journal of Biotechnology* 13(7), pp.834–43.

Nuwamanya, E. *et al.* 2014b. Biochemical and secondary metabolites changes under mois-
    ture and temperature stress in cassava (*Manihot esculenta* Crantz). *African Journal of
    Biotechnology* 13(31), pp.3173–86.

Nyaboga, E. *et al.* 2013. Unlocking the potential of tropical root crop biotechnology in east
    Africa by establishing a genetic transformation platform for local farmer-preferred
    cassava cultivars. *Frontiers in Plant Science* 4. doi:10 3389/fpls 2013 00526.

O'Connell, D. *et al.* 2007. *Biofuels in Australia – Issues and Prospects*. Publication No.
    07/071. Canberra: Rural Industries Research and Development Corporation.

Ogwok, E. *et al.* 2012.Transgenic RNA interference (RNAi)-derived field resistance to
    cassava brown streak disease. *Molecular Plant Pathology* 13, pp.1019–31.

Okogbenin, E. *et al.* 2013. Phenotypic approaches to drought in cassava: review. *Frontiers
    in Physiology* 4. doi:10.3389/fphys.2013.00093.

Philips, T. *et al.* 2006. *The Nigerian Cassava Industry: Statistical Handbook*. Ibadan,
    Nigeria: IITA.

Poramacom, N. *et al.* 2013. Cassava production, process and related policy in Thailand.
    American International Journal of Contemporary Research 3(5), pp.43–51.

Prakash, A. 2005. *Cassava: International Market Profile*. Background paper for the World
    Bank Competitive Commercial Agriculture in Sub-Saharan Africa (CCAA) study.
    [Online]. [Accessed 11 February 2016]. Available from: http://siteresources.worldbank.
    org/INTAFRICA/Resources/257994-1215457178567/Cassava_Profile.pdf

Quaye, W. *et al.* 2009. Characteristics of various cassava processing methods and the
    adoption requirements in Ghana. *Journal of Root Crops* 35(1), pp.59–68.

SADC (Southern African Development Community) Trade. 2012. *Trade Information Brief:
    Cassava*. Trade and Industrial Policy Strategies and Australian Agency for International
    Development (AusAid) Partnership. [Online]. [Accessed 11 February 2016]. Available
    from: http://www.sadctrade.org/files/Cassava-Trade-Information-Brief.pdf.

Snodgrass, D. 2014. *Agricultural Transformation in Sub-Saharan Africa and the Role of
    the Multiplier*. Michigan State University International Development Working Paper
    No. 135. [Online]. [Accessed 11 February 2016]. Available from: http://fsg.afre.msu.
    edu/papers/idwp135.pdf.

Star-COLIBRI. 2011. *Joint European Biorefinery Vision for 2030*. Star-COLIBRI-Strategic
    Targets for 2020 – Collaboration Initiative on Biorefineries. [Online]. [Accessed 11

February 2016]. Available from: http://www.forestplatform.org/files/Star_COLIBRI/ Vision_document_FINAL.pdf

Taylor, N.J. *et al.* 2012a. A high-throughput platform for the production and analysis of transgenic cassava (*Manihot esculenta*) plants. *Tropical Plant Biology* 5, pp.127–39.

Taylor, N.J. *et al.* 2012b. The VIRCA Project: virus resistant cassava for Africa. *GM Crops & Food* 3(2), pp.93–103.

Tonukari, N.J. 2004. Cassava and the future of starch. *Electronic Journal of Biotechnology* 7(1), pp.5–8.

Tran, T. *et al.* 2007. Gelatinization and thermal properties of modified cassava starches. *Starch/Stärke* 59, pp.46–55.

Turyagyenda, L.F. *et al.* 2013. Physiological and molecular characterization of drought responses and identification of candidate tolerance genes in cassava. *AoB PLANTS* 5:plt007. doi:10.1093/aobpla/plt007.

Vanderschuren, H. *et al.* 2007. Engineering resistance to geminiviruses – review and perspectives. *Plant Biotechnology Journal* 5, pp.207–20.

Wang, H. *et al.* 2013. Integration process of biodiesel production from filamentous oleaginous microalgae *Tribonema minus*. *Bioresource Technology* 142, pp.39–44.

Wang, X. 2007. *China's Corn Processing Industry: Its Future Development and Implications for World Trade*. Presentation. National Grain & Oils Information Centre, China. [Online]. [Accessed 11 February 2016]. Available from: http://www.agfdt.de/ loads/st07/wangabb.pdf

11 Europe and Africa

Biofuels for sustainable energy and mobility in the EU and Africa

Francis X. Johnson and Yacob Mulugetta

Introduction

The use of biofuels in motorized transport began more than a century ago, and was promoted by automobile industry pioneers such as Henry Ford and Rudolph Diesel (Kovarik, 1998; Knothe, 2001). The story of biofuels has been one of boom and bust since then, attracting interest during periods of high oil prices and later for environmental concerns, but fading away in the face of other priorities. Today's global dependence on petroleum fuels is now understood as being unsustainable in social, economic and environmental terms. Yet substitution efforts have proceeded slowly even in advanced economies that have the resources required. At the same time, biofuels have become more intertwined with other uses of land, water and biomass and are increasingly inseparable from the overall bioeconomy as well as the complex issues associated with rural development and climate change.

The EU and sub-Saharan Africa (SSA) have special economic and political ties for geographical and historical reasons, and this relation has also impacted the development of biomass resources and biofuels (Johnson and Rosillo-Calle, 2007). Thus biofuels in the EU and SSA can be discussed in the same context due to potentially strong relations in markets, investment, financing and policies. Just as is the case with biotechnology and biosciences in general, the pathways followed by African countries are often linked to those in the EU. At the same time, there are complementarities to be exploited through trade and investment (Mathews, 2007). As the bioeconomy develops globally, it is instructive to look at these developments from the lens of biofuels markets and policies in the EU and SSA so as to identify how biofuels can support a more sustainable future in the EU and Africa as well as globally.

Historical overview

There were many European countries that tested biofuels (mainly ethanol and methanol) and even mandated their use during periods of scarcity in the 1930s and during World War II. The era of cheap petroleum fuels in the 1950s put an end to biofuels initiatives and there was little effort to revive them until the oil crises of the 1970s. The EU did not launch its first serious biofuel policy initiatives until the Biofuels Directive of 2003 (EC, 2003). At that time, only a few countries such as Sweden had significant experience with biofuels; the Swedish programme included not only automobiles but also ethanol-fuelled buses to reduce urban air pollution. Swedish energy/transport policies are now aimed at achieving oil independence by 2030 (Sanches-Pereira and Gómez, 2015). Some EU countries, particularly Germany, supported and subsidized the use of rapeseed biodiesel on a significant scale; biodiesel is more highly valued in the EU than bioethanol due to the dominance of diesel engine automobiles.

The history of biofuels for transport in Africa is shorter but is quite novel in certain respects. A number of African countries experimented with alcohol fuels in the late 1970s, with Zimbabwe and Malawi notable for establishing nationwide ethanol blending programmes (Watson, 1990; Johnson and Matsika, 2006). The energy security logic for biofuels is strong in these two landlocked countries that face additional hardship and costs for imported petroleum. Malawi is the only African country whose biofuel (ethanol) programme has been uninterrupted since its inception (Johnson and Silveira, 2014). More recently, there has been considerable interest throughout Africa in vegetable oil crops to replace diesel, particularly jatropha and palm oil. Jatropha was widely touted for its ability to grow in marginal soils and/or with less rainfall, but has not achieved economic profitability (Gasparatos *et al.*, 2015). Considerable effort would be required to upscale jatropha to an industrial crop; in spite of the difficulties, it may nevertheless be of potential future interest (von Maltitz *et al.*, 2014).

Biofuels now account for just 3 per cent of transport energy globally, although the share is considerably higher in certain countries such as Brazil and the US (BP, 2015). Biofuels markets – and the policies that have stimulated them – have historically been closely tied to rising and falling oil prices and energy security concerns: a rapid expansion in global biofuels production accompanied rising oil prices in the past decade (Figure 11.1). Yet the rationale for biofuels – in developed and developing countries alike – has also expanded to include climate change, agricultural innovation and rural development. At the same time, sustainability concerns over land and water arose as well as social concerns for conflicts with food security and traditional land tenure.

The EU Renewable Energy Directive (EU-RED) of 2009 set targets of 10 per cent renewable energy in the transport sector and had some wide-reaching effects on biofuels markets in the EU and globally (EC, 2009). In light of EU-African trade linkages, companies and farmers in Africa (or those investing in Africa) viewed EU biofuels as a new export market opportunity due to lower land and labour costs along with the fact that liquid fuels and feedstocks are portable and tradable. Although developing countries have a significant comparative advantage, biofuel feedstocks nevertheless tend to be sourced within the EU due to member state agricultural support along with perceived economic and environmental risks for imports.

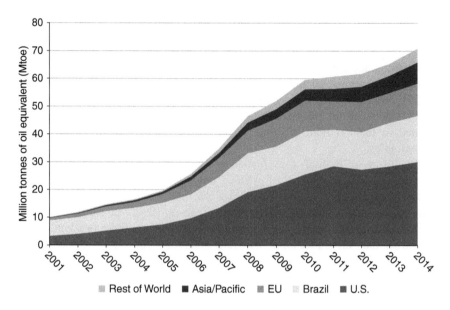

Figure 11.1 Biofuels use in various world regions (BP, 2015)

Biomass resources and potential

Unlike fossil fuels, biomass for the production of biofuels is widely distributed around the world, with the exception of deserts and some mountainous areas. Climate, soils and related ecological conditions are major determinants of the physical potential when it comes to land-based biofuels. The biophysical potential forms the basis for estimating economic potential, which depends on competing uses and population density along with key cost factors of land, labour, water and nutrients. Bioenergy potential estimates rely on many assumptions, which can be complex to harmonize for comparison purposes (Batidzirai *et al.*, 2012).

A brief overview is given in Table 11.1 for some key crops. Qualitative descriptions are used as there can be significant variation across species and varieties; the performance of particular crops can be highly location-specific and can also vary with the management approach. The various cultivars adopted in different world regions can have quite different requirements and performance. The vast field of agricultural breeding, including conventional, molecular and genetic modification (GM) methods, is premised on efforts to enhance the characteristics for particular applications, locations and/or climatic conditions (Chapter 3, this volume).

In general, the medium to long-term biophysical potential is greater in African countries compared with European countries due to favourable climates. The transformative socioeconomic potential is also higher in Africa (Lynd *et al.*, 2015). Country-level assessments of bioenergy potential suggest that a number of

Table 11.1 Characteristics of selected biofuels crops

	Type	Photo-synthetic pathway	Latitude range	Frost tolerance	Drought tolerance	Rainfall requirement	Energy yield	GHG balance	Direct competition with food production	Potential synergies with food production
Sugar crops										
Sugarcane	Perennial	C$_4$	37°N – 31°S	poor	poor	high	very high	excellent	minimal	some
Sweet sorghum	Annual	C$_4$	adapted widely	poor–moderate	excellent	low–moderate	high	good–excellent	depends on variety	yes
Starch crops										
Cassava	Perennial	C$_4$	30°N – 30°S	poor	good	moderate	moderate	good	yes	yes
Maize	Annual	C$_4$	adapted widely	poor	poor–moderate	moderate	moderate	low–moderate	yes	yes
Wheat	Annual	C$_3$	adapted widely	good	moderate	moderate	low	low–moderate	seasonal	yes
Oil crops										
Jatropha curcas	Perennial	C$_3$ + CAM	tropical and sub-tropical	moderate	excellent	low–moderate	moderate	good	minimal	some
Oil palm	Perennial	C$_3$	10°N – 10°S	none	dry periods tolerated	very high	very high	good	yes	some
Soya bean	Annual	C$_3$	adapted widely	poor–moderate	poor–moderate	moderate	low	moderate	depends on market	yes
Rape	Annual	C$_3$	temperate	moderate–good	moderate (winter variety)	moderate	moderate	low–moderate	depends on market	yes
Castor oil	Perennial/annual	C$_3$	tropical	poor	excellent	moderate	moderate	moderate	minimal	some
Lignocellulosic										
Eucalyptus	Perennial	C$_3$	adapted widely	moderate	good	low–moderate	high	high	no	no
Switchgrass	Perennial	C$_4$	adapted widely	good	good	moderate	very high	excellent	no	no
Poplar	Perennial	C$_3$	temperate	excellent	moderate	moderate	moderate	moderate–high	no	no
Willow	Perennial	C$_3$	temperate	excellent	moderate	moderate	moderate	moderate–high	no	no
Miscanthus	Perennial	C$_4$	adapted widely	excellent	good	moderate	very high	excellent	no	no

Source: Adapted from El Bassam, 2010; de Vries *et al.*, 2010; FAO/UNEP, 2011

southern African countries, particularly Mozambique, South Africa and Zambia, have quite high potential (Deng *et al.*, 2015). For well-developed crops in southern Africa such as sugarcane, the potential for the entire southern Africa region is roughly on the same order as Brazil (Johnson and Seebaluck, 2012; Watson, 2011). With the exception of a few countries such as South Africa and Mauritius, land is not a limiting factor since the levels of transport fuel use per capita are quite low. Furthermore, there are other markets for liquid biofuels, such as industrial applications and household cooking (Utria, 2004; Johnson and Matsika, 2006; Rogers *et al.*, 2013). For advanced biofuels in EU countries, Germany, France and Poland appear to have the highest potential (Deng *et al.*, 2015). The EU faces greater land constraints although the current EU targets and sustainability requirements are not binding in terms of land availability (Treesilvattanakul *et al.*, 2014).

Food vs fuel or food and fuel?

A distinction is generally made between first generation (1G) biofuel crops and advanced generations of biofuels crops, including second generation (2G) crops. Sugar and starch crops as well as oilseed crops are considered 1G crops, whereas lignocellulosic crops (Table 11.1) are 2G. However, this distinction is misleading for two main reasons. First, 2G biofuels are associated more with the conversion process than the feedstock; thermochemical or gas to liquid biofuels (Fischer–Tropsch) results in 2G biofuels but can be obtained from many different feedstocks. Second, implementation platforms can use the same crop to simultaneously produce 1G and 2G biofuels: in the case of sugarcane, 1G bioethanol is obtained from direct fermentation while 2G ethanol is obtained through lignocellulosic conversion of bagasse (IEA, 2009).

As shown in Table 11.1, the choice of crop is important in avoiding conflicts across food, energy and water objectives and in some cases can exploit synergies across the objectives (Rosillo-Calle and Johnson, 2010). First generation or food-based biofuels crops can impact food prices, although the magnitude of these impacts seems to be much smaller than was estimated after the 2007–8 price spikes (Timilsina, 2014). Food security impacts must be assessed in terms of supply and demand and in relation to both biophysical and socioeconomic factors; there can be synergies just as easily as there can be conflicts between food and fuel, while in other cases there will be little net effect (BEFS, 2010; Osseweijer *et al.*, 2015).

Production and conversion pathways

Thanks to scientific and technological advances during the past decade or so, the raw materials for production of biofuels have been or can be based on an extremely wide variety of sources, including agricultural wastes, municipal wastes, oilseeds, sugar and starch crops and woody biomass. The variety of available production pathways and conversion platforms is increasing each year and it is primarily economic factors that determine which options are used and at what scales. Figure 11.2 provides an overview of the different conversion platforms that are available.

In addition to the technical complexity of the various options, there are economic and organizational factors such that choosing among the various feedstocks and conversion routes becomes an inherently complex task (FAO/UNEP, 2011):

- There is no one-to-one mapping between feedstocks and conversion routes or between conversion routes and energy carriers or products. Consequently system-based evaluation is needed to analyse combinations of options in addition to analysing specific options.
- There are various co-products obtained in almost all paths, which have potential applications that must also be considered if cost-effectiveness is to be prioritized.
- Some pathways result in fuels and co-products across different energy carriers, including heat, mechanical power, electricity, liquid fuels, gaseous fuels and hydrogen; while this can be an advantage in resource utilization and efficiency, taking advantage of the different carriers requires more sophistication in coordinating markets/demand as well as in technical capacity for supporting infrastructure.

The significance of co-products is also among the reasons that biofuels are becoming increasingly linked to the bioeconomy and biosciences (Chapter 2, this volume). This inherent complexity calls for considerable technical expertise in evaluating and comparing various feedstock/conversion platforms. African countries and Least Developed Countries (LDCs) more generally will require capacity-building support to overcome such challenges.

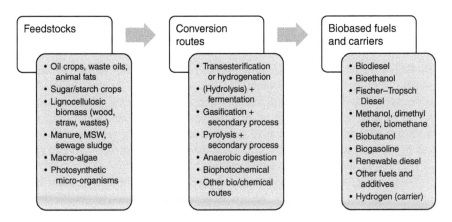

Figure 11.2 Feedstocks, conversion routes and fuels, products or energy carriers (Adapted from IEA, 2009)

Table 11.2 Liquid fuels for different feedstocks and end-uses or applications

End-use/ feedstock:	Woody biomass	Herbaceous (grasses, cereals)	Oil-bearing	Other/mixtures
Liquid (generally for transport)	• Lignocellulosic ethanol • Fischer–Tropsch fuels • Methanol	• Ethanol • Biobutanol	• Biodiesel	• Ethanol (from municipal waste and other sources) • Biogasoline (from algae)
Liquid (other sectors or options)	• Pyrolysis oil	• Black liquor • Ethanol gel • Heavy (fusel) oils	• Straight vegetable oil	• DME • Industrial oils/ applications

Source: Adapted from FAO/UNEP, 2011

It should also be noted that there are other end-use sectors besides transport that must be considered in order to match biofuels supply with the most valued and sustainable centres of demand. In the EU, the term *bioliquids* has been coined to refer to uses of biofuels outside the transport sector, which may include industrial and various non-mobile applications. Some examples are given in Table 11.2. In the African and LDC context, one of the most interesting applications is the use of bioethanol and other bioliquids for household cooking, which offer health and climate benefits (Goldemberg *et al.*, 2004; Utria, 2004; Grieshop *et al.*, 2011). Replacement of traditional biomass could also help to reduce women's drudgery, improve labour productivity and create new opportunities for income-generating activities (Oparaocha and Dutta, 2011; Sovacool, 2012). Introduction of stoves using bioethanol has attracted interest in countries such as Ethiopia (Rogers *et al.*, 2013). The analysis of trade-offs between monetary and non-monetary attributes reveals some willingness to pay for household benefits of cleaner fuels, such as reduced smoke and improved safety (Takama *et al.*, 2012).

Assuring environmental sustainability

Biofuels involve more complicated supply chains than other renewable energy sources (Figure 11.3). The strength of the weakest link in the chain affects economic feasibility while sustainability and GHG emissions must be assessed across the entire chain. Evaluating the sustainability of biofuels therefore requires a considerable amount of data on conditions across all these components, which can be difficult to obtain or track in some developing countries (Amigun *et al.*, 2011; Pacini *et al.*, 2013; Treesilvattanakul, 2014).

The EU-RED included sustainability requirements for biofuels that were applicable regardless of whether the feedstocks were sourced within or outside the EU (EC, 2009). Such provisions departed from conventional greenhouse gas (GHG) emission accounting under the United Nations Framework Convention on Climate Change (UNFCCC) in which emissions responsibility is associated with

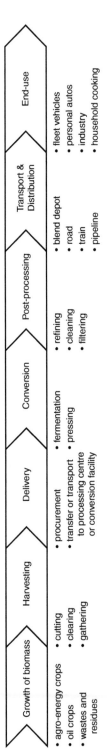

Figure 11.3 Biofuels supply chain (Adapted from FAO/UNEP, 2011)

the country of final use (Pena *et al.*, 2010). Users of imported biofuels in the EU became effectively responsible for GHG emissions associated with land use or other physical processes occurring in the source country; some responsibility for emissions reductions was thereby shifted to exporting countries (Johnson, 2011). The EU market was attractive for African countries due to duty-free status, but at the same time the EU sustainability requirements were difficult for them to meet due to a lack of administrative and technical capacity. Sustainable biofuels have not been able to attract the expected price premium and thus LDCs would have to absorb the additional costs (Pacini *et al.*, 2013).

The successful Brazilian model for biofuels contributed to considerable global optimism concerning environmental impacts and GHG emissions as well as its contributions to agriculture and development goals. By the 1990s, Brazil offered a viable model for the development of alternative fuels as a substitute for gasoline. Although the Brazilian programme was originally aimed at energy security and agricultural development, the excellent GHG balances it achieved further propelled interest in replicating the Brazilian model (Goldemberg and Guardabassi, 2010).

While the carbon emissions and reduction of GHG are often seen as the leading environmental considerations related to biofuels, there are a number of other environmental concerns that have importance in the local and national context. Some of these include water quality and quantity, air pollution, soil degradation and biodiversity concerns. Regarding water quantity, some biofuels are very water-intensive, and the average water footprint of bioenergy production is generally larger than gasoline production (Wu *et al.*, 2009; Fingerman *et al.*, 2010; ERD, 2012). However, the relationship between biofuels production and water use is also highly dependent on location, the specific feedstock, production methods and supply chain aspects, underlining the need to monitor the effects of biofuels production on water and land use more closely. Similar provisions would need to be made to monitor the impact of biofuel production on water and air quality and soil resources.

Clearly, environmental factors are prominent in shaping consumer country policies which partly explains the keen interest in biofuels around the world. For the producing countries in the South, socioeconomic factors such as poverty alleviation, rural development, and employment creation, and energy security are seen as key policy drivers to stimulate the biofuels sector. Socioeconomic factors are thus generally seen as more important in African biofuels development policies; however, access to global markets often requires the capacity to prove fulfilment of sustainability criteria that arise from the EU or US. Trade agreements could be one way to address this imbalance of market power (Westberg and Johnson, 2014).

Socioeconomic impacts

The emergence of biofuels at the interface between agriculture and energy led to considerable debates around social, economic and cultural issues. The expansion in biofuels at a time when concerns around food security are high on the development agenda highlights the core potential conflicts for developing countries, but there are also many other issues that arise related to land tenure, local vs national interests and low bargaining power of poor farmers in rural areas. A considerable hype was created during the early to mid-2000s, giving the impression that biofuels offered a silver bullet (panacea), able to provide a sustainable source of fuel that could be grown domestically but that could also have numerous ancillary benefits on carbon emissions, economic development and poverty alleviation (Gasparatos *et al.*, 2015). It must also be noted that there can be significant socioeconomic issues in EU countries; in particular, the emergence of biofuels markets has been one of the few opportunities that benefits farmers and rural areas in an era when urbanization has depopulated the countryside in much of the EU. Nevertheless, the situation is less controversial within Europe since agricultural systems and actors are already integrated into political and economic systems at national level. By contrast, in developing countries, biofuels crops intersect with practices of subsistence farmers and offer excellent development opportunities when done well (Egbendewe-Mondzozo, 2014). Three particular aspects are especially worth highlighting in the African context: poverty reduction and rural development, land acquisition and tenure, and gender issues.

Poverty reduction

The development of biofuels occurs in the rural areas where some of the poorest communities live, often engaging in small-scale and subsistence farming practices (Amigun *et al.*, 2011). Thus, the pro-poor benefits of increasing income per capita from expanding biofuel programmes has been an important political driver across Africa. To this end, a number of models have been proposed. Biofuels were seen to boost rural development and poverty reduction directly by providing income from employment in plantations or sub-contracted selling of feedstock (essentially a cash crop) from smallholders, as well as boosting rural development indirectly through the provision of locally renewable energy that can boost other productive activities (Gasparatos *et al.*, 2015). However, one challenge identified by Amigun *et al.* (2011) is to understand how equity and quality of life are impacted by biofuel developments in the affected communities. They argue that countries such as South Africa and Mozambique are committed to promote biofuels mainly in response to national poverty alleviation agendas, but whether biofuel development will contribute significantly to poverty alleviation requires further investigation.

Land acquisition and tenure

The land-intensiveness of biofuels compared to other energy sources means that land is normally a central question in biofuels programmes, which have tended towards large-scale rather than small holder-based initiatives (Van Eijck *et al.*, 2014). Different land tenure arrangements can be observed across countries, which will influence the way in which biofuels programmes are designed. The issue of foreign investment for land across Africa has underlined the need for workable legal frameworks of land ownership that limit disputes and ensure local benefits from these activities and transactions. Furthermore, it must be borne in mind that access to land is closely linked to the right to adequate food, water, grazing or fishing grounds, and forest products for the most vulnerable groups. To this end, it is critical to acknowledge that land users are not necessarily the same as land owners, and in many cases the actual users lack properly defined land rights, as in the case of pastoralists in parts of East Africa (AETS Consortium, 2013).

Gender matters

Women across Africa are responsible for securing livelihoods for their household through multiple activities, including doing the majority of the labour-intensive work in the field. Thus, there is a potential for biofuels programmes to either harm or assist women in creating opportunities that would benefit them directly (Karlsson and Banda, 2009). Given the dominance of policy attention to large-scale biofuel plantations, Amigun *et al.* (2011) argue that men and women within the same household as well as male- and female-headed households could face different risks, particularly with regard to their access to and control of land and other productive assets. In addition, their different levels of participation in decision-making and socioeconomic activities mean that biofuels programmes will have differential impacts on men and women. Much of this lies in the different levels of access to land between men and women. For example, in Cameroon, while women undertake more than 75 per cent of agricultural work they own less than 10 per cent of the land, with similar disparities identified in Tanzania, Kenya and Nigeria (UNICEF, 2007). Furthermore, general lack of access to formal credit schemes for women and the general tendency for female-run households to be pushed to marginal lands means that some structural disadvantages limit women's development prospects. The emergence of biofuels could either exacerbate these conditions or create new opportunities for women, and so how programmes are designed will determine the quality of the outcomes.

Enabling policies: investment, infrastructure and institutions

The three I's – investment, infrastructure and institutions – are crucial for the creation of economically viable and environmentally sustainable biofuels markets. The challenges exist for both the EU and Africa but are characterized by radically different driving forces and different policy priorities. A fundamental difference is of course the weaker regional institutions in Africa compared to the EU and the difficulties that arise in reconciling national agendas with regional priorities. The low level of infrastructure and the difficulty in attracting investment in nearly all African countries makes it much more complicated to translate the physical and economic biofuels potential into market developments. Realizing the potential depends also on political structures and governance capacity, where African countries face much greater constraints due to political instability and/or weak institutions (WGBU, 2009). There have nevertheless been some exceptions at regional level, such as the strong push by the Economic Organisation of West African States (ECOWAS) towards a common biofuels policy framework for West Africa (ECOWAS, 2012). It is also interesting to note that the Southern African Development Community (SADC) was the first region after the EU to craft a regional biofuels policy (Gnansounou *et al.*, 2007).

Biofuels investment in the EU and abroad increased considerably between the time of the Biofuels Directive of 2003 and the EU-RED of 2009, especially since oil prices were increasing throughout this period. Some member states provided production subsidies or incentives that allowed set-aside lands under the Common Agricultural Policy (CAP) to be redirected towards biofuels crops. Supporting technical infrastructure nevertheless lagged except for those that had already invested in fuel blending (e.g. Sweden) or technical standards (e.g. Germany). However, the timing of the EU-RED was unfortunate, as the financial crisis of 2008–9 hit the biofuels industry rather hard. Investment was further dampened by controversies surrounding the socioeconomic and environmental impacts of biofuel feedstocks, particularly those imported from developing countries where land-grabbing, food security and GHG emissions from land use change were seen as significant concerns (Johnson, 2011). The revisions to the EU-RED that capped biofuels from food crops at 7 per cent constituted one of the main responses to these concerns. Investment is also constrained by uncertainty over accounting for Indirect Land Use Change (ILUC), which is associated with emissions that occur when displaced food production results in land use change and emissions elsewhere. The ILUC approach has raised awareness but is not sufficiently robust to support mitigation strategies (Finkbeiner, 2014).

Conclusions

Although biofuels have been used in transport for over a hundred years, the past decade has been eventful. Policy goals related to climate change, energy security and rural development led to the emergence of new biofuels markets and regulations around the world. In the EU, initial enthusiasm was followed by a backlash due to concerns over land use change, food security and GHG emissions. In SSA, where EU market developments are closely monitored for export opportunities, considerable experimentation has taken place in rural areas where farmers can benefit from new market opportunities. Regional and national efforts in Africa have focused on improving the physical and institutional infrastructure as well as addressing sustainability concerns raised by the EU. The bioscience agenda in the EU calls for greater investment in advanced biofuels, whereas African LDCs can still reap considerable benefits from first generation biofuels by investing in improved yields, careful selection of crops and varieties and better management of overall biomass resources. Cooperation both in science/research and policy/ implementation between the EU and African LDCs could greatly improve the chances for biofuels to become a vibrant part of the bioeconomy and a major contributor to future sustainable energy and transport pathways.

References

AETS Consortium. 2013. *Assessing the impact of biofuels production on developing countries from the point of view of Policy Coherence for Development – Final Report, EU.* Contract No. 2012/299193, FWC COM 2011 - Lot 1 – Studies and Technical Assistance in all Sectors.

Amigun, B. *et al.* 2011. Biofuels and sustainability in Africa. *Renewable and Sustainable Energy Reviews* 15, pp.1360–72.

Batidzirai, B. *et al.* 2012. Harmonising bioenergy resource potentials – methodological lessons from review of state of the art bioenergy potential assessments. *Renewable and Sustainable Energy Reviews* 16, pp.6598–630.

BEFS (Bioenergy and Food Security). 2010. *Bioenergy and Food Security (BEFS) Analytical Framework, Tanzania Case Study.* [Online]. Rome: Food and Agriculture Organisation (FAO) of the United Nations. [Accessed 2 September 2015]. Available from: http://www.fao.org/bioenergy/foodsecurity/befs/en/

BP. 2015. *BP Statistical Review of World Energy.* [Online]. [Accessed 2 September 2015]. Available from: http://www.bp.com/en/global/corporate/about-bp/energy-economics/statistical-review-of-world-energy.html

Deng, Y.Y. *et al.* 2015. Country-level assessment of long-term global bioenergy potential. *Biomass and Bioenergy* 74, pp.253–67.

de Vries, S.C. *et al.* 2010. Resource use efficiency and environmental performance of nine major biofuel crops, processed by first-generation conversion techniques. *Biomass and Bioenergy* 34(5), pp.588–601.

EC (European Commission). 2003. *Directive 2003/30/EC of the European Parliament and of the Council of 8 May 2003 on the promotion of the use of biofuels or other renewable fuels for transport.* Brussels: Official Journal OJL 123/42.

EC (European Commission). 2009. *Directive 2009/28/EC of the European Parliament and of the Council, of 23 April 2009, on the promotion of the use of energy from renewable sources and amending and subsequently repealing Directives 2001/77/EC and 2003/30/EC.* Brussels: Official Journal OJL 140/16.

ECOWAS (Economic Organisation of West African States). 2012. *Economic Organisation of West African States (ECOWAS) Bioenergy Programme. ECOWAS Centre for Renewable Energy and Energy Efficiency (ECREEE).* [Online]. [Accessed 2 September 2015]. Available from: www.ecreee.org

Egbendewe-Mondzozo, A. 2014. Bioenergy done right for jobs and economic growth in Africa: dealing with land, biofuels and food security issues. *Biofuels* 5(4), pp.379–84.

El Bassam, N. 2010. *Handbook of Bioenergy Crops: A Complete Reference to Species, Development and Applications.* London: Earthscan.

ERD (European Report on Development). 2012. *Confronting Scarcity: Managing Water, Energy and Land for Inclusive and Sustainable Growth.* [Online]. [Accessed 2 September 2015]. Available from: http://erd-report.eu/erd/

FAO/UNEP. 2011. *Bioenergy Decision Support Tool.* [Online]. Rome: Food and Agriculture Organization of the United Nations (FAO). [Accessed 2 September 2015]. Available from: http://www.bioenergydecisiontool.org/

Fingerman, K.R. *et al.* 2010. Accounting for the water impacts of ethanol production. *Environmental Research Letters* 5(1), 014020.

Finkbeiner, M. 2014. Indirect land use change – help beyond the hype? *Biomass and Bioenergy* 62, pp.218–21.

Gasparatos, A. *et al.* 2015. Biofuels in sub-Saharan Africa: drivers, impacts and priority policy areas. *Renewable and Sustainable Energy Reviews* 45, pp.879–901.

Gnansounou, E. *et al.* 2007. Sustainable liquid biofuels for transport: the context of the Southern Africa development community (SADC) (No. GR-GN-REPORT-2007-001). [Online]. [Accessed 8 September 2015]. Available from: http://infoscience.epfl.ch/record/121498

Goldemberg, J. *et al.* 2004. A global clean cooking fuel initiative. *Energy for Sustainable Development* 8(3), pp.5–12.

Goldemberg, J. and Guardabassi, P. 2010. Ethanol: can the success of Brazil be replicated? *Biofuels* 1(5), pp.663–5.

Grieshop, A.P. *et al.* 2011. Health and climate benefits of cookstove replacement options. *Energy Policy* 39(12), pp.7530–42.

IEA (International Energy Agency). 2009. *Bioenergy – a sustainable and reliable energy source: a review of status and prospects.* [Online]. [Accessed 2 September 2015]. Available from: http://www.ieabioenergy.com/wp-content/uploads/2013/10/MAIN-REPORT-Bioenergy-a-sustainable-and-reliable-energy-source.-A-review-of-status-and-prospects.pdf

Johnson, F.X. 2011. Regional-global linkages in the energy-climate-development policy nexus: the case of biofuels in the EU Renewable Energy Directive. *Renewable Energy Law and Policy Journal* 2, pp.91–106.

Johnson, F.X. and Matsika, E. 2006. Bioenergy trade and regional development: the case of bio-ethanol in southern Africa. *Energy for Sustainable Development* 10(1), pp.42–53.

Johnson, F.X. and Rosillo-Calle, F. 2007. *Biomass, Livelihoods and International Trade: Challenges and Opportunities for the EU and Southern Africa.* Stockholm Environment Institute (SEI) Report 2007-01 [Online]. [Accessed 2 September 2015]. Available from: http://www.sei-international.org/publications?pid=718

Johnson, F.X. and Seebaluck, V. 2012. *Bioenergy for Sustainable Development and International Competitiveness: The Role of Sugar Cane in Africa.* London: Routledge.

Johnson, F.X. and Silveira, S. 2014. Pioneer countries in the transition to alternative transport fuels: comparison of ethanol programmes and policies in Brazil, Malawi and Sweden. *Environmental Innovation & Societal Transitions* 11, pp.1–24.

Karlsson, G. and Banda, K. 2009. *Biofuels for Sustainable Rural Development and Empowerment of Women: Case Studies from Africa and Asia.* [Online]. Leusden: ENERGIA Secretariat. [Accessed 2 September 2015]. Available from: http://energia.org/wp-content/uploads/2015/06/68-Biofuelsfor-sustainable-rural-development-and-empowerment-of-woman.pdf

Knothe, G. 2001. Historical perspectives on vegetable oil-based diesel fuels. *Inform* 12, pp.1103–7.

Kovarik, B. 1998. Henry Ford, Charles F. Kettering and the fuel of the future. *Automotive History Review* 32, pp.7–27.

Lynd, L.R. *et al.* 2015. Bioenergy and African transformation. *Biotechnology for Biofuels* 8(1), pp.8–18.

Mathews, J. 2007. Biofuels: what a biopact between North and South could achieve. *Energy Policy* 35, pp.3550–70.

Oparaocha, S. and Dutta, S. 2011. Gender and energy for sustainable development. *Current Opinion in Environmental Sustainability* 3(4), pp.265–71.

Osseweijer, P. *et al.* 2015. Bioenergy and food security. In: Souza, G.M. *et al.* (eds). *Bioenergy & Sustainability: Bridging the Gaps.* [Online]. Paris: SCOPE. [Accessed 2

September 2015]. Available from: http://www.bioenfapesp.org/scopebioenergy/index.php

Pacini, H. *et al.* 2013. The price for biofuels sustainability. *Energy Policy* 59, pp.898–903.

Pena, N. *et al.* 2010. *Conquering space and time: the challenge of emissions from land use change.* InfoBrief No. 27. [Online]. Bogor: Center for International Forestry Research (CIFOR). [Accessed 2 September 2015]. Available from: http://www.cifor.org/library/3269/conquering-space-and-time-the-challenge-of-emissions-from-land-use-change/

Rogers, C. *et al.* 2013. Sweet nectar of the Gaia: lessons from Ethiopia's 'Project Gaia'. *Energy for Sustainable Development* 17(3), pp.245–51.

Rosillo-Calle, F. and Johnson, F.X. 2010. *Food versus Fuel: An Informed Introduction to Biofuels.* London: ZED Books.

Sanches-Pereira, A. and Gómez, M.F. 2015. The dynamics of the Swedish biofuel system toward a vehicle fleet independent of fossil fuels. *Journal of Cleaner Production* 96, pp.452–66.

Sovacool, B.K. 2012. The political economy of energy poverty: a review of key challenges. *Energy for Sustainable Development* 16(3), pp.272–82.

Takama, T. *et al.* 2012. Evaluating the relative strength of product-specific factors in fuel switching and stove choice decisions in Ethiopia: a discrete choice model of household preferences for clean cooking alternatives. *Energy Economics* 34(6), pp.1763–73.

Timilsina G.R. 2014. Biofuels in the long-run global energy supply mix for transportation. *Philosophical Transactions of the Royal Society of London A: Mathematical, Physical and Engineering Sciences* 372, No. 2006:20120323.

Treesilvattanakul, K. *et al.* 2014. Application of US and EU sustainability criteria to analysis of Biofuels-Induced Land Use Change. *Energies* 7(8), pp.5119–28.

UNICEF. 2007. *The State of the World's Children 2007: Women and Children, the Double Dividend of Gender Equality.* [Online]. [Accessed 2 September 2015]. Available from: http://www.unicef.org/publications/index_36587.html

Utria, B. 2004. Ethanol and gel fuel: clean renewable cooking fuels for poverty alleviation in Africa. *Energy for Sustainable Development* 8(3), pp.107–14.

Van Eijck, J. *et al.* 2014. Global experience with jatropha cultivation for bioenergy: an assessment of socio-economic and environmental aspects. *Renewable and Sustainable Energy Reviews* 32, pp.869–89.

von Maltitz, G. *et al.* 2014. The rise, fall and potential resilience benefits of jatropha in Southern Africa. *Sustainability* 6(6), pp.3615–43.

Watson, H.K. 2011. Potential to expand sustainable bioenergy from sugarcane in southern Africa. *Energy Policy* 39(10), pp.5746–50.

Watson, P.J. 1990. Malawi experience in fuel ethanol production and utilization. *International Sugar Journal* 92(1096), pp.59–61.

Westberg, C.J. and Johnson, F.X. 2014. The path not yet taken: bilateral agreements to promote sustainable biofuels under the EU Renewable Energy Directive. *Environmental Law Reporter* 44, pp.10607–29.

WGBU (German Advisory Council on Global Change). 2009. *Future Bioenergy and Sustainable Land Use.* London: Earthscan.

Wu, M. *et al.* 2009. Water consumption in the production of ethanol and petroleum gasoline. *Environmental Management* 44(5), pp.981–97.

Part IV

Broadening the bioscience innovation agenda

12 The potential of biosciences for agricultural improvement in Africa and Europe

Looking forward to 2050

Denis J. Murphy

Introduction

This chapter will focus mainly on the application of new bioscience discoveries to crop production over the coming decades. Current applications of new gene-based technologies are discussed in Chapter 3. During the next few decades, agriculture will be required to play an increasingly central role in providing renewable resources to a growing global population that could reach as much as 13 billion by 2100 (Gerland *et al.*, 2014). In addition to providing food, agriculture is an important source of many other renewable products including textiles, building materials, medicines, lubricants, oleochemicals, livestock feed, and biofuels (Murphy, 2007a, 2010). The major priority of agriculture will always be the provision of sufficient food. However, in what is predicted to be an era of rising demand for other crop-based resources, there will be increasing competition for scarce arable land from non-food crops such as cotton, fodder/feed crops and, possibly, from some biofuel crops (Long *et al.*, 2015).

It is likely that these additional demands on agricultural outputs will be coupled with higher levels of climatic variation and environmental degradation that may directly impact crop yields. This situation will be exacerbated by increased threats from new pathogens and pests (Bebber *et al.*, 2014). Such threats to food production will be especially severe in Africa where the human population is predicted to reach 2.4 billion by 2050 (Population Reference Bureau, 2014). Africa is also the region where current models predict some of the highest likelihoods of reduced yields of staple food crops due to climate change and man-made factors such as increased soil salinity and decreased water availability during the period from 2015–50 (Wheeler and Braun, 2013; Africa Progress Panel, 2015; Suweis *et al.*, 2015). It seems therefore that there are formidable challenges facing agriculture and that any new tools provided by bioscience R&D could be of immense benefit (Ricroch and Hénard-Damave, 2015).

Why the GM issue is unlikely to be so important by 2050

In many respects GM (genetic manipulation or genetic engineering) is simply a more precise and rapid method for the downregulation of undesirable genes or the introduction and/or upregulation of desirable genes (see also Chapter 3). For many traits such modifications can also be achieved by employing breeding technologies that are not classified as GM. Examples include the use of DNA-damaging chemicals or exposure to gamma radiation from nuclear reactors in order to induce mutations in plant genomes. Such relatively crude and non-selective methods have been used in plant breeding since the 1930s and as a result tens of thousands of new non-GM commercial varieties have been produced without any controversy (Murphy, 2007b). Another non-GM technology involves the forced mating of a crop with a distantly related species in order to produce a hybrid plant with useful characters. Neither this so-called 'embryo rescue' nor the induced mutagenesis techniques outlined above can be thought of as anything other than non-natural breeding methods in much the same way as GM is often described (Murphy, 2007a, 2007b). In reality, of course, all types of breeding are non-natural interventions used by humans since the dawn of agriculture to control the genetics of other species rather than allowing them to evolve via Natural Selection.

Probably the major distinction between GM and other modern so-called 'non-natural' breeding methods is that new GM varieties can be protected by patent legislation that cannot be used in the case of non-GM varieties. This means that the developer of the new GM variety has ownership of the plants and their progeny and can stop them being propagated for reuse by growers. However, this situation has been changing since the beginning of commercial GM farming in the 1990s when GM crops were mostly developed by private sector multinational companies and grown in industrialized countries. By 2015, over half of all GM crops were being grown in developing countries, including several countries in Africa. There has also been an increasing tendency for such crops to be developed by public sector institutions in developing countries and to be distributed for humanitarian purposes. An example is golden rice developed by IRRI (International Rice Research Institute) in the Philippines and scheduled for release to farmers in 2016–17 (Kowalski, 2015; Moghissi *et al.*, 2015). As developing countries produce new varieties of GM crops with traits, such as improved nutritional quality, drought tolerance and disease resistance, it will become increasingly difficult to defend the 1990s-era argument that GM crops represent a tool for the imposition of global food hegemony by Western governments and multinationals (Engdahl, 2007).

Genome editing technologies – a game changer?

By the 2050s, biological advances will have made it much easier to manipulate genomes in more radical and precise ways than were possible with traditional late twentieth-century GM technologies. For example, in the mid-2010s several new and potentially revolutionary forms of plant and animal (including humans) GM technologies known as 'genome editing' were developed. Probably the most powerful is the CRISPR (Clustered, Regularly Interspaced, Short Palindromic Repeats) system (Bhaya *et al.*, 2011; Hsu *et al.*, 2014; Mao *et al.*, 2013). In 2015, the CRISPR/Cas9 system was described in a *Nature* article as 'the biggest game changer to hit biology since PCR' (Ledford, 2015). Applying this method to crop improvement has opened up many new possibilities for radical genome modifications (Belhaj *et al.*, 2015; Zhang *et al.*, 2014). Genome editing will greatly accelerate crop and livestock breeding by precise and predictable genetic modifications directly in elite individuals and will also enable simultaneous modification of multiple traits.

This means that breeders will progress well beyond the random insertion of single or small numbers of genes into a genome (as in traditional GM) to the highly precise insertion into a defined location of large numbers of genes, chromosome segments or pseudo-segments encoding entire metabolic pathways into virtually any plant species. Methods such as TALEN (Transcription Activator-Like Effector Nucleases) and CRISPR/Cas9 can be used for gene knockouts, for example to eliminate unwanted genes that adversely affect food quality or confer susceptibility to pathogens or that divert metabolism away from valuable end products. An example reported in 2014 was the use of both TALEN and CRISPR/Cas9 to target the genes of the mildew-resistance locus in wheat. This resulted in the production of plants resistant to powdery mildew disease, which is a serious crop disease (Wang *et al.*, 2014). Genome editing and other methods will be increasingly used to create transgenic livestock with improved quality and yield as well as for reduced environmental footprints (such as methane emissions) and for production of valuable high-value products including pharmaceuticals (Laible *et al.*, 2015).

Precise nucleotide exchanges using oligonucleotide donor sequences can also be used to modify the regulatory sequences upstream of genes that determine agricultural performance leading to improved crop yields. In some cases it will be possible to re-programme genes so that they are expressed in different organs at much higher rates. For example, seed-specific genes regulating storage lipid accumulation could be re-programmed to function in leaves or roots in order to generate high levels of oil in such vegetative tissues (Murphy, 2014b; Vanhercke *et al.*, 2013). The oil could be used for food or fodder, as a source of renewable oleochemicals for industry, or even for biofuels. By 2050, it is almost certain that entire metabolic pathways will be transferred to the plant and tissue of choice so that some crops could become low-cost production systems for industrial green chemicals including high-value specialty chemicals (Murphy, 2014b), nutraceuticals such as omega-3 oils (Napier *et al.*, 2015), cellulases and other industrial proteins (Hahn *et al.*, 2014), and pharmaceuticals such as vaccines, antibodies and drugs (Murphy, 2007c).

Another significant aspect of the new genome editing systems is that it can be virtually impossible to detect resultant modifications in a genome. This is in contrast to conventional late-twentieth-century GM methods where the presence of novel DNA can be readily detected (Ledford, 2015; Lunshof, 2015). Therefore some new GM plants may not carry any proof whether they were produced either via a GM-type technology or via one of several non-GM technologies that could have been used instead. This development has the potential to undermine the entire framework that is currently used for the regulation of GMOs because, for example, it would become impossible to distinguish between a new plant variety that has arisen via spontaneous mutation from a plant produced via deliberate mutagenesis in the lab or a GM plant that has been modified by genome editing.

Legislators in Europe have been slow to respond to such developments. As early as 2007 the European Commission appointed an expert panel to advise it on the ever-expanding plant-breeding toolbox, but the panel's report, submitted in 2012, was never published and there is little evidence of awareness amongst policymakers of the potentially momentous nature of these new technologies (Anon, 2015). Unless the situation changes radically in the next few decades, by 2050 we may face a scenario where the rest of the world, including Africa, is benefiting from new breeding technologies and new genomic advances (some initiated by European researchers) while Europe itself has become a backwater in terms of applied crop breeding and biotechnology.

Genomics will play a major role in crop improvement

Already, by the early 2000s, the application of modern genomics in agriculture was beginning to have direct impacts on crop breeding and food security. One example is the decrease in the cost of DNA sequencing by more than 1 million-fold between 2000 and 2015. For example, the cost of the first sequenced human genome was US$300 million; by 2015 the cost was US$1–3,000 and this was predicted to drop to US$100 by 2017. Advances in next generation sequencing technologies are now enabling the genomes of even comparatively minor crops to be characterized (Edwards and Batley, 2010). This is driving new discoveries relating to crop yield/quality performance and responses to the abiotic environment and to biotic threats such as pests and diseases. In turn, it will underpin identification and manipulation of the genes that regulate such traits in crops so that by 2050 it can be expected that virtually all crop plants and many wild plants will be fully sequenced and available for the deployment of advanced molecular breeding technologies such as genome editing.

The availability of detailed genetic maps and full genome sequence data has already enabled breeders to develop DNA-based molecular markers that are reducing the time required for bringing new varieties to market by many years, including in African crops. In particular, the use of single nucleotide polymorphisms (SNPs) for marker-assisted selection can reduce the time required to develop a new crop variety by as much as 3–5 years. These advances will enable farmers to increase overall crop yields and to address sustainability criteria, while also being able to respond to environmental threats such as climate change and more immediate anthropogenic issues such as salinization and lack of moisture (Zhang *et al.*, 2008; Ashraf *et al.*, 2008). Sustainability issues include the use of energy-intensive and environmentally impacting chemical inputs such as fertilizers, pesticides, fungicides and herbicides. By the 2050s, biological versions of many of these inputs will be in routine use, for example inbuilt insecticides such as Bt proteins and biofertilizers in the form of nitrogen-fixing soil bacteria (Murphy, 2011a, 2011b).

Impacts of genomic technologies in Africa

During the 2010s, the impact of genomic technologies on agricultural systems in developing countries was rather mixed. In some of the more rapidly expanding economies such as India, China, Brazil, Malaysia and South Africa, uptake of these technologies has been relatively rapid, but in much of sub-Saharan Africa it was much slower. However, as we have seen from other areas such as DNA sequencing, the costs and resource-intensity of these genomics-related technologies will steadily decline with time. Such technologies will also become increasingly easy to use which will greatly facilitate their dissemination to regions with less advanced knowhow and infrastructure. Dissemination of plant-related genomic technologies will be especially important for parts of sub-Saharan Africa where there are potentially great gains to be won in terms of increasing crop yield and quality. In future it would be beneficial if there could be improved knowledge sharing, collaborative breeding platforms and the targeting of genomic tools to improve staple smallholder crops in developing countries.

One issue that is especially acute in Africa is that many of the most important staples grown by smallholders are so-called 'orphan crops'. These crops have yet to benefit from many aspects of modern breeding technologies, including genomics (Dawson and Jaenicke, 2006). Many are grown in parts of sub-Saharan Africa where a combination of poverty, poor infrastructure, corruption and lack of security have seen crop yields stagnate or even decline. While a few countries such as Kenya and Uganda are now making good progress in some areas, the overall picture is patchy and there is still a large gulf between those relatively disadvantaged areas of the developing world that are most exposed to food insecurity and the rest of the world where there is room for cautious optimism. Although orphan crops suffer from very low yields and may be severely impacted by environmental changes, they have considerable scope for significant genetic improvement for yield, quality and resilience using new genomic approaches that include bioinformatics (Armstead *et al.*, 2009).

An example of a way forward is the African Orphan Crops Consortium (World Agroforestry Centre, 2015). This is an international effort to improve the nutrition, productivity and climatic adaptability of some of Africa's most important food crops, helping to decrease the malnutrition and stunting rife among the continent's rural children. With the endorsement of the African Union, the goal is to sequence, assemble and annotate the genomes of 100 traditional African food crops and to lodge the resulting information into the public domain. These 'orphan crops' are species that were neglected by researchers and industry because they are not economically important on the global market. Table 12.1 shows the variation in cassava yield in major African producer countries as an example of the potential to improve 'orphan crops'. There are many factors behind the wide variation in cassava yield but poor agronomic practice and lack of access to improved varieties are among the most important. With modern genomics-assisted breeding, yields can be increased to as much as 30 tonnes/ha, which is more than 15-fold higher than in countries such as Sudan and Burkina

Table 12.1 Variability in yields in sub-Saharan African cassava production in 2014

This table shows the pronounced productivity gap for cassava yields between countries in sub-Saharan Africa. Cassava yields in other parts of the world tend to be much higher than all of these values. Lack of access to modern breeding expertise is a major factor behind such yield variations.

Selected country	Yield of cassava tonnes/ha
Burkina Faso	1.3
Chad	10.4
Congo DR	8.0
Gambia	3.7
Guinea	8.6
Malawi	23.4
Mali	14.6
Mauritius	15.0
Niger	18.4
Nigeria	7.7
Sudan	2.2
Uganda	3.3
Zambia	4.6
Zimbabwe	4.6
Average for entire region	**8.38**

Source: FAOSTAT, 2015

Faso. By focusing on such orphan crops it should be possible to make significant gains in overall food production in sub-Saharan Africa by the 2050s.

Radical redesign of crop architecture and composition

Crop plants come in various sizes and shapes and in many cases much of the biomass is not useful either for edible or other purposes. One of the greatest potential achievements of the twenty-first century could be the use of bioengineering to rationally redesign both the overall architecture of crop plants and the composition of their useful organs, such as seeds or fruits. To some extent breeders have been doing this for many centuries but the approach has been largely empirical and reliant on the chance identification of useful naturally occurring mutations. The new genetic technologies will enable breeders to deliberately alter the size, shape and composition of a given crop or organ to maximize yield and/or quality and to enable the plant to be managed and harvested more efficiently. In a recent example, the expression of a barley transcription factor gene in rice caused the reallocation of carbon from root to shoot biomass. The new rice plants had higher starch yields and lower methane emissions than conventional rice (Su *et al.*, 2015).

One of the key factors that contributed to the success of the Green Revolution in the late twentieth century was the development of new cereal varieties carrying semi-dwarf mutations. The resulting plants were much shorter than historic cereals and were able to divert resources into producing larger grains instead of growing tall stems. The semi-dwarf trait results from changes in gibberellin pathway genes that regulate cell expansion and elongation during plant growth (Hedden, 2003). Efforts are already underway to create dwarf versions of non-cereal crops and the knowledge of which genes to target will considerably assist this work. Breeders have also produced dwarf, espalier versions of apple plants that are trained to grow like vines of about 2 metres in height rather than 10–20-metre tall trees. These espalier apple plants produce more fruit and can be harvested mechanically, which saves greatly in terms of labour costs and fruit spoilage.

One globally important tree crop that would greatly benefit from a dwarf form is the African oil palm, which originated in the west of Africa but is now mainly grown in Southeast Asia (Murphy, 2014a). Oil palm already feeds some 2–3 billion people around the world and is by far the most efficient oil-producing crop with yields 4–10 fold higher than temperate oilseeds such as soybean, sunflower or rapeseed. During the 2010s, oil palm cultivation began to increase in its former African heartland and it is likely that by 2050 it will once again become a major crop in western Africa and the Congo basin. This process will be greatly accelerated if dwarf varieties can be produced with 2–3 fold higher yields and much greater ease of harvesting compared to the current trees where the fruit bunches can be more than 20 metres above the ground (Murphy, 2014a).

Domesticating new crops

We need to domesticate new crops because over half of global food calories are provided by only four major crops, namely rice, wheat, maize and potato (Murphy, 2011b). Each of these four crops was domesticated over 10,000 years ago and, because they provide such a high proportion of human food intake, any setback in their production due to pest/disease outbreaks, climatic change or other factors could spell disaster for large numbers of the global population. Since 2000 there has been a significant increase in the emergence and spread of new pest/disease threats to agro-ecosystems. One example is the rapid spread from Uganda of the virulent Ug99 strain of wheat stem rust fungus that went on to devastate wheat crops throughout Africa and the Middle East (Singh *et al.*, 2011). Within Europe in the 2010s, there have also been several serious new disease outbreaks in important tree species including olive blight, larch phytophthora disease and ash dieback.

One of the best ways to increase resilience from pest/disease and climatic threats to our food supply would be to domesticate entirely new crops. There are many non-crop plants that could potentially yield considerable amounts of food, providing they are domesticated into forms that are amenable to agriculture. This process is analogous to the taming of selected wild animals into livestock species such as cattle and sheep. Recent discoveries have recently revealed the genetic basis of the key domestication processes that have enabled people to convert wild plants into productive crops over the last ten millennia (Gepts, 2014; Weeden, 007). Historically,

domestication was an empirical process relying on relatively rare spontaneous mutations in the tiny number of species that now make up our staple crops. However, many
other potentially valuable species have proved recalcitrant to domestication despite
centuries of efforts by farmers and breeders (Murphy, 2007a).

By using the new knowledge about domestication genomics we can create a
range of new crops designed for the twenty-first century (Murphy, 2011b). For
example, recent surveys have highlighted some of the many indigenous green
vegetables in Africa that are often informally used in local areas but have
received virtually no attention from breeders (CTA and FARA, 2011; Cernansky,
2015; National Research Council, 2006). Plants such as jute mallow (*Corchorus
olitorius*), moringa (*Moringa oleifera*) and spider plant (*Cleome gynandra*) are
sources of protein and/or micronutrients that could be improved by breeding and
made available across the continent and beyond. Historically very few major
commercial crops have come from Africa and there is still a huge reservoir of
biodiversity that will doubtless be tapped in order to increase overall food
production, and equally importantly, to address issues of micronutrient deficiency
that still afflict much of the continent (Habwe *et al.*, 2009; Yang and Keding,
2009). In addition to new species of annual crops, there are many perennial plants
that could be usefully domesticated as sources of food, fibre and fuel. Perennial
crops provide additional beneficial functions that are often labelled as 'ecosystem
services'. Examples of such functions include sequestering of carbon, increased
soil organic content, and much reduced soil disturbance, nutrient leakage, soil
erosion and water evaporation. A major advantage of domesticating existing
African plants, instead of growing imported crop species, is that the native plants
will be pre-adapted to the climate and pest/disease threats in their native regions
and tend to be more resilient in the face of future threats.

What are the key future targets for genomics-assisted
crop improvement?

1. Short-term target groups of crop traits that need to be addressed
immediately are:

- increasing overall yields of crop product(s), especially for food use;
- improving the quality of crop products in relation to their particular end use.
  For example many staple crops are currently deficient in key nutrients ranging from vitamins to essential minerals such as iron and zinc;
- improving resource effectiveness of crop production system, optimizing the
  use of inputs such as nutrients, water and labour.

These are the key trait groups that should be targeted for short/medium-term
priority over the next 5–15 years (see also Chapter 3). Improving these traits has
the potential both to increase food production and to reduce requirements for
further expansion of farmland. Therefore they can reduce the overall environmental footprint of agriculture. They can also be implemented quickly in

conjunction with improved input strategies (Murphy, 2011a). Improving the nutritional quality of existing crops is an important objective for both European and African consumers. One example is the development of new oilseed varieties that contain very long chain omega-3 polyunsaturates. These lipids are not normally present in higher plants and have historically been derived from marine sources, especially increasingly scarce and expensive fatty fish such as trout and salmon. Omega-3 fats are regarded as deficient in the modern Western diet so their presence in vegetable oils is likely to produce significant health benefits at the population level (Napier *et al.*, 2015).

2. Medium-term (i.e. by 2020–30) breeding and management targets could include:

- abiotic stress tolerance: e.g. drought, flooding, heat, cold and salinity;
- pathogen tolerance: especially to new fungal, oomycete, viral and bacterial diseases;
- pest tolerance: especially to newly evolved pesticide-resistant insects;
- widespread deployment of genomic surveillance methods for pest/disease outbreaks;
- development of new agro-industrial crops and crop systems to sustainably supply the chemical industry sector with renewable raw materials and useful biomass.

These are mostly complex multigenic traits that will require further investment in crop-focused R&D in order to generate new real-world field varieties of modified crops. However, the availability of genome editing technologies plus the genomic advances described above mean that researchers should be able to provide the biological tools for breeders to address such traits over a 2–3 decade timescale from the present day. The breeding of inherent tolerance (i.e. genetically determined within the plant itself) to biotic threats in crops will be particularly valuable in terms of agricultural sustainability. This is because such plants will not require the use of biocide chemicals, such as fungicides, insecticides, herbicides, etc., which will thereby reduce overall costs and the environmental footprint of the crop (Murphy, 2011b). Genomic advances will also enable the rapid and accurate detection of pest/disease outbreaks in cropping systems (Thynne *et al.*, 2015).

3. Longer term target traits (i.e. by the 2050s and beyond) will include more radical alterations to the structure and performance of major crops. Some of the most important target traits include:

- modifying crop architecture to maximize yield and harvestability, e.g. via dwarfing;
- increasing nitrogen and phosphorus uptake by major crops, including the introduction of nitrogen fixation into crop species that currently require supplementation by external nitrogen in the form of fertilizers;

- increasing the efficiency of CO_2 uptake during photosynthesis, e.g. by engineering Rubisco and the C4 pathway of photosynthesis (Covshoff and Hibberd, 2012);
- introducing apomixis, i.e. the ability of plants to produce fertile seeds without pollination, into major crop groups in order to facilitate breeding and propagation;
- focus much more effort on orphan crops that have high yield potential, especially in Africa;
- domesticate new crops to increase the overall resilience of the global food-producing system in the face of increased biotic and abiotic threats;
- development of perennial resource-efficient crop systems able to mitigate climate change and consequences of pollution.

Summary

Between now and 2050, Europe and Africa will need to confront many challenges to their agricultural systems and particularly the question of food security. Crop yields will be increasingly threatened by factors including climatic change, pest/disease outbreaks and environmental degradation. The good news is that modern bioscience is continually progressing and is producing new tools that can be used to improve agricultural output in order to meet these challenges. In particular, the use of genome editing and genomics technologies has the scope to vastly increase crop yield, quality and biodiversity.

Over recent decades there has been a great deal of bad news and pessimism about African agriculture. For a variety of reasons the region was unable to match the truly spectacular yield gains made in the rest of the developing world as part of the momentous Green Revolution in the twentieth century. This was followed by more decades of unrest, poor management and a lack of investment in modern breeding and outreach methods. More recently, however, there have been signs that the rhetoric may be changing and there may be grounds for cautious optimism for African breeders, farmers and consumers (Sanchez, 2015). This may be the first glimmer of a new dawn for both Europe and Africa in terms of making full use of the burgeoning toolkit now available for breeders and agronomists.

References

Africa Progress Panel. 2015. *Power People Planet: Seizing Africa's Energy and Climate Opportunities, Africa Progress Report 2015*. [Online]. [Accessed 4 August 2015]. Available from: http://app-cdn.acwupload.co.uk/wp-content/uploads/2015/06/APP_REPORT_2015_FINAL_low1.pdf

Anon. 2015. Seeds of change. The European Union faces a fresh battle over next-generation plant-breeding techniques. Editorial. *Nature* 520, pp.131–2.

Armstead, I. *et al.* 2009. Bioinformatics in the orphan crops. *Briefs in Bioinformatics* 10, pp.645–53.

Ashraf, M. *et al.* 2008. Some prospective strategies for improving crop salt tolerance. *Advances in Agronomy* 97, pp.45–110.

Bebber, D.P. *et al.* 2014. The global spread of crop pests and pathogens. *Global Ecology and Biogeography* 23, pp.1398–407.

Belhaj, K. *et al.* 2015. Editing plant genomes with CRISPR/Cas9. *Current Opinion in Biotechnology* 32, pp.76–84.

Bhaya, D. *et al.* 2011. CRISPR-Cas systems in bacteria and archaea: versatile small RNAs for adaptive defense and regulation. *Annual Review of Genetics* 45, pp.273–97.

Cernansky, R. 2015. Super vegetables. *Nature* 522, pp.146–8.

Covshoff, S. and Hibberd, J.M. 2012. Integrating C_4 photosynthesis into C_3 crops to increase yield potential. *Current Opinion in Biotechnology* 23, pp.209–14.

CTA (Technical Centre for Agricultural and Rural Cooperation) and FARA (Forum for Agricultural Research in Africa). 2011. *Agricultural Innovations for Sustainable Development. Contributions from the Finalists of the 2009/2010 Africa-wide Women and Young Professionals in Science Competitions.* Accra: CTA and FARA, s.n., pp.8–16

Dawson, I.K. and Jaenicke, H. 2006. *Underutilised Plant Species: The Role of Biotechnology. International Centre for Underutilised Crops Position Paper No. 1.* [Online]. Colombo: International Centre for Underutilised Crops (ICUC). [Accessed 4 August 2015]. Available from: https://books.google.com.my/books?id=nsnkdqS3reUC&lr=

Edwards, D. and Batley, J. 2010. Plant genome sequencing: applications for crop improvement. *Plant Biotechnology Journal* 8, pp.2–9.

Engdahl, W.F. 2007. *Seeds of Destruction – The Hidden Agenda of Genetic Manipulation.* Montreal: Global Research.

Gepts, P. 2014. The contribution of genetic and genomic approaches to plant domestication studies. *Current Opinion in Plant Biology* 18, pp.51–9.

Gerland, P. *et al.* 2014. World population stabilization unlikely this century. *Science* 346, pp.234–7.

Habwe, F.O. *et al.* 2009. Iron content of the formulated East African indigenous vegetable recipes. *African Journal of Food Science* 3, pp.393–7.

Hahn, S. *et al.* 2014. A novel and fully scalable *Agrobacterium* spray-based process for manufacturing cellulases and other cost-sensitive proteins in plants. *Plant Biotechnology Journal* 13, pp.708–16.

Hedden, P. 2003. The genes of the Green Revolution. *Trends in Genetics* 19, pp.5–9.

Hsu, P.D. *et al.* 2014. Development and applications of CRISPR-Cas9 for genome engineering. *Cell* 157, pp.1262–78.

Kowalski, S.P. 2015. Golden rice, open innovation, and sustainable global food security. *Industrial Biotechnology* 11, pp.84–90.

Laible, G. *et al.* 2015. Improving livestock for agriculture – technological progress from random transgenesis to precision genome editing heralds a new era. *Biotechnology Journal* 10, pp.109–20.

Ledford, H. 2015. CRISPR, the disruptor. *Nature* 522, pp.20–4.

Long, S.P. *et al.* 2015. Feedstocks for biofuels and bioenergy. In: Souza, G.M. *et al.* (eds). *Bioenergy & Sustainability: Bridging the Gaps.* [Online]. São Paulo: SCOPE, pp.302–47. [Accessed 5 August 2015]. Available from: http://bioenfapesp.org/scopebioenergy/images/chapters/bioenergy_sustainability_scope.pdf

Lunshof, J. 2015. Regulate gene editing in wild animals. *Nature* 521, p.127.

Mao, Y. *et al.* 2013. Application of the CRISPR-Cas system for efficient genome engineering in plants. *Molecular Plant* 6, pp.2008–11.

Moghissi, A.A. *et al.* 2015. Golden rice: scientific, regulatory and public information processes of a genetically modified organism. *Critical Reviews in Biotechnology* doi: 10.3109/07388551.2014.993586

Murphy, D.J. 2007a. *People, Plants, and Genes: The Story of Crops and Humanity.* Oxford: Oxford University Press.

Murphy, D.J. 2007b. *Plant Breeding and Biotechnology: Societal Context and the Future of Agriculture.* Cambridge: Cambridge University Press.

Murphy, D.J. 2007c. Improved containment strategies in biopharming. *Plant Biotechnology Journal* 5, pp.555–69.

Murphy, D.J. 2010. Manipulation of oil crops for industrial applications. In: Singh B.P. (ed.). *Industrial Crops and Uses.* Wallingford, UK: CABI Press, pp.183–206.

Murphy, D.J. 2011a. Current Status and Options for Crop Biotechnologies in Developing Countries. In: *Biotechnologies for Agricultural Development.* [Online]. Rome: FAO, pp.6–24. [Accessed 5 August 2015]. Available from: http://www.fao.org/docrep/014/i2300e/i2300e.pdf

Murphy, D.J. 2011b. *Plants, Biotechnology, and Agriculture.* Wallingford, UK: CABI Press.

Murphy, D.J. 2014a. The future of oil palm as a major global crop: opportunities and challenges. *Journal of Oil Palm Research* 26, pp.1–24.

Murphy, D.J. 2014b. Using modern plant breeding to improve the nutritional and technological qualities of oil crops. *Oilseeds & Fats Crops and Lipids* 21, D607. doi:10.1051/ocl/2014038.

Napier, J.A. *et al.* 2015. Transgenic plants as a sustainable, terrestrial source of fish oils. *European Journal of Lipid Science and Technology* doi:10.1002/ejlt.201400452.

National Research Council. 2006. *Lost Crops of Africa: Volume II: Vegetables.* Washington: National Academies Press.

Population Reference Bureau. 2014. *World Population Datasheet.* [Online]. [Accessed 5 August 2015]. Available from: http://www.prb.org/pdf14/2014-world-population-datasheet_eng.pdf

Ricroch, A.E. and Hénard-Damave M.C. 2015. Next biotech plants: new traits, crops, developers and technologies for addressing global challenges. *Critical Reviews in Biotechnology* doi: 10.3109/07388551.2015.1004521.

Sanchez, P.A. 2015. En route to plentiful food production in Africa. *Nature Plants* 1, pp.1–2.

Singh, R.P. *et al.* 2011. The emergence of Ug99 races of the stem rust fungus is a threat to world wheat production. *Annual Review of Phytopathology* 49, pp.465–81.

Su, C. *et al.* 2015. Expression of barley SUSIBA2 transcription factor yields high-starch low-methane rice. *Nature* 523, pp.602–6.

Suweis, S. *et al.* 2015. Resilience and reactivity of global food security. *Proceedings of the National Academy of Sciences* 112, pp.6902–7.

Thynne, E. *et al.* 2015. Phytopathogen emergence in the genomics era. *Trends in Plant Science* 20, pp.246–55.

Vanhercke, T. *et al.* 2013. Metabolic engineering of plant oils and waxes for use as industrial feedstocks. *Plant Biotechnology Journal* 11, pp.196–210.

Wang, Y. *et al.* 2014. Simultaneous editing of three homoeoalleles in hexaploid bread-wheat confers heritable resistance to powdery mildew. *Nature Biotechnology* 32, pp.947–51.

Weeden, N.F. 2007. Genetic changes accompanying the domestication of *Pisum sativum*: is there a common genetic basis to the 'domestication syndrome' for legumes? *Annals of Botany* 100, pp.1017–25.

Wheeler, T. and Braun, J. 2013. Climate change impacts on global food security. *Science* 341, pp.508–13.

World Agroforestry Centre. 2015. *African Orphan Crops Consortium*. [Online]. [Accessed 10 August 2015]. Available from: http://africanorphancrops.org/

Yang, R.Y. and Keding, G.B. 2009. Nutritional contributions of important African indigenous vegetables. In: Shackleton, C.M. *et al.* (eds). *African Indigenous Vegetables in Urban Agriculture.* London and Sterling, VA: Earthscan, pp.105–44.

Zhang, H. *et al.* 2008. Soil bacteria confer plant salt tolerance by tissue-specific regulation of the sodium transporter HKT1. *Molecular Plant Microbe Interactions* 21, pp.737–44.

Zhang, H. *et al.* 2014. The CRISPR/Cas9 system produces specific and homozygous targeted gene editing in rice in one generation. *Plant Biotechnology Journal* 12(6), pp.797–807.

13 The need for international bioscience collaboration and a shared agenda

John Komen and Julius Ecuru

Introduction – modern bioscience presents opportunities for Africa

> It is no secret that Africa's history has been marked by a development narrative in which the benefits from science, technology and innovation have been enjoyed by few, instead of being seen as tools for the development of all citizens. Today this is changing and Africa's leaders view science, technology and innovation as critical to human development, global competitiveness and ecological management.
>
> (Juma and Serageldin, 2007, p.xv)

Science, technology and innovation (STI) policies are currently at the heart of national development discussions in Africa. Across the continent, governments are beginning to actively support STI development as a tool for modernizing agriculture and agro-industry, and ensuring environmental sustainability (Brenner *et al.*, 2010). In all Eastern African countries STI policies are beginning to take root. Some countries like Tanzania are reviewing their science and technology (S&T) policies, while other countries like Uganda have prepared strategies and plans for their implementation. In Kenya the policy and legal framework already in place has given rise to the Commission of Science, Technology and Innovation as the coordinating entity in conjunction with the Innovation Agency, and has launched the National Research Fund equivalent to 2 per cent of gross domestic product. The challenge is efficiently implementing these ideas and translating them into real impact. This renewed emphasis on STI as a driver for economic growth and development reflects the African Union (AU) commitment to advancing S&T on the continent and addresses the goals of the AU's Science, Technology and Innovation Strategy for Africa (STISA) 2024 (African Union, 2014).

Expectations regarding enhanced STI investments are spurred by optimism over Africa's economic prospects. With particular reference to agricultural development, Juma (2010) notes:

> African agriculture is currently at a crossroads, at which persistent food shortages are compounded by threats from climate change. But … Africa faces three major

opportunities that can transform its agriculture into a force for economic growth: advances in science and technology; the creation of regional markets; and the emergence of a new crop of entrepreneurial leaders dedicated to the continent's economic improvement.

Arguably, the African continent could have a competitive edge in developing a bioresource-based economy. Already, revolutionary advances in the field of biosciences are changing the conditions for the utilization of biological resources worldwide. The application of modern biosciences is, for example, assisting in crop and animal breeding and improving efficiency in the production of disease and pest-resistant cultivars for small-scale farmers. Advances in the field of biosciences present new agro-processing opportunities, and lead to diversification of smallholder production and the creation of market opportunities for resource-poor famers. And this would increase demand for local crops, thereby improving rural livelihoods. Furthermore, bioscience innovations help agro-processing industries to be more efficient and sustainable where agricultural waste can be converted into valuable products such as feed, bioenergy and other valuable by-products.

In most countries in sub-Saharan Africa (SSA), the necessary organizations and policies seem to be in place, such as enabling policy and legal frameworks, and science councils that coordinate and fund R&D efforts and increasingly provide support to bioscience start-ups and small companies. However, despite these promising developments there is still a long way to go for bioscience capacity building and innovation in Africa. Frequently cited challenges to bioscience capacity development in Africa are covered elsewhere in this book, such as lack of financial support and venture capital, the need for well-trained human resources, and stifling government policies and regulations. In this chapter, we argue that international bioscience collaboration goes a long way in addressing a number of key challenges, especially in terms of securing technology access, funding, R&D capacity development and bioscience business skills. Collaboration with European R&D organizations is essential in our view, considering the lead role that European research has in the biosciences and its close historic ties with African universities and public research organizations.

Rationale for international bioscience collaboration: driving forces

Stating that international collaboration represents a growing share of scientific and other R&D activities worldwide may be a platitude; still, it is important to acknowledge this phenomenon when discussing bioscience capacity development in Africa. Various studies have demonstrated that international collaboration in science and technology continues to grow (see, for example, Wagner, 2006). Particularly in emerging economies, the international and regional networks created by international collaborative bioscience projects offer important opportunities to acquire funding, knowledge and skills for local development and for scientific infrastructure development. As much of the analysis on international science collaboration is based on scientometric analysis, it is striking that most African countries – with the exception of South Africa and, until recently, Egypt – do not feature at all in global overview studies.

According to Leydesdorff *et al.* (2013), one driver of international collaboration in science has been the efforts in Europe to stimulate collaboration within the European Union across sectors and nations, and with third countries; but this development is also observed at the global level, notably in the United States and other advanced industrial nations for reasons driven by the demands of science. Mass data storage, scientific 'grand challenges', easy access to electronic communications, and less expensive international travel may also be among the drivers and facilitators. In addition, an increasing number of governments in emerging economies invest purposefully in the 'internationalization' of their R&D sector. Economic and policy objectives often add to the importance of international collaboration for emerging economies, particularly those in Africa, in terms of:

1. bridging the North–South technological divide and gaining access to cutting-edge technologies;
2. access to financing for R&D – in many SSA countries, donor agencies provide over 50 per cent of total investments in R&D;
3. capacity and skills development through, for example, training and exchange programmes abroad and skills development in grant proposal writing and project management as well as bio-entrepreneurship;
4. opening up of new businesses and trade relationships with advanced economies.

A closer look at international collaboration based on an analysis of co-authorship patterns in African research shows that scientific papers produced by African academics in collaboration with international partners grew by 66 per cent over a recent five-year period (Pouris and Ho, 2014). It should be noted that most of the collaboration is with the USA, France and the UK, the three countries that are also the largest funders of bioscience research in Africa, with emphasis on research priorities in agricultural science and medicine. While these priorities may be justified given the prevailing development challenges, the authors also suggest that governments and research institutes in Africa are too often *recipients* of international collaborative programmes rather than equal *partners* who provide unique skills or resources. This dependency on international scientific collaboration has the inherent risk that research priorities are determined externally, and may not properly address other scientific disciplines and national or sub-regional development goals. According to Pouris and Ho (2014, p. 2183), 'the continent suffers from subcritical research systems and collaboration dominance'.

Whereas the research cited above presents a number of important policy questions, the key question remains how African countries can maximize benefits from international bioscience collaboration while ensuring they respond to local priorities and policy goals. With this as a backdrop, this chapter will focus on lessons learned from selected cases of international bioscience collaboration with a view to deriving policy recommendations that will support Africa's continued evolution from recipient to an equal partner.

Bioscience development in sub-Saharan Africa: benefits from international collaboration

Against the background sketched in sections 1 and 2 above, there is a growing number of initiatives aimed at international bioscience collaboration and partnering with Eastern African research organizations. It is beyond the scope of this chapter to summarize these initiatives; instead, we will present two cases, described below, that illustrate ways in which international collaboration responds to regional and national research priorities and policy objectives.

A regional approach to capacity development and bio-innovation: the BecA-ILRI Hub and Bio-Innovate

Bioscience development is recognized by the AU as a strategic niche for the continent, especially SSA, which is rich in genetic resources and is largely agrobased. The AU Commission highlights the need to improve crop productivity, value addition and resilience to climate change, which are the challenges affecting smallholder farming communities in SSA. In the early 2000s, the AU through the African Bioscience Initiative (ABI) set out to establish regional centres of excellence in modern bioscience. The Bioscience East and Central Africa Hub at the International Livestock Research Institute (BecA-ILRI Hub) in Nairobi, Kenya, is one such centre. The other is the Southern African Network of Biosciences (SANBio) in South Africa, and two more to be operationalized for West and North Africa. The Bio-Innovate programme that has been co-hosted with BecA at ILRI is an initiative that was also established to actualize ABI objectives by supporting bioscience innovation activities in Eastern Africa.

The BecA-ILRI Hub is a co-creation of the AU's New Partnership for Africa's Development (NEPAD) and ILRI, with initial support from the Canadian Government, to provide world-class technology platforms to support research and capacity development in modern bioscience within Eastern and Central Africa. Serving 18 countries, the BecA-ILRI Hub has emerged to be a strong collaborative arena not only for scientists within the region, but also with scientists outside Africa, particularly Europe, North America and Australia. BecA-ILRI technology platforms serve African scientists in areas of genomics and genotyping services, plant transformation, diagnostics (for plant and animal diseases) and food safety assessments. The BecA-ILRI Hub, through its African Bioscience Challenge Fund Fellowships (ABCFs), has assisted in capacity development of more than 500 scientists and researchers (with 33 per cent female representation) from African universities and agricultural research institutes between 2010 and 2014. This is a small number considering the enormous need for modern bioscience capacity development in the region. Furthermore, nearly 80 per cent of those trained scientists have come from more advanced research systems in countries such as Ethiopia, Kenya, Uganda, Rwanda and Tanzania (Dalberg Global Development Advisors, 2014). So far this represents only a handful of countries in the BecA region. The BecA-ILRI Hub is supported with grants from the Swedish Government through Sida, the Australian Government and British Government. It also receives support from the Bill and Melinda Gates Foundation, Syngenta Foundation for Sustainable Agriculture, CGIAR centres as well as African governments.

Already, the BecA-ILRI Hub lays a good foundation for Africa–EU partnerships, especially for programmes that have a regional outlook. Capacity development in bioscience is expensive and takes a long time to reach fruition. However, sustained support to the BecA-ILRI Hub since 2002, when it was first established, is helping to achieve the AU agenda for sustainable agricultural production and overcome malnutrition and possible negative effects of climate change. With more than US$50 million worth of current investments in high throughput molecular instrumentation, the BecA-ILRI Hub emerges as a regional centre to promote North–South as well as South–South collaboration in the advancement of bioscience for Africa's development. Most regional governments and development partners may find BecA-ILRI Hub an attractive model for strengthening regional integration in science and technology.

The Bio-Innovate programme was established to support bioscience research and innovation activities in the Eastern African region. The programme has applied a uniquely regional approach in executing bioscience innovation projects that allows for regional problems to be solved by joint teams that traverse country boundaries. In addition to allowing for cross pollination of ideas and solutions from different institutions and scientists with different perspectives that results in solutions that are applicable and readily adaptable, this approach allows for ease of exchange of biological and human resources across the region. With around 400 partners from within and outside the region participating in the first phase, the programme has provided a platform for international collaborators to identify and collaborate with partners in the region that has not only contributed to the generation of bio-innovations but also enhanced the scientific capacity of local researchers. More about Bio-Innovate is discussed in Chapter 15.

Maximizing the benefits from international collaboration: the case of Uganda

When considering ways to maximize benefits from international bioscience collaboration, there is a wide range of examples from international agricultural research programmes, some of which are presented elsewhere in this book. As described by Sengooba and Komen (2011), a relevant case in point to reaping the benefits from collaboration is presented by Uganda, which is illustrative for many other countries in SSA. In Uganda an internationally supported, integrated programme for technology transfer and capacity development in agricultural biotechnology and associated policy development has been implemented over the last decade. This is spearheaded by national research and policy-making organizations and financially supported by the Government of Uganda, multilateral and bilateral donor agencies. Uganda is now regarded as a regional hub for agricultural biotechnology innovations and connected with a range of international projects and programmes aimed at developing relevant agricultural innovations. In recent years, a range of genetically modified (GM) crops have been developed and tested for priority traits including those summarized in Table 13.1 (Namuddu and Ecuru, 2014).

The five key factors contributing to progress in international agricultural biotechnology programmes in Uganda in the last ten years can be summarized as follows (Sengooba and Komen, 2011):

1. *Working on a priority commodity and trait*: Research on banana proved to be a most effective entry point for Uganda in advanced agricultural biosciences. In Uganda, more than 12 million people depend on banana for food and income. The crop is grown on about 1.5 million hectares of land, which represents about 38 per cent of total arable land in the country. Farmers rank banana as their most important staple for various reasons including availability of harvest through the year and the relatively low production costs. The most devastating production constraints that have become increasingly serious over the years are black Sigatoka, weevils and nematodes and more recently also the bacterial wilt. These four biotic constraints are very difficult to overcome through conventional approaches hence transformation technology is a welcome option to explore. Under these circumstances the application to field test GM Sigatoka-resistant banana was embraced by policymakers and scientists considering that it could be a solution to a serious farmers' problem. Having been originally developed at the University of Leuven in Belgium, it was also appreciated that the materials needed to be evaluated under field conditions in Uganda where the product was expected to be grown.

2. *Scientific and infrastructure capacity*: The Uganda agricultural research system embraced biotechnology towards the end of the 1990s when the then Director General of the National Agricultural Research Organization decided to join the international agricultural research consortium under the Consultative Group on International Agricultural Research (CGIAR). This decision was tied to a request for support to biotechnology capacity development, including plant transformation technology for Uganda. An international project on 'Novel approaches to the improvement of banana production in Eastern Africa – the application of biotechnological methodologies' was developed and implemented between the banana network

Table 13.1 GM crops under development in Uganda, 2016

Crop	Trait of interest	Status	National and international partners
Banana	Bacterial wilt resistance	Confined Field Trial (CFT), multilocational – ongoing	• National Agricultural Research Organisation (NARO) • International Institute of Tropical Agriculture (IITA) • African Agricultural Technology Foundation (AATF)
Banana	Black sigatoka resistance	CFT – completed	• NARO • AATF
Banana	Pro-vitamin A, iron content	CFT – ongoing	• NARO • Queensland University of Technology (QUT)
Banana	Nematode and weevil resistance	CFT – ongoing	• NARO • Leeds University • International Institute for Tropical Agriculture (IITA)
Cassava	Cassava mosaic disease virus	CFT – completed	• NARO • Donald Danforth Plant Science Center (DDPSC)
Cassava	Cassava mosaic disease virus, cassava brown streak disease virus resistance	CFT, multi-locational trials – ongoing	• NARO • DDPSC • IITA
Cotton	Bollworm resistance, herbicide tolerance	CFT, multi-locational trials – completed	• NARO • Monsanto
Maize	Insect resistance (stemborer)	CFT – completed	• NARO • AATF
Maize	Drought tolerance	CFT – completed	• NARO • AATF
Maize	Drought tolerance and insect resistance (stacked genes)	CFT, multi locational – ongoing	• NARO • AATF
Rice	Nitrogen use efficiency, salt tolerance, water use efficiency	CFT – ongoing	• NARO • AATF
Sweet potato	Weevil resistance	Greenhouse – completed	• NARO • International Potato Center (CIP)
Potato	Potato blight resistance	CFT – ongoing	• NARO • CIP

Source: Namuddu and Ecuru (2014) – updated 2016; Chambers *et al.* (2014)

of Bioversity International, National Agricultural Research Organisation –
Kawanda Agricultural Research Institute (NARO-KARI), Uganda; Catholic
University of Leuven (KU Leuven), Belgium; Forestry and Agricultural
Biotechnology Institute, University of Pretoria (FABI), South Africa; and
the University of Leeds, UK. This project focused on highland bananas,
which is an important staple food for the country. Several PhD scientists
were trained in various universities with a focus on molecular biology
and banana transformation technology. Phase II of this project focused on
developing GM East African highland bananas with resistance to banana
weevil and nematodes in Uganda. Under this project, human resource
development in biotechnology went hand in hand with constructing a
well-equipped biotechnology laboratory at NARO-KARI, so that when
the trained officers returned they had good facilities to continue conducting molecular biology research. At the time of establishing the molecular
biology laboratory, NARO-KARI already had a modern tissue culture
facility. On that foundation, a biosafety containment facility level II was
constructed and technical guidelines defined. In addition to the biosafety
facility, a biotechnology centre was supported to establish a confinement
facility to enable field testing of GM plants under appropriate confinement
conditions.

3. *A supportive policy framework and enabling regulatory environment*:
    The Government of Uganda has been a consistent and strong supporter
    of the judicious introduction and application of agricultural biotechnology
    research in the country. In 2002, the Uganda National Council for Science
    and Technology (UNCST) formulated a proposed national policy on bio-
    technology and biosafety aiming to build and strengthen national capacity
    in biotechnology through research and development; promote the utilization
    of biotechnology products and processes as tools for national development;
    and provide a regulatory and institutional framework for safe and sustainable
    biotechnology development and application. Following stakeholder consul-
    tations and multisectoral reviews, Cabinet approved the policy in April 2008.
    The policy confirmed government's balanced position on biotechnology and
    genetically modified organisms (GMOs), and that the best way to evalu-
    ate potential benefits and risks is to have the necessary research and risk/
    safety assessment capacity in place. This overall position is reflected in the
    country's regulatory framework. In recent years, UNCST in collaboration
    with international development partners has had a leading role in formulat-
    ing guidelines and standard operating procedures (SOPs) for field testing;
    supporting a functional national biosafety committee (NBC); training regula-
    tors and scientists in environmental risk assessment, risk management and
    biosafety compliance; and facilitating international and regional collabora-
    tion. In order to establish a fully comprehensive regulatory framework,
    a Biotechnology and Biosafety Bill (2012) was tabled in Parliament in
    November 2013 and has gone through various rounds of parliamentary and
    stakeholders' review.

4. *Effective communication with stakeholders*: While building up R&D and regulatory capacity, programme partners were mindful of the needs of policymakers and the public in general to get information on biotechnology and biosafety. A communication strategy was developed by UNCST to guide the procedure and process for the transfer of relevant knowledge and information to diverse audiences, and to promote public awareness and participation in discussions around biotechnology, field testing and the development of the biosafety framework in general. The critical audiences within the Ugandan context were defined as: i) the media (print, broadcast, electronic, multimedia); ii) policy makers (legislators and regulatory bodies); iii) scientists; iv) agricultural extension workers; v) the private sector (seed companies, processors, exporters); and vi) general public (consumers, farmers). Each of these audiences requires specific communication approaches and activities tailored to suit their information needs. The communication strategy identified gaps in the transfer of biotechnology information and knowledge to these audiences and on this basis, facilitated audience segmentation and setting objectives for communicating to the different groups. The communication strategy was implemented by partners each taking a lead role where they had comparative advantage or core responsibility. UNCST was responsible for monitoring implementation of the overall communication strategy.

5. *Financial resources and networking*: As noted in the sections above, Uganda has benefited from strong international support in developing its national capacity for agricultural sciences and biosafety. This includes leading bilateral donor agencies such as Sida/Sweden (through BIO-EARN and Bio-Innovate, among others) and USAID, multilateral donors such as the Global Environment Facility (GEF) support to the national biosafety framework, as well as private foundations such as the Bill and Melinda Gates Foundation. However it would be a mistake to regard the process as externally driven, as the leadership and coordination roles are clearly performed by national agencies and organizations (NARO, UNCST), ensuring that international support is aligned to the national agenda and does not lead to duplication of efforts. Building biotechnology and biosafety capacity requires funding. By providing an enabling environment for modern agricultural research, Uganda is very well connected in a range of international agricultural biotechnology programmes, which have all contributed to establishing R&D infrastructure and training.

Lessons learned: success factors in international bioscience collaboration

A partial, qualitative analysis such as presented in this chapter points to a number of success factors in international bioscience collaboration. While some of these may appear obvious, they remain critical considerations in establishing productive partnerships, and in moving from 'collaboration dominance' to collaboration on equal terms. The main lessons are as follows:

1. *Contribute to shared agendas around mutually agreed priorities, with clear product focus*: The case study from Uganda illustrates the importance of science collaboration around a clear and specific priority programme, in this case the national banana improvement programme. This approach allowed for planning around a well-defined end product, defining specific intermediate milestones. Too often, priority areas for scientific collaboration are very loosely defined, both in donor countries and in recipient countries. Particularly in emerging scientific disciplines, such as advanced biosciences, selecting a limited number of improved products as a target – rather than broadly defined thematic areas – greatly enhances the chances of success and ultimate impact. There is no need to embark on new priority setting exercises, as many countries have determined theirs as part of formulating STI policies and agricultural development plans, often as part of CAADP. The key here is to make the connection with an established programme on a product or technology of vital importance, and to avoid a top-down approach to priority setting.

2. *Adopt an integrated approach to bioscience collaboration and capacity development*: Whereas many international bioscience programmes focus on R&D and technology transfer, they must be accompanied by supporting activities toward training and skills development; infrastructure development; and fostering a conductive policy and regulatory framework. The cases described above clearly confirm the critical importance of such supporting measures. They contribute directly to any programme's results and impact, and indirectly to the longer-term sustainability of efforts through well-organized local institutions and knowledgeable individuals.

3. *Sustained and diversified funding*: Connected with point (2) above, a long-term perspective must be adopted on financially supporting R&D and capacity development in biosciences. Several leading donor agencies, including Sida, USAID and the Gates Foundation, have adopted such an approach, in many cases encouraged by a strong commitment from governments in partner countries, such as Uganda. This country's own investment in the banana improvement project initially spurred funding from USAID, which was swiftly followed by investments from the Bill and Melinda Gates Foundation, Government of Japan, and other bilateral and multilateral donor agencies. Over time, the expansion and maintenance of newly developed R&D infrastructure, and the employment of personnel trained as part of international programmes, are gradually absorbed into national plans and budgets in so doing building long-term sustainability.

Addressing remaining constraints

While the above sections emphasize (potential) benefits from active participation in international bioscience programmes, as African countries are starting from a low resource base, a number of constraints remain that should be addressed by governments and government-supported institutions. From our perspective, the main ones are:

Policy and legal coherence and implementation: An increasing number of African governments have formulated and adopted supportive policies on STI emphasizing capacity development in biosciences including biotechnology. Uganda's National Science, Technology and Innovation Policy (2009) is a relevant example, which is complemented by a specific National Biotechnology and Biosafety Policy (2008). As in many other countries there is no shortage of policies and plans, but actual policy implementation remains a challenge. This is especially the case for R&D funding, which has generally remained stationary at low levels. For example, while Uganda set ambitious goals for agricultural development as part of government's Development Strategy and Investment Plan, overall spending on public agricultural R&D stood at 1.22 per cent of GDP in 2011 with modest growth rates in prior years (Beintema *et al.*, 2014), and overall government investment in agriculture (around US$122 million in 2011) falls way below the 10 per cent of GDP mark as agreed under CAADP. In the case of Kenya, the Science, Technology and Innovation Act of 2013 that lays down the legal framework stipulating the STI activities and a research fund equivalent to 2 per cent of GDP is currently being operationalized. Uganda and Kenya exemplify the efforts being made by SSA countries to support STI activities. However, a lot clearly needs to be done in this respect.

In addition to policy implementation, coherence of these policies as well as legal and institutional frameworks should be considered. For example, while STI policies and national biotechnology policies fully recognize the potential from new technologies for economic development, the adoption of new technologies is often stifled by protective regulatory frameworks. Frequently, applications for contained use or confined field testing are required to meet disproportionally high regulatory hurdles, in some cases full Environmental Impact Assessments (EIA). In other cases, biogas schemes that are promising at pilot scale are prevented from up scaling due to unfavourable national energy regulations. Such examples point to the need for more coherent and coordinated policy frameworks.

Being part of collaborative projects can be demanding in terms of management, communication, reporting and networking. In order to benefit from regional and international collaboration, African institutions need to further develop R&D management capacities to handle collaborative projects. This includes sound and efficient institutional policies, administrative processes and capacities to facilitate the management of intellectual property, mechanisms for exchange of staff and material and resources between institutions in different countries.

Continued low level of S&T investments: As a result of patchy implementation of policy goals and legal frameworks, research funding depends heavily at present on external funding, by bilateral and multilateral donors and philanthropic foundations. To correct this bias, it would be necessary for governments to increase their own funding and, in parallel, to provide incentives for private investment in research. At the same time, it would be necessary to provide incentives to stimulate the development of technology markets and, in particular, the creation of local enterprises. These might include: the provision of matching funds for product development, innovation funds, 'bridging finance' mechanisms, and the provision of micro-credit in support of local entrepreneurs. Dependence on external funding can be a double-edged sword in the sense of enabling researchers to pursue personal interests, often with short timelines dictated by donor conditions, which may be at variance with long-term, national research priorities. Similarly, donor priorities may differ from national priorities. Again, one way of minimizing inherent conflict would be for governments to provide clear policies and guidance with respect to national R&D priorities and strategies.

Challenges to bio-business development: Recent studies (for example, Virgin *et al.*, 2015) conducted as part of the Bio-Innovate programme in Eastern Africa point to business opportunities and emerging private-sector interest in commercial applications of biosciences, such as in wastewater treatment and micropropagation of high-value crops. However, these same studies confirm the wide range of challenges to further business development. This is exacerbated by the fact that bioscience innovation funding tends to be concentrated on the R&D phase of the innovation cycle, with little to no rigour and funding towards large-scale testing and validation as well as commercialization. While the dominance of public and donor funding continues, more innovative approaches are required for bioscience innovations. This would imply a greater focus on forging links between the public research institutes and other public and private actors who might play the role of 'technology brokers' or 'intermediaries' to bring bioscience applications to market. It would also imply greater efforts to provide seed funding and venture capital specifically to promote bio-business development. Relevant examples of recently launched, innovative investment schemes are managed by the Alliance for a Green Revolution in Africa (AGRA), such as the Africa Enterprise Challenge Fund, and the Scaling Seeds and Other Technologies Partnership.

Conflicting signals from EU member countries: Specifically when collaboration with EU countries is involved, the conflicting policies and messages at EU level regarding bioscience development can be a complicating factor. Whereas the EU has very supportive policy and strategy documents regarding the need to move towards a bioeconomy, decision-making at EU level on practical applications is often based on perceptions rather than facts. As such, bans in EU member countries were effected on the cultivation of genetically modified (GM) plants, for political reasons, and on the use of a certain class of plant pesticides (neonicotinoids) for suspected negative effects on bee populations. The way this affects R&D capacity development in Africa is analysed in more detail in Chapter 19 of this volume. Clearly, while a growing number of African countries are developing an active interest in plant biotechnology including genetic modification, it is virtually impossible to pursue this as part of EU-funded programmes.

Recommendations and conclusion

The contribution from bioscience innovation to economic and social development is undisputed, and reflected in numerous STI policies and policy statements across Africa. The above sections serve to illustrate this point, as well as the critical role of international collaboration and technology transfer. While the potential is strong, governments in Africa can provide specific interventions and incentives in order to ensure actual innovation, i.e. the timely adoption of bioscience technologies in production and value-added processes.

Proposed priorities for policymakers are:

First, to encourage participation by public- and private-sector researchers and R&D organizations in international science programmes. This is an excellent way to build innovation clusters (e.g. for plant biotechnology in the case of Uganda) and national champions for bioscience innovations. Participation in international programmes (such as is the case for banana in Uganda) that respond to national development goals, should first of all be secured via co-funding arrangements in cash and in kind. Apart from financial support, it is important that governments formally endorse international partnerships at high political level and ensure that the regulatory framework fosters collaboration and international technology transfer.

Second, it is a common observation that technology transfer and innovation are constrained by government regulations, institutional policies and administrative processes; such constraints must be lifted. For example inflexible regulations have impacted upstream activities by hampering international technology transfer as well as laboratory supplies and importation of plant materials for testing and downstream processes leading to proven technologies not reaching the productive stages among others.

Last but not least, STI policy objectives must be matched by real funding allocations. Despite solid economic growth in recent years, government investments in S&T generally and agricultural research in particular have remained at very low levels. Reversing this trend will be critical in strengthening STI capacities and ultimately decreasing 'collaboration dominance'.

References

African Union. 2014. *On the Wings of Innovation. Science, Technology and Innovation Strategy for Africa 2024. STISA-2024.* Addis Ababa: African Union.

Beintema, N. *et al.* 2014. *Agricultural R&D Indicators Factsheet: Uganda.* Washington, DC: International Food Policy Research Institute.

Brenner, C. *et al.* 2010. *Fostering Bioscience Innovation: Lessons from BIO-EARN.* Kampala: East Africa Regional Programme and Research Network for Biotechnology, Biosafety and Biotechnology Policy Development.

Chambers, J.A. *et al.* 2014. *GM Agricultural Technologies for Africa: A State of Affairs. Report of a Study Commissioned by the African Development Bank.* Washington, DC: International Food Policy Research Institute.

Dalberg Global Development Advisors. 2014. *The Beca-ILRI Hub Africa Biosciences Challenge Fund (ABCF) Capacity Building Evaluation.* Final report, April 2014.

Juma, C. 2010. *The New Harvest: Agricultural Innovation in Africa.* New York: Oxford University Press.

Juma, C. and Serageldin, I. 2007. *Freedom to Innovate: Biotechnology in Africa's Development. A Report of the High-level African Panel on Modern Biotechnology.* Addis Ababa / Pretoria: African Union (AU) / New Partnership for Africa's Development (NEPAD).

Leydesdorff, L. *et al.* 2013. International collaboration in science: the global map and the network. *El Profesional de la Información* 22(1), pp.87–94.

Namuddu, A. and Ecuru, J. 2014. Case study – Uganda. In: Keetch, D.P. *et al.* (eds). *Biosafety in Africa: Experiences and Best Practices.* East Lansing, MI: Michigan State University.

Pouris, A. and Ho, Y.S. 2014. Research emphasis and collaboration in Africa. *Scientometrics* 98, pp.2169–84.

Sengooba, T. and Komen, J. 2011. Capacity development for agricultural biotechnology and biosafety decision making: facilitating implementation of confined field trials in Uganda. In: *Proceedings of the International Conference on Agro-biotechnology, Biosafety and Seed Systems in Developing Countries.* Kampala, Uganda, March 2010, pp.9–17.

Virgin, I. *et al.* 2015. *Supporting Bioscience Innovation Systems in Eastern Africa: An Assessment of Key Processes in Four Bio-Innovate Technology Systems,* SEI. Working Paper. 2016–6. [Online]. Stockholm. Stockholm Environment Institute [Accessed 8 June 2016]. Available from: https://www.sei-international.org/publications?pid=2956.

Wagner, C.S. 2006. International collaboration in science and technology: promises and pitfalls. In: Box, L. and Engelhard, R. (eds). *Science and Technology Policy for Development, Dialogues at the Interface.* London: Anthem Press.

14 The social and economic challenges for a bioeconomy

Richard D. Smart and Justus Wesseler

Introduction

Developing a sustainable bioeconomy in Europe and Africa is a key societal challenge. Meeting this multifaceted challenge requires both technical and socioeconomic competencies that are able to exploit economic opportunities, design effective government policies, facilitate public communication and address cultural differences.

The bioeconomy has many definitions (see Chapter 1) and is complex, involving biological, technical, social and economic dimensions. Its activities range from primary to tertiary production and include supplying a number of services. The bioeconomy's scope can be harnessed to find sustainable solutions to society's interwoven challenges such as food security, natural resource scarcity, fossil resource dependence and climate change (EC, 2012). The success of the bioeconomies in Europe and Africa depends on advancements in the biological and technical sciences and timely action by politicians to implement enabling policies.

This chapter focuses on selected socioeconomic challenges facing the bioeconomies of Europe and Africa. Despite the macro-level differences between these regions' bioeconomies, both are internally heterogeneous – contributing to the complexity of the demands they face.

We start by describing each region's bioeconomy followed by a qualitative analysis of their main challenges and opportunities using a SWOT (strengths, weaknesses, opportunities and threats) analysis, which is followed by investigating:

- steps for ensuring that bioscience research and development (R&D) (public and private) contribute to sustainable development;
- the public and private sectors' roles and the power relations between them;
- factors affecting innovation diffusion;
- uncertainties and how can they be addressed;
- the impact of globalization, and how governance issues can be addressed.

We conclude the chapter by discussing possible pathways to success.

The bioeconomies of Europe and Africa

Description

Europe's bioeconomy is embracing a knowledge-intensive phase. Its market size has been assessed to be worth about €2 trillion providing 22 million jobs, which constitutes about 9 per cent of the European Union's (EU's) labour force (Table 14.1) as of 2009. There is scope for growth and improvement through innovation – contributing to the region to remain globally competitive (McCormick and Kautto, 2013). The development of 'innovation-friendly framework condi-tions' is expected to support the sustainable growth of the bioeconomy (EC, 2014, p.3), especially as it needs enabling policies (Carus *et al.*, 2011, p.9; Wesseler and Kalaitzandonakes, 2011) reducing regulatory burdens (e.g. Wesseler *et al.*, 2015). The sustainability of the bioeconomy strategy is chal-lenged because of its potential adverse impact on the environment (Co-operative Research on Environmental Problems in Europe, 2011), while innovations within the bioeconomy such as herbicide-tolerant and insect resistant-crops have contributed to reduce negative impacts on the environment (through the reduced use of agrochemicals, amongst others) (Wesseler and Smart, 2014), and are expected to continue to do so (Wesseler, 2015).

The turnover of Africa's bioeconomy is substantially smaller than that of the EU (Table 14.1). We emphasize that these data ignore that the shadow economy

Table 14.1 The sector turnover of the bioeconomies of the EU and Africa for 2009

Sector	Turnover (billion €)	
	EU[1]	*Africa*
Food	965	no reliable data
Agriculture	381	136[2,3]
Paper/Pulp	375	0.1[2,4]
Forestry/Wood Industry	269	2.2[2,4]
Fisheries and Aquaculture	32	1.5[2,5]
Biochemicals and Plastics	50	export only 4.6[2,7]
Enzymes	0.8	export only 0.7[2,8]
Biofuels	6	0.5[2,9]
Total	2,078.8	145.6

Source:
[1] EC, 2012
[2] Conversion used: €1 = US$1.4 (X-RATES, 2015)
[3] Gross production value (FAOSTAT, 2015)
[4] FAOSTAT (2015)
[5] FAO (2015)
[6] FAO (2014)
[7] Organic chemicals and plastics and articles thereof (African Development Bank Group, 2015)
[8] Albuminoids, modified starches, glues, enzymes (African Development Bank Group, 2015)
[9] Biodiesel, ethanol production (African Development Bank Group, 2015); prices estimated from OECD/FAO (2011)

plays a much larger role in Africa than in Europe. A large proportion of Africa's population (*c.* 70 per cent) relies on agriculture for employment and income (Paarlberg, 2009). Sub-Saharan Africa (SSA) is, according to the Global Hunger Index, the most malnourished region globally (von Grebmer *et al.*, 2014). Projections to 2030 show that the largest relative gains in the world's population are expected in SSA (OECD, 2009). The agricultural sector contributes 60 (up to 90 per cent in some countries) and 25 per cent to Africa's total employment and gross domestic product, respectively. In the first decade of the twenty-first century, Africa accounted for 2.8 and 2.5 per cent of global exports (mostly unprocessed) and imports, respectively. Africa's growth rate was about 4 per cent in 2013 (5 per cent for SSA), better than that of the global economy (3 per cent) thus demonstrating the continent's economic prospects. Noteworthy is that growth performance is inconsistent across Africa, which reflects differences in stages of economic development, availability of natural resources, climate, and political and social stability (OECD/AfDB/UNDP, 2014).

SWOT analysis

A qualitative analysis of the bioeconomies of Europe and Africa using the SWOT technique helps to identify internal strengths and weaknesses, and external opportunities and threats (Armstrong, 2012, p.752) considered important for achieving a successful and sustainable bioeconomy. The results (Table 14.2) reflect each region's contrasting phase of economic development with Europe 'developed' and Africa 'developing'. Europe's strengths: born from a high level of formal education (expertise, skilled labour) with a well-established logistics and communication infrastructure; few, stable currencies; a reliable judicial system; and strong institutions (banks, input suppliers, knowledge transfer), are contrasted by Africa's weaknesses resulting from lower levels of formal education (Obonyo *et al.*, 2011); inadequate infrastructure; a poor judiciary; food insecurity; pockets of political instability; asymmetrical and obstructing regulations (Paarlberg, 2009); costly supply chains (Chambers *et al.*, 2014); low investments in bioscience R&D; multiple currencies with volatile exchange rates (Kirchner, 2014); and poor information networks (World Bank, 2006). Africa's strengths include its 'enormous transformative potential' (Chambers *et al.*, 2014, p.7), abilities to cope with and to adapt to crises (Hall and Clark, 2010), and the availability of land and labour for developing value-adding activities. Europe's weaknesses are reflected by its demography (aging population, low birth rates (Eurostat, 2014)), stifling regulatory policies and divergent views on green biotechnology. Opportunities exist for bilateral cooperation between Europe and Africa, especially for developing the latter's bioeconomy by adapting existing technology. Threats to Europe's bioeconomy stem from regulations (Wesseler and Kalaitzandonakes, 2011) and a loss of expertise and investments to more accommodating and developed bioeconomies such as that of the United States (Dunwell, 2014; Malyska and Twardowski, 2014), whereas Africa is vulnerable due to its weak position in the global economy, inaction by its political leaders and weak governance.

Table 14.2 A qualitative SWOT (strengths, weaknesses, opportunities, threats) analysis of the bioeconomies of Europe and Africa

Europe	Africa	Europe	Africa
Strengths (endogenous)		*Weaknesses (endogenous)*	
• Favourable climate for biomass production	• Relatively inexpensive land for development	• Limited possibilities for expanding primary production	• Low levels of education (literacy, numeracy), low investments in human capital
• High average levels of education	• Availability of relatively inexpensive labour	• Relatively expensive land and labour	• Limited expertise for R&D
• Skilled labour force	• Institutional willingness for improvement	• Aging population, low birth rates	• Unfavourable ratio of skilled to unskilled labour
• Well-functioning judicial system	• Ability for coping with crises	• Slow pace of innovation	• Political instability (regional) and lethargy
• Developed logistics infrastructure (road, rail, port)	• Ability to adapt	• Low R&D investments	• Weak judicial systems
• High-tech communications infrastructure	• 'Islands' of willingness to improve	• Stifling policies for green biotechnology	• Net importer of food (insecure)
• Coordinated framework for policy-making	• Favourable regulations and business environment for foreign fixed investments (some countries)	• Divergent views on green biotechnology	• Expertise, capacity asymmetries for biosafety and other regulations
• Strong institutions for policy implementation	• Biobased production and agriculture a key pillar in the economy in many countries	• Weak networking between science, education, industry	• Divergent views on green biotechnology
• Large customer base for innovations		• Incoherent and uncoordinated polices for moving Europe towards a modern bioeconomy	• Weak information networks
• Low number of currencies			• Poor performance of public sector providing basic services and infrastructure
• Strong biotech (red, grey, white) sector			• Inadequate infrastructure
• High level of R&D expertise and allied infrastructure			• Large distances to ports for international trade, weak supply chains
• Food secure			• Slow (in some cases: none) regulatory mechanisms and weak institutions
			• Falling per capita public spending on agricultural science
			• Internal trade barriers, asynchronous regulations
			• Productivity, earnings: vulnerable to weather

(Continued)

Table 14.2 (Continued)

Europe	Africa	Europe	Africa
Opportunities (exogenous)		*Threats (exogenous)*	
• Expertise available for identifying opportunities in Africa • Strong ties with African countries • Africa presents many opportunities for cooperation with Europe Potential for: • job creation • resource- and energy-efficient, climate-smart productive agricultural systems • integrating into global markets • value-adding activities • improving productivity • recycling energy and material flows	• Strong ties with Europe, common languages, religions, similar time zones • Foreign direct investment in the bioeconomy, especially in developing value chains • Capacity for bilateral cooperation in R&D • Potential for adopting foreign innovations Potential for: • job creation; value-adding • increasing agro-productivity, fish production • connecting smallholder farmers to markets, value chains and agro-processing • revitalizing rural communities • modernizing the African agro-processing sector • converting agro-waste to useful products	• Asynchronous regulations with offshore trading partners • Loss of human capital/expertise to competitors • Competition from other developed regions	• Productivity, earnings: vulnerable to international commodity markets • Volatile exchange rates • Risk-averse policies of foreign investors • Negative influence of politicians and lobbyists from abroad • Asynchronous regulations with offshore trading partners • Trading barriers of offshore trading partners • Changing offshore consumer attitudes, preferences

Socioeconomic issues of the bioeconomy

Research and development (R&D): for whom and the role of the public and private sectors

The private sector's role in the bioeconomy includes: R&D, developing expertise, bringing innovations (products, services) to the market, cooperating with the public sector, providing employment and contributing to economic growth and development. An increasing proportion of R&D in the bioeconomy is done in the private sector and in small and medium enterprises (SMEs) in particular (OECD, 2009). Their primary target is developing and commercializing bioscience technologies for 'high' profit markets. The public sector plays an important role in the 'low' profit, region-specific and local bioscience innovations that are important for small-scale farmers. An African example is the public sector's involvement in genetically engineering bananas for resistance to bacterial wilt (African Agricultural Technology Foundation, 2015a).

A strong public and private sector research base is necessary for developing human capital, making promising knowledge-intensive bioscience technologies widely available, for addressing social and environmental needs, and shortening the time from R&D to market. This can be organized by the public as well as the private sector or by public–private partnerships (PPPs). The public sector plays a significant role – particularly in Africa – in adopting and disseminating innovations to agricultural (especially smallholder farming systems) and agro-processing actors, and for addressing societal needs such as food security, adaptation to climate change and protecting the environment. Although public R&D is important for inclusive knowledge development, innovation and deployment, public organizations have often been less effective in shifting ideas and technologies beyond research. Linking public and private institutions through various kinds of innovation platforms, as is the aim of the EU's Knowledge and Innovation Community Food4future (2020Horizon, 2015) for example, is expected to improve the chances of innovations reaching a broader set of market actors. These links can stimulate bioeconomic activity and the establishment of new enterprises and governments can support initiatives fostering such linkages and knowledge exchange (Schmid *et al.*, 2012).

Thriving SMEs generally promote diversification and establish a base for economic growth (The Banking Association South Africa, 2014). SMEs constitute 95 per cent of firms in SSA, but their contribution is meaningful only when a country is in a persistent phase of economic growth (Fjose *et al.*, 2010). Despite many SMEs in Africa facing high market risks, being trade oriented and infrequently engaged in R&D and innovation efforts, examples of successful SMEs in the biotechnology sector are presented in a feature article by Al-Bader *et al.* (2009). SMEs form the backbone of the EU's economy comprising about 99 per cent of all businesses (EC, 2015). Here, they are more engaged in innovation and R&D, but are negatively affected by regulatory barriers, and in the case of genetically modified (GM) crops, by negative public and political perceptions (Wesseler, 2014).

Public and private institutions often cooperate in public–private partnerships by pooling complementary resources and expertise. European examples include the Bio-Based Industries (BBI) Joint Undertaking (BBI, 2016) and the *Top Sectoren* strategy in The Netherlands (Top Sectoren, 2016). Spielman and Zambrano (2013, p.198) point out that in Africa these 'valuable learning and information-exchange opportunities' are often stifled by regulatory hurdles, and institutional and organizational barriers. Thus governments exercise market power as they control the approval processes of innovations (Wesseler and Zilberman, 2014).

When PPPs form, it is crucial that actors discuss and agree upon framework conditions beforehand, as demonstrated by an *ex ante* study on introducing GM cotton in Uganda. Establishing clarity about the participants in seed propagation and distribution and the government's involvement as a price broker both for the technology fee and the final product contributed to the project's success (Horna *et al.*, 2013).

Scholars (Moschini and Lapan, 1997; Falck-Zepeda *et al.*, 2000) and international organizations are concerned that private multinationals could exercise monopolistic power in developing countries by, for example, charging unfair prices for their products or limiting access to innovation. Moreover, negative views exist about the increased involvement of the private sector in this arena as 'one more example of corporate control of agriculture and its activities' (Falck-Zepeda *et al.*, 2013, p.5). Well-planned projects with good governance could quell these concerns – especially as preventing them would deny Africans access to much-needed innovations. According to Chambers *et al.* (2014), in Africa there is much scope for the private sector's involvement in biotechnology.

Although the public sector has initially been the major player in the innovation process in Africa for GM crops (Sithole-Niang *et al.*, 2004), the private sector was responsible for bringing them to the market. South Africa developed strategies in 2001 and 2013 for public sector involvement in, and for the creation of incentives for, growing its biotechnology sector (Department of Science and Technology, 2013). Importantly, a number of PPPs in Africa are involved with bioscience projects for developing solutions for local challenges (e.g. field testing in Kenya of maize developed for drought and insect resistance) (Chambers *et al.*, 2014), demonstrating a sharing of power. In the EU, the public and private sectors are divesting from crop genetic engineering mainly because of stifling regulations and adverse public opinion (Dunwell, 2014), with the possibility of negatively affecting other parts of the bioeconomy.

In summary, an increasing proportion of bioscience R&D is being done by the private sector: a trend that many fear may exclude some farming communities and value chain actors – especially in Africa – from the benefits of innovations. A more inclusive bioeconomy could be developed by, amongst others, increasing funding for public R&D, strengthening its linkages to markets and private sector actors, and lowering regulatory hurdles (for more details see e.g. Juma *et al.*, 2007). This could broaden the R&D agenda and promote a sustainable, more resource-efficient, inclusive and climate-smart agricultural and agro-processing sector on both continents.

Sustainable implementation of bioscience R&D

Translating and implementing bioeconomy strategies and R&D agendas varies among countries, stakeholders and actors. Europe and Africa can benefit from developing a common understanding, strategies, actions, plans and visions about what a modern bioeconomy should lead to, how to get there, and importantly, take action.

The bioeconomy is responding to the increased demand for food, bioresources for renewable energy and fuels, biobased products and materials, and processing, and the need for reducing greenhouse gas emissions (European Commission, 2012; Pfau *et al.*, 2014). R&D has primarily been targeted at the agricultural and renewable energy sector, especially in the EU (Schmid *et al.*, 2012), although the focus has recently shifted to chemicals and materials.

A successful bioeconomy can be developed by focusing R&D so that outcomes can be sustainably implemented (EC, 2012; OECD, 2009). No single 'recipe' for success exists. Importantly, the sustainable use of natural resources – many of which are public goods – must be integrated into these plans (Schmid *et al.*, 2012). Therefore such work would reveal – on a case-by-case basis – information about where the greatest challenges (including economic, social, political, environmental) lie along the most important value chains, the R&D and institutional capacities, the available resources and the regulatory environment. Actors, and in particular the private sector, would then be able to prioritize, plan, coordinate and schedule R&D activities, and identify where capacity-building for extension services and institutions needs to be established (or strengthened) for sustainably implementing bioscience-derived solutions. The EU's new Bio-Based Industries Joint Undertaking, a PPP referred to earlier, provides funding for biobased innovations, including demonstration and flagship projects.

The level of development and focus of Europe's bioeconomy are more advanced than that of Africa, where for example, food security is still a priority. In Europe, the following are current focus areas: renewable energy, bioplastics, plant-produced pharmaceuticals, and recycling. Public R&D funds have been prioritized for providing solutions to key societal demands, such as improving the resource and energy efficiency of the agricultural sector, making it climate smart and more environmentally friendly under the Horizon 2020 research programme including broadening the diversity of agricultural products produced and involving new industrial value chain actors in the search for new agro-products. Although solving the challenge of food security in Africa remains a priority for its bioeconomy, developing other promising areas (e.g. the pharmaceutical sector) can provide important contributions towards economic growth and in particular attract much needed foreign direct investments.

In the bioeconomy, actors' opinions become important for developing strong supply chains. Efficient and effective communication platforms can help reduce potential R&D overlaps or duplications, better identify opportunities for cooperation (establishing PPPs, for example) and communicate with consumers

(Chambers *et al.*, 2014) and other stakeholders to inform them about current bioscience developments and how they can benefit from them.

Europe has capacity for providing Africa with expertise for training personnel for specific tasks such as the establishment of innovation platforms and aiding with establishing appropriate structures (e.g. integrated supply chains). Such cooperation can aid technology transfer by accelerating capacity building and contributing to the sustainable implementation of innovations. Spielman and Zambrano (2013, p.199) suggest incentivizing closer public–private collaboration for public-interest research, and where ventures could be 'spun off from public research agencies'. Furthermore, proven methods like the 'honest broker' model can be used where non-profit third-party organizations like The Bill and Melinda Gates Foundation, The Syngenta Foundation for Sustainable Agriculture, and UK aid 'facilitate interactions between the sectors, manage the research, and assume responsibility for the use of proprietary knowledge and technology' (see for example African Agricultural Technology Foundation, 2015b).

Socioeconomic issues that the EU's bioeconomy strategy focuses on include job creation, increasing competitiveness, sustainability, knowledge and skills transfer, involving society, research, developing infrastructure and improving supply chains (EC, 2012). This strategy's value lies in its effective implementation. South Africa is the only African country that has a formalized bioeconomy strategy, the benefits of which will be limited if commercialized innovations cannot be exported because of weak demand and/or regulatory hindrances/deficiencies with trading partners. Immediate steps, according to Chambers *et al.* (2014), for Africa to reduce these obstructions include finding ways for eliminating confusion about bioscience innovations, coordinating regulatory initiatives, building regional regulatory harmonization and developing confidence in national regulatory frameworks. Finally, a coordinated multidisciplinary bioeconomy development plan at regional level could form the foundation for the growth of Africa's bioeconomy.

In both regions, social innovation in the bioeconomy needs to be strengthened. This 'bottom up', interactive, social process can be used for empowering groups that are facing common problems (e.g. inadequate rural development contributing to declining local populations, sinking service levels from government, an uncompetitive agricultural sector) to seek solutions, and for rehabilitating dysfunctional (rural) markets (Schmid *et al.*, 2012). An important aspect in this context is to pay attention to strengthening individual rights and to avoid an authoritarian 'knowing it all' approach to, in particular, avoid mistakes made in the past (see e.g. Easterly, 2014).

Another related aspect is to avoid having a too narrow view on the bioeconomy that may result in excluding approaches linked to agro-ecology that centre around 'enhancing farmers' knowledge of natural resources' (Birch *et al.*, 2010). In our view a successful bioeconomy strategy has to build on farmers' knowledge. We see this as being a natural synergy for improving the efficiency of natural resource use.

Innovation diffusion

An innovation usually results from translating an idea into a commercially available good or service for which customers are willing to pay. Innovation diffusion is a complex 'process by which an innovation is communicated through certain channels over time among the members of a social system' (Rogers, 1962, p.79). It is influenced by, amongst others, societal values, everyday practices, infrastructure, local economy, technical knowledge and social self-identity.

Adopting an innovation is a crucial element of its diffusion and is affected by factors such as tacit knowledge (Nightingale, 2012), tradition, religion, laws, environment, lifestyle, human behaviour (Prasad, 2011), availability of information, administrative decisions, government interventions, market price and 'thresholds of perceived profitability and risk being crossed' (Scandizzo and Savastano, 2010, p.156). McCormick and Kåberger (2005) distinguish between technological, organizational and social innovation; sometimes the former two are seen as being a part of social innovations (BEPA, 2011). Nevertheless, understanding the links between these can contribute to formulating sustainable bioeconomy strategies.

A key challenge in the transition towards a modern bioeconomy is how bioscience innovations reach the market. The question of demand and the connected market externalities will be challenges in this sphere.

In Africa, constraints for adopting and deploying bioscience innovations include:

- a low level of formal education;
- unfavourable conditions for entrepreneurship development (e.g. weak or no markets, unfavourable and disconnected policy regimes, financing and credit constraints).

Similarly, in Europe the main constraints are connected to stringent regulatory systems, but favourable conditions for entrepreneurship and access to financing prevail.

Innovation diffusion is strongly influenced by economic incentives (Horna *et al.*, 2013), whereas doubts spawned from ungrounded fears have a negative impact (Fok *et al.*, 2007). In Africa, it is structurally impeded by deficiencies in its biosafety regulatory capacity, incoherent regulatory instruments, and in some cases, the weak enforcement of regulatory procedures (Obonyo *et al.*, 2011) and slow regulatory processes (if existing at all (Spielman and Zambrano, 2013)). Similar problems exist in Europe, but they are less pronounced.

In Africa, farmers' adoption of bioscience innovations such as improved seed varieties depends on their access to, interaction with, and the arrangement of input and output markets, together with their access to credit and technical support. When these markets are deficient (Gouse *et al.*, 2005; Fok *et al.*, 2007), innovation diffusion is hampered. And from work done in Greece, Genius *et al.* (2013, p.328) concluded that 'both extension services and social learning are strong determinants of technology adoption and diffusion, while the effectiveness of each of the two informational channels is enhanced by the presence of the other'.

In summary, innovation diffusion is affected by many interacting socioeconomic factors and actors. In Africa, access to finance, technical support and markets are important for farmers adopting bioscience innovations. Governments, through their regulations, can either hamper or promote innovation diffusion. The prospect of innovations bringing financial benefits stimulates their diffusion.

Addressing uncertainties in the bioeconomy

One cannot predict what innovations will be discovered, how consumers will respond to them, how politicians will continue to exercise their power through regulations, or what will determine political decisions. But, as previously mentioned, a modern bioeconomy can contribute to solving current socioeconomic and environmental challenges.

Socioeconomic uncertainties can hamper the growth and development of the respective bioeconomies of Europe and Africa. Addressing some key issues can contribute to overcoming these uncertainties:

- financing and funding the transition towards a bioeconomy;
- sharing of information on the social, economic and environmental effects of a modern bioeconomy;
- frameworks for assessing socioeconomic risks and benefits of bioscience innovations; and
- a coherent bioeconomy policy strategy.

Financial incentives and the ease of conducting business can promote the private sector's involvement in the bioeconomy, where numerous opportunities for developing innovations exist. But, when regulations are too burdensome – especially for SMEs – the private sector's involvement is often limited to multinational firms.

In Africa, little information for making informed decisions about the bioeconomy is available. Linked to this is the uncertainty of how to consistently keep high-level, influential politicians informed and motivated to act. Targeting research to find answers to explicit questions on the socioeconomic impact of moving towards a bioeconomy is one route to take. Information about the potential social and economic impacts of introducing an innovation can be garnered from *ex ante* studies, which can also be used to model the impacts of precautionary regulations (e.g. Wesseler and Zilberman, 2014). Their estimates show that a decade's delay in the authorization of 'Golden Rice' (rice genetically engineered to contain vitamin A) by the Indian regulators may have resulted in at least 1.4 million cases of blindness. In a more recent study Zilberman *et al.* (2015) estimated the forgone benefits for delays in the approval of corn (maize), rice and wheat to be between about 33 and 77 billion US$ per year. Assessing and weighing potential/perceived benefits with risks of innovations may contribute to easing current negative public perceptions about them (e.g. Kikulwe *et al.*, 2013), but will not result in immediate policy change.

A conflict-free and stable political environment facilitates economic growth. Where conflicts and political turmoil exist, avenues for neutralizing them need to be sought. Such a path may be paved by the bioeconomy through developing value chains in which jobs are created, food production is raised and earnings are improved. We do not know when Africa's politicians will show sufficient urgency to put policies in place that promote local bioscience-derived innovations. The consequences of their inaction has been quantified by socioeconomic studies on the forgone benefits caused by these delays (e.g. Zilberman *et al.*, 2015; Kikulwe *et al.*, 2014) and observed by visiting affected areas such as those in Uganda suffering from the destruction of banana plantations by bacterial wilt.

Globalization and governance

Globalization 'has effects on the environment, on culture, on political systems, on economic development and prosperity, and on human physical well-being in societies around the world' (The Levin Institute, 2015). At this macro level, governance is needed for enhancing the prosperity and viability of Europe and Africa. Protection from exploitation and unfair competition, which could result in joblessness, the dispossession of property and the loss of biodiversity, for example, is important (Richardson, 2012).

Governance encompasses strategies, policies, regulations and controlling bodies that are ideally shaped via participatory, transparent and knowledge-driven processes. Governance takes place at the firm level through self-regulatory mechanisms (e.g. setting of quality standards and formal contracts) and nationally and internationally through standards and laws. Disputes at an international level could be resolved through litigation. Governance issues play a core role in the efficient functioning of the bioeconomy, especially as it influences the commercial fate of innovations.

Modern biosciences have the potential to link smallholder farmers to markets, value chains and agro-processing opportunities locally and abroad. Thus, bioscience innovation can assist African countries to establish better connections with regional and global trading markets, which in turn would enhance their agricultural sectors. Similarly in Europe, investments in bioscience innovations targeted at the agricultural and agro-processing sectors can improve their global competitiveness (EC, 2012). Strengthening local knowledge and capabilities by complementing it with outside expertise and teaching can contribute to enhancing diversity and complexity, thereby adding resilience to the bioeconomy (Schmid *et al.*, 2012).

Domestic policies in one region can have a negative impact on another (e.g. subsidies for cotton in the USA have rendered its production in parts of SSA uncompetitive (Sumner, 2013)). Unharmonious regulations or the lack thereof (e.g. very few African countries currently authorize genetically engineered crops) and exchange-rate fluctuations, border controls and other forms of governance (e.g. fishing quotas, restrictions on logging natural forests, climate-change policies, biosafety regulations and bioenergy policies) hamper trade and disturb the power relations between trading partners. These disequilibria can be addressed via bilateral negotiation, third-party mediators, or in the case of serious disputes, the International Court of Justice, and lead to improvements in governance and hence to a more productive bioeconomy.

In short, globalization means that the bioeconomies of Europe and Africa are impacted by international actors and cross-border governance issues. Governance is necessary for ensuring a balance of power between actors in the bioeconomy, promoting prosperity especially in rural areas and preventing exploitation.

Pathways to success

No 'one-fits-all' path for innovation success in the biosciences exists. Each region will have to tailor pathways unique to its circumstances for sustainably developing its bioeconomy. The successful implementation of technical solutions will largely depend upon the institutional environment and public acceptance. Socioeconomic and technical challenges and opportunities of bioeconomies must be addressed simultaneously (Fok *et al.*, 2007). Schmid *et al.* (2012, p.47) underline the need for socioeconomic research 'to inform strategies, pathways and stakeholder cooperation towards sustainability goals'. Pathways to success require a conflict-free and stable political environment.

Europe and Africa at policy level can benefit from formulating and implement- ing bioeconomy plans that coordinate their internal approaches and actions with clear visions, aims, schedules and systems for measuring and monitoring their progress to implement corrective action when needed, and have policies targeted at supporting sustainable bioeconomic development. Immediate action and bold leadership are often required to translate these plans into tangible outputs to benefit society. Influential leaders in government, education and business need to address the bioeconomy challenges together proactively, as was done in Berlin in November 2015 (Global Bioeconomy Summit 2015, 2015), otherwise their global competitiveness will be compromised and welfare lost as opportunities and their benefits will be lost to competitors from other regions (e.g. the United States and Asia).

Africa can benefit from the establishment of an open-source bioeconomy information system to facilitate efficient decision-making (Chambers *et al.*, 2014; Spielman and Zambrano, 2013). Existing infrastructure and expertise of a regional organization such as the African Development Bank could be used and further developed for this purpose (African Development Bank Group, 2014, p.148).

Governments could stimulate their bioeconomies through policies such as preferential procurement programmes and providing financial incentives for initiatives that will be of long-term benefit to society such as climate-smart farming or the generation of 'green' electricity. Important for Africa will be to combine this with strengthening the rights of local people, and to increase investments in education so that knowledge about the bioeconomy can expand and be applied to solve local challenges. An increase in public and private sector R&D

investments and capacities (infrastructure and expertise) is needed to accelerate innovation development in the bioeconomy – traditionally a sector with low R&D investments, especially in Africa.

The EU is speeding-up its efforts in promoting bioscience entrepreneurship and innovation for it to remain globally competitive. In Africa, current efforts could be enhanced by introducing new financing models and establishing strategically located bioscience and business incubator parks. Adopters of innovations need access to financial and technical support in the form of credit and extension services, respectively. More investments in communication and transport infrastructure are needed in Africa for coordinating and transporting produce in rural areas to markets and value-adding facilities.

Hardy agricultural value chains across a spectrum of commodities can be helpful. These will yield economic and social knock-on effects like catalysing job creation (especially in rural areas) and contributing to regional stability. Improved production in the cotton industry and higher coffee exports from northern Uganda and Rwanda, respectively, serve as recent, inspiring examples (OECD/AfDB/UNDP, 2014).

In Africa, implementation of secure land tenure systems is important to avoid controversies about land use such as 'land grabbing'. Fair and equitable employment conditions need to be upheld to prevent the exploitation of workers. Support for women farmers needs to be enhanced to improve gender inequality by including them in economic and education activities, amongst others. Value-added activities need to be established in rural areas to keep the bioeconomy decentralized and sustainable (World Bank, 2012; Pfau *et al.*, 2014; Wiggins *et al.*, 2015), and to reduce pressure on urbanization.

Europe and many African countries need to lighten their regulatory 'millstones' (Chambers *et al.*, 2014; Spielman and Zambrano, 2013) for authorizing innovations, especially genetically engineered crops. This, together with improved public acceptance of biotechnology, are crucial challenges facing the success of these regions' bioeconomies. McCormick and Kautto (2013) highlight participatory governance (general public and key stakeholders) and commitments to innovation by government (via 'pro-active' policies (Hall and Clark, 2010, p.322)) and industry for promoting a competitive bioeconomy.

Africa has the potential to overcome its capacity, expertise and funding limitations by centralizing risk assessment (Adenle *et al.*, 2013), harmonizing regulations and facilitating cooperation through regional economic communities (Chambers *et al.*, 2014). Africa could reap the benefits of existing innovations approved elsewhere by adopting them without lengthy and costly regulatory delays, which could generate substantial immediate economic benefits (e.g. Kikulwe *et al.*, 2011). Having practical and implementable biosafety regulations is one way of achieving this.

We have identified and summarized some of the more important hurdles that need to be overcome for facilitating pathways leading to the successful development of the bioeconomies of Europe and Africa. There are many unknowns and fears, but a knowledge-based bioeconomy has the potential for yielding a net positive effect on the socioeconomic situation in Europe and in Africa. This will, in part, depend upon these regions having a sufficiently broad innovation agenda deploying new technologies and products benefitting the majority of the population, empowering peoples' rights and especially those of smallholder famers in Africa. Ultimately, well-planned, targeted and rights-based interdisciplinary actions with a sustainable focus are needed for these bioeconomies to sustainably advance.

References

2020Horizon. 2015. *Food4future KIC*. [Online]. [Accessed 29 February 2016]. Available from: http://www.2020-horizon.com/Food4future-KIC-i2125.html

Adenle, A. *et al.* 2013. Status of development, regulation and adoption of GM agriculture in Africa: views and positions of stakeholder groups. *Food Policy* 43, pp.59–166.

African Agricultural Technology Foundation. 2015a. Progress and planning meeting held for Bacterial Wilt Resistant Banana project. [Online]. [Accessed 18 May 2015]. Available from: http://banana.aatf-africa.org/news/latest-news/progress-and-planning-meeting-held-bacterial-wilt-resistant-banana-project

African Agricultural Technology Foundation. 2015b. About us. [Online]. [Accessed 18 May 2015]. Available from: http://aatf-africa.org/about-us

African Development Bank Group. 2014. *Guidelines for Building Statistical Business Registers in Africa. Laying the Foundation for the Harmonization of Economic Statistics Programs*. [Online]. [Accessed 15 February 2016]. Available from: http://www.unsiap.or.jp/e-learning/el_material/sna/1501_SBR_MYS/Guidelines_for_Building_Statistical_Business_Registers_in_Africa.pdf

African Development Bank Group. 2015. [Online]. [Accessed 5 May 2016]. Available from: http://opendataforafrica.org/

Al-Bader *et al.* 2009. Small but tenacious: South Africa's health biotech sector. *Nature Biotechnology* 27(5), pp.427–45.

Armstrong, M. 2012. *A Handbook of Human Resource Management Practice* (12th edition). London: Kogan Page.

BBI (Bio-Based Industries). 2016. Bio-based industries joint undertaking website. [Online]. [Accessed 17 February 2016]. Available from: http://bbi-europe.eu/

BEPA (Bureau of European Policy Advisers). 2011. *Empowering People, Driving Change. Social Innovation in the European Union*. Luxembourg: Publications Office of the European Union.

Birch, K. *et al.* 2010. Sustainable capital? The neoliberalization of nature and knowledge in the European 'knowledge-based bio-economy'. *Sustainability* 2(9), pp.2898–918. [Accessed 15 February 2016]. Available from: http://www.mdpi.com/2071-1050/2/9/2898

Carus, C. *et al.* 2011. *Level Playing Field for Bio-based Chemistry and Materials: Policy Paper on Bio-based Economy in the EU*. [Online]. Huerth: Nova-Institute. [Accessed 2 June 2015]. Available from: http://www.greengran.eu/download/Policy%20paper%20on%20Bio-based%20Economy%20in%20the%20EU.pdf

Chambers, J.A. *et al.* 2014. *GM Agricultural Technologies for Africa: A State of Affairs*. [Online]. Washington: International Food Policy Research Institute and African Development Bank. [Accessed 15 February 2016]. Available from: http://ebrary.ifpri.org/utils/getfile/collection/p15738coll2/id/128215/filename/128426.pdf

Co-operative Research on Environmental Problems in Europe. 2011. *Agricultural Innovation: Sustaining What Agriculture? For What European Bio-Economy?* Project-wide final report. [Online]. [Accessed 15 February 2016]. Available from: http://crep-eweb.net/wp-content/uploads/2011/02/crepe_final_report.pdf

Department of Science and Technology, South Africa. 2013. *The Bio-economy Strategy.* [Online]. [Accessed 15 February 2016]. Available from: http://www.dst.gov.za/images/ska/Bioeconomy%20Strategy.pdf

Dunwell, J.M. 2014. Genetically modified (GM) crops: European and transatlantic divisions. *Molecular Plant Pathology* 15, pp.119–21.

Easterly, W. 2014. *The Tyranny of Experts: Economists, Dictators, and the Forgotten Rights of the Poor.* New York: Basic Books.

EC (European Commission). 2012. *Innovating for Sustainable Growth: A Bioeconomy for Europe.* [Online]. [Accessed 15 February 2016]. Available from: http://ec.europa.eu/research/bioeconomy/pdf/bioeconomycommunicationstrategy_b5_brochure_web.pdf

EC (European Commission). 2014. *Case Studies of Market-making in the Bioeconomy.* [Online]. [Accessed 15 February 2016]. Available from: http://ec.europa.eu/research/bioeconomy/pdf/where-next-for-european-bioeconomy-case-studies-0809102014_en.pdf

EC (European Commission). 2015. *Fact and Figures about the EU's Small and Medium Enterprise (SME).* [Online]. [Accessed 18 May 2015]. Available from: http://ec.europa.eu/small-business/policy-statistics/facts/index_en.htm

Eurostat. 2014. *Statistics Explained: Population Structure and Ageing.* [Online]. [Accessed 10 November 2014]. Available from: http://epp.eurostat.ec.europa.eu/statistics_explained/extensions/EurostatPDFGenerator/getfile.php?file=2001:4CA0:2703:0:513F:A8DC:5F57:21A3_1415633924_25.pdf

Falck-Zepeda, J. *et al.* 2000. Surplus distribution from the introduction of a biotechnology innovation. *American Journal of Agricultural Economics* 82(2), pp.360–9.

Falck-Zepeda, J. *et al.* 2013. Introduction and background. In: Falck-Zepeda, J. *et al.* (eds). *Genetically Modified Crops in Africa: Economic and Policy Lessons from Countries South of the Sahara.* Washington, DC: IFPRI.

FAO (Food and Agriculture Organization of the United Nations). 2014. *Fisheries and Aquaculture Circular No. 1093 FIPS/C1093 (En).* [Online]. [Accessed 5 May 2016]. Available from: http://www.fao.org/3/a-i3917e.pdf

FAO (Food and Agriculture Organization of the United Nations). 2015. Fisheries and Aquaculture Information and Statistics Service. [Online]. [Accessed 5 May 2016]. Available from: http://www.fao.org/fishery/statistics/global-aquaculture-production/en

FAOSTAT (Food and Agriculture Organization of the United Nations, Statistics Division). 2015. [Online]. [Accessed 5 May 2016]. Available from: http://faostat3.fao.org/home/E

Fjose, S. *et al.* 2010. *SMEs and Growth in Sub-Saharan Africa: Identifying SME Roles and Obstacles to SME Growth.* [Online]. MENON-publication No. 14/2010. [Accessed 15 February 2016]. Available from: http://www.norfund.no/getfile.php/Documents/Homepage/Reports%20and%20presentations/Studies%20for%20Norfund/SME%20and%20growth%20MENON%20%5BFINAL%5D.pdf

Fok, M. *et al.* 2007. Contextual appraisal of GM cotton diffusion in South Africa. *Life Science International Journal* [Online]. 1(4), pp.468–82. [Accessed 15 February 2016]. Available from: http://hal.archives-ouvertes.fr/docs/00/17/65/46/PDF/GMC_Sudaf_Indus_1007_preprint.pdf

Genius, M. *et al.* 2013. Information transmission in irrigation technology adoption and diffusion: social learning, extension services, and spatial effects. *American Journal of Agricultural Economics* 96(1), pp.328–44.

Global Bioeconomy Summit 2015. 2015. *Making Bioeconomy Work for Sustainable Development*. [Online]. Communiqué Global Bioeconomy Summit 2015, Berlin. [Accessed 15 December 2015]. Available from: http://gbs2015.com/fileadmin/gbs2015/Downloads/Communique_final_neu.pdf

Gouse, M. *et al*. 2005. Bt cotton in KwaZulu Natal: technological triumph but institutional failure. *AgBiotechNet* 7(134), pp.1–7.

Hall, A. and Clark, N. 2010. What do complex adaptive systems look like and what are the implications for innovation policy? *Journal of International Development* [Online]. 22(3), pp.308–24. [Accessed 15 February 2016]. Available from: http://dx.doi.org/10.1002/jid.1690

Horna, D. *et al*. 2013. Genetically modified cotton in Uganda: an ex ante evaluation. In: Falck-Zepeda, J. *et al*. (eds). *Genetically Modified Crops in Africa: Economic and Policy Lessons from Countries South of the Sahara*. Washington, DC: IFPRI, pp.61–97.

Juma, C. *et al*. 2007. *Freedom to Innovate: Biotechnology in Africa's Development*. [Online]. Addis Ababa, Ethiopia, Pretoria: African Union, New Partnership for Africa's Development. [Accessed on 16 December 2015]. Available from: http://belfercenter.ksg.harvard.edu/publication/17382/freedom_to_innovate.html

Kikulwe, E.M. *et al*. 2011. A latent class approach to investigating developing country consumers' demand for genetically modified staple food crops: the case of GM banana in Uganda. *Agricultural Economics* 42, pp.547–60.

Kikulwe, E. *et al*. 2013. Benefits, costs, and consumer perceptions of the potential introduction of a fungus-resistant banana in Uganda and policy implications. In: Falck-Zepeda, J. *et al*. (eds). *What Role for Genetically Modified Crops in the African Countries South of the Sahara?* Washington, DC: IFPRI, pp.99–141.

Kikulwe, E. *et al*. 2014. Incremental benefits of genetically modified bananas in Uganda. In: Castle, D. *et al*. (eds). *Handbook on Agriculture, Biotechnology and Development*. Cheltenham: Edward Elgar, pp.793–807.

Kirchner, C.H. 2014. Estimating present and future profits within the Namibian hake industry: a bio-economic analysis. *African Journal of Marine Science* 36(3), pp.283–92.

Malyska, A. and Twardowski, T. 2014. The influence of scientists, agricultural advisors, and farmers on innovative agrobiotechnology. *AgBioForum* 17, pp.84–9.

McCormick, K. and Kåberger, T. 2005. Exploring a pioneering bioenergy system: the case of Enköping in Sweden. *Journal of Clean Production* 13, pp.1003–14.

McCormick, K. and Kautto, N. 2013. The bioeconomy in Europe: an overview. *Sustainability* 5(6), pp.2589–608.

Moschini, G. and Lapan, H. 1997. Intellectual property rights and the welfare effects of agricultural R&D. *American Journal of Agricultural Economics* 79(4), pp.1229–42.

Nightingale, P. 2012. Tacit knowledge. In: Arena, R. *et al*. (eds). *Handbook of Knowledge and Economics*. Cheshire: MPG Books Group, pp.383–402.

Obonyo, D. *et al*. 2011. Identified gaps in biosafety knowledge and expertise in sub-Saharan Africa. *AgBioForum* 14(2), pp.71–82.

OECD (Organisation for Economic Co-operation and Development). 2009. *The Bioeconomy to 2030. Designing a Policy Agenda*. Paris: OECD, pp.322.

OECD (Organisation for Economic Co-operation and Development) / AfDB (African Development Bank Group) / UNDP (United Nations Development Programme). 2014. *African Economic Outlook 2014: Global Value Chains and Africa's Industrialisation*. [Online]. [Accessed 22 October 2014]. Available from: http://dx.doi.org/10.1787/aeo-2014-en

OECD/FAO (Organisation for Economic Co-operation and Development / Food and Agriculture Organization of the United Nations). 2011. *OECD-FAO Agricultural Outlook 2011–2020.* [Online]. [Accessed 5 May 2016]. Available from: http://dx.doi.org/10.1787/agr_outlook-2011-en

Paarlberg, R. 2009. *Starved for Science: How Biotechnology Is Being Kept Out of Africa.* Cambridge, MA: Harvard University Press.

Pfau, S.F. *et al.* 2014. Visions of sustainability in bioeconomy research. *Sustainability* 6(3), pp.1222–49.

Prasad, S. 2011. *Controversies in Acceptance of Genetically Modified Food by European Union: Symptoms of Conflicts in Diffusion of an Innovation.* [Online]. Master of Arts Thesis, University of Missouri-Columbia. [Accessed 15 February 2015]. Available from: https://mospace.umsystem.edu/xmlui/bitstream/handle/10355/11501/research.pdf?sequence=3

Richardson, B. 2012. From a fossil-fuel to a biobased economy: the politics of industrial biotechnology. *Environment and Planning C: Government and Policy* 30(2), pp.282–96.

Rogers, E. 1962. *Diffusion of Innovations.* Glencoe, IL: The Free Press.

Scandizzo, P. and Savastano, S. 2010. The adoption and diffusion of GM Crops in United States: a real option approach. *AgBioForum* 13(2), pp.142–57.

Schmid, O. *et al.* 2012. The bio-economy concept and knowledge base in a public goods and farmer perspective. *Bio-based and Applied Economics* 1(1), pp.47–63.

Sithole-Niang, I. *et al.* 2004. Putting GM technologies to work: public research pipelines in selected African countries. *African Journal of Biotechnology* 3(11), pp.564–71.

Spielman, D. and Zambrano, P. 2013. Policy, investment, and partnerships for agricultural biotechnology research in Africa: emerging evidence. In: Falck-Zepeda, J. *et al.* (eds). *Genetically Modified Crops in Africa: Economic and Policy Lessons from Countries South of the Sahara.* Washington, DC: IFPRI, pp.198–200.

Sumner, D.A. 2013. *Effects of Farm Subsidies for the Rich on Poor Farmers.* [Online]. UC, Davis: University of California Agricultural Issues Center and Agricultural and Resource Economics. [Accessed 15 February 2016]. Available from: http://aic.ucdavis.edu/publications/farm%20subsidy%20and%20the%20poor.pdf

The Banking Association South Africa. 2014. *Small & Medium Enterprise.* [Online]. [Accessed 20 November 2014]. Available from: http://www.banking.org.za/index.php/our-industry/small-medium-enterprise/

The Levin Institute. 2015. *What is Globalization?* [Online]. [Accessed 15 February 2016]. Available from: http://www.globalization101.org/what-is-globalization/

Top Sectoren. 2016. Top Sector website. [Online]. [Accessed 17 February 2016]. Available from: http://topsectoren.nl/

von Grebmer, K. *et al.*, 2014. *2014 Global Hunger Index: The Challenge of Hidden Hunger.* [Online]. Bonn, Washington DC and Dublin: Welthungerhilfe, International Food Policy Research Institute and Concern Worldwide. [Accessed 15 February 2016]. Available from: http://dx.doi.org/10.2499/9780896299580

Wesseler, J. 2014. Biotechnologies and agrifood strategies: opportunities, threads and economic implications. *Bio-based and Applied Economics* 3(3), pp.187–204.

Wesseler, J. 2015. *Agriculture in the Bioeconomy. Economics and Policies.* Wageningen, NL: Wageningen University.

Wesseler, J. and Kalaitzandonakes, N. 2011. Present and future EU GMO policy. In: Oskam, A. *et al.* (eds). *EU Policy for Agriculture, Food and Rural Areas*, Second Edition. Wageningen: Wageningen Academic Publishers, pp.323–32.

Wesseler, J. and Smart, R. 2014. Environmental impacts. In: Falck-Zepeda, J. *et al.* (eds). *Socio-economic Considerations in Biotechnology Regulation*. New York: Springer, pp.81–95.

Wesseler, J. and Zilberman, D. 2014. The economic power of the Golden Rice opposition. *Environment and Development Economics* 19(6), pp.724–42.

Wesseler, J. *et al.* 2015. Introduction special issue 'The Political Economy of the Bioeconomy'. *German Journal of Agricultural Economics* 64(4): 209–11.

Wiggins, S. *et al.* 2015. *Competitive or Complementary? Industrial Crops and Food Security in sub-Saharan Africa*. [Online]. London: Overseas Development Institute. [Accessed 2 June 2015]. Available from: http://www.odi.org/sites/odi.org.uk/files/odi-assets/publications-opinion-files/9633.pdf

World Bank. 2006. *Enhancing Agricultural Innovation: How to Go Beyond the Strengthening of Research Systems*. [Online]. [Accessed 15 February 2016]. Available from: http://siteresources.worldbank.org/INTARD/Resources/Enhancing_Ag_Innovation.pdf

World Bank. 2012. *World Development Report. Gender Equality and Development*. Washington, DC: World Bank.

Zilberman, D. *et al.* 2015. The loss from underutilizing GM technologies. *AgBioForum* 18(3), pp.312–19.

15 Two decades of European-African bioscience collaboration

From BIO-EARN to Bio-Innovate

Ivar Virgin and Allan Liavoga

Introduction

In Africa, the ability of countries on the continent to adapt modern biosciences to local needs and propel the development of knowledge-based bioeconomies needs to be strengthened. Adopting and deploying bioscience technologies will require active support from African governments and a dynamic African research for development (R4D) and innovation sector. In addition to government, intra regional and international collaborations as well as functional multidisciplinary innovation platforms will also be key factors in ensuring that the new biosciences benefit Africa (CAAST-Net Plus, 2014). Building capacity in Africa through network programmes has indeed many advantages, such as:

- sharing of scarce R4D infrastructure and key competences to avoid duplication and leverage available resources;
- jointly producing regional public goods while reducing transaction costs and enhancing economies of scale;
- bringing new knowledge and technologies to a broad set of institutions and creating a critical mass of skilled scientists and policy researchers;
- establishing partnerships not only with actors in the region but also international collaborators interested in working with African partners on bioscience innovation issues.

In this chapter the success but also the challenges encountered by two of the largest African bioscience R4D and innovation collaboration programmes are described: the Eastern Africa Regional Programme and Research Network for Biotechnology, Biosafety and Biotechnology Policy Development (BIO-EARN) and the Bio-resources Innovations Network for Eastern Africa Development (Bio-Innovate).

An integrated approach to bioscience capacity building

Both the BIO-EARN and the Bio-Innovate Programmes were tailored to build bioscience R&D and innovation capacity in eastern Africa. BIO-EARN, supported from 1999 to 2010, had its major focus on R4D capacity building. Bio-Innovate, initiated in 2010 as a successor, largely builds on knowledge and technologies developed under BIO-EARN, focusing on creating and strengthening innovation platforms and disseminating bioscience technologies to various end-users.

The overall aim of both programmes has been to develop a comprehensive regional network of scientists, private sector actors and policymakers that would form a solid base for R4D collaboration, innovation and policy development. A key feature in both programmes is their integration of technology, policy issues and capacity building into project activities. Human capacity building included training in bioscience policy analysis, handling of intellectual property issues, basic elements of business development as well as studies on innovation structures. This approach has been successful at facilitating dialogue between scientists and policymakers and in initiating strong public–private partnerships leading to a comprehensive and integrated capacity-building process. The link between researchers in Europe, with a focus on Swedish researchers and researchers in Africa, has also been a strong feature in both programmes.

BIO-EARN and Bio-Innovate have been unique in Africa in that they have not only been able to link agricultural, environmental and industrial biosciences in the same programme but also insights on how to move bioscience R4D and innovations developed by the public sector further along the innovation chain, towards market introduction, in the eastern Africa region. Figure 15.1 depicts a chronology of activities that spans the different phases of the two programmes

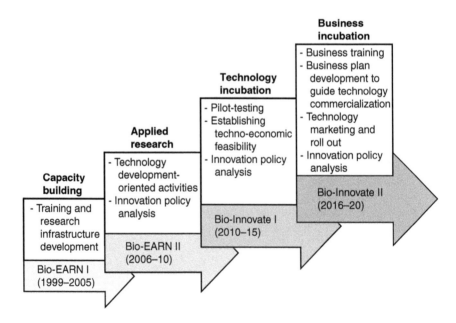

Figure 15.1 The evolution of the BIO-EARN and Bio-Innovate programmes

from 1999 to date and into the future. It has taken over 15 years for some of these R4D ideas to be conceptualized, developed and validated as potentially commercially useful bioscience technologies. It will take a few more years, additional funding and incubation for these promising technologies to be impactful on the ground. This is a reflection of the challenges affecting bio-innovation processes in the region, some of which are highlighted later in this chapter. The experiences of both programmes reinforce the importance for African governments and development partners to have a long-term approach to investments in bioscience R4D and innovation to reap the benefits from modern biosciences.

The BIO-EARN Programme

Background

The BIO-EARN programme was developed by the Stockholm Environment Institute (SEI) in close collaboration with eastern African institutions. Funding for BIO-EARN came from the Swedish International Development Cooperation Agency (Sida) which invested 160 million SEK (20 million US$) covering the period 1999–2010. The goal of the programme was to develop capacity and competencies to effectively use and integrate modern biotechnology in agriculture, industry and in environmental management in Ethiopia, Kenya, Tanzania and Uganda.

The first and second phases of the BIO-EARN programme (1999–2005) focused on building human and infrastructural capacity for using advanced agricultural, environmental and industrial biotechnology, and on developing biopolicy and biosafety regulatory skills. Six Swedish research institutions closely collaborated with eastern African partners in developing new capacities and knowledge that provided an avenue for advanced biotechnology and biosafety training at MSc and PhD levels. In these first two phases, activities centred around 20 biotechnology and biosafety PhD projects and a series of technical training workshops and policy seminars. A positive evaluation in 2004 resulted in a third and final BIO-EARN phase running from 2006 to 2010. As a result, nine regional research consortia were created, involving science and business actors, engaged in research and development (R&D) with a focus on crop productivity, value addition and agro-processing, waste treatment and conversion.

BIO-EARN Impact

BIO-EARN's outputs and impact were monitored and assessed both internally and externally with key impact areas as described below.

R&D outputs

BIO-EARN developed knowledge, technologies and products in the following areas:

1. increased crop productivity using advanced biotechnology tools enabling the selection of sorghum and millet cultivars more tolerant to drought, pests or poor soils;
2. production of disease-free planting materials for coffee, enset, sweet potatoes, sorghum and bananas;
3. value addition and modern agro-processing technologies for cassava, sorghum and millet.
4. Agro-waste treatment and conversion of waste to useful products, including converting slaughter house, sisal and fish processing waste to products such as biogas, biofertilizers and commercially attractive fatty acids.

In all the BIO-EARN projects, there were advances in collaborative research, product and technology development manifested through the more than 90 peer-reviewed publications developed through the projects. Even though none of the potential technologies were commercially disseminated, several of these technologies were further developed and refined under Bio-Innovate (see case studies below).

Trained core of bioscience leaders

One of the most important achievements of the BIO-EARN was the training of a new cadre of young scientists. In total BIO-EARN trained 31 eastern African PhDs and 36 MScs.

Equally important for BIO-EARN was the high percentage of trained researchers retained in their home institutions, which has contributed significantly to strengthening local and national bioscience innovation capacity. A majority of these graduates are now senior researchers training the next generation of scientists and generating funding opportunities. They have also expanded their regional and international networks extensively and are building new research groups.

Given their exposure to biotechnology policy issues a substantial number of the PhD graduates are also engaged in national policy development and decision-making systems.

Building R&D infrastructure

Besides the human factor, a well-equipped and managed R&D infrastructure is a necessity for countries that wish to take part in the bioscience revolution. BIO-EARN contributed significantly to the setting up of functional, well-equipped laboratories in 17 key eastern African institutions. Approximately US$5 million was invested in infrastructure support for:

*   improved research facilities;
*   modern research equipment;
*   provision of laboratory consumables including procedures and robust channels for procuring and importing necessary chemicals and reagents.

A case in point, illustrative of all network institutions and countries is Makerere University in Uganda where BIO-EARN contributed substantially to the improvement of research infrastructure and equipment. These investments had significant spill-over effects in terms of enabling new teaching programmes at Makerere University. The infrastructural improvement enhanced network partners' ability to compete for national and international R&D grants.

Strengthening research management capabilities

Being part of collaborative projects can be demanding in terms of management, communication, reporting and networking. BIO-EARN network members went through extensive training in research management and undertook short courses in science and proposal writing, strengthening the capabilities of local institutions to participate as equal partners in international and regional R4D collaborative initiatives. BIO-EARN also supported development of institutional research policies, technology transfer and benefit-sharing structures, administrative routines and capacities to facilitate the exchange of staff and material and other resources between institutions in different countries.

Towards an enabling policy environment

The programme stimulated the much-needed dialogue between policy makers and scientists on key bio-policy issues, both nationally and regionally, contributing to a more enabling environment for bioscience adoption, innovation and technology dissemination. This included support in the following areas:

- biosafety risk assessment capacity of GM crops;
- product development partnerships between academia and the private sector;
- assisting network institutions to develop technology transfer structures including institutional Intellectual Property (IP) policies, capacity to manage IP and development of appropriate contractual agreements regulating ownership of IP and sharing of potential benefits arising from the R&D projects;
- analysis of the bioscience innovation systems in the region and recommendations on how these innovation systems could be made more functional and better contribute to sustainable development;
- assessments of the potential socioeconomic benefits emanating from the various BIO-EARN projects, assisting policymakers in the region to perform cost–benefit analysis of using biosciences.

An efficient platform for collaboration

BIO-EARN catalysed and developed regional links among a number of collaborative initiatives in the region through graduate student exchange programmes allowing for experience sharing in science and policy. BIO-EARN was also an efficient mechanism for linking eastern African researchers and public R&D institutions to suitable partners in the private sector and international centres of excellence.

The programme also demonstrated the benefit of building strong collaborative links with researchers in Europe, particularly in Sweden, benefiting institutional development in eastern Africa but also in Sweden. Swedish researchers were able to develop skills and mechanisms that enabled them to contribute to solving problems in Africa.

The Bio-Innovate Programme

Background

The Bio-resources Innovations Network for Eastern Africa Development (Bio-Innovate) Programme is a regional initiative established to support bioscience research and innovation activities in eastern Africa. The programme, initiated in 2010, succeeded BIO-EARN and is supported by Sida with funding of 90 million SEK (12 million US$) and modest matching funds from the private sector. Phase I of the programme ended in 2015 with a second phase to begin in 2016.

Bio-Innovate has deployed a regional competitive multi-country, multidisciplinary and multi-stakeholder innovation funding mechanism assembling critical players along the innovation chain to catalyse the translation of bioscience research outputs into scalable and impactful innovations. Altogether, the programme has supported nine multidisciplinary innovation and policy consortia involving 57 implementing partners drawn from research organizations/academia, private sector and other delivery agents in the six eastern Africa countries of Burundi, Ethiopia, Kenya, Rwanda, Tanzania and Uganda.

The programme is applying an innovation system approach recognizing that active information flow among actors, enterprises and institutions is key to innovation processes (Lundvall, 1992). The programme recognizes that public research organizations and academia in eastern Africa have limited capability to move research outputs along the innovation chain primarily due to the absence of effective technology and business incubation mechanisms necessary to steer technological solutions to the marketplace in the region.

Bio-Innovate is therefore tailored to provide specific services to support innovation processes spearheaded by public research organizations in partnership with the private sector in the eastern Africa region. This support includes project management backstopping, technology incubation, intellectual property audits and freedom to operate assessment, feasibility and techno-economic analysis, capacity building at both technical and business level as well as innovation policy analysis.

The technology innovation platform created by Bio-Innovate provides mechanisms in which technologies could transit from the more controlled laboratory and academic experimental environment to be tested and applied in the 'real world'.

On the two occasions that Bio-Innovate has been reviewed, independent reviewers acknowledged that the technology development aspects of the programme were largely successful in linking academic and business partners. However, the reviewers also noted 'application of entrepreneurial thinking and stronger, more balanced partnerships with the private sector would enable the programme to gain greater traction in satisfying its mission objectives' (Crouch and Bloch, 2013, p.ix). The reviewers therefore called for a stronger business development orientation throughout the programme to assist the most commercially attractive technologies to attract further private sector investments thereby increasing their chances of being deployed and adopted at scale.

Bio-Innovate Phase II will draw lessons and build on Phase I with more resources geared towards supporting the business aspects of the innovation projects. Phase II will partner with business incubation expertise to create a functional bioscience innovation platform able to move bio-innovations all the way to the market.

Case study: Higher productivity returns from root crops

Sweet potato and cassava are important food security crops in Africa. Despite their great potential to alleviate malnutrition and poverty, and despite being priority crops in eastern African agricultural research programmes, cassava and sweet potato are still underdeveloped with very low productivity.

Under the BIO-EARN programme a project was started whose key objectives were to produce sweet potato and cassava varieties with improved yields and nutritional value, and with resistance to viral diseases such as cassava brown streak virus disease (CBSVD) and sweet potato virus disease (SPVD) which can cause yield losses of more than 90 per cent. Other objectives were to develop more efficient methods for understanding, diagnosing and managing serious crop diseases and to establish methods for producing disease-free seedlings.

During BIO-EARN, after a series of selections 15 promising sweet potato varieties were tested in Uganda before their final release through the national variety release committee. Building on these achievements, the project was supported further under Bio-Innovate where protocols and procedures for rapid multiplication of sweet potato tissue culture plants in the laboratories, screen-houses and in the field were developed and have been adopted by micro-propagation companies in Uganda and Kenya. A model seed system for delivery of sweet potatoes involving private micro-propagation companies, research centres and entrepreneurial farmers that enables poor farmers to access disease-free clean planting material was pilot-tested in Kenya and Uganda. This is exemplified by Mawesse Ronald, a sweet potato farmer from Kikoota Village, Mpigi District, Uganda, who says 'Since I started using clean and improved sweet potato vines from a local sweet potato tissue culture seedling multiplier, my production has increased from 3 tonnes per acre to 8 tonnes. I started sweet potato farming in 2009 and with money from it I have built myself a house, gotten married and am now able to support my wife and child'.

Bio-Innovate Impact

Bio-Innovate's primary goal has been to create effective partnerships along the innovation chain necessary to take technologies to end users. The programme has demonstrated that it is possible to create bioscience innovation platforms around specific technologies that bring together the public and private sectors to generate and move the bio-innovations along the innovation chain.

Building on BIO-EARN the programme similarly supported three strategic areas of biosciences:

- increased crop productivity for traditionally strategic staple crops including sorghum, finger millet, cassava and sweet potato using advanced biotechnology tools and application of biopesticide technology to help farmers adapt to climate change as well as tackle disease and pest challenges in an environmentally sustainable manner;
- sustainable mechanisms of adding value to local agro-produce, focusing on traditional grains and legumes;
- managing and converting agro-waste to useful products such as biogas, food and biofertilizer.

In total eight technologies and supporting processes were developed and refined, five of which can trace their origins from BIO-EARN. Some of these technologies have been validated by regulatory authorities in the respective countries and adopted by market actors at pilot scale, and are ready for commercialization and scale-up provided that the business cases are sufficiently attractive and financed. The two case studies in this chapter depict the link between the two programmes in moving bio-innovations further along the innovation chain to the market.

Innovation outputs

The projects funded by Bio-Innovate have moved in varied ways along the innovation chain from the laboratory to the market, and at the end of the first phase of the programme period they can be roughly placed in the following product development stages:

- concept validation stage;
- pilot-testing stage;
- commercialization stage.

1. Technologies reaching concept validation level
These are technologies that were proven to work well in a controlled experimental environment i.e. laboratory or experimental field.

- Fifteen promising drought-tolerant finger millet lines were identified in Ethiopia, Kenya and Tanzania and one line that is very early maturing and drought tolerant was recommended for varietal release in Kenya and another in Ethiopia.

- Six hundred and thirty-four finger millet landraces and 121 cross-compatible wild accessions were collected, conserved and characterized and will be invaluable sources of desirable genetic material for future crop improvement in the region.
- Novel stay-green sorghum lines were identified in Ethiopia and will be used in breeding for drought tolerance.
- Advanced bioscience breeding tools were developed, leading towards a more efficient breeding process that generates higher yielding finger millet varieties with resistance to biotic and abiotic stresses. The process of integrating these tools into national breeding programmes is now underway.

2. Technologies reaching pilot-testing level

These are technologies that were proven to work well when pilot-tested in expected conditions and environment with the participation of end users.

- At least 20 varieties of sweet potato and nine of cassava exhibiting disease resistance and drought tolerance adaptable to diverse agro-ecological zones in Kenya, Uganda, Ethiopia and Tanzania were identified and tested in farmers' fields.
- A model seed system for delivery of vegetatively propagated crops (sweet potatoes) involving private micro-propagation companies, research centres and entrepreneurial farmers that enable rural farmers to access disease-free clean planting material was tested in Kenya and Uganda.
- Improved protocols and procedures for rapid multiplication of sweet potato tissue culture plants in the laboratories, screen-houses and in the field were developed and have been adopted by micro-propagating companies in Uganda and Kenya.
- Fungal-based biopesticides products have been developed for tomatoes, maize and eggplant and proven to work in farmers' fields. Two of these products have been registered in Kenya, Tanzania and Ghana.
- Five prototype food products have been developed from sorghum including a non-alcoholic clear malt drink, instant and composite flours, snack bars and puffs. Three of the products, i.e. clear malt drink, instant sorghum flour and composite sorghum flour, are already on the market at pilot-scale in Tanzania, Uganda and Ethiopia respectively.
- Technologies for producing mushrooms from sisal and coffee post-harvest waste in Tanzania and Kenya have been pilot-tested.
- Technology for producing biogas, fertilizer and reusable water from slaughterhouse and tannery wastewater that also removes 99 per cent of the pollutants has been pilot-tested in Uganda and Ethiopia respectively.

3. Technologies reaching commercialization level

These technologies were proven to work at full-scale and/or were adopted and used in commercial settings.

- Seven new varieties of canning beans that are drought tolerant and disease resistant and that meet industrial processing requirements have been validated by regulators and registered in Kenya and Ethiopia, and ten are expected to be released by the end of 2016 in Ethiopia, Tanzania, Rwanda and Burundi. Farmers have been contracted by food-processing companies on a pilot-scale in the first season to grow the new lines in Kenya.
- A full-scale integrated wastewater treatment system has been installed at a banana-processing brewing factory in Tanzania generating biogas and biofertilizer.

Case study: Turning agro-waste into biogas, fertilizer and water for irrigation

The technology to purify agro-wastewater using wetlands was conceptualized and tested at experimental level during BIO-EARN. This idea was developed and refined further to an integrated process that combines wetland technology with waste conversion to additionally produce bioenergy and biofertilizer, and was pilot-tested under Bio-Innovate.

Banana Investment Limited (BIL) is located at the heart of a rural community in Arusha, Tanzania, and processes 25 metric tonnes of peeled ripe bananas per week to produce wine in a process that also produces about 400 m^3 of wastewater per day. This agro-processing company was considered an environmental problem like many agro-processing factories in eastern Africa before the intervention of the Bio-Innovate supported project. The factory was not properly treating its wastewater from the banana wine manufacturing process and discharged it into the nearby river Kijenge. Due to protests from the community, the government through the environmental regulatory agency threatened to close down the facility unless action was taken by management to treat the waste. The company also unsustainably used 3,600 m^3 of wood fuel and diesel oil to run the factory costing the company in excess of US$50,000 per year.

All this began to change in 2011 after scientists from the University of Dar es Salaam, with support from Bio-Innovate, started the development of an integrated wastewater treatment facility for the processing plant. 'The purpose of our engagement with this project was to show that environmental problems can be solved through modern biosciences and by proper collaboration and integration with academia', says Professor Karoli Njau of University of Dar es Salaam, the team leader.

Through Bio-Innovate support and additional investment by BIL in the order of US$170,000, a full-scale integrated wastewater treatment system has been installed at the processing facility that treats 100 per cent of the agro-industrial waste and generates 100 m^3 of biogas gas per day that is used to substitute a significant portion of the energy that was hitherto produced from diesel and wood fuel. A certificate of compliance has been issued to BIL by regulators certifying that the treated wastewater meets Tanzanian environmental standards and can be used for irrigation of crops. The treated water has therefore been redirected for reuse in a fish pond and irrigation in neighbouring agricultural farms.

'Before, our problem was that we had too much waste causing a whole range of problems. Today with the new treatment facility converting waste to useful products, I feel like we are producing too little waste', says Mr Adolf Olomi, the company's managing Director.

Innovation policy analysis

The programme conducted targeted innovation policy analysis with the aim of identifying bottlenecks for innovation uptake. Some of the outputs included:

- an assessment of the programme from an innovation system perspective that revealed the need for specific policies, incentives, business incubation and financial mechanisms for bio-innovation in the region;
- a review of science, technology and innovation (STI) policies in eastern Africa that revealed that while all countries in the region have STI policies, their broad nature makes them ineffective;
- specific intervention strategies on policy and regulatory incentives for adoption of innovative solutions for agro-industrial wastewater management and utilization of biopesticides for Kenya, Uganda, Ethiopia and Tanzania.
- publication of the book *Bio-Innovate: Fostering a Bioeconomy in Eastern Africa* discussing what needs to be done for countries in the region to transform into vibrant bioeconomies.

Capacity building

Transiting into knowledge-based bioeconomies by countries in eastern Africa requires R&D infrastructure with the capacity for research translation, i.e. knowledge and knowhow to create value from R&D as well as managing intellectual assets, business development and bioentrepreneurship.

Bio-Innovate applied an integrated approach to capacity building that embedded training activities into product development activities. The programme's capacity development ranged from highly technical fields like bioinformatics and genomics for breeders to intellectual asset management and fundamentals of business development. The actors in the programme were also exposed to results-based management tools that enhanced the project management capacity.

Training and awareness-raising activities involved more than 400 scientists, market actors and policymakers directly connected to the activities in the nine consortia projects. At the student level 38 MScs and seven PhDs were graduated through the programme. Another outcome linked to the capacity-building activities was the publication of over 50 peer-reviewed articles in international journals.

Bio-Innovate also supported targeted R&D infrastructural development in some participating public research organizations. As an example, three food-processing research units in three institutions in Kenya, Tanzania and Uganda had their old equipment upgraded, and as a consequence of their partnerships with private processing companies they developed and they pilot-marketed new canning bean varieties, sorghum extruded products and a beverage in the three countries.

Governance of the programmes

The two programmes have supported bioscience innovation and capacity-building activities in eastern Africa (see Figure 15.1) for the past 16 years. During the initial seven years (1999–2006), BIO-EARN was coordinated by the Stockholm Environment Institute (SEI) in collaboration with the Uganda National Council for Science and Technology (UNCST). To mark the regional eastern Africa ownership, the management and coordination of BIO-EARN was transferred to the Inter-University Council for East Africa (IUCEA) in Uganda (2006–9). In 2010 BIO-EARN changed its name to Bio-Innovate to signify a change in strategic focus from a research capacity-building orientation to product-oriented innovation activities. In an effort to enhance the administration of the programme and leverage synergies with other initiatives in the bioscience space in the region, Bio-Innovate was hosted at the International Livestock Research Institute (ILRI) in Nairobi, Kenya. In both programmes a designated Programme Management Office handled the day-to-day management with support from a technical advisory committee that provided implementation oversight to the programme, peer review of the competitive grant scheme and monitoring.

The partners involved, drawn from academia, governments, private sector and civil society in the region have jointly formulated funding priorities and projects in the two programmes to ensure local relevance. The close dialogue that has been cultivated over the years between researchers and policymakers also enabled the programmes to be anchored at the national policy-making level.

Lessons learned and future prospects

Multi-country, multifaceted programmes like BIO-EARN and Bio-Innovate, involving a wide range of research and policymaking institutions, yield a rich set of lessons relevant for current and future bioscience initiatives. Key lessons learned include the following:

Building collaborative platforms can be a useful tool for development

Building an inclusive regional network around competitively funded R4D and innovation projects, with strong regional ownership, leadership and technical backstopping from international collaborators, can lead to impressive results. Network initiatives, such as BIO-EARN and Bio-Innovate, that strongly link public research organizations and market actors can dramatically improve the chances of eastern African farmers, agribusiness practitioners and agro-processors to benefit from the rapidly advancing field of biosciences.

The importance of south–south–north partnerships

Networking and innovation platforms involving south–south–north partnerships can catalyse the adoption of strategic technology and application of knowledge to local needs. In both programmes, there has been an exchange of useful knowhow amongst the regional partners and also from global collaborators from Sweden, China, Denmark, Finland, Netherlands, India, USA and Germany, thus enhancing key capacities and technology transfer as well as innovation processes.

The crucial role of business and market input in the design of innovation projects

A problem in both programmes was a focus on technical and scientific aspects in the initial project design with limited emphasis on market prospects, techno-economic analysis and clear business strategies. Poor mechanisms for market feedback during the development of products were also a key barrier in this regard.

Developing and deploying innovations needs sufficient resources and incubation

For the large majority of BIO-EARN and Bio-Innovate projects, impressive advances were made in collaborative R&D and technology development that was well targeted to a potential market demand. However, the high barrier in up-scaling and commercializing R&D results has been a major problem resulting in a very slow pace of deployment. The capacity for business development and sourcing of financial partners and investors to support commercialization and/or deployment of technologies were inadequate and are largely lacking in the region which severely restricts innovation efforts in eastern Africa. This points to the need for business incubation support able to assist innovation actors with business development, market research, techno-economic analysis and connection to additional financing to support up- and out-scaling as well as commercialization.

Long-term strategy and government commitment crucial to support innovation

Innovation is a long-term, non-linear and complex process, difficult to predict and manage. All innovations encounter unexpected barriers, experience unforeseen events and go through setbacks as they move through the 'Valley of Death' (Barr *et al.*, 2009). Access to long-term support and capital enabling improvement of products and the innovation processes in an iterative manner is often crucial for success. Of importance here is the longevity and follow through of donor and government support.

Sida provided valuable and strategic long-term support to both BIO-EARN and Bio-Innovate. Moving the innovations in these programmes to commercialization and large-scale application will however require continued support and funding. Such support could come from donors such as Sida, but should also increasingly come from other actors, including governments in the region, development banks and the private sector.

It is also critical that there is real ownership by the national governments in the region that translates beyond in-kind support to complement donor funding. This will ensure that successful programmes such as BIO-EARN and Bio-Innovate transform into sustainable entities or structures able to catalyse bioscience innovation over time.

Conclusions

BIO-EARN and Bio-Innovate illustrate the benefits of building functional innovation platforms, integrating both technical and business capacity development as well as policy analysis. The programmes also demonstrate the benefits of building strong collaboration links between researchers in Europe and eastern Africa which in turn support institutional development in the two regions.

The programmes have successfully demonstrated that the region has good capacity to develop biobased innovations and that the private sector is eager to participate if it is adequately incentivized. However, more needs to be done, particularly by national governments, to develop supportive ecosystems for bioscience innovation to thrive and translate to development and impact.

In terms of supporting bioscience innovations in the region and linking R&D in academia with economic development, lessons learned from BIO-EARN and Bio-Innovate are of great value. A key message here is that apart from strengthening R&D efforts, future programmes and innovation initiatives also need a more pronounced focus on and investment in building bio-businesses, entrepreneurial capacity and market dissemination pathways. This could be done through professional incubation of innovation actors to support up-scaling, marketing capability and links to durable financing mechanisms.

References

Barr, S.H. *et al.* 2009. Bridging the valley of death: lessons learned from 14 years of commercialization of technology. *Education Academy of Management Learning & Education* 8(3), pp.370–88.

CAAST-Net Plus. 2014. *Africa-EU Research Collaboration on Food Security: A Critical Analysis of the Scope, Coordination and Uptake of Findings.* [Online]. [Accessed 9

October 2015]. Available from: http://caast-net-plus.org/object/news/1212/attach/CN__ FoodSecurityReport_v7.pdf

Crouch, J. and Bloch, P. 2013. *Bio-Innovate Program Mid-Term Review Report 2013.* [Online]. Stockholm: SIDA. [Accessed 26 February 2016]. Available from: http://www. sida.se/globalassets/publications/import/pdf/en/bio-innovate-program-mid-term-review-report-2013_3501.pdf

Lundvall, B-Å. *et al.* 1992. National systems of production, innovation and competence building. *Research Policy* 31, pp.213–31.

Part V

Transitions to a modern bioeconomy

Analysis of policies

16 European strategies and policies getting towards a bioeconomy

Dirk Carrez

Introduction

In Europe, resource utilization, Greenhouse Gas (GHG) emissions, recyclability and sustainability are important drivers in developing supporting policies. In addition, industrial development has become an important driver in the last few years, just as in South East Asia, Brazil and China.

The development of an innovative and sustainable bioeconomy is influenced by many different factors, among others the political framework conditions in which such a sector is built. In this chapter, we have a closer look at how Europe and its member states handle the development of the bioeconomy politically.

Bioeconomy strategies in the European Union (EU) and its member states

In the last few years we have seen a growing number of governments worldwide developing a strategy and action plan to support the development of a sustainable and competitive bioeconomy. In Europe, the European Commission and several member states have developed a specific strategy.

EU

In February 2012, the European Commission adopted a strategy and action plan entitled *Innovating for Sustainable Growth: A Bioeconomy for Europe* to shift the European economy towards greater and more sustainable use of renewable resources (EC, 2012). The plan focuses on three key aspects: developing new technologies and processes for the bioeconomy, developing markets and competitiveness in bioeconomy sectors, and pushing policymakers and stakeholders to work more closely together.

The European Commission also formed a Bioeconomy Panel in 2013. The aim is to take a holistic viewpoint of the bioeconomy and build bridges between the different policy areas, sectors and stakeholders to ensure its coherent development. The Bioeconomy Observatory on the other hand collects and presents the latest data and information about the bioeconomy, including statistics on investments in research, policy mapping, bioeconomy country profiles, data visualization and analytical reports (EC, 2016).

Although many actions still need to be implemented, some progress was made already. In the area of innovation, the financial support for bioeconomy-related research under Horizon 2020 will be in the region of €4.3 billion, which represents an increase of over 100 per cent compared with the previous European Research and Innovation Programme, and a specific public–private partnership for biobased industries (BBI-JU) was launched in 2014 (Biobased Industries Initiative, 2016). Investments in pilot plants, as well as demonstration infrastructure can now be supported by the Regions via the Regional Development and the Rural Development funds as well as by the BBI-JU.

EU-wide methods for the calculation of the Environmental Footprint of Products and Organisations were adopted by the Commission on 9 April 2013 (EC, 2013a, 2013b). Data collection on environmental sustainability assessment is also part of the Bioeconomy Observatory activities, while some EU-funded projects were launched to create tools for GHG calculations for biofuels, as well as biomass.

Mandated standardization work is currently being performed by the European Committee for standardization in order to develop methodological standards for biobased products with regard to biobased content, biodegradability and functionalities.

A European public–private partnership for the Biobased Industries

The European Bio-based Industries Initiative Joint Undertaking (BBI-JU) is a new public–private partnership (PPP) which was launched in 2014. The establishment of this PPP in Europe is meant to address the issues of the so-called 'valley of death' that are thought to inhibit European bioeconomy development. The PPP was brought into force with a total budget of €3.7 billion for biobased innovation from 2014–24. €975 million of this is EU funds, with the other €2.7 billion from private investments (EC, 2014).

The PPP has an emphasis on higher added value. The key is to develop new biorefining technologies to sustainably transform renewable natural resources into biobased products, materials and fuels.

Individual member states

Meanwhile, several member states have created and published strategies or plans on how to meet the potentials of the bioeconomy, while other member states have started designing their specific strategy. Concerning the implementation, some countries made more progress, such as Germany and the Netherlands, while others still have to start. Although not exhaustive, Table 16.1 summarizes and compares the different bioeconomy strategies in Europe, indicating some key elements.

Table 16.1 Overview and comparison of European bioeconomy strategies

	European Union	Germany	Netherlands	Belgium (Region of Flanders)
Strategy	Innovating for Sustainable Growth: A Bioeconomy for Europe (EC, 2012)	The National Bioeconomy Research Strategy 2030 (BMBF, 2011); National Policy Strategy on Bioeconomy (BMEL, 2014)	Hoofdlijnennotitie Biobased Economy (Dutch Cabinet, 2012)	The Vision and Strategy for a Sustainable and Competitive Bioeconomy in 2030 (Flemish Government, 2013)
Framework and objective	The production of renewable resources of land, fisheries and aquaculture and their conversion into food, products or energy. An innovative and low-emission economy, reconciling demands for sustainable agriculture and fisheries, food security, and the sustainable use of renewable biological resources for industrial purposes, while ensuring biodiversity and environmental protection.	The framework is the agricultural economy and all manufacturing sectors and associated services that utilize biological resources. To become a dynamic research and innovation centre for biobased products, energy, processes and services. To meet responsibilities for global nutrition, as well as protection of the climate, resources and the environment.	The transition of the economy from fossil raw materials towards an economy based on renewable biomass as a raw material. From a 'fossil-based' towards 'biobased' economy.	The production of biomass and the various ways in which this biomass and its residual streams are subsequently used. To become one of the top regions in Europe for innovation and research relating to the bioeconomy, where the available biomass streams will be used according to an accepted cascade.
Main actions	Investment in research, innovation and skills for the bioeconomy. Development of markets and competitiveness in bioeconomy sectors. Reinforced policy coordination and stakeholder involvement.	Sustainable production and provision of renewable resources. Growth markets, innovative technologies and products. Processes and value-adding networks.	Sustainable use of biomass, an integrated policy, knowledge and innovation, clear and transparent sustainability criteria.	A coherent policy that supports a sustainable bioeconomy. Excellent education, training, and research and innovation in bioeconomy. To produce and use biomass optimally and sustainably across the entire value chain. Strengthening of markets and competitiveness.

(Continued)

Table 16.1 (Continued)

	Sweden	UK	Norway	Ireland
Focus	R&D, sustainability, innovation, competitiveness, job creation, economic growth, coherent policy framework, stakeholder participation.	Sustainability (including biomass vs food security), competitiveness, innovation, economic growth, integrated policy, education.	Sustainable use of biomass and agricultural biomass production, sustainable production processes, innovation, integrated policy.	Sustainability, innovation, market introduction, competitiveness, education, integrated policy.
Coordination	The European Bioeconomy Panel	The Bioeconomy Council	The High-Level Group Biobased Economy	Interdepartmental Working Group (IWG)
Strategy	Swedish Research and Innovation Strategy for a Biobased Economy (FORMAS, 2012)	Building a High Value Bioeconomy (UK Government, 2015)	Norwegian Industrial Biotech Network (Industrial Biotech Network Norway, 2012); BioNAER – Research Programme on Sustainable Innovation in Food and Biobased Industries (The Research Council of Norway, 2012)	Developing the Green Economy in Ireland (FORFAS, 2009)
Framework and objective	A sustainable production of biomass to enable increased use within different sectors of society. The objectives are to reduce climate effects and the use of fossil-based raw materials, obtain an increased added value for biomass materials, and to optimize the value and contribution of ecosystem services to the economy.	Producing energy, fuels and chemicals from waste-derived feedstocks.	Support of companies in developing their advantage and to enhance innovation.	Promote green sectors that drive exports and job creation, and make of Ireland a hub for green enterprise, by building a sustainable bioenergy sector, fostering R&D in renewables.

Main actions	Stimulating cross-industry collaboration, supporting the growth of research and innovation environments, and accelerating development, verification and commercializations of new biobased solutions.	To support the transition towards a more circular economy, encouraging a more sustainable and efficient approach to resource use and management. Support R&D of technologies and biorefineries, continuing to encourage investment in the development and demonstration of technologies, processes and facilities. Development of a skilled workforce. Support businesses by ensuring the right policy and incentives framework is in place, ensuring that actions are coordinated across government.	Enhancing innovation in Norwegian enterprises and industry. Securing development in rural areas. Transforming ideas into successful business cases. Promote interaction between enterprises, knowledge communities and R&D institutions.	Building the ideas economy. Promote green sectors and deliver green zones and green international financial services sector. Create world-class research and human capital. Remove hurdles for the development of the green economy.
Focus	Sustainability, biomass production, R&D and innovation, market introduction.	Innovation, skills, economic growth, policy, sustainability.	Innovation, competitiveness.	Enterprise, innovation, economic growth, competitiveness.
Coordination	User Forum	Industrial Biotechnology Special Interest Group (IB-SG)		

(Continued)

Table 16.1 (Continued)

	Finland	Belgium (the Walloon region)	France	Denmark
Strategy	Sustainable Growth from Bioeconomy – The Finnish Bioeconomy Strategy (Finnish Ministry of Employment and the Economy, 2014)	Le 'Coq Vert' (Belgium Biobased Industries Consortium, 2013; GreenWin, 2013)	French National Reform Programme 2011–2014 (French Government, 2011)	Agreement on Green Growth (Danish Government, 2009)
Framework and objective	To increase the yield of the bioeconomy from the present €60 billion to €100 billion and to create 100,000 new bioeconomy jobs by 2025	Valorization of non-food biomass streams (co-products, waste, residues, etc.) and second generation biorefineries.		To ensure that a high level of environmental and climate protection goes hand in hand with modern and competitive agriculture and food industries.
Main actions	Creating a competitive operating environment for growth in the bioeconomy. Creating new bioeconomy business activities through risk financing, bold experiments and transcending boundaries between different sectors. Upgrading the bioeconomy knowledge base by developing education and research activities.	Identification of priority R&D projects, support training, investment stimulation and attracting of foreign investors.	Setting up regional 'competiveness clusters' (cfr. IAR)	The agricultural sector as a supplier of green energy, support investments in new green technologies, develop a more value-creating food industry.
Focus	Innovation, competitiveness.	Innovation, competitiveness.	R&D and innovation, competitiveness.	Environmental sustainability.
Coordination				

We notice here that the focus of interest may vary from one country to another. A number of countries such as Germany and Finland have adopted a broader approach to bioeconomy as a whole, while most countries – such as the Netherlands, Sweden and some regions in France – lay an emphasis on a particular biobased part of it (the non-food aspects). By contrast, Norway and the United Kingdom concentrate their attention primarily on industrial biotechnology and biorefineries. A number of countries such as Denmark and Ireland have not developed a specific strategy for the bioeconomy to date, but have incorporated elements in support of this into a broader approach with the aim of stimulating 'green growth'. Very strikingly, most countries took the initiative to start developing a specific vision and strategy for the bioeconomy at the urgent request of stakeholders (industry, scientific world, agricultural organizations, etc.).

Although the most important action point seems to be related to supporting 'innovation' (in the broadest sense of the term), most authorities are designing an 'integrated' policy. For instance, while the accent in the Netherlands is on biomass production, innovation, sustainability and a consistent policy, Sweden places an emphasis on innovation, market introduction, SME support and a general supporting policy. Germany in its turn has established a national 'Bioeconomy Council' with focus on economy, innovation, education and policy.

An important part of most strategies involves establishing and supporting a specific cluster and/or public–private partnership. Examples thereof are BE-BASIC in the Netherlands, the regional clusters in Germany (such as CLIB2021 and BIOM WB) and France (IAR).

Recently, we have also noticed an increase in the number of partnerships between the clusters and PPPs in Europe, or even with regions outside Europe. A clear example, which is also supported by the European Commission, is the ERA-Net Industrial Biotechnology. Norway and the United Kingdom have agreed to jointly support research in the field of industrial biotechnology and biorefinery development. The French cluster IAR has formed official partnerships with the Wagralim cluster (Wallonia), CLIB2021 (Germany), and clusters from Canada, Finland and Hungary, while BE-BASIC (the Netherlands) has signed cooperation agreements with Brazil, Malaysia, the United States and Vietnam.

European policy regimes affecting the development of a bioeconomy

Renewable energy and biofuels

The legislation and policy on bioenergy and biofuels is determined at both EU and member state level. The Renewable Energy Directive of 2009 is calling for a mandatory target of a 20 per cent share of renewable energies in the EU energy mix by 2020, and by the same date each member state must ensure that 10 per cent of total road transport comes from 'renewable energy', including biofuels and biogas, as well as hydrogen and electricity. In addition, to stimulate the use of the so-called second-generation biofuels, biofuels from waste, residues, non-food cellulosic material and lignocellulosic material will count double towards achieving the renewable energy transport target (EC, 2009).

In 2014, The EU Energy Council reached political agreement on the draft amendment to the Renewable Energy Directive and the Fuel Quality Directive to reflect concerns over the sustainability and GHG-reduction benefits of some biofuels. The agreement acknowledges and addresses the Indirect Land Use Change (ILUC) phenomenon.

In 2015, the European Parliament and the member states agreed to reform the EU's biofuel policy by capping conventional biofuels at 7 per cent and setting a non-binding advanced fuels target and to take on a non-binding 0.5 per cent target for advanced biofuels. The compromise also amends EU renewable energy and fuel quality laws to take into account the additional greenhouse gas emissions arising from indirect land-use change caused by biofuels production.

Biobased products and materials

In contrast to biofuels and bioenergy, there is currently no European policy framework to directly support biobased materials, although the European Commission's Lead Market Initiative (LMI) for Bio-based Products could be a good example of a synchronized approach to stimulating demand for these products. In 2008, the Commission set up an expert group composed of representatives from national governments, industry and academia, entitled the Ad-hoc Advisory Group for Bio-based Products. At the end of 2009, the Ad-hoc Advisory Group agreed on measures that make use of the four LMI demand-side instruments, namely regulation, public procurement, standardization and complementary measures (Ad-hoc Advisory Group for Bio-based Products, 2009). The Expert Group published in 2011 a financing and a communication paper (Ad-hoc Advisory Group for Bio-based Products, 2011a, 2011b). Although most of the recommendations still need to be implemented, progress was made in the area of research and innovation, public procurement and standards. In particular, the progress with a concrete agenda to develop industry standards that set out the environmental and other credentials of biobased products is a welcomed development for improving market conditions and provides a critical link to advancing public procurement and communication efforts. Within the European Committee for Standardization (CEN), a Technical Committee is working on this mandate, which is CEN/TC 411 'Bio-based Products'. Their work includes establishing industry standards for measuring and declaring biobased content of products, developing a common methodology for Life Cycle Assessment, labelling and information to consumers and a methodology for information about the sustainability of biomass production (CSES, 2011).

As a follow up, the European Commission launched in 2013 a new Expert Group for Bio-based Products. The main tasks of the Group are to monitor and reflect on the implementation of the LMI priority recommendations, to identify and monitor demand-side policy actions conducive to the market uptake of biobased products (standardization, public procurement, labelling), and the mapping of activities and exchange of good practices at regional, national, international and EU-level. Progress of this new group however is very slow.

Non-specific policies

There are a number of other non-specific policies and European Directives that may have an important impact on the development of the bioeconomy, but where links to the bioeconomy are not effectively or sufficiently made. Examples of such policies are the Resource Efficiency Roadmap (EC, 2011) proposing ways to increase resource productivity and decouple economic growth from resource use and its environmental impact, and the Directive 94/62/EC (1994) on Packaging and Packaging Waste which, to date, does not provide incentives for bioplastics packaging, and its ambiguous definitions concerning organic waste management for compostable bioplastics provide insecurity to the market.

In 2015 the European Parliament voted new rules to reduce the use of lightweight non-biodegradable plastic bags drastically, and asked the European Commission to propose labelling and marking measures for an EU-wide recognition of biodegradable and compostable plastic bags by 2017.

Feedstock-related policies and the European policy toward GMOs

Europe's agricultural policy

The Common Agricultural Policy (CAP) is the most important policy in Europe that has an impact on the availability and price of feedstock also for industrial (non-food) use. The original CAP combined a direct subsidy payment for crops and land that could be cultivated with price support mechanisms, including guaranteed minimum prices, import tariffs and quotas on certain goods from outside the EU. As of 2004, energy crop support of €45/ha was available in the EU15 for the production of energy crops on basic land. It was assumed that biomass production for energy will be stimulated by strong demand due to the policy targets for biofuels (EC, 2010). There are a variety of instruments in the so-called second pillar of the CAP, the rural development policy, which address both the supply and use of bioenergy. Some examples are: support for biogas production facilities, perennial energy crops, processing of biomass towards energy, installations and infrastructure for renewable energy from biomass.

The European Commission, the Parliament and the member states revised the CAP in 2013. Support for science and innovation is a key element, as well as the greening of agriculture by incentivizing sustainable farming practices. However, the proposed greening measures are limited to nature preservation practices (EC, 2013c), do not specifically mention the bioeconomy and are not at all linked to the EU bioeconomy strategy.

The EU sugar regime

The EU sugar regime was introduced in 1968 as part of the CAP, covering the production and marketing of beet and sugar cane within EU member countries. Sugar is a major feedstock for the production of biobased materials via fermentation processes. Today, the European sugar market is divided into quota sugar and out-of-quota sugar, which includes industrial sugar. The European sugar market is fully isolated from the rest of the world because imports are subject to very high duties. In 2017, the EU Common Organisation of the Market in the sugar sector will bring an end to production quotas by country and market price support. It is expected that this will make significantly more sugar available on the European market at much more competitive prices, which could strongly boost the feedstock access of producers of biobased chemicals.

Europe policy towards GMOs

EU legislation foresees that no GMO can be cultivated in the EU if it has not received a prior authorization, following a thorough risk assessment which involves the national evaluation agencies and the European Food Safety Authority (EFSA), in order to ensure safety for human and animal health and for the environment.

Today, only one GM maize – MON 810 – is commercially cultivated in the EU. This product's genetic modification aims to protect the crop against a harmful pest – the European corn borer – and was authorized in 1998. The MON 810 maize is only cultivated in five member states (Spain, Portugal, Czech Republic, Romania and Slovakia). It represents 1.56 per cent of the 9.6 million hectares of maize cultivated in the EU, and 0.26 per cent of the 57.4 million hectares of GM maize cultivated worldwide. In 2010, a GM starch potato, known as 'Amflora' potato, was authorized for cultivation and industrial processing in the EU, but since 2011 it has no longer been cultivated in the EU.

There are two key rules which govern GMOs in the EU: a directive used for the authorization of GMO products in the EU and a regulation used on food and feed made from GMO products that have been authorized. The producer must request authorization from a national competent authority. The national authority then informs the European Food Safety Authority (EFSA), which is mandated to conduct a scientific assessment and report to the Commission. The Commission then submits its decision on the matter to the Council. In the event that the Council does not reach a majority for or against authorization, the matter is handed back to the Commission, which is free to authorize the GMO based on a special regulatory procedure.

In 2009, 13 member states asked the Commission for more flexibility to decide not to cultivate GMOs on their territory. This is why, in 2010, the Commission adopted a proposal to the European Parliament and to the Council to offer additional possibilities to member states to ban or restrict the cultivation of GMOs on part of or all their territory, based on their national circumstances, and without affecting the EU authorization system. In July 2011, the European Parliament issued a positive first reading opinion with amendments and after several years, the Council adopted on 12 June 2014 a political agreement which will allow the co-legislators to get one step closer towards the adoption of the proposal. Under the new legislation, which came into force in 2015, EU member states will be able to ban or restrict cultivation of GMOs on their territory, but they will not be able to block the authorization process at EU-level. The new rules give member states a two-step possibility for refusing GMO cultivation: first, during the EU authorization process, they will be able to adjust the geographical scope of the cultivation, and second, if a crop is authorized by the Commission, they will be able to restrict or prohibit cultivation on their territory. The directive gives member states the possibility to ban GMO cultivation on environmental grounds, but also for other reasons, such as socioeconomic impact or public policy, and they will no longer need to provide new evidence of risk to health or the environment.

It is evident that these new rules sacrifice the internal market in favour of a patchwork of national bans, and that failing to uphold the EU-wide approval of safe GMOs will indirectly damage jobs, growth, innovation and competitiveness in certain areas of the bioeconomy.

In order to secure a sustainable supply of renewable biomass for the production of biobased products and energy, initiatives to strengthen European plant breeding in general, irrespectively of choice of breeding technology, are needed. The European Technology Platform (ETP) 'Plants for the Future' has put together Research, Education and Innovation action plans that explain how the plant sector can support the development of a sustainable bioeconomy (ETP 'Plants for the Future, 2015).

Discussion and conclusions

Considerable progress has been made to support the bioeconomy in Europe. The EU as well as many member states and regions have developed specific strategies to support the bioeconomy. Although the implementation is still going on, the first results are visible: a higher budget for the bioeconomy is foreseen in Horizon 2020, Europe's largest Research and Innovation programme, and a specific public–private partnership has been set up with a total budget of €3.7 billion.

A striking issue is that there seems to be a weak link or even mismatch between strategies and the policy regimes in Europe. While strategies both in EU and many member countries are clear on creating strong innovative biobased economies, polices to support this are often instable, incoherent, uncoordinated and in some areas even stifling. An example of this is that, compared to biofuels and bioenergy, other products and materials from renewable resources receive a minimal amount of support. Assistance for biomaterials, biobased products and biochemicals is basically limited to R&D efforts and general declarations of intent, while bioenergy benefits from a variety of market instruments, such as feed-in quotas, tax reductions, crop support, market introduction programmes, etc. It is critical for the development of biomaterials, bioplastics and biochemicals that coherent support systems and policies are put in place for all possible applications within the bioeconomy in order to maximize the potential for developing added-value products and related employment opportunities and to ensure the access of high-value industries to a guaranteed volume of feedstock at affordable costs.

The focus on biofuels and bioenergy creates a strong market distortion for a broader use of biomass, meaning that producers of biomaterials and biobased products are increasingly hard-pressed to find a secure and affordable supply of feedstock for their products. In addition, it became almost impossible in Europe to cultivate GM crops, even for non-food use. And where the EU may give the green light for certain applications based on extensive assessment by an independent institute, member states now have the possibility to block all possible cultivation. As a result, future development of the European biobased sector will be subject to a high degree of uncertainty, mainly depending on crop yields and land availability, unbalanced policy support and a GMO policy stifling innovation.

So a major hurdle for a more diversified use of biomass is that much of the current biomass feedstock is used to produce electricity due to the many incentives in place for this, which has the effect of creating an uneven playing field for all other applications. It is, therefore, important to create a more balanced marketplace for all types of biobased products, and this will require more stable, but also broader and non-exclusive market-oriented policies.

In the short term, market demand certainty is a significant challenge. Currently, there is an important market within the bioeconomy for biofuels, which has been created by policy incentives. However, the policy is not stable – it is changing – which is a major hurdle for new investments in biofuel production. From this, it is clear that whether this direction will be either with or without policy incentives, stability and predictability is the key to attracting investment, and that is the same for all biobased products.

A last hurdle, which has now almost been overcome, concerns access to finance. In the past, the issue was that not enough funding existed. That has now changed, with money available through the European Investment Bank (EIB), Horizon 2020, the new BBI public–private partnership, the Structural Funds, and even private banks. Accessibility, however, remains an issue. The funding is fragmented and the procedures involved from one institution to the next, or from one region to another, are different, and the process of applying for funds can also be very long-winded and complex. This is a much different environment to that seen in the USA, for instance, where things are much more harmonized.

To conclude, in order to develop a sustainable and competitive bioeconomy in Europe, it is necessary:

- to implement completely the European and national bioeconomy strategies, in order to introduce a long-term, stable and transparent policy and incentive framework to promote the bioeconomy;
- to improve the access to feedstock at a competitive price, and to facilitate the appropriate use of wastes and residues;

- to improve and facilitate the access to finance by simplifying and harmonizing the procedures between the different funding organizations, whether they be European, national or regional;
- to develop a fairer playing field between biobased alternatives, such as bioenergy, biofuels and biobased products and materials.

References

Ad-hoc Advisory Group for Bio-based Products. 2009. *Taking Bio-based from Promise to Market: Measures to Promote the Market Introduction of Innovative Bio-based Products.* [Online]. European Commission Enterprise and Industry. [Accessed 13 August 2015]. Available from: http://bookshop.europa.eu/en/taking-bio-based-from-promise-to-market-pbNB3109225/%20

Ad-hoc Advisory Group for Bio-based Products. 2011a. *Lead Market Initiative on Bio-based Products: Financing Paper.* [Online]. [Accessed 22 February 2016]. Available from: http://ec.europa.eu/DocsRoom/documents/8878

Ad-hoc Advisory Group for Bio-based Products. 2011b. *Lead Market Initiative on Bio-based Products: Recommendations on Communication.* [Online]. [Accessed 22 February 2016]. Available from: http://ec.europa.eu/DocsRoom/documents/8879

Biobased Industries Initiative. 2016. [Online]. [Accessed 21 February 2016]. Available from: http://bbi-europe.eu/

BMBF (German Federal Ministry of Education and Research). 2011. *National Research Strategy Bioeconomy 2030. Our Route Towards a Biobased Economy.* [Online]. [Accessed 19 February 2016]. Available from: https://www.bmbf.de/pub/Natinal_Research_Strategy_BioEconomy_2030.pdf

BMEL (German Federal Ministry of Food and Agriculture). 2014. *National Policy Strategy on Bioeconomy: Renewable Resources and Biotechnological Processes as a Basis for Food, Industry and Energy.* [Online]. [Accessed 19 February 2016]. Available from: http://www.bmel.de/SharedDocs/Downloads/EN/Publications/NatPolicyStrategyBioeconomy.pdf?__blob=publicationFile

CSES (Centre for Strategy & Evaluation Services). 2011. *Final Evaluation of the Lead Market Initiative: Final report Annex B.4 – Bio-based Products: The Elaboration of New European Standards.* Sevenoaks, UK: Centre for Strategy & Evaluation Services.

Danish Government. 2009. *Agreement on Green Growth.* [Online]. [Accessed 19 February 2016]. Available from: http://eng.mst.dk/media/mst/69152/Danish%20Agreement%20on%20Green%20Growth_300909.pdf

Dutch Cabinet 2012. *Hoofdlijnennotitie Biobased Economy.* Kamerstuk 02-04-2012, EL&I.

(EC) European Commission. 2007. *A Lead Market Initiative for Europe.* COM(2007) 860 final. Brussels, 21.12.2007.

EC (European Commission) 2009. *Council Directive (EC) 2009/28/EC of 23 April 2009 on the promotion of the use of energy from renewable sources and amending and subsequently repealing Directives 2001/77/EC and 2003/30/EC.* Official Journal of the European Union L140/16, 5.6.2009.

EC (European Commission). 2010. *Overview of the CAP Health Check and the European Economic Recovery Plan. Modification of the RDPs.* Luxembourg.

EC (European Commission). 2011. *Roadmap to a Resource Efficient Europe.* COM(2011) 571 final. Brussels, 20.9.2011.

EC (European Commission). 2012. *Innovating for Sustainable Growth: A Bioeconomy for Europe*. COM(2012) 60, final. Brussels, 13.2.2012.

EC (European Commission). 2013a. *Recommendation on the Use of Common Methods to Measure and Communicate the life cycle Environmental Performance of Products and Organisations*. 2013/179/EU. Brussels, 9.4.2013.

EC (European Commission). 2013b. *Building the single market for green products - facilitating better information on the environmental performance of products and organisations*. COM(2013) 196 final. Brussels, 9.4.2013.

EC (European Commission). 2013c. *Overview of CAP Reform 2014–2020*. [Online]. Agricultural Policy Perspectives Brief No. 5 (December 2013). [Accessed 22 February 2016]. Available from: http://ec.europa.eu/agriculture/policy-perspectives/policy-briefs/05_en.pdf

EC (European Commission). 2014. *Council Regulation (EU) No 560/2014 of 6 May 2014 Establishing the Bio-based Industries Joint Undertaking*. [Online]. [Accessed 22 February 2016]. Available from: http://eur-lex.europa.eu/legal-content/EN/TXT/?uri=CELEX%3A32014R0560

EC (European Commission). 2016. *Bioeconomy Observatory*. [Online]. [Accessed 19 February 2016]. Available via: http://ec.europa.eu/research/bioeconomy/

ETP (European Technology Platform) 'Plants for the Future'. 2015. *Summary of Action Plans to 2020 – Growing a Prosperous Future for the European Union*. [Online]. [Accessed 22 February 2016]. Available from: http://www.plantetp.org/images/stories/stories/documents_pdf/Plant%20ETP_SummaryActionPlans.pdf

Finnish Ministry of Employment and the Economy. 2014. *Sustainable Growth from Bioeconomy: The Finnish Bioeconomy Strategy*. [Online]. [Accessed 22 February 2016]. Available from: https://www.tem.fi/files/40366/The_Finnish_Bioeconomy_Strategy.pdf

Flemish Government. 2013. *Bioeconomy in Flanders: The Vision and Strategy of the Government of Flanders for a Sustainable and Competitive Bioeconomy in 2030*. [Online]. [Accessed 19 February 2016]. Available from: https://www.vlaanderen.be/nl/publicaties/detail/bioeconomy-in-flanders

French Government. 2011. *French National Reform Programme 2011–2014*. [Online]. [Accessed 19 February 2016]. Available from: http://ec.europa.eu/europe2020/pdf/nrp/nrp_france_en.pdf

FORFAS (National Policy Advisory Board for Enterprise, Trade, Science, Technology and Innovation). 2009. *Developing the Green Economy in Ireland. High-Level Group on Green Enterprise*. [Online]. [Accessed 19 February 2016]. Available from: https://www.djei.ie/en/Publications/Publication-files/Developing-the-Green-Economy-in-Ireland-01-12-09.pdf

FORMAS (The Swedish Research Council for Environment, Agricultural Sciences and Spatial Planning). 2012. *Swedish Research and Innovation Strategy for a Biobased Economy*. [Online]. [Accessed 22 February 2016]. Available from: http://www.formas.se/PageFiles/5074/Strategy_Biobased_Ekonomy_hela.pdf

GreenWin. 2013. *'Le Coq Vert' Project: Towards a Biobased Economy in Wallonia*. [Online]. [Accessed 19 February 2016]. Available from: http://www.coqvert.be/

Industrial Biotech Network Norway. 2012. *Virksomhetsplan for Industrial Biotechnology Network – Norway (Network Vision and Strategy)*. [Online]. [Accessed 22 February 2016]. Available from: http://www.indbiotech.no/content/network-vision-and-strategy

The Research Council of Norway. 2012. *Sustainable Innovation in Food and Biobased industries – BIONAER*. [Online]. [Accessed 19 February 2016]. Available from: http://www.forskningsradet.no/prognett-bionaer/Home_page/1253971968569

UK Government. 2015. *Building a High Value Bioeconomy. Opportunities from Waste.* [Online]. [Accessed 19 February 2016]. Available from: https://www.gov.uk/government/uploads/system/uploads/attachment_data/file/408940/BIS-15-146_Bioeconomy_report_-_opportunities_from_waste.pdf

17 Getting towards an African bioeconomy

Julius Ecuru

Introduction

Africa seeks accelerated growth and transition from a peasant to a modern society, where scientific knowledge, technology and innovation drive economic growth and development. This aspiration for increased growth and transformation is widely emphasized in the national development plans and strategies (Government of Uganda, 2013). These country plans provide a 20 to 30-year horizon by which the countries should achieve at least middle-income status – a middle-income country is one whose annual gross national income per capita is between US$1,045 and US$12,736 (World Bank, 2016).

Therefore, a continued focus on growth, and in particular, ways of increasing employment opportunities for the youth and women, are crucial for Africa to achieve its medium and long-term aspirations. The rapid urbanization (up to 5 per cent or more per annum) and a growing middle class in the continent is an opportunity to reckon with because of the demand created for value-added products and consumer services (World Economic Forum, 2015). At the same time, Africa's labour market is growing by more than 20 million people annually (African Development Bank, 2015).

These evolving circumstances point to the need for Africa to shift away from solely depending on the extractive natural resource industry to a more value-added knowledge-based economy. The agricultural and related biosciences offer some of the greatest opportunities for the continent to foster a knowledge-based African bioeconomy. This is not far fetched and is within reach of the continent. For example, as of now, modern bioscience is advancing in several countries (especially in sub-Saharan Africa) and providing the means to add value to natural resources and create opportunities for investments in new knowledge-intensive bioenterprises. Modern bioscience encompasses a range of techniques that involve working with or studying living organisms or their parts usually at genetic, molecular or atomic and subatomic level as well as developing novel biobased products for use as medicine, or improved plant varieties, or industrial processing or environment and pollution control.

This chapter highlights the support mechanisms, which should be in place for Africa to become one of the important players in the global bioeconomy. The chapter is divided into sections. The following section shows the supportive policy framework in Africa. The subsequent one identifies opportunities for developing an African bioeconomy. Other sections discuss bioscience innovation systems as precursors of a bioeconomy, the role of the university and importance of regional economic cooperation in contributing to a vibrant African bioeconomy. The chapter concludes with some policy recommendations for moving Africa towards a knowledge-based bioeconomy.

African policies in support of an African bioeconomy

Africa's Agenda 2063 (AUC, 2014a) and related policies of the African Union (AU), such as the Science, Technology and Innovation Strategy for Africa (STISA-2024) (AUC, 2014b), the Africa Biosciences Initiative (ABI), the Comprehensive Africa Agriculture Development Programme (CAADP) and Science Agenda for Agriculture in Africa (S3A), provide the framework for an African bioeconomy (NEPAD, 2003; AUC, 2014c; FARA, 2014). The AU Agenda 2063 points towards a transformed continent with citizens empowered not only to meet their needs but also to contribute to global development.

The NEPAD, which was adopted in Lusaka, Zambia, in 2001 as a technical body of the AU, provides leadership and guides nation states in efforts towards achieving the goals of the AU Agenda 2063, not least for enhancing Africa's growth, development and participation in the global economy. One of NEPAD's priorities is investment in modern bioscience (NEPAD, 2006). The ABI in particular calls for more research and capacity development in biodiversity, biotechnology and indigenous knowledge. The new STISA-2024 promotes science, technology and innovation as the main drivers of economic and human development across the continent. It has the following specific goals: 1) eradicating hunger and achieving food and nutrition security; 2) preventing and controlling diseases; 3) enhancing physical and intellectual communication; 4) protecting space; 5) living together – building the community; and 6) creating wealth.

CAADP is another framework by NEPAD for a coordinated investment in agriculture for social and economic development. It has prioritized its actions in four pillars namely: 1) extending area under sustainable land management and reliable water control systems; 2) improving rural infrastructure and trade-related capacities for market access; 3) increasing food supply and reducing hunger; and 4) agricultural research, technology dissemination and adoption. Pillar 4 specially aims for accelerated gains in productivity, which, among other things, requires renewing the ability of agricultural research systems to efficiently and effectively generate and adapt new knowledge and technologies, including biotechnology, to Africa. Many of the bioscience research and innovation programmes in the continent, together with research and development in the agricultural and environmental sciences, anchor on CAADP pillar 4. An example is the Science Agenda for Agriculture in Africa (S3A), which is a coordinated initiative of the Forum for Agricultural Research in Africa (FARA). S3A provides the rationale for increasing investment in science and technology, particularly to make the food and agricultural sector more productive and efficient so as to guarantee food and nutritional security. Priority themes for S3A include, among others, sustainable production in major farming systems, food systems and value chains, agricultural biodiversity and natural resources management, sustainable intensification, modern genetics and genomics, and climate change (FARA, 2014).

Furthermore, the African Union Commission (AUC) has highlighted five strategic foundations of the agriculture future for Africa as follows: 1) increased production and productivity, driven by a solid science agenda; 2) increased value addition and access to functioning markets and trade in a competitive agricultural sector which captures the growing market opportunities and increases the share of intra-African trade to at least 50 per cent of the continent's total agri-food trade by 2025, within a continental free-trade area supported by an effective external tariff scheme that strengthens regional preference in agri-food by 2019; 3) food and nutrition security for all African citizens by 2025; 4) resilience to climate change and other risks affecting African agriculture through strong integration of climate change adaptation in agricultural investment plans; and 5) public–private engagement and investment financing based on Africa's own resources and resourcefulness underpinned by continued action by member states to deliver on commitments made in the Maputo 2003 Declaration, and sustaining the CAADP momentum (AUC, 2014c).

The above initiatives are building blocks of an African bioeconomy from the policy front. They support the design and implementation of strategies and plans as well as investments in agriculture and related biosciences that should move Africa to a modern society.

Opportunities for an African bioeconomy

Africa is endowed with natural resources, especially genetic resources, which are the backbone of a bioeconomy. This coupled with the vast arable land area (about 60 per cent of the continent), (World Bank, 2015a) provides opportunities for agri-business development and high-value products based on genetic resource utilization (Byerlee *et al.*, 2013). The millions of people in Africa who directly depend on the natural resources for their survival, e.g. through smallholder farming, traditional medicine and other social amenities, could explore alternative resource utilization and new business opportunities brought about by value addition to these resources, thereby helping to conserve them. Otherwise, the rising African population will continue to exploit the rich bioresources in an unsustainable way, which does not significantly improve livelihoods. A big advantage of a sustainable African bioeconomy is that it has potential to gain more value from Africa's genetic resources, while ensuring that the resources are conserved for future generations.

The question, then, for Africa is 'How could an African bioeconomy increase economic growth in an inclusive and sustainable manner?' Various viewpoints may be expressed on this question. However, it is clear that developing an African bioeconomy will require addressing constraints to agricultural productivity and profitability. The main ones include: finding new methods to breed for resistance to pest and diseases; improving crops and livestock to be resilient to declining soil fertility and climate change; and finding scientific and technological solutions for enhancing productivity on marginal lands and fragile ecosystems. In this regard, therefore, new plant-breeding tools become necessary to develop crop varieties that are resistant to disease and resilient to climatic change. Similarly, tools for improved livestock breeding and health are necessary as well as improved feed and forage. Suffice to say that African countries that are investing in modern bioscience are getting better prepared to meet their future food, feed and bioenergy demands. Such countries will also most likely reap the early benefits of the emerging regional and global markets of value-added biobased products and services. Investing in modern bioscience that fosters a bioeconomy also helps Africa diversify its sources of growth, e.g. through increased value addition opportunities, agro-processing and agri-business development. It is one way to ensure that growth becomes inclusive and actually improves living standards in Africa (Byerlee *et al.*, 2013).

Globally, the sustainable development goals (SDGs) are poised to support and create opportunities for increased investment in modern bioscience for poverty reduction, wealth creation and social wellbeing. By all means, therefore, an African bioeconomy remains an attractive endeavour for a number of reasons: first, as already indicated above, Africa is rich in genetic resources, which provide the raw materials for high value and specialist industries. Second, globally there is a rising demand for renewable bioresources brought about by rapid globalization and climatic change. Global trade in biobased products is expected to be on the rise as countries embrace the goals of sustainability. Third, modern bioscience is rapidly advancing, and new bioscience tools are now increasingly available at affordable prices to African scientists and organizations. The ongoing investment in infrastructure, e.g. electricity and roads, further reduces the cost of doing business and not least the maintenance costs of high throughput equipment in Africa. Fourth, over the years, the continent has trained a critical mass of scientists in the field of bioscience, who are able to provide leadership in the development of an African bioeconomy (Juma, 2011). Therefore, the technological advantage for Africa is that it can leverage all these opportunities and possibilities to develop a vibrant African bioeconomy and leapfrog into a modern society as soon as possible.

Functional bioscience innovation systems a precursor of an African bioeconomy

Functional bioscience innovation systems are the foundation for a bioeconomy. Bioscience innovation systems are networks of people and organizations that interact and learn from one another in the process of developing technology, or adding value to a product or in processing local crops and other bioresources. The concept of innovation systems has been discussed since the late 1980s and early 1990s, when it was first introduced by Freeman (Freeman, 1995), Lundvall

(Lundvall *et al.*, 2002) and Nelson (Nelson, 1995). It recognizes that innovation is a non-linear process, which involves multidisciplinary actors with common interests.

Innovation system thinking is increasingly applied in African policymaking processes, as well as in framing and developing technological programmes. A case in point is the Bio-Innovate Programme, described in Chapter 15, which has successfully applied the concept of innovation systems to develop new plant-breeding tools, waste-treatment technologies, value-added products from agro-produce, and policy analysis (Bio-Innovate Africa, 2015). The Programme has supported numerous projects in eastern Africa since 2010, most of which address the needs of smallholder farmers and agro-processors in the region.

Innovation systems are shaped, defined and held together by norms, traditions, standards and governing relationships in a particular setting (Oyelaran-Oyeyinka and Sampath, 2007). This is highly relevant for Africa, where these systems are still being constructed, and where there is need for policy flexibility in adapting and adopting new practices. A functional African bioscience innovation system is needed, which would create the conditions and links among important actors in the public sector, private sector and civil society with respect to knowledge, technological development and diffusion. More importantly, in Africa such a system would connect smallholder farmers to agro-processors and value chains regionally and globally. Such connection is not only necessary for creating new business opportunities, but also enhancing productivity and profitability of the smallholder farmers, who account for over 75 per cent of agricultural production in most parts of the continent (Salami *et al.*, 2010).

African universities play a vital role in the African bioeconomy

Universities play an important role in the development of nations. Across Africa, there is a rise not only in the numbers of universities created but also an increase in student enrolment. Within East Africa alone, there are more than 170 universities, enrolling over 700,000 students annually (IUCEA, 2014). These numbers are still extremely low when compared with the average percentage tertiary school enrolment in the rest of the world, especially Asia and Latin America (World Bank, 2015b; World Bulletin, 2014). As Figure 17.1 shows, tertiary school enrolment has continued to increase, but at a much lower rate compared with East Asia and Pacific, and Latin America and Caribbean nations.

In many African countries, government-aided schools and universities have prioritized science, technology, engineering and mathematics education. Science and engineering career programmes are emphasized at the universities. The challenge for the African university, however, is to ensure that the graduates they produce have skills sets, which match the demands of the labour market. Moreover, the university should focus on producing graduates who are not only qualified technically, but also who have an entrepreneurial mindset to be able to translate scientific knowledge into business opportunities.

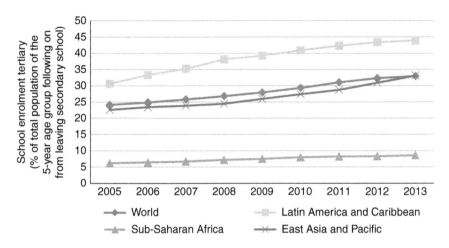

Figure 17.1 Tertiary school enrolment in sub-Saharan Africa compared with other regions (World Bank, 2015b)

If well facilitated, universities in Africa can catalyse a rapid evolution of an African bioeconomy and specifically support the creation of new biobased enterprises/firms, or could significantly enhance the competitiveness of the existing ones. Unfortunately, universities and higher education institutions in general are still poorly resourced. Most universities cannot afford world-class scientific infrastructure and scholastic materials necessary to produce the highly competitive and productive graduate. They are often overwhelmed by the need to absorb the high numbers of post-secondary students. Most universities also focus on attracting high numbers of students at the undergraduate levels in order to bridge the funding gap. African governments, therefore, have a challenge to balance the need to absorb more young people into university education with the need for quality in teaching and research. There is need for a collective longer term strategy to address this challenge.

Ongoing efforts by, for example, the African Development Bank (AfDB) and other development partners to improve quality and excellence in the African higher education system are commendable but still insufficient to meet the continent's present and future growth needs. The AfDB is focusing on enhancing skills and technology for competitiveness and employment opportunities. Kenya, Malawi and Uganda have so far received higher education, science and technology funding support from the Bank for the period 2012–17 (Kunene, 2013). With initial funding from the Carnegie Foundation, the Regional Initiative in Science and Education (RISE) of the Science Initiative Group at the Institute for Advanced Study in the USA has supported nearly 200 PhD and MSc graduates in science and engineering in 17 countries across Africa since 2008 (RISE, 2015).

Additionally, long-term bilateral cooperation in training and research capacity development has been instrumental in contributing to economic growth and development in Africa. For example, the Swedish International Development Cooperation Agency (Sida) bilateral research cooperation with national universities in Ethiopia, Mozambique, Rwanda, Tanzania and Uganda has enhanced research capacities of these universities by more than four times since 2000. The latter has focused on building research infrastructure, institutional policy reforms, MSc, PhD as well as post-doctoral training. Taking the example of Makerere University in Uganda, between 2000 and 2020, Sida would have offered Makerere University approximately US$98 million, training nearly 600 staff of public universities at Masters and PhD levels in the two decades (Muhindo, 2016). Arguably, this long-term and sustained investment has enabled Makerere University to rank among the top three universities in Africa in 2015 according to the Times Higher Education World University Rankings (Bothwell, 2015). Post-graduate training does not only enable the generation of knowledge locally but also helps in transfer and utilization of the global scientific knowledge resources that are essential for poverty eradication, inclusive growth and sustainable development. The continent needs more of such initiatives to achieve its Agenda 2063.

Therefore, universities in Africa are well positioned to play an enhanced role in the African bioeconomy. However, the governments should have incentives that attract entrepreneurial faculty and students from the universities to start up new ventures, especially in value addition and agri-business. As Etzkowitz and Dzisah (2007, p.3) observed, 'the potential for future economic development increases lies with the rich research potential and students within higher educational institutes'. Students at universities together with their faculty are an ever-renewing source of new ideas.

Regionalism good for an African bioeconomy

Scientific cooperation should be strengthened within Africa as well as between Africa and the rest of the world. However, greater regional cooperation within Africa is key to opening up opportunities for investment and knowledge exchange across the continent. In this respect, regional collaborative programmes in bioscience become crucial mechanisms for regional cooperation. Some of the programmes, which appear to have made significant strides contributing to an African bioeconomy include, *inter alia*, Biosciences Eastern and Central Africa – International Livestock Research Institute (BecA-ILRI) Hub for modern bioscience research and capacity building; Bio-Innovate programme for translation of research outputs into innovations for societal use; The Regional Universities Forum for capacity building in agricultural sciences; and Association for Strengthening Agricultural Research in East and Central Africa (ASARECA) for strengthening national agricultural research systems. While, in some respects, these programmes actualize the continental aspirations within the regional economic groupings, a continuing challenge is to ensure that they link well with national programmes.

Policy recommendations

Going forward, developing an African bioeconomy requires a concerted effort of African governments, development partners and the private sector to undertake the following:

First, there is need for policies that respond to needs of the community and to sustainability goals, which also guarantees a future for generations to come. If this is agreeable, then policies should not stifle scientific progress that is intended to move the continent towards a knowledge-based bioeconomy. Rather, policies should be enabling. Furthermore, while the continent seems to have scores of science and technology policies, these policies are often too broad in their scope and lack clarity. Such broad policies may be difficult to implement. It is better to have science, technology and innovation policies with clear goals and expected measurable outcomes as well as more evident incentives. In this regard, specific bioeconomy policies and strategies may be necessary. For example, a Pan African Bioeconomy Strategy (PABS) may help focus investments in bioscience research and innovation in the continent. Such a strategy may also clarify intellectual property management issues, taxation regimes, etc., that are essential for creating an environment conducive to business development and growth, not least for promoting a knowledge-based bioeconomy.

Second, there should be innovative financing mechanisms for research and innovation for a knowledge-based bioeconomy. The current financing mechanisms, which are predominantly through commercial banks, have unfavourable terms and conditions for new and apparently risky start-up bioscience businesses. Additionally, the private sector in most parts of Africa is still young and weak, and neither invests sufficiently in research and development, nor in projects aimed at bringing research products to market. It is extremely difficult at the present times to get financing for proof of concept for technologies or prototype development, not least in the life sciences field. Therefore, for the time being, African governments should play a leading role in providing innovative financing, such as research and development funds, innovation funds or public venture capital funds. This type of home-grown initiative by African governments would be the foundation for regional and international collaboration in research and innovation and inevitably nurtures local talent and spurs creativity and innovation in the community, including the private sector.

Third, products and firms that produce the products must be competitive. This means that firms should innovate, and new firms should emerge. The latent potential of scientists in the universities should be tapped by letting interested scientists who want to go into business to take leave of absence to try out their luck in the business and entrepreneurial world. These scientists who potentially have business acumen can be supported through well-structured, active and professional business incubation services for creative and innovative bioscience-based business cases, ideas or technologies.

Conclusion

A synergy between continental initiatives under the NEPAD Agency and other organs of the African Union, regional programmes under the regional economic communities, and research and innovation initiatives within nation states, particularly at the universities, is desirable for developing an African bioeconomy. As a matter of policy, efforts are needed to integrate continental initiatives within states. However, this may happen best when there are strong institutions and systems within countries. Strong state institutions can make resources available to complement regional and continental cooperative research and innovation programmes. Special attention should be given to the role of public policy organizations as well as industry and universities in facilitating utilization and diffusion of bioscience-based technologies. These organizations should focus on creating a functional bioscience innovation system that promotes a vibrant African bioeconomy.

References

African Development Bank. 2015. *African Economic Outlook 2015.* [Online]. [Accessed 12 February 2016]. Available from: http://www.africaneconomicoutlook.org/fileadmin/uploads/aeo/2015/PDF_Chapters/Overview_AEO2015_EN-web.pdf

AUC (African Union Commission). 2014a. *Agenda 2063: The Africa We Want.* [Online]. [Accessed 12 February 2016]. Available from: http://www.agenda2063.au.int/en/sites/default/files/agenda2063_popular_version_05092014_EN.pdf

AUC (African Union Commission). 2014b. *On the Wings of Innovation. Science, Technology and Innovation Strategy for Africa. 2024 Strategy, STISA-2024.* Addis Ababa: African Union.

AUC (African Union Commission). 2014c. *Report of the AU Joint Conference of Ministers of Agriculture, Rural Development, Fisheries and Aquaculture.* [Online]. [Accessed 14 February 2016]. Available from: http://rea.au.int/en/sites/default/files/Final%20Report%20of%20the%20AUC%20Joint%20Conf%20Ministers_AgriRuralDevFisheriesAquaculture_20_05_2014.pdf

Bio-Innovate Africa. 2015. *Bio-resources Innovations Network for Eastern Africa Development.* [Online]. [Accessed 12 February 2016]. Available from: http://www.bioinnovate-africa.org/success-stories/

Bothwell, E. 2015. *Top 30 African Universities: Times Higher Education Reveals Snapshot University Ranking.* [Online]. [Accessed 14 February 2016]. Available from: https://www.timeshighereducation.com/news/top-30-african-universities-times-higher-education-reveals-snapshot-university-ranking

Byerlee, D. *et al.* 2013. Growing Africa – Unlocking the Potential of Agribusiness: Main Report. [Online]. Washington, DC: World Bank. [Accessed 14 February 2016]. Available from: http://documents.worldbank.org/curated/en/2013/03/17427481/growing-africa-unlocking-potential-agribusiness-vol-1-2-main-report

Etzkowitz, H. and Dzisah, J. 2007. The triple helix of innovation: towards a university-led development strategy for Africa. *African Technology Development Forum* 4(2), pp.3–11.

FARA (Forum for Agricultural Research in Africa). 2014. *Science Agenda for Agriculture in Africa (S3A).* Accra: FARA.

Freeman, C. 1995. The national system of innovation in historical perspective. *Cambridge Journal of Economics* 19, pp.5–24.

Government of Uganda. 2013. *Uganda Vision 2040*. Kampala: Government of Uganda.

IUCEA (Inter-University Council for East Africa). 2014. *Report from a Study Establishing the Status of Higher Education Qualification Systems and their Contributions to Human Resources Development in East Africa.* Kampala: IUCEA.

Juma, C. 2011. *The New Harvest: Agricultural Innovation in Africa.* New York: Oxford University Press.

Kunene, B. 2013. AfDB's initiatives in higher education. Presentation at the Regional Initiative in Science and Education, 2013 Annual Meeting, Johannesburg. [Online]. [Accessed 14 February 2016]. Available from: https://sig.ias.edu/sites/sig.ias.edu/files/AfDB's%20initiatives%20in%20HE.pdf

Lundvall, B.-Å. *et al.* 2002. National systems of production, innovation and competence building. *Research Policy* 31, pp.213–31.

Muhindo, C. 2016. 167 public university lecturers get scholarships. *NewVision.* [Online]. 10 February 2016. [Accessed 15 February 2016]. Available from: http://www.newvision.co.ug/new_vision/news/1416846/167-public-university-lecturers-scholarships

Nelson, R.R. 1995. Co-evolution of industry structure, technology and supporting institutions, and the making of comparative advantage. *International Journal of the Economics of Business* 2(2), pp.171–84.

NEPAD (New Partnership for Africa's Development). 2003. *Comprehensive Africa Agriculture Development Programme (CAADP).* Pretoria: NEPAD.

NEPAD (New Partnership for Africa's Development). 2006. *Africa's Science and Technology Consolidated Plan of Action.* [Online]. [Accessed 14 February 2016]. Available from: http://www.nepad.org/system/files/ast_cpa_2007.pdf

Oyelaran-Oyeyinka, B. and Sampath, P.G. 2007. *Innovation in African Development: Case Studies of Uganda, Tanzania and Kenya, a World Bank Study.* Washington, DC: World Bank. pp.1–67.

RISE (Regional Initiative in Science and Education). 2015. RISE: In Numbers. [Online]. [Accessed 14 February 2016]. Available from: https://sig.ias.edu/rise/in-numbers-2015

Salami, A. *et al.* 2010. *Smallholder Agriculture in East Africa: Trends, Constraints and Opportunities.* [Online]. Tunisia: African Development Bank. [Accessed 14 February 2016]. Available from: http://www.afdb.org/fileadmin/uploads/afdb/Documents/Publications/WORKING%20105%20%20PDF%20d.pdf

World Bank. 2015a. *Arable Land (% of land area). Data.* [Online]. [Accessed 14 February 2016]. Available from: http://data.worldbank.org/indicator/AG.LND.ARBL.ZS/countries

World Bank. 2015b. *World Bank Data: School Enrolment, Tertiary (% gross).* [Online]. [Accessed 14 February 2016]. Available from: http://data.worldbank.org/indicator/SE.TER.ENRR

World Bank. 2016. *Country and Lending Groups.* [Online]. [Accessed 14 February 2016]. Available from: http://data.worldbank.org/about/country-and-lending-groups

World Bulletin. 2014. *E. Africa Suffers World's Lowest University Enrolment.* [Online]. [Accessed 14 February 2016]. Available from: www.worldbulletin.net/news/137826/e-africa

World Economic Forum. 2015. *The Africa Competitiveness Report 2015.* [Online]. [Accessed 14 February 2016]. Available from: http://www3.weforum.org/docs/WEF_ACR_2015/Africa_Competitiveness_Report_2015.pdf

18 Intellectual property challenges for a bioeconomy

Rosemary Wolson

Introduction

Intellectual property rights (IPRs) provide a mechanism for incentivizing and rewarding innovative activity by granting creators and innovators exclusive rights to enjoy the benefits of their innovation and decide how it is used, for a limited period of time. The intellectual property (IP) system aims to strike a balance between the private rights of innovators to be recognized and rewarded for their innovative behaviour, and the broader rights of society to get access to and benefit from the products of innovation. Much debate centres on the extent to which this balance is in fact being achieved. In particular, there is concern that the system favours technology producers in the developed world to the detriment of developing countries. In most sectors of the biotechnology industry, strong IP protection is viewed as crucial to enable recoupment of the large investments that are required to bring new products to market, and this is certainly true in the area of agricultural biotechnology. This means that much of the new technology is proprietary, held by large organizations in both the public and private sectors. As a result, concerns have been raised about the impact of this trend on efforts to build a bioeconomy in developing countries.

Strong views have been expressed by stakeholders across the spectrum on the role of IP in promoting access to technology as well as domestic innovation in developing countries. At one end, proponents of a strong IP regime emphasize the importance of IPRs as a tool to incentivize R&D investment and innovative activity. At the other end, critics of a strong IP system point to the barriers to access created by IPRs in developing countries and call for IPRs to be abandoned in favour of a more open approach.

Arguably, neither of these views alone offers a viable means of promoting food security by getting modern biotechnology solutions into the hands of African farmers and onto African tables, nor to stimulate the development of African biotechnology to solve local problems, eliminate poverty, promote competitiveness and improve quality of life. However, a range of practical options exists (both regulatory and contractual) to help navigate the complex IP landscape, improving access to relevant biotechnology in Africa and helping to realize the innovative capabilities of African researchers and farmers.

Perspectives on IP: unpacking the issues

By examining in more detail the various issues and perspectives which have a bearing on the role of IP in building a bioeconomy in Africa, the relevance and validity of these can be better understood.

The impact of IPRs on innovation in general

Clear evidence demonstrating a direct causal link between the role of patents in promoting innovation is hard to come by, and several studies show that sometimes patents may in fact stifle innovation (Mercurio, 2014). This makes the task of crafting enabling IP policies quite onerous, especially for developing countries characterized by a weaker private sector, lower levels of innovation and conflicting advice received from lobby groups promoting diverse agendas.

Yet, irrespective of the complexities of this environment and the mixed evidence available to draw on in formulating appropriate policies, it has become non-negotiable for countries wishing to participate in the multilateral trade system and to extract value from their indigenous biological resources and traditional knowledge to implement IP systems that comply with certain mandated minimum requirements.

Do IPRs incentivize developed countries to develop solutions for developing country needs?

There is little evidence to suggest that IPRs have played a major role in encouraging developed country organizations to perform R&D to solve the problems that are most pressing to developing countries. The profitability of markets tends to drive the research agenda, making the smaller economies and poorer consumers of developing country markets less attractive to focus on. This is borne out for example by looking at the early genetic modification traits to reach the market, aimed mostly at large commercial farmers. While these traits may also have some application or offer some benefit for developing country farmers, including small-scale farmers, there are arguably other traits which might on balance be of higher priority and hold greater promise for achieving higher impact in the developing world.

Do IPRs promote innovation in developing countries?

For developing countries, resources (in the form of funding, infrastructure and skills) are often in short supply, serving to limit the scale of innovation that can take place. In the absence of a healthy pipeline of new technologies, strong IPRs become much less significant in promoting innovation. In the short to medium term, introduction of a new IP regime is likely to be of greater benefit to foreign entities that are ensured protection for their technologies, than for local organizations who will be developing fewer technologies worth protecting.

Do IPRs create a barrier to entry for the products of biosciences R&D in developing countries?

The products of biotechnology are often subject to a multitude of patents, covering any combination of methods, processes, formulations, materials, genes and genetic sequences, seeds and plants, molecules, tools, kits, techniques and reagents. This is sometimes referred to as a 'patent thicket': 'a dense web of overlapping intellectual property rights that a company must hack its way through in order to actually commercialize new technology' (Shapiro, 2001, p.120). Golden Rice is a commonly cited example of this. The rice, biofortified with pro-Vitamin A, was developed with a humanitarian purpose in mind, aiming to reduce Vitamin A deficiency. A freedom-to-operate study showing that the production of Golden Rice was covered by over 40 patents held by several different organizations raised concerns about the viability of taking this to market (Kryder *et al.*, 2000). Because of the humanitarian use objectives, however, licence fee waivers were obtained from all patent holders.

On the one hand, this illustrates that even where a particular solution is covered by numerous patents, this need not be a barrier to entry for the product concerned. On the other hand, though, the transaction costs involved in hacking through a patent thicket cannot be underestimated and could well act as a deterrent in getting other less high profile technologies to market. Expert legal and technical knowledge is required to carry out comprehensive freedom-to-operate studies and negotiate the acquisition of rights from the various individual rights holders. This might prove beyond the reach of smaller or less experienced technology producers. Where one is dealing with technologies which have a less clear-cut humanitarian objective (including those with dual application for both commercial and humanitarian use), patent holders might prove more reluctant to waive licence fees. Finally, as a postscript to this example, it must be noted that Golden Rice is not yet available on the market for reasons unrelated to IP.

The costs of obtaining patent protection also have to be taken into account. Developing country innovators wishing to patent new technologies they develop are likely to encounter resource constraints, both in the form of finances to cover the costs of patent prosecution and maintenance, as well as in finding qualified local patent attorneys. Enforcing patent rights can also be challenging, especially if these have to be defended against more powerful players with deeper pockets.

Can IPRs be used to promote the protection of and generation of value from indigenous knowledge?

Indigenous knowledge (IK) is a potential area of competitive advantage for many developing countries, yet harnessing the benefits of this has proved elusive. Much IK has been developed over centuries, and passed down through generations, evolving over time with further developments. Some IK is held by individuals, but much of it is collectively held by one or more communities. Some IK remains highly confidential, but many uses of IK have been documented. This can create the perception that this knowledge is in the public domain and free for anyone to use, thus failing to recognize or reward the contributions made by the IK holders. Instead, those who appropriate and beneficiate IK (typically in developed countries) may be entitled to claim IPRs over the products or processes they develop based on IK without acknowledgment or compensation to the IK holders.

It is therefore recognized that mechanisms are needed to provide legal protection for IK, in order to govern its preservation, use and exploitation, the prevention of misappropriation and the equitable sharing of benefits. Various challenges are presented, though, when attempts are made to use the established IP legal regime to protect IK. For example, knowledge or material that has been in existence for a long time will not be considered novel (this being a requirement for obtaining many types of IPRs). Where IK is kept secret, obtaining IPRs will require disclosure of the IK concerned, and it will enter the public domain on expiry of the IPR. The western IP system is based on the premise that individual creativity and innovation should be encouraged and rewarded and does not always cater for collective or communal rights. Furthermore, the costs of and complex processes for obtaining IP protection can be prohibitive for many IK holders. Additional measures are therefore needed to supplement conventional IPRs in order to ensure better recognition and protection of IK and IK holders (Correa, 2001; Hansen and VanFleet, 2003).

Is it a feasible alternative to make technologies freely available without IP restrictions?

It is sometimes suggested that those involved in producing technologies aimed at developing country markets should choose not to pursue IP protection and instead make their technologies available without restriction to all who can potentially benefit from them. Unfortunately, though, this is seldom an effective method of ensuring that they reach their intended beneficiaries in developing countries (CGIAR Consortium Office, 2011). Without a dedicated technology transfer strategy, end-users are unlikely to know that a new technology exists, how to access it or how it may be of benefit to them. And where there is no opportunity to profit from the exploitation of a new technology, it is difficult to mobilize the funding and institutional support needed to ensure uptake.

Governance of IPRs in agricultural biotechnology

Many roots of the complexities associated with IPRs and development can be traced to the international governance system. Several multilateral treaties and conventions regulate agriculture, plant genetic resources, trade and IP. These create a fairly complicated set of overlapping and intersecting rules, which together shape the international landscape for agricultural innovation, and ultimately food security. These can broadly be categorized into two types of regime: i) those based on IPRs, which tend to recognize and reward individual innovation, and ii) those based on equity/conservation, in terms of which plant genetic resources are viewed as national assets ('sovereign property') that can be exploited for collective benefit in order to incentivize conservation (Aoki and Luvai, 2007). IPR regimes include Trade-Related Aspects of Intellectual Property Rights (TRIPS) and the International Union for the Protection of New Varieties of Plants (UPOV), and equity/conservation regimes include the Convention on Biodiversity (CBD) and the International Treaty on Plant Genetic Resources for Food and Agriculture (ITPGRFA).

This proliferation of regimes has created an environment conducive to 'forum shopping', where different actors select the arena where they are most likely to successfully promote their interests and prevail in achieving their strategic objectives. As a result, different states and organizations representing different constituencies dominate in different fora, leading increasingly to inconsistencies and contradictions in the rules established in each. Most often, developed countries hold sway in the fora that promote IPR regimes, while developing countries exert more influence in those which espouse equity/conservation regimes. The IPR regimes are generally characterized by stronger language, which leads to more enforceable obligations, whereas the language in the equity/conservation regime instruments tends to be vaguer, making substantive implementation harder. This can pose challenges for the implementation of international obligations into national law, create tensions in bilateral relationships, and ultimately complicate attempts to develop coherent national policies.

TRIPS

Membership of the World Trade Organization (WTO) requires member states to sign up to TRIPS as a condition for participating in the multilateral trade system. While evidence of the impact of the global trade system on various WTO member states (especially developing countries) is not unequivocally positive, it appears that the benefits are deemed to exceed the costs of participation, as attested to by current membership of WTO numbering 161 member states, and more than 20 observer states in (or expected to begin soon) the process of accession. TRIPS sets minimum standards of IP protection that member states are expected to incorporate into national law, including the requirement that member states offer protection for plant genetic resources through patents, plant variety protection or other *sui generis* rights. This means that failure to provide any form of protection for living organisms as a principle would not be considered TRIPS-compliant.

For many developing countries, TRIPS necessitated introducing new legislation or significantly strengthening existing IP protection offered. Since levels of domestic innovation are relatively low in most developing countries, the inevitable consequence of such measures is that the main beneficiaries of this system are foreign players seeking protection for the goods and services they bring into these markets. In an effort to counteract the potentially negative impact of this, TRIPS therefore also contains provisions that are intended to address the inherent imbalances between – for the most part – developed country technology producers and developing country technology users. These include the introduction of exceptions and flexibilities that can be invoked by developing countries in speci-fied circumstances and provision for technical assistance to be offered by devel-oped countries to developing countries. Least developed countries were given an extended deadline for the implementation of their TRIPS obligations into national law (which has been further extended to 2021). Notably, TRIPS includes strong enforcement mechanisms through its dispute settlement framework, in terms of which breaches attract trade sanctions. By linking IP to international trade, it is felt by some that TRIPS serves more to protect the interests of those who domi-nate the international trade system than to promote innovation globally (Barton *et al.*, 2007).

UPOV

The UPOV Convention establishes a multilateral framework for the protection of new plant varieties aimed at encouraging plant breeding by granting plant breed-ers' rights for plant varieties which are new, distinct, uniform and stable. Certain uses of the propagating material (and in some cases, harvested material) of a plant variety require authorization from the holder of the breeders' right, but private and non-commercial use, experimental use and use for the purpose of breeding other varieties are not covered by the protected right. The Convention has been revised periodically. The most recent revision (1991 Act), to which new members would be required to accede, is considered overall to be more advantageous to the commercial plant breeding industry and less favourable for farmers and the infor-mal seed sector.

While few African countries are UPOV members (only Kenya, South Africa and Tunisia), a number have either initiated the procedure for accession or sought assistance from UPOV in developing UPOV Convention-based legislation. Two regional IP organizations, the African Intellectual Property Organization (OAPI) (17 member states) and the African Regional Intellectual Property Organization (ARIPO) (19 member states) have recently adopted instruments for plant variety protection which conform to UPOV requirements. The Southern African Development Community (SADC) has also drawn up a UPOV-aligned draft protocol for harmonization of plant variety protection in the region. While the benefits of harmonization with international standards are touted by some (UPOV, 2002), concern has been expressed by many civil society organizations who believe that this approach does not serve the best interests of the region. They are calling for alternatives to be considered, which would be more effective in combating biopiracy, protecting farmers' rights and responding to the needs of a large informal seed sector (de Jonge, 2014).

CBD

The CBD has three interlinked objectives, namely i) the conservation and ii) sustainable use of biological diversity and iii) the sharing of benefits arising out of such use. The CBD treats biological resources as sovereign property of states and confers on member states both the responsibility to conserve their biological diversity as well as the right to benefit from the utilization of their national biological resources. The mechanism proposed by the CBD for providing access and sharing benefits is bilateral, involving contracts between the states of origin of the material concerned (or local communities within member states from whom the material is sourced) and parties wishing to use the material.

The Nagoya Protocol to the CBD, on Access to Genetic Resources and the Fair and Equitable Sharing of Benefits Arising from their Utilization, provides a legal framework for access and benefit-sharing to supplement the CBD principles. There is concern that the requirements for implementation are quite onerous and could in fact ultimately stifle rather than promote effective conservation and use of biological resources, thereby reducing the opportunities for member states to reap the expected benefits (Chartered Institute of Patent Attorneys, 2015).

ITPGRFA

The ITPGRFA establishes a multilateral framework to facilitate access to plant genetic materials for 64 important crops by farmers, plant breeders and researchers from member states to use for the purposes of research, breeding and training for food and agriculture, in exchange for sharing benefits derived from the commercial use of such resources with the countries of origin. No IPRs may be claimed over material in the form in which it is received. The Treaty provides for the protection of farmers' traditional knowledge, participation by farmers in relevant national decision-making processes and equitable benefit-sharing (to be given effect by member states in national law). However, its success both in creating a substantial open access pool of plant genetic resources and in encouraging the adoption of substantive farmers' rights has arguably been limited as a result of vague and weak language that has failed to ensure meaningful implementation of its principles by member states (Beck, 2010).

IP options to help promote the creation of a bioeconomy in African countries

Developing countries striving to develop and access technologies that can promote development and improve the lives and livelihoods of their citizens need appropriate tools and capabilities to navigate the overlapping instruments and fora of the international governance regime and the practical constraints imposed by the complex IP landscape. Solutions are needed to reduce transaction costs and lower barriers, draw on inherent strengths and competitive advantage, and be feasible to implement in the local environment. This requires a combination of appropriate regulatory interventions, incentives and contractual arrangements that complement one another. Different actors and institutions in the innovation ecosystem will be responsible for shaping and adopting different policies and practices, dictating that policymakers, the private sector, academia and researchers, and civil society work collaboratively and supportively.

An enabling regulatory environment

The national IP regulatory framework should be responsive to domestic needs. Accession to relevant international treaties and conventions should be carefully considered, and available flexibilities should be exploited when implementing obligations under such treaties and conventions into national law.

- Plant variety protection
  Plant variety protection regimes should promote food security and protect local farming systems (which typically rely on seed saving and informal seed exchange between farmers). This will generally require a combination of incentives for both commercial seed suppliers (to ensure that they develop optimal varieties for a particular environment) and informal agriculture (to safeguard the ability of subsistence and small-scale farmers to sustain their families and communities and to reward them for the contributions they make to conserving germplasm). This could potentially be achieved by adopting a *sui generis* hybrid framework that incorporates many of the UPOV concepts, while simultaneously catering to the needs of small-scale farmers by means of some changes to UPOV-based protection, thereby striking a balance between the demands of the different constituencies (de Jonge, 2014).

- Protection of IK
  Various mechanisms can be explored to supplement the conventional IP regime and address some of the limitations encountered in applying it for the purposes of IK protection. Defensive mechanisms can be used to prevent unauthorized claims of rights and exploitation without rewarding or acknowledging IK holders. IK registries can be used to document IK, thereby preventing patent rights being claimed over pre-existing IK. Patent law may require that any IK-based inventions disclose the origin of such IK, or that proof of legal acquisition of such IK be furnished, to assist patent examiners in determining whether the requirements of novelty and inventive step are met, and/or in ensuring that equitable sharing of benefits takes place with IK holders. Positive protection in the form of *sui generis* legal rights for IK holders can also be introduced. This may take the form of a property regime of exclusive rights (akin to other forms of IPR), or of a liability regime, in terms of which the IK would be made available to anyone who wished to use it, subject to compensating IK holders fairly. Where applicable, customary law may also provide a basis for protection of IK (Tobin, 2013).

- Compulsory licensing
  Compulsory licensing involves a grant of licence rights to a third party by an authority without the consent of the patent holder. Compulsory licensing is provided for in TRIPS as well as in most national patent legislation, subject to stipulated conditions (including adequate compensation for the patent holder), which may differ from country to country (subject to TRIPS requirements). It is generally intended to counteract the abuse of patent rights, in cases where a patent holder is failing to satisfy the market, particularly in

times of national need. Compulsory licensing is rarely invoked by developing countries, but in appropriate cases can be a tool for ensuring access to technology on reasonable terms. Sometimes the threat that a compulsory licence may be issued can encourage a patent holder to enter into voluntary licences.

IP management options for overcoming IP-related barriers

In addition to legislative interventions, various initiatives have been adopted or proposed to overcome some of the obstacles posed by IPRs. Some options to consider are discussed here. These are not exhaustive and features of some overlap with others.

- Open source licensing models
  The principles underlying the free and open source software movement can be drawn on to expand access to biotechnologies. This involves making technologies available on a non-exclusive basis for anyone to use, provided that they adhere to the agreed terms of sharing, including the obligation to share improvements made to the technologies acquired under the framework concerned on the same terms. This facilitates freedom-to-operate and can apply to both patented and unpatented technologies, and both commercial and not-for-profit use.
- Compensatory liability rules
  This can be referred to as a 'take and pay' regime, in terms of which anyone is permitted to access and use material or technology held by someone else, on condition that the provider of the material or technology concerned is fairly compensated for the benefits the user receives. This reduces transaction costs while incentivizing material and technology holders to offer easy access with the assurance that compensation will be forthcoming (Reichman and Lewis, 2005).
- Cross-licensing, patent pools and clearinghouses
  Cross-licensing, patent pools and clearinghouses are intersecting mechanisms that can help reduce transaction costs associated with accessing patented technology, particularly in areas with high patent density and where patents covering essential standards exist. *Cross-licensing* involves two or more patent holders agreeing to license one another rights under their respective patents. This concept can be taken further into a *patent pool*, in terms of which multiple patent holders pool their respective patents for the purpose of making them available to one another and to third parties on stipulated terms and conditions (Krattiger, 2004). Certain patent pools might operate as *clearinghouses*, taking in IP from multiple patent holders, licensing it out to users, and collecting and distributing licence fees.
- Socially responsible licensing
  Socially responsible licensing (SRL) facilitates the availability of technologies for underserved populations at affordable cost. It aims to ensure that profitable markets can be tapped in developed countries, while concurrently

promoting access in developing countries on favourable terms, by applying segmented licensing provisions. SRL is typically driven by technology transfer offices at public research institutions or mandated by funders.

- Innovation prizes

  Innovation prizes can take many different forms but usually involve a financial incentive for solving a defined problem or meeting a challenge or objective. Prizes have been proposed as an alternative to IPRs, in terms of which in lieu of patents, government would provide cash incentives after the fact to reward certain types of socially beneficial innovation that can then be made available to consumers at reduced cost. Many prizes are also increasingly being offered by philanthropic organizations and companies to achieve different goals (Bays *et al.*, 2009). These do not necessarily preclude IPRs, but instead provide a framework governing how and to whom the IP in the solution will be licensed or transferred (e.g. InnoCentive, 2016; XPRIZE, 2016).

Capacity development

IP management capacity can play an important role in accelerating the uptake of biosciences in developing countries (Hennessey *et al.*, 2014). Biotechnology is a very research-intensive, IP-rich field which calls for a thorough practical understanding of IP issues. Collaboration is recognized as a prerequisite for successful biotechnology R&D, as individual organizations are rarely able to access all the tools, materials, technologies and/or expertise they need from internal sources alone. This is particularly true of developing country R&D organizations. Effective IP management capability becomes very important to facilitate such collaborations. IP terms in collaboration agreements need to be negotiated to achieve fair outcomes for all partners while at the same time ensuring that the IP developed in the course of the collaboration can be exploited without too many restrictions. This can be a complex process and projects can often be held up as a result of parties being unable to reach agreement on IP terms. The chances of this are however reduced when the negotiations are carried out by those with IP knowledge and experience.

Developing country research organizations also need capabilities to evaluate, recognize the value of and seek appropriate protection for their own IP. In some cases this IP can be commercialized, either directly by the originating organization or through a process of technology transfer, in which IP would typically be licensed to a company with the resources to take a product or service to market based on the IP concerned, or to a start-up company established for the purpose of exploiting the IP. For successful commercialization, the licensee in most cases will have to invest substantially in activities such as further development, obtaining regulatory approvals or certification, packaging and marketing. Without a patent to keep competitors out of the market for a period of time, a prospective licensee might be unwilling to make the necessary investment. Venture capitalists and others investing in start-ups have similar concerns, and often a strong patent position will be a prerequisite for attracting early stage investment. Without the necessary investment, the new technologies will be unlikely to reach the market. For those that do, their impact is likely to be sub-optimal if they are inadequately financed.

Capacity is then also needed to generate value from such IP. It can also be used as a bargaining chip to access complementary technology owned by others, which might be needed to use one's own IP effectively (e.g. through a cross-licensing arrangement), or as an 'entrance fee' to participate in public–private partnerships, multi-party collaborations or patent pools. Often, a condition for participation in large consortia requires a contribution of background IP to open the doors to substantial R&D funding as well as other benefits that arise out of such relationships, including access to IP and technology held by other consortium members, as well as capacity development.

Conclusion

IP issues will continue to generate debate and pose challenges for the creation of a successful African bioeconomy. The obstacles are generally surmountable. Gaining access to IP is rarely the major hurdle in getting biotechnology to African researchers, farmers, entrepreneurs, communities and consumers. Without simultaneously transferring know-how and/or show-how, the IP may not be adopted optimally or at all by the intended beneficiaries. Issues might also arise in respect of sub-optimal supply chains, distribution networks, regulatory regimes or user acceptance. It is therefore important not to view IP in isolation, but rather to take a more holistic approach with a thorough understanding of the full value chain, so that interventions and institutional support can be appropriately targeted at weak links.

But even while recognizing that IP is only 'one piece of the puzzle', it remains vital that strong capacity be developed in Africa to deal effectively with IP issues in order to ensure that IP does not become a barrier to the development of, and access to, relevant biotechnology. The real impact of IPRs in a particular environment must be distinguished from the rhetoric, to enable appropriate policies and strategies to be crafted that will ultimately be able to promote the establishment of a sustainable bioeconomy capable of delivering effective solutions to local problems.

There is a critical need for productive collaborations and creative partnerships between the public, private and academic sectors, where Africa takes greater initiative in shaping the research agenda, investing in it and implementing the results. Creative forms of collaboration and partnership can be facilitated and supported with appropriate contractual frameworks that are of mutual benefit to all parties. This can, though, only be accomplished by a strong cohort of IP-literate and IP-articulate African stakeholders across the spectrum, who have mastered the legal and technical complexities of IP. This will contribute to ensuring that Africa is well-placed to reap the benefits that biotechnology offers.

References

Aoki, K. and Luvai, K. 2007. Reclaiming 'common heritage' treatment in the international plant genetic resources regime complex. *Michigan State Law Review*, pp.35–70.

Barton, J.H. *et al.* 2007. *Views on the Future of the Intellectual Property System*. ICTSD Programme on Intellectual Property Rights and Sustainable Development Selected Issue Briefs No. 1. Geneva: International Centre for Trade and Sustainable Development.

Bays, J. *et al.* 2009. Using prizes to spur innovation. *McKinsey Quarterly*. [Online]. [Accessed 11 February 2016]. Available from: http://www.mckinsey.com/insights/innovation/using_prizes_to_spur_innovation

Beck, R. 2010. Farmer's rights and open source licensing. *Arizona Journal of Environmental Law & Policy* 1(2), pp.167–218.

CGIAR Consortium Office. 2011. *The Intersection of Public Goods, Intellectual Property Rights, and Partnerships: Maximizing Impact for the Poor*. Briefing paper. Montpellier: CGIAR Consortium of International Agricultural Research Centers.

Chartered Institute of Patent Attorneys. 2015. *Briefing Note on the Nagoya Protocol: New Laws that May Damage Public Health and UK Science*. [Online]. [Accessed 15 January 2016]. Available from: http://www.cipa.org.uk/policy-and-news/briefing-papers/the-nagoya-protocol-to-the-convention-on-biological-diversity/

Correa, C.M. 2001. *Traditional Knowledge and Intellectual Property: Issues and Options Surrounding the Protection of Traditional Knowledge: A Discussion Paper*. Geneva: Quaker United Nations Office.

De Jonge, B. 2014. Plant variety protection in sub-Saharan Africa: balancing commercial and smallholder farmers' interests. *Journal of Politics and Law*. [Online]. 7(3). [Accessed 15 August 2015]. Available from: http://dx.doi.org/10.5539/jpl.v7n3p100

Hansen, S.A. and VanFleet, J.W. 2003. *Traditional Knowledge and Intellectual Property: A Handbook on Issues and Options for Traditional Knowledge Holders in Protecting their Intellectual Property and Maintaining Biological Diversity*. Washington, DC: American Association for the Advancement of Science (AAAS) Science and Human Rights Program.

Hennessey W.O. *et al.* 2014. Practice driving policy: agbiotech transfer as capacity building. In: Smyth, S.J. *et al.* (eds). *Handbook on Agriculture, Biotechnology and Development*. Cheltenham and Northampton: Edward Elgar, pp.314–42.

InnoCentive. 2016. InnoCentive website. [Online]. [Accessed 11 February 2016]. Available from: http://www.innocentive.com

Krattiger, A.F. 2004. Financing the bioindustry and facilitating biotechnology transfer. *IP Strategy Today* 8, pp.1–45.

Kryder, R.D. *et al.* 2000. *The Intellectual and Technical Property Components of Pro-vitamin A Rice (Golden Rice): A Preliminary Freedom-to-Operate Review*. ISAAA Brief No. 20. Ithaca, NY: ISAAA.

Mercurio, B. 2014. *TRIPs, Patents and Innovation: A Necessary Reappraisal?* E15Initiative. Geneva: International Centre for Trade and Sustainable Development (ICTSD) and World Economic Forum 2014.

Reichman, J.H. and Lewis, T. 2005. Using liability rules to stimulate local innovation in developing countries: application to traditional knowledge. In: Maskus, K.E. and Reichman, J.H. (eds). *International Public Goods and Transfer of Technology Under a Globalized Intellectual Property Regime*. Cambridge: Cambridge University Press, pp. 337–66.

Shapiro, C. 2001. Navigating the patent thicket: cross licenses, patent pools, and standard-setting. In: Jaffe, A.B. *et al.* (eds). *Innovation Policy and the Economy Vol I.* Cambridge: MIT Press, pp.119–50.

Tobin, B.M. 2013. Bridging the Nagoya compliance gap: the fundamental role of customary law in protection of indigenous peoples' resource and knowledge rights. *Law, Environment and Development Journal.* [Online]. 9(2), pp.142–62. [Accessed 11 February 2016]. Available from: http://www.lead-journal.org/content/13142.pdf

UPOV (International Union for the Protection of New Varieties of Plants). 2002. *International Harmonization Is Essential for Effective Plant Variety Protection, Trade and Transfer of Technology. UPOV Position based on an Intervention in the Council for TRIPS, on September 19, 2002.* [Online]. [Accessed 23 December 2015]. Available from: http://www.upov.int/export/sites/upov/about/en/pdf/international_harmonization.pdf

XPRIZE. 2016. XPRIZE website. [Online]. [Accessed 11 February 2016]. Available from: http://www.xprize.org

19 Europe and Africa

How European policies influence bioscience adoption in Africa

John Komen

Introduction

As early as 2003, the Nuffield Council on Bioethics (2003, p.xvii) stated that:

> The freedom of choice of farmers in developing countries is being severely challenged by the agricultural policy of the European Union (EU). Developing countries might well be reluctant to approve GM crop varieties because of fears of jeopardising their current and future export markets. They may also not be able to provide the necessary infrastructure to enable compliance with EU requirements for traceability and labelling.

The report continues to conclude that: 'There is a considerable imbalance between the hypothetical benefits afforded by the EU policy for its own citizens, and the probable and substantial benefits that could be afforded to developing countries' (p.xviii).

The critical analysis of EU policies on biotechnology adequately sums up European influence on the adoption of modern bioscience in Africa. While this may be one obvious example of Europe's influence in Africa, regarding the adoption of GM crops, it is representative of European policies and policy decisions with serious negative impacts on scientific and economic development in Africa.

This chapter provides examples of the type of EU policy inconsistencies that influence policymaking in Africa regarding biosciences in general, and modern biotechnology in particular, and attempts to explain the key factors involved in their negative impacts in Africa. Recommendations point to actions that can be taken at the national, sub-regional and international (EU–Africa) levels to address this challenge.

Europe's importance to African agriculture

Due to preferential trade agreements with former colonies in Africa, the Caribbean and Pacific (ACP), the European Union is a major export market for countries in sub-Saharan Africa (SSA). It is generally estimated that around 40 per cent of SSA's agricultural exports is destined for Europe. This figure confirms the important role of Europe in African development, and also points to the impact that EU policy decisions can have on the continent. For example, in 2012, the EU's drastic lowering of maximum residue levels (MRLs) of certain pesticides used in horticultural production, immediately resulted in a sharp reduction of Kenya's horticulture exports to the EU (Hortidaily, 2013).

Europe also extends its influence in Africa through development assistance. In 2012 the EU (27 member states and the European Commission combined) was the largest provider of development aid in the world, contributing more than half of all Official Development Assistance (ODA) worldwide. Overall 43 per cent or €25.3 billion of the EU's ODA was targeted to Africa in 2011. Africa is the main continent targeted by EU development assistance: African countries received close to €24 billion of ODA from EU aid instruments over the period 2007–12. The European Development Fund (EDF), providing an average funding level of €3.7 billion per year, is the main instrument for the EU's cooperation with 79 ACP countries including 48 countries from SSA (European Development Fund, 2016).

Also in the agricultural biosciences, the ties between Europe and Africa remain close. The EU policy communication 'Agenda for Change' (EC, 2011) identifies sustainable agriculture as a key driver of poverty reduction and economic development. More recent EU policy communications identify nutrition with an emphasis on children and women, and resilience to food security crises as particular challenges. These challenges are addressed through the AR4D – Agricultural Research for Development programme, among other instruments. It is interesting to note that the straightforward need to increase agricultural productivity in ACP countries is hardly mentioned in EU policy documents. This is somewhat surprising as low productivity has especially affected basic African food crop production. It can be assumed, however, that a good deal of EU AR4D funding addresses productivity challenges. Between 2010 and 2013, of a total investment of €320 million around 29 per cent of funds were channelled through the Consultative Group on International Agricultural Research (CGIAR) international agricultural research centres and another 8 per cent through non-CGIAR international centres. In addition, some 20 per cent of funding is allocated to Africa-based Sub-regional Research Organisations (SROs) in order to support their agricultural research agendas (EC, 2014).

Incoherent EU policies affect Africa's development

The Common Agricultural Policy: more open market, but less accessible

There are a number of often-cited policy paradoxes in Europe, which have significant negative effects on developing countries particularly those in Africa. The most notable example is the EU's Common Agricultural Policy (CAP), which was originally designed to provide the EU population with high-quality food at reasonable prices, while ensuring a reasonable standard of living for its farmers. Initially, the main policy instrument used involved production subsidies and price support to farmers, leading to surpluses and international trade distortions (dumping). Totalling nearly €60 billion per year, the EU's farm budget consumes some 40 per cent of the EU's €130 billion annual spending. A long-drawn process of CAP reform resulted in a gradual shift from production subsidies to more direct income support to EU farmers. Generally, this has allowed EU agricultural commodity prices to fall significantly, making them much more competitive on world markets including African markets (Goodison, 2009). This has undermined domestic agricultural production across African countries – while European farmers are protected from lower prices through direct income support. This is compounded by a general eroding of so-called preferential trade agreements for ACP countries, for instance leading to lower export value for important African cash crops such as sugar and bananas.

A critical element of CAP reform is the shift from quantity to quality of production, driven by the need to cut back on subsidies for production and export, and by food safety concerns and changing patterns of food consumption in affluent Europe. According to Goodison (2009), the dominant trend is that while EU markets are in principle becoming *more open*, they are also becoming *less accessible* as stricter food safety and higher quality standards increase the costs of serving the EU market. The example of Kenyan horticultural exports cited above is one case to illustrate this trend. In addition, recent EU regulations on aflatoxin levels in imported cereals, groundnuts and fruits have effectively blocked such developing country exports to the EU (Masip *et al.*, 2013).

At the same time, it must be stated that more rigorous food safety regulations can in principle drive innovations in the food industry in Africa, but only when they are implemented in parallel with a targeted technical assistance programme. An interesting case in point is the fish industry in Uganda, where the introduction of strict sanitary standards created a crisis in the industry in the late 1990s, with widespread loss of jobs, livelihoods and export revenues. The EU, in partnership with other international donors, helped the sector to recover by providing technical assistance to the government. Activities involved collaboration across the entire value chain – suppliers, fish-processing firms, buyers – foreign companies, policymakers, as well as international development agencies. National authorities supported technological change by strengthening the inspection process through increased oversight and by designating and approving laboratories. They helped improve infrastructure and sanitary conditions at transportation sites and provided the knowledge infrastructure for proper handling, packaging and transport of fish. This programme enabled the Ugandan fish industry to improve the quality of their products and comply with international standards.

Europe's policy inconsistencies affect bioscience adoption

In the EU, the concept of a Knowledge-Based Bioeconomy (KBBE) is now a central element in the EU Commission's science and innovation policy and research programmes, acknowledging that the European bioeconomy has an approximate market size of around €2 trillion, employing more than 22 million people (EC, 2012). As also described in Chapter 1, a KBBE is defined as the art and science of transforming biological resources into new, sustainable, eco-efficient and value-added products. In essence, it is the coming together of biology, chemistry, material sciences, genomics and information technology to better utilize natural resources in agriculture and industry. Among many other EU member states, Germany, as a leading country in the biosciences, established a Bioeconomy Council in 2009 that guides the country's National Research Strategy Bioeconomy 2030. In each European policy document, biotechnology and the life sciences generally are identified as essential components of a KBBE strategy.

Despite these policy goals, biotechnology R&D in Europe is stifled by a combination of onerous and lengthy regulatory procedures and political, rather than scientific decision-making processes. While a detailed analysis of EU regulations for biotechnology products falls outside the scope of this chapter (but see also Chapter 16), it is sufficient to point to facts such as:

- Regulatory compliance for a new genetically modified (GM) crop can cost up to €11 million (Kalaitzandonakes *et al.*, 2007) and requires many years of review (EuropaBio, 2014). According to life-science industry data, a scientific opinion by the European Food Safety Agency (EFSA) now takes over five years, up from less than two years in 2006 (EuropaBio, 2015). The extensive duration of the safety assessment adds further to undue delays in the GMO approval process at the political level, resulting in asynchronous approvals and impacting global commodity trade.
- The last product receiving commercial planting approval in 2010, a starch-modified potato ('Amflora'), took 13 years to go through the EU regulatory review and approval process.
- Currently, as of July 2015, over 40 GM applications are pending at EFSA awaiting risk assessment and a scientific opinion. The oldest product currently in the system has been awaiting EFSA's scientific opinion for more than eight years. As a comparison, in 2011 the average time required for a complete GM product approval was around 25 months in the USA, 27 months in Brazil and 30 months in Canada (EuropaBio, 2015).
- The situation sketched above is compounded by Europe's constraining policies for co-existence of GM crops with conventional agriculture, and extremely low thresholds for low-level, adventitious presence of GMOs in imported agricultural commodities.

Recent reform proposals by the EU Commission, while formally aimed at breaking the deadlock over GM decision-making by giving a stronger voice to individual member countries, have actually created more confusion and a breakdown of a common EU policy on GM crops. The Commission's proposals boil down to amending the genetically modified organism (GMO) legislation in order to extend the grounds on which member states could restrict or prohibit the cultivation of EU-authorized GMOs on their territory ('opt outs'). Member states are now legally able to restrict or prohibit GMO cultivation on their territory (or part of it) on social, ethical or economic grounds, provided that such measures are justified on the basis of compelling, 'non safety' reasons other than the risk to human or animal health and the environment, that is, criteria other than those assessed by the European Food Safety Authority (EFSA) in its risk assessment. This only applies, however, to GMOs for cultivation and not to GM food and feed, which represent the majority of the authorizations granted in the EU (EC, 2015). As a result, the majority of EU member states have already declared a ban on GMO production in their territories; as other member states will continue GM crop production, the Commission's decision has effectively abandoned its common policy on biotechnology and created issues regarding intra-EU trade in agricultural products.

The EU's perceived GMO-free status

Contrary to popular belief, countries in the EU are not against GMOs or 'GMO free'. While the cultivation of GM crops is limited to insect-resistant maize, which is predominantly planted in Spain, the EU has approved a wide range of GM products for direct consumption by humans and animals despite the lengthy and unwieldy approval procedures. This includes GM soybeans, cotton, maize, oilseed rape and sugar beet. Consequently, the EU trading bloc imports massive quantities of GM commodities mainly for animal feed use. About 70 per cent of soybean meal consumed in the EU is imported and 80 per cent of this meal is produced from GM soybeans. On average, EU imports of soybean meal and soybeans amount to US$9 billion and US$6.5 billion per year, respectively (USDA FAS, 2013). So, although it has to comply with very strict labelling rules, and long drawn-out decision-making procedures, trade involving GM products with EU countries has clearly not been deterred. In fact, the EU farms out its GM crop production to large agricultural exporting countries such as Argentina, Brazil, Canada and the USA.

Nevertheless, trade concerns associated with the EU's perceived 'GMO-free' status are often cited in SSA as a reason for taking a precautionary approach to biotechnology crop adoption, which may result in forgone benefits for farmers and society at large and have a negative impact on a country's food security situation. A closer look at real versus perceived trade risks is essential in this debate. In recent years, for example, research commissioned by the Common Market for East and Southern Africa (COMESA) analysed the issue in more detail. Using international trade data, the COMESA-supported project 'Regional Approach to Biotechnology in East and Southern Africa' calculated the export losses that might be incurred for six selected country cases if the commercial planting of GMOs were to begin and if all the agricultural exports of these countries that might possibly be considered 'GM' would then be rejected by all importers in Europe. The analysis confirmed that if European importers would reject all exports from the region that might possibly be GM or GM-derived (e.g. animal products that could have been raised with GM feed), the total monetary value of all commercial exports lost would still be quite small (Paarlberg, 2006).

The commercial export risks from planting GMOs were found to be small because the agricultural crops most heavily exported from Africa to Europe (e.g. coffee, tea, sugar, bananas, cocoa, oil palm, groundnuts, and other fruits and vegetables) are crops not yet being developed nor grown for commercial marketing in GM form anywhere in the world. So even the most sensitive importers would have no reason to reject them after an African country began planting crops such as GM cotton or maize, which are currently in the regulatory pipeline in several countries in Africa and are commercially planted in a few African countries. Moreover, most GM cotton and maize events that are currently produced commercially worldwide have received clearance from EFSA and are approved for planting (GM maize) or for importation into the EU for direct use as food, for feed, or for processing.

A recent, detailed analysis in East Africa (Komen and Wafula, 2013) concludes that the degree of trade risk associated with the prospective commercial adoption of GM crops such as maize, cassava, cotton and bananas – which are among those currently being tested in confined field trials in Kenya and Uganda – is first and foremost an intraregional issue and poses little cause for concern. First, as argued above, various GM varieties of maize and cotton are traded worldwide and are generally accepted for processing as food, feed and fibre. Moreover, the value and volume of exports to 'GM-sensitive' destinations, such as the EU, are very small and in most cases negligible.

However, simply dismissing the perceived GMO trade risks as irrational fears would be naïve. For instance, a recent study conducted by the International Food Policy Research Institute (IFPRI), based on stakeholder interviews across Africa, confirmed the strong influence from European agri-food retailers and supermarket chains that have adopted their own 'GM-free' standards. For instance, Gruère and Sengupta (2009) report that GM-free certification is required for exports of tea from Kenya to the United Kingdom, while it is commonly known that GM tea has not been developed or commercialized anywhere in the world. They also find reports of organic producer groups in Kenya believing that producing GM field crops would jeopardize their exports of horticultural products. The Kenya Organic Agriculture Network, for example, expressed concerns that the introduction of GM varieties of maize or cotton would affect market access for horticultural products that are organically produced. Yet gene flow, or 'contamination' from maize or cotton to horticultural products, cannot occur because the products are not biologically compatible.

Another case cited by Gruère and Sengupta (2009) involves beef production and exports from Namibia to the EU, which was affected by a temporary ban by EU food retailers in 2000 due to rumours that beef cattle in Namibia had been fed with GM maize. While technically there is no regulation whatsoever prohibiting beef or other meat products being produced with GM feed in the EU – on the contrary, the EU imports massive amounts of GM feed each day – this nevertheless resulted in a moratorium on GM feed in Namibia that continues up to today. As recent as May 2014, the managing director of Namibian Dairies was quoted saying:

We export our beef products to the European Union, where the use of GMOs is also banned. The EU forms our largest beef export market and if we were to allow the use of GMOs, it would put the beef industry under tremendous strain and the effects on our local economy would be grave.

(Graig, 2014)

While this statement may be unfounded, it very well illustrates the fact that developing countries are forced to adopt ever more restrictive GMO policies under EU pressure.

Finally, it should be noted that even EU officials amplify the myth that Europe is against GMOs or GM-free. As recent as May 2014, the head of the EU delegation in Nairobi, Kenya, claimed that 'Kenyan farmers will find it difficult to find markets in the EU if the country adopts genetically modified crops' (OFAB, 2014). While this statement was publicly corrected at a later stage, it does exemplify how widespread such perceptions are.

The challenges to EU policy coherence

Considering the above examples, it is no surprise that criticism has been raised that policy incoherence and lack of coordination among European countries is having negative effects on African farmers. Particularly the European policy – or lack thereof – on GM crops has had a negative influence on adoption of the technology particularly in Africa. This is not just related to the policy as such, but also to the way it is presented to African policymakers by EU officials and EU-supported NGOs.

Obviously, with 28 member states and a range of EU institutions influencing and shaping development policy, a certain level of policy incoherence can be expected. But the difference between EU policy goals such as for the KBBE and for the EU–Africa partnership and actual decision-making on agriculture in general and biotechnology in particular warrants further explanation. Aerni (2014) approaches this paradox in his essay introducing 'wellness sustainability', meaning the urban elites' desire to feeling right with regard to what we eat, say, read or think. The attitude to food and food production is reflected in the 'food sovereignty' movement, which embraces the preservation of small-scale, low-input agriculture and the right of people to choose their own food system, and categorically rejects modern agricultural technology and associated phenomena such as plant breeders' rights. Food sovereignty is a central concept for EU-based NGOs, who have a strong presence in SSA and regularly mount campaigns against modern agriculture, biotechnology and related policies on, for example, biosafety or plant breeders' rights. In March 2015, the UK newspaper *The Independent* reported on how ActionAid-Uganda campaigns against modern biotechnology and a proposed national biosafety bill by spreading misinformation claiming biotech crops would cause cancer (Redfern, 2015). Although ActionAid's UK headquarters stated that this should not have happened, local campaigns continue to spread misinformation about agricultural biotechnology and the proposed biosafety bill. This is not an isolated example from Uganda but illustrative for similar campaigns in West Africa (Ghana, Nigeria, Burkina Faso), East Africa (Kenya, Tanzania) and Southern Africa (Malawi, South Africa).

Ironically, such campaigns are often directly or indirectly financed by EU subsidies. Generally, NGOs are raising substantial amounts of private donations for anti-biotechnology campaigns and they are effective in lobbying at EU level and with national governments. In addition, as one example, Friends of the Earth Europe receives around €750,000 each year from EU environmental funds (Friends of the Earth Europe, 2014) and is one of the most vocal anti-biotechnology groups in the EU and worldwide – actually spreading information and positions regarding a GMO-free Europe that go against official EU policies and EU research findings. Another source of funds for anti-biotechnology campaigns in Africa is through European 'development NGOs' which receive a significant part of their funding from official development aid budgets. Their influence is also felt by the food industry, which claims their own GMO-free private standards rather than becoming the subject of anti-biotechnology protests against their products or supermarkets.

As Aerni (2014) rightly argues, the undue influence of EU policies and decisions, and anti-science activism in Africa is contrary to the essence of the Paris Declaration on Aid Effectiveness. This declaration was signed in 2005 by members of the Organisation for Economic Co-operation and Development (OECD). They agreed that priorities for food security and agricultural policies should be set by governments in recipient countries. However it is broadly felt that development aid priorities are not fully aligned with Africa's development priorities, such as those laid down in the Comprehensive African Agricultural Development Programme (CAADP).

Conclusions and policy recommendations

In a recent report by the European Academies Science Advisory Council (EASAC) (EASAC, 2013, p.23), it is concluded that:

> In several African countries where there has been an active debate about biotechnology, European influences have not necessarily been helpful and some have hindered the introduction of GM crops. Negative political sentiment in the EU has influenced the political acceptance process in Africa, and this impact has been compounded by the perceived loss of trade when EU countries did not accept GM products from abroad.

As argued in this chapter and elsewhere in this book, economic ties between the EU and SSA remain strong, in terms of trade, development aid, foreign direct investment and R&D collaboration. These factors explain the strong influence that Europe has on policy decisions in Africa, particularly regarding bioscience and biotechnology development. As for modern biotechnology, a coalition of EU officials, retail companies and activist NGOs convey messages that Europe rejects GMOs, keeps a GMO-free status and that Africa's agricultural exports would be jeopardized if GM crops were approved for commercial release. To

African policymakers, the political reality of these paradoxes and inconsistencies surrounding the EU's biotechnology policies, for cultivation and commodity imports, is a major challenge.

This situation contributes to the often observed disconnect between national biotechnology policies and biosafety laws and regulations in Africa. While national biotechnology policies in African countries generally contain policy statements that recognize the potential contribution of modern biotechnology for meeting socioeconomic development goals, their biosafety regulations sometimes have stringent provisions that will undermine efforts to meet broader developmental and food security goals. Such provisions are often drafted against the backdrop of Europe's perceived GMO-free status. The disconnect can be addressed by establishing a coordinated framework for biotechnology and biosafety regulation, involving ministries and regulatory agencies responsible for agriculture, environmental protection, science and technology, and trade and industry.

As far as actual trade risks are concerned, recent studies point to a high concentration of agricultural trade (exports as well as imports) within SSA while the volume and value of exports to GM-sensitive countries is relatively low. Clearly, agricultural trade involving GM crops can be addressed early enough by regional regulatory dialogues and by accelerating the processes of developing common, Pan African biosafety policies, in order to mitigate any bottlenecks to market access. Given that the current regional integration initiatives in Africa – such as those spearheaded by COMESA – pay much attention to trade in key agricultural commodities and the need to minimize tariff and non-tariff barriers, matters concerning decision-making on GM crops can be adequately mainstreamed into the regional integration policies and instruments.

Common African policies and positions on biotechnology and biosafety, as recently adopted by the COMESA Council of Ministers, will be a great asset in consultations with EU partners. It would greatly help achieving a mutual understanding of the benefits and potential (trade) risks associated with biotechnology adoption, and avoid the continuation of fear-mongering and spread of misinformation in Africa. Policy forums such as the EU–Africa Partnership and CAADP would be instrumental in effectively addressing their agricultural development priorities in development assistance programmes, and to tackle issues related to policy incoherence. Since CAADP is a primarily growth-oriented agricultural development agenda, aimed at increasing agriculture growth rates to a minimum of 6 per cent per year, it will be critical to ensure that the EU's support policies and regulatory decisions are in line with this important goal.

References

Aerni, P. 2014. The great misunderstanding of the global food crisis. In: Heap, R.B. and Bennett, D.J. (eds). *Viewpoints: Africa's Future … Can Biosciences Contribute?* Cambridge: Banson/B4FA, pp.76–87.

EASAC (European Academies Science Advisory Council). 2013. *Planting the Future: Opportunities and Challenges for Using Crop Genetic Improvement Technologies for*

Sustainable Agriculture. EASAC Policy Report 21. Halle: European Academies Science Advisory Council.

EuropaBio. 2014. *Undue Delays in EU Authorisation of Safe GM Crops.* [Online]. [Accessed 18 February 2016]. Available from: http://www.europabio.org/positions/undue-delays-eu-authorisation-safe-gm-crops

EuropaBio. 2015. *Increasing Timelines for Risk Assessment of GMOs in EFSA.* [Online]. [Accessed 18 February 2016]. Available from: http://www.europabio.org/positions/risk-assessment-gmos-efsa

EC (European Commission). 2011. *Increasing the Impact of EU Development Policy: An Agenda for Change.* COM(2011) 637 final. Brussels: European Commission.

EC (European Commission). 2012. *Innovating for Sustainable Growth: A Bioeconomy for Europe.* [Online]. [Accessed 15 February 2016]. Available from: http://ec.europa.eu/research/bioeconomy/pdf/bioeconomycommunicationstrategy_b5_brochure_web.pdf

EC (European Commission). 2014. *Research & Innovation. Food and Nutrition, Security / Sustainable Agriculture.* [Online]. European Commission, Directorate General Development and Cooperation – EuropeAid. [Accessed 22 February 2016]. Available from: https://ec.europa.eu/europeaid/sites/devco/files/guide-approach-paper-ar4d-2014_en_0.pdf

EC (European Commission). 2015. *Communication from the Commission to the European Parliament, the Council, the European Economic and Social Committee and the Committee of the Regions. Reviewing the Decision-making Process on Genetically Modified Organisms (GMOs).* COM(2015) 176 final. Brussels: European Commission.

European Development Fund. 2016. Website of the European Commission International Cooperation and Development European Development Fund. [Online]. [Accessed 18 February 2016]. Available from: https://ec.europa.eu/europeaid/funding/funding-instruments-programming/funding-instruments/european-development-fund_en

Friends of the Earth Europe. 2014. Friends of the Earth Europe financial information. [Online]. [Accessed 18 February 2016]. Available from: https://www.foeeurope.org/sites/default/files/other/2015/foee_financial_information_2014.pdf

Goodison, P. 2009. *The Impact of Common Agricultural Policy (CAP) Reform on Africa-EU Trade in Food and Agricultural Products.* Policy Notes 2009/7 – Special Issue on the EU Africa Partnership Strategy. Wageningen: Technical Centre for Agricultural and Rural Cooperation.

Graig, A. 2014. *Dairies versus GMO.* [Online]. Informanté, 5 May. [Accessed 18 February 2016]. Available from: http://www.informante.web.na/dairies-versus-gmo.14003

Gruère, G. and Sengupta, D. 2009. *Biosafety Decisions and Perceived Commercial Risks: The Role of GM-free Private Standards.* IFPRI Discussion Paper 00847. Washington, DC: International Food Policy Research Institute.

Hortidaily. 2013. Kenya: chemical ban hits vegetable exports to the EU market. [Online]. [Accessed 18 February 2015]. Available from: http://www.hortidaily.com/article/950/Kenya-Chemical-ban-hits-vegetable-exports-to-the-EU-market

Kalaitzandonakes, N. *et al.* 2007. Compliance costs for regulatory approval of new biotech crops. *Nature Biotechnology* 25(5), pp.509–11.

Komen, J. and Wafula, D.W. 2013. *Trade and Tribulations: An Evaluation of Trade Barriers to the Adoption of Genetically Modified Crops in the East African Community.* A Report of the CSIS Global Food Security Project. Washington, DC: Center for Strategic and International Studies.

Masip, G. *et al.* 2013. Paradoxical EU agricultural policies on genetically engineered crops. *Trends in Plant Science* 18(6), pp.312–24.

Nuffield Council on Bioethics. 2003. *The Use of GM Crops in Developing Countries: A Follow-up Discussion Paper.* London: Nuffield Council on Bioethics.

OFAB (Open Forum on Agricultural Biotechnology in Africa). 2014. *EU Head of Delegation in Kenya Says Yes to GMOs.* [Online]. [Accessed 18 February 2016]. Available from: http://ofabnews.ofabafrica.org/?p=175

Paarlberg, R. 2006. *Toward a Regional Policy on GMO Crops among COMESA / ASARECA Countries.* RABESA Regional Workshop Policy Options Paper. Nairobi: African Centre for Technology Studies.

Redfern, P. 2015. ActionAid criticises Ugandan counterpart for saying GM crops cause cancer. *The East African*, 24 March.

USDA FAS (United States Department of Agriculture, Foreign Agricultural Service). 2013. *EU-27 Agricultural Biotechnology Annual.* Global Agricultural Information Network (GAIN) Report Number FR9142. Washington, DC: United States Department of Agriculture, Foreign Agricultural Service.

Part VI

Way forward

Progressing towards European and
African bioeconomies

20   Conclusions and key messages

Ivar Virgin and E. Jane Morris

While global economic growth during the last two decades has lifted billions out of poverty, its rewards have been unequally distributed and it has brought unprecedented environmental impacts. Urgent development challenges remain and one of the most critical is to meet future increasing demands for food, feed and bioresources in a way that does not threaten our planet and the wellbeing of future generations. This is also emphasized in the post-2015 Sustainable Development Goals (SDGs) which stress that growth must not only be sustainable but also inclusive and equitable.

In view of the increasing global demands for bioresources, in this book we call for countries to make a rapid and radical conversion to sustainable bioeconomies. With this as a point of departure, the book covers many aspects of the development of knowledge-based bioeconomies and the use of modern biosciences as a tool for a more sustainable future: a future where we are able to use modern technology, including bioscience innovation, to tailor-make resource-efficient and climate-smart agricultural production, agro-processing and value chains. A future where we, through knowledge-based governance, are able to move towards knowledge-based bioeconomies assisting us to reach the SDG targets.

At the same time, we recognize that bioeconomies should not be seen in isolation. Bioscience must play its part alongside other technological fields (wind, solar, water management systems, conservation agriculture, precision farming, etc.) to achieve sustainable development while at the same time responding to climate change.

The chapters in this book have taken the reader on a journey to explore the prospects for how bioscience innovation can help countries in Africa and Europe to move towards resource-efficient agriculture and sustainable bioeconomies. Chapter 1 set the scene and explained the focus on Africa and Europe, as well as delving into some of the terminology used in the book. Chapter 2 introduced us to the fact that the era of plentiful and cheap resources is coming to an end, and in which agriculture and ecosystem services are under increasing pressure. We are not even meeting present needs in a sustainable way, and yet we are faced with a predicted dramatic increase in demand for bioresources, driven by the increasing world population as well as by the need to reduce our dependence on fossil fuels. The need to reduce dependence on fossil fuels represents a particular challenge for developing countries which seek to continue on a development trajectory while feeding their growing populations, despite the financial resources to be provided to these under the United Nations Framework Convention on Climate Change.

Following on from the introductory chapters, Chapters 3–11 have described how knowledge-based bioeconomies and the rapid advances in bioscience could promote sustainable production of renewable biological resources and the conversion of these resources and waste streams into value-added products, such as food, feed, fibre biobased products and bioenergy. Modern bioscience has great potential to deliver a new 'doubly green revolution' in agriculture, by means of a 'gene revolution'. This book covers many examples of modern bioscience applicable today, but also covers future prospects that are even more exciting. Examples that could be implemented today include the introduction of a variety of improved crops with relevance to African farmers (see Chapter 5), crops to mitigate climate change (Chapter 7), crops as feed stocks for the chemical and pharmaceutical industries (Chapters 8 and 9), and value-added products from primary produce or agricultural waste such as bioenergy from cassava or sorghum, or agricultural wastes and agro-industrial residues such as bagasse (Chapters 9–11).

In Chapter 1 we stressed that food security is a fundamental priority in a sustainable bioeconomy, and challenged stakeholders to develop multifunctional bioeconomies where production of renewable non-food/feed products supports increased production and availability of food at local and global levels. We alluded to the 'food vs fuel' debate, which is a particular concern in terms of its potential impact on food security in developing countries. This is addressed in more detail in Chapter 11. While second generation biofuels offer the potential for conversion of lignocellulosic crop wastes to ethanol or methane (biogas), this technology is still not optimal. Nevertheless progress is being made, and moreover a number of highly sustainable perennial feed stocks for cellulosic fuels have been identified that could be grown on a wide range of lands, including semi-desert and alienated soils where no food crops could be grown (Somerville and Long, 2015).

Looking toward the longer term, Chapter 12 shows what the future could hold as rapidly developing new bioscience techniques promise crops with major modifications in their architecture and metabolism to sustainably increase crop yields and crop quality in an era of climate change. Of particular importance is the need for crops that can cope with increasingly erratic climate conditions, which are more difficult to cope with than for instance a persistent but stable low rainfall situation.

Throughout the book, the situations of Europe and sub-Saharan Africa (SSA) have been compared and contrasted, and opportunities for mutual learning and collaboration have been identified. In Joachim von Braun's Foreword to the book, he points to the opportunities for strategic partnership between Europe and Africa, with Africa being rich in biomass resources with a growing science capacity, while Europe is rich in science capacity but has a limited biomass resource base. He emphasizes that the development of bioeconomies requires a global strategy, and needs to be internationally coherent.

While there is a broad recognition of the need for sustainable bioeconomies on both continents, the policies and strategies to deliver a bioeconomy have been more clearly articulated in Europe than in most African countries. Social, policy and governance issues in connection with a move towards knowledge-based economies need to be addressed on both continents, as discussed in detail in Chapters 14, 16 and 19. An essential component of such policies is the need for Europe and Africa to embrace and support innovation as a tool for increasing agricultural productivity, food security and sustainability, as described in Chapters 4, 6 and 17. However, this requires that we broaden the R&D agenda, and invest in public R&D platforms ensuring that the new biology is made available to a broader set of actors than today, and that technologies reach the end user rather than ending up on the shelf. Technologies and the innovation agenda today are largely in the hands of the multinationals, therefore, as described in Chapters 2 and 14, more funding and support of public sector-driven innovation (including public–private partnerships) is needed. This will require strong political commitment to adequately support the public sector, particularly in Africa.

In Europe the basic capacity and the structure for bioscience innovation is largely in place, but further investment and policy regime adjustments are needed if Europe is to realize the visions outlined in the European Strategy and Action Plan, *Innovating for Sustainable Growth: A Bio-economy for Europe*. In Africa, efforts in many areas are needed to strengthen the structure for bioscience innovation. In addition to government support and national development efforts, regional collaboration, international research initiatives and multidisciplinary innovation platforms will also be key factors in ensuring that the new biosciences benefit Africa (see Chapters 15 and 17). There are promising examples of synergies and collaboration between Europe and Africa that could be nurtured and grown through instruments such as the European Framework Programmes and the European Development Fund. There are also significant regional differences that need to be taken into account, and bioscience innovations need to be developed that are adapted to local needs while remaining globally relevant.

Both Africa and Europe need to support innovation structures and a policy environment ensuring that the promises of modern bioscience effectively and safely contribute to more resource-efficient, climate-smart, resilient agricultural production and processing systems. Figure 20.1 shows the various steps in the chain from research to market diffusion and indicates the various points of intervention where sound policies and support mechanisms can make a difference.

Both Europe and Africa need to support the process of moving promising and appropriate biosciences from the lab to the market. This would mean, in the case of Europe, new policy coherent regimes, and credible, science-based and transparent regulatory frameworks that do not stifle, but instead encourage bioscience innovation. It would also mean efforts to more effectively link the chemical-processing sector to the agricultural sector. In the case of Africa it would mean supportive policies, but also business incubation and support to

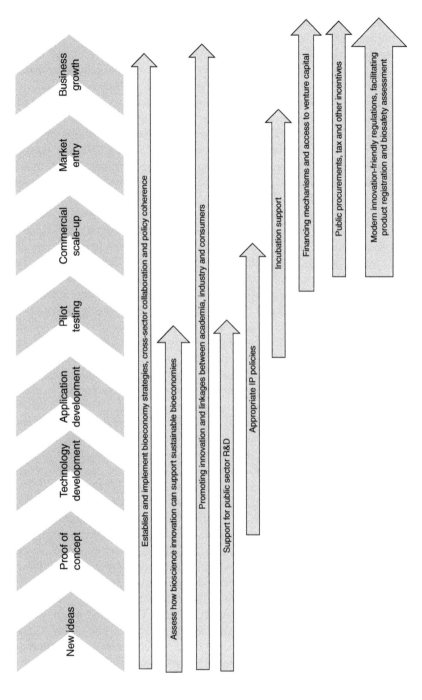

Figure 20.1 Steps in the chain from research to market diffusion

financing mechanisms able to fund up-scaling and roll out of appropriate bioscience technologies supporting a broad set of farming, value addition and agro-processing systems. Both continents need to guard against those who promote anti-science views that can act as a barrier to the introduction of new technologies.

In summary, the main messages in the book are that:

- The growing global demand for food, feed and biobased renewable material is changing the conditions for agricultural production worldwide. At the same time, the revolutionary achievements in the field of biosciences are contributing to a transition whereby biobased alternatives for energy and materials are becoming more competitive (see Chapters 2, 3, 4, 8, 11, 12).
- There is a wide gap between what agricultural biosciences and genetic engineering can do in principle and the extent to which bioscience technologies have been deployed to improve the efficiency and sustainability of current farming systems (see Chapters 5, 6, 9).
- Modern biosciences have a great potential to contribute towards sustainable development both in Europe and in Africa (see Chapters 5, 7, 9, 10) but ...
- ... this will not happen until we broaden the R&D agenda, invest in public R&D platforms ensuring that the new bioscience is made available to a broader set of actors than today, and address social, policy and governance issues that are hampering progress towards sustainable bioeconomies (see Chapters 2, 14, 16).
- Important contributions have been made in ensuring that the new biosciences are made available to countries in SSA, especially East Africa and South Africa (see Chapters 5, 9, 13, 15), but ...
- ... more targeted investments in R&D, buisness development, intellectual property management and policy research are needed to ensure that the new biosciences effectively and safely contribute to more resource-efficient, climate-smart, resilient agricultural systems worldwide and towards the transition to sustainable bioeconomies (see Chapters 14, 18).
- The successful development of a sustainable bioeconomy will be determined not only by technical developments, but also by government policies, public opinion, social and economic benefits, governance of innovation and cultural differences (see Chapters 14, 17, 19).
- There are promising examples of synergies and collaboration between the North (as exemplified by Europe) and the South (as exemplified by Africa), which could be nurtured and grown (see Chapters 13, 15), but ...
- ... there are also significant regional differences which need to be taken into account, and bioscience innovations need to be developed that are fit for purpose and adapted to local needs while remaining globally relevant (see Chapters 2, 8, 9, 10).

Many of the issues and challenges are similar for both continents. A number of key questions emerge, which may stimulate further discussion and strategy development, and where collaboration and communication between the best minds on both continents would be beneficial. These include questions such as:

- How can countries in Africa be supported to use bioscience innovation and knowledge-based economies as tools for inclusive and sustainable economic growth?
- How can Europe use bioscience innovation as an engine for improved resource effectiveness and reduced dependency on fossil fuels and realize the visions outlined in the European Strategy and Action Plan, *Innovating for Sustainable Growth: A Bio-economy for Europe?*
- How to balance sustainability with the increasing resource requirements of a growing world population?
- How to balance the multiple potential uses of bioresources for food, feed, fuel, fibre, chemicals, etc.?
- How can public policy strengthen the conditions for bioscience innovation and the development of bioeconomies?
- How to make sustainability and resource efficiency important breeding and development targets for public and private sector-driven innovation efforts?
- How to make sure that modern gene technologies and biosciences are supporting an inclusive innovation agenda involving a broader set of actors to improve other crops than maize, soya and cotton for a larger set of end users than today?
- How to ensure that the social and environmental factors governing the development of sustainable bioeconomies are successfully addressed?
- How to ensure that a bioeconomy is indeed sustainable in all circumstances?

In addressing the last question, it should be recognized that the development of bioeconomies in both continents does not necessarily provide a guarantee of sustainable development. Interdisciplinary assessments of various bioeconomy pathways are needed to identify and weigh benefits, risk, conflict of interest and corresponding mitigation. Because bioeconomy research can be considered a multidisciplinary field, a recognition and consideration of insights from a broad set of disciplines and stakeholders is necessary. It is important to analyse all activities within the bioeconomy, for example, using lifecycle analysis tools to value their contribution to sustainability. Such assessments may not only evaluate existing processes, but should also be used to choose the most beneficial applications for the future bioeconomy, so that an optimal contribution to sustainability can be reached. This is a key area that could benefit from collaboration between Europe and Africa.

There is no single, one-size-fits-all solution for how to promote a bioeconomy. Indeed, there may be a number of possible pathways to success for each individual innovation system in each country. Nevertheless, we feel that there are a number of common issues that, if addressed by the policymaking community, would substantially increase the chances of success. We therefore conclude the book by proposing below a set of action points for Africa and Europe respectively, that address the priorities, taking into account the current status on each of the continents.

10-point action plan for Africa

1. *Take ownership of the opportunities offered by the bioscience revolution* to catalyse improvements in health, agricultural productivity, agro-processing and environmental sustainability on the continent. This requires African countries to balance an often inappropriately large focus on perceived biosafety risks with the potential benefits of modern bioscience. Adoption of technologies responding to local needs through national and regional investments in R&D and innovation structures can also offset the perceived dominance of multinational companies that has resulted in the stigmatization of much of modern bioscience. Local hubs of innovation with local ownership can play a key role here.

2. *Establish and implement national and/or regional bioeconomy strategies*, based on local strengths and opportunities that support the medium and long-term development goals. This includes the need for coherent and coordinated policies in support of a knowledge-based bioeconomy. This may also include African-driven assessments on how the new biosciences and a new generation of biotechnology crops, agro-processing and value chains could benefit countries in Africa. Such assessments should also include the consideration of socioeconomic issues in the development of the African bioeconomies.

3. *Ensure that all relevant government sectors work together* to agree on priorities in sectors affected by the bioeconomy. This includes sectors such as agriculture, energy, transport, industry, health and environment.

4. *Provide mechanisms for meaningful public sector support* to bioscience research and innovation, to enable scientists to focus on country priorities and to avoid the situation where scientists and innovators are at the mercy of priorities dictated by donor funding.

5. *Broaden the innovation agenda.* Build and sustain capacity in the public R&D sector with highly trained scientific and technical staff with capacity to link to market actors, and create opportunities and incentives for them to be engaged in innovation activities. This also includes providing support to entrepreneurship and enabling scientists to interact with the market actors.

6. *Develop incubation services and 'technopark'* infrastructures and services to assist emerging innovation actors with product and enterprise development for different types of market (commercial markets but also low profit markets with high social impact). This includes provision of a range of different services such as intellectual property management, business plan development, techno-economic feasibility studies, partner matching and access to capital.

7. *Implement enabling policies and regulatory frameworks* that create demand for the commercialization of bioscience technologies, including certification and quality and environmental standards, public procurement efforts,

tax incentives and government initiatives. This could also include enabling policies and frameworks for promoting inclusive innovation involving and serving the poor.

8. *Establish a comprehensive financing mechanism framework* for bringing bioscience technologies to the market along the growth path, from small incubation grants, matching grants, soft loans, 'angel' investment, public and private equity/venture capital and commercial loans from specialized banks.

9. *Support transparent and knowledge-based governance* aided by close interaction between scientists, politicians and, where relevant, industry to address hurdles that need to be overcome for the development of bioeconomies and to support scientific literacy amongst policymakers to ensure that the benefits are realized.

10. *Strengthen international partnerships and collaborations* within Africa, with Europe and with the rest of the world to ensure that African countries tap into the best available expertise. This includes the provision of substantial and long-term support by African governments to their own national R&D and innovation actors ensuring their ability to collaborate internationally and with partners from Europe. In this way, modern bioscience could be harnessed to Africa's vast knowledge of indigenous farming practices and its wealth of lesser-known crops. African countries should develop and support permanent institutions and mechanisms catalysing international collaboration, such as regional bioscience innovation and bioeconomy platforms. Such catalysing mechanisms would make it easier to link to potential European public and private sector collaborators and also to develop new knowledge and technologies benefitting a broad set of African actors. Such platforms may also enable African actors to more effectively link to European R&D and innovation efforts such as the EU Horizon 2020 R&D programme.

10-point action plan for Europe

1. *Address uncoordinated and mismatched strategies and policies that hamper the development of a bioeconomy.* Coherent policies and strategies that support and coordinate all sectors of the bioeconomy are needed. This includes progressive strategies to foster biobased development and limit dependence on fossil fuels. Incentives should support a broadening of biobased applications for use of agricultural and forestry produce rather than emphasizing one segment (e.g. biofuels) at the expense of others (e.g. green industrial chemicals).

2. *Ensure that policies and regulations keep up with technology development.* While European countries are still sitting on the fence or even banning the introduction of GM crops grown widely elsewhere in the world, the technology is moving fast and Europe is ill prepared to deal with the next generation of GMOs produced using genome editing tools. This would include modern and innovation-friendly regulation of biotechnology crops, as well as stimulating and catalysing the development of new productive, resource-efficient

and climate-smart agricultural crop production systems. Such a regulatory system would benefit a broader range of innovations and biotechnology crops, including those developed in the public sector.

3. *Increase investment in modern agricultural research and innovation* to support sustained and sustainable growth in agricultural productivity, delivering yield increases while minimizing the need for agricultural inputs and addressing the need for climate change adaptation.

4. *Streamline fragmented funding schemes* to support bioscience innovation and minimize the time and complexity of applying for funds, which severely hampers the process of publicly funded bioscience research and development.

5. *Develop incentives and improved business models for roll-out of the bio-economy*, considering that the transition will involve a radical move away from dependence on fossil fuel and 'business as usual', where new capital investment and partnerships will be essential. This includes strong linkages and incubating public R&D and private sector actors ensuring that the promises of the new biology can be adopted and used in European farming systems. Such incubation and incentive systems could also be introduced and harmonized with the goals supported in the EU framework for Common Agriculture Policy (CAP).

6. *Support a more entrepreneurial approach to farming* whereby entrepreneurs including farmers are encouraged to innovate and commercialize new sustainable agricultural products and services broadening the base of crops and income sources rather than being at the mercy of a 'top-down' social planning approach.

7. *Improve science communication and science advice* to the European Commission (EC) and national governments, as well as to the public at large, and implement science capacity development for politicians. While the appointment of the High Level Group of Scientific Advisors of the EC Scientific Advice Mechanism is to be commended, it is noteworthy that this group does not include anyone with an agricultural background or with any involvement in bioeconomy development. The EC needs to promote discussion on strategies, visions and roadmaps on how modern technology, including the use of modern bioscience, can contribute to a biobased European economy. In concert there is also a need for improved public communication and consultation so that both the potential benefits and challenges in the transition to a bioeconomy are well understood and widely discussed.

8. *Undertake new research and assessments on how bioscience innovation could support a sustainable European bioeconomy.* This would include assessments on how the new biosciences and a new generation of biotechnology crops, agro-processing and value chains could benefit a sustainable European bioeconomy. Such assessment should also strengthen the consideration of socioeconomic issues in the development of the bioeconomy.

9. *Align European donor funding to Africa with priorities of the recipient countries* in line with the Paris Declaration on Aid Effectiveness. Europe should

avoid shaping recipient priorities in a way that is in line with European priorities, particularly with regard to enabling African farmers and African public R&D breeding platforms to make use of modern biosciences including the introduction and use of genetically modified crops.

10. *Further build on partnerships with Africa (by selecting targeted countries)* that are balanced and mutually inclusive, so that the bioeconomies of European and African countries develop synergistically and can reinforce each other. Separate support for R&D collaboration between European and African private sector actors should also be provided. The Roadmap produced by the EU-Africa High Level Policy Dialogue Expert Working Group on food and nutrition security and sustainable agriculture could form the basis for future partnerships, fostering the collaboration between academic and private sector partners on both continents, and also link to various funding institutions and financial mechanisms.

As can been seen from these two sets of action points there are many similarities and possibilities for European and African collaboration. The implementation of these action plans could lead both continents towards the 'high road' of successful and sustainable bioeconomies, as opposed to the 'low road' where humankind continues to overuse the world's resources which by reference to the definition of sustainable development 'compromises the ability of future generations to meet their own needs'.

References

EU-Africa High Level Policy Dialogue Bureau. 2015. *Roadmap towards a Jointly Funded EU-Africa Research & Innovation Partnership, with an Initial Focus on Food and Nutrition Security and Sustainable Agriculture.* [Online]. [Accessed 22 December 2015]. Available from: https://caast-net-plus.org/attach/HLPD_roadmap_Experts_ WG_proposal_final_version_27th_April.pdf

Somerville, C.R. and Long, S.P. 2015. The future of biofuel and food production in the context of climate change and emerging resource stresses. *The Bridge, National Academy of Engineering* Summer, pp.32–40.

Index

For Product Safety Concerns and Information please contact our EU
representative GPSR@taylorandfrancis.com
Taylor & Francis Verlag GmbH, Kaufingerstraße 24, 80331 München, Germany

www.ingramcontent.com/pod-product-compliance
Ingram Content Group UK Ltd.
Pitfield, Milton Keynes, MK11 3LW, UK
UKHW021012180425
457613UK00020B/913